CRITICISM AND FICTION
AND OTHER ESSAYS

W. D. Howells.

CRITICISM AND FICTION

AND OTHER ESSAYS

BY W. D. HOWELLS

Edited with Introductions and Notes by

CLARA MARBURG KIRK

and

RUDOLF KIRK

GREENWOOD PRESS, PUBLISHERS
WESTPORT, CONNECTICUT

Library of Congress Cataloging in Publication Data

Howells, William Dean, 1837-1920.
   Criticism and fiction.

   Reprint of the 1959 ed. published by New York University Press, New York.
   1. Fiction--History and criticism--Collected works.
2. American fiction--History and criticism--Collected
works. 3. Criticism--Collected works. I. Title.
[PN3451.H6 1977]   809.3   76-57973
ISBN 0-8371-9460-1

Originally published in 1959 by New York University Press,
New York

Reprinted with the permission of New York University Press

Reprinted in 1977 by Greenwood Press, Inc.   76-57973

Library of Congress catalog card number

ISBN 0-8371-9460-1

Printed in the United States of America

"*The life of any man of letters who has lived long with strong convictions becomes part of the literary history of his time, though the history may never acknowledge it.*"

W. D. HOWELLS

North American Review
October, 1912

PREFACE

❧❧

DURING the past half century few American writers have been so constantly—one is tempted to say so intentionally—misunderstood as William Dean Howells, who in the last quarter of the nineteenth century was regarded by most readers as our foremost man of letters. Various causes for this misunderstanding may be found—social, economic, political, literary, and religious —but the principal one may be that his critical essays have lain hidden in the files of magazines and have been neglected even by most students of our literature. Because these statements of Howells' views and opinions have gone unread, many attitudes and beliefs have been attributed to him that he never harbored and, indeed, explicitly repudiated. It is with the hope that a true conception of Howells' ideas, especially as they concern literature, may be gained by a reading of a substantial selection of his essays that the present volume has been produced. We are not sure that these essays, read alone, would in this day and generation carry their message as they once did. For this reason we have included introductions to explain matters that may be helpful to the present-day reader. But beyond anything we may write about Howells, the student must turn to the sources of the late nineteenth century to understand the background against which he wrote. If he does so, he will go further in correcting common misconceptions than is possible from a mere reading of the essays.

We have attempted, with reasonable fidelity, to adhere to Howells' text in matters of spelling, grammar, and punctuation. A few obvious errors, probably those of typesetters, have been emended in the interest of clarity and consistency. In the notes we have identified only those names and references that cannot be found in such readily available books as *Webster's Collegiate*

Dictionary or the *Oxford Companions to English and American Literature.*

In the introductions to Howells' essays we have made use of many sources without giving title and page reference. The reason for this seemingly cavalier treatment of the reader is that we have been dependent on so many different writers—both contemporaries of Howells and later students of him and his age— that we should not have known where to insert a reference and where to leave the source to the knowledge of the reader. In general, we are heavily in debt to the three bibliographies compiled by George Arms and William M. Gibson: *A Bibliography of William Dean Howells,* 1948; "Selected Bibliography," in *Representative Selections of William Dean Howells,* edited by the present authors in the "American Writers Series," 1950; and "Books and Articles on W. D. Howells, 1950–1956," *Howells Sentinel,* No. 3, March 4, 1957. In addition to these sources, we have of course made use of reference books and magazine and newspaper files.

The frontispiece, reproduced from the first edition of *Criticism and Fiction,* was originally made from a photograph of Howells at the age of forty-one, taken at Belmont, Massachusetts, in 1878. It appeared in the February, 1881, issue of *Harper's,* as a headpiece to an article entitled "Literary and Social Boston," with the engraver's name, "Goetze," in the lower right-hand corner. The artist was probably E. Goetze, a painter and engraver of the time. The later engraver who retouched the plate for *Criticism and Fiction* substituted his own initials "N.D.N." for the name of the original artist.

We are indebted to a great many scholars for help during the years we have been studying Howells. At the head of the list stand the two friends named above, with whom we have exchanged Howellsian news through conversations, notes, and our published writings. They have always been ready to go over our typescripts and lend us the benefit of their great knowledge. Others to whom we owe thanks are the late C. Rexford Davis, Remigio U. Pane, Albert W. Holzmann, and Helmut von Erffa, all of Rutgers University. We wish to express our appreciation of the patient and

PREFACE

cheerful proofreading of the text by our sister, Anita Marburg Lerner.

We also particularly thank Professor W. W. Howells of Harvard University for granting us permission to reproduce letters and essays by his grandfather W. D. Howells that are still in copyright. Anyone wishing to make use of this material must secure permission from Professor Howells.

We have been most hospitably received in the Firestone Library at Princeton University and in the New York Public Library. To the Rutgers University Library we are obligated for constant favors. We are particularly indebted to Gilbert Kelley and his reference staff.

To the Rutgers Research Council we wish to express our appreciation for confidence reposed in us, as demonstrated by grants-in-aid.

C. M. K.
R. K.

Rutgers University
October, 1958

INTRODUCTION

FOR over half a century William Dean Howells profoundly influenced the literary taste of the United States. He helped the American reader recover from a subservient respect for "the classics," especially those of a romantic flavor, by directing his attention to the great realistic writers of Italy, France, Spain, Russia, and the Scandinavian countries. Through editorial columns, first of the *Atlantic Monthly* and then of *Harper's Magazine,* he patiently, humorously, and wisely talked to a widening circle of men and women concerning the importance of truth in literature. As early as 1872 Howells had declared his allegiance to "Real Life" in *Their Wedding Journey*—"Ah, poor Real Life, how I love thy foolish and insipid face." When Howells opened the door of "The Editor's Study" of *Harper's* in January, 1886, he invited his readers, still delighting in the sensational novels of Oüida and Charles Reade, "to regard our life without the literary glasses so long thought desirable, and to see character, not as it is in other fiction, but as it abounds outside of all fiction."

From 1886 to 1892 Howells' voice became more insistent; every month from "The Editor's Study" it could be heard "perpetually thundering at the gates of Fiction in Error." It is from these *Harper's Magazine* essays that Howells selected the little volume, *Criticism and Fiction,* with which he blasted the "historical romance" before he left his editorial chair in 1892. In Part I of this book will be found, in its entirety, *Criticism and Fiction,* which for too long has been out of print. In its own day this small book became the center of a literary controversy that raged for many years on both sides of the Atlantic. "In our country," Howells wrote in mock despair over the popularity of such novels as *Quo Vadis* and *When Knighthood Was in Flower,* "nothing of late has been heard but the din of arms, the horrid tumult of the swashbuckler swashing on his buckler." *Criticism and Fiction* is Howells' answer to "the welter of overwhelming romance," from Scott to Lew Wallace, as well as his reply to the arguments for naturalism, which seemed to Howells only another form of romanticism. It is with this vehement expression of critical theory that one must begin a study of Howells' part in the battle for realism of the 1880's and 1890's. A careful reading of this manifesto shows that the issues raised are not dead, though the language used is of another generation.

Part II, "European Masters," includes Howells' essays on European writers who helped form his—and our—concept of realism. As a child Howells taught himself not only Latin and Greek, but also German, French, Spanish, and Italian, and was therefore able to profit by his four years abroad as a young consul in Venice and to maintain during all his life an eager interest in the current literature of Europe, where, throughout the century, realism in literature and art developed as an aspect of political and social change. Howells' literary views, published in most of the leading journals of the day, influenced the literary taste of Americans and drew them closer to the vast European movement. The eager reading of European masters that followed suggested to American writers the richness of their native material, realistically conceived. The Continental novelists teach us to imitate nature, Howells reminded his readers. "Every plant now bearing good and nourishing fruit" is of that seed, he said. The lesson Howells learned from his reading of Björnson, Turgenev, Tolstoy, Valdés, Hardy, Zola, and many others was that the greatest beauty is always associated with the greatest truth. To Howells the "romantic" approach seemed both unethical and unbeautiful. "To be single in the aim to represent life as one has seen and known and felt it, that is the great thing." Howells' "literary passions" were wide enough to include poetry and drama as well as fiction, and to see in Ibsen, for instance, another great advocate of truth in literature, whose purpose was, like that of the realist in fiction, to understand the impulses of ordinary people. These European masters, these "literary divinities" who became "the cult of the Study," Howells tirelessly inter-

INTRODUCTION

preted to an American public still reading aloud Scott, Dickens, and Thackeray.

Part III, "American Writers," reflects the large-minded sympathy that enabled Howells to form a host of associates by whom he was influenced and whom in turn he influenced. The list of literary figures is impressive, and to it many more names could be added. "I knew Hawthorne and Emerson and Walt Whitman; I knew Longfellow and Holmes and Whittier and Lowell; I knew Bryant and Bancroft and Motley; I knew Harriet Beecher Stowe and Julia Ward Howe; I knew Artemus Ward and Stockton and Mark Twain; I knew Parkman and Fiske," said Howells to the large audience gathered to celebrate his seventy-fifth birthday. How many more names and faces must have passed through his mind as he spoke! For the procession of "literary friends and acquaintance" was a long one. In over fifty years of critical appraising Howells frequently welcomed writers now forgotten—who today reads a novel of Henry Ward Beecher?—and occasionally failed fully to appreciate writers acclaimed by a later generation, such as Whitman and Melville. But he held out a welcoming hand to so many young writers when they stood most in need of support that one has no difficulty in understanding why he came at last to be known as the Dean of American Letters. "How truly generous and humane is the Dean of American Letters," wrote Theodore Dreiser, who in 1900 as a young reporter interviewed the established novelist and critic. Dreiser added, "The great literary philanthropist, I call him." A genuine pleasure in the flash of truth in the writing of another made Howells recognize at once the power of Mark Twain, the redheaded stranger from the West who shocked literary Boston by his irreverencies; enabled him to welcome Bret Harte to his Cambridge home in spite of his swaggering pretensions; moved him to urge the publishing of Henry James's stories in the *Atlantic* when Fields hesitated; impelled him to walk from publisher to publisher with a privately printed copy of Stephen Crane's *Maggie* in his hand and to write the first American review of it when the book finally was published in England. Howells was, in Dreiser's words, " 'the lookout on the watch tower' straining for a first glimpse of approaching genius." Perhaps because

Howells was himself both a novelist and a critic, he took a peculiar delight in his editorial contact with young writers: "I do not know how it is with other editors who are also authors," he wrote, "but I can truly say for myself that nothing of my own which I thought fresh and true ever gave me more pleasure than that I got from the like qualities in the work of some young writer revealing his power."

Under the title "Further Critical Issues" will be found, in Part IV, Howells' ranging critical views. Here he is concerned with the place of a writer in a capitalistic society; with the relationship between the teacher and the critic; with the new opportunities for novelists accompanying the growth of the country in the 1890's; with the subtle interrelation of poetry and prose; and finally with the past and future of American literature.

"I like to look the facts in the face," Howells observed of himself. To his contemporaries, that is what he succeeded in doing in his long struggle to prove to his generation that truth is more arresting than falsehood in the writing both of novels and of criticism.

CONTENTS

❦

CONTENTS

PART III: American Writers

CONTENTS

PART IV: Further Critical Issues

CRITICISM AND FICTION
AND OTHER ESSAYS

PART I

CRITICISM AND FICTION*

INTRODUCTION

THE book *Criticism and Fiction* was well named by Howells, for the belief in realism expressed in this essay grew from his own experience as critic and novelist. Because he continued to write both reviews and essays as well as fiction for over fifty years; because he talked with, encouraged, criticized, and enjoyed the friendship of almost all the men and women writing in this country from 1866 to 1920; because his serialized novels and monthly book notices were discussed in front parlors and clubs as well as in editorial offices, his concept of realism is, one might say, securely built into the fabric of American fiction, and it deserves from students of American literature today a careful reappraisal. What realism meant to him is fully expressed in *Criticism and Fiction*.

But before turning to a reading of this long essay, which has never been reprinted in full since Howells' day, it is important to know how he himself felt about his critical reviews and hence about criticism in general, and how the issues raised in his monthly column in *Harper's Magazine* became part of the literary discussions of the times.

One is left in no doubt as to Howells' attitude toward book reviewing. "Criticism I have not cared for, and often I have found it repulsive," Howells candidly admitted on more than one occasion. But from his early days as a young reporter on the *Ohio State Journal* to the half-finished essay on Henry James, which he was

* *The notes to Part I begin on p. 375. These have been supplied by the authors to provide the reader with the background of some of Howells' references.*

writing at the time of his death, Howells' critical comment on his fellow writers continued to flow. The novels that issued year by year from his amazingly creative mind with equal regularity might be taken as illustrations of the quest for the realism defined in *Criticism and Fiction*.

The tension between Howells the critic and Howells the novelist was felt by him at the very outset of his career. As assistant editor and then editor of the *Atlantic Monthly* from 1866 to 1881, Howells wrote well over four hundred critical reviews; during this same period he published a series of successful novels, ranging from *Their Wedding Journey* (1872) to *A Modern Instance* (1882), reflecting his own development as a novelist, from the delicate irony of the travel sketch to the serious analysis of a new kind of heroine realistically conceived. Commenting on this period of his life in "Recollections of an Atlantic Editorship," Howells remarked: "I never liked writing criticism, and never pleased myself in it; but I should probably have kept writing most of the *Atlantic* notices to the end, if my increasing occupation with fiction had not left me too few hours out of the twenty-four for them." Howells "grew more and more a novelist and needed every morning for fiction," so that gradually the work of editing was "pushed into a corner."

The double burden of criticism and fiction led Howells to the verge of a breakdown and forced him to resign from the *Atlantic* in 1881. He traveled abroad for a time, and he wrote a succession of novels, plays, essays, travel sketches, and poems, only to resume his duties as critic when he took over the column "The Editor's Study" in *Harper's Monthly Magazine* in January, 1886. From this time until he gave up "The Editor's Study" in 1892, his critical views became more clearly defined as his concern with social conflict found expression in such novels as *The Minister's Charge* (1887) and *Annie Kilburn* (1889). Whether this deepening sense of the urgency of realism, both in criticism and in fiction, was borne in upon him because of the quickening effect of life in New York, or because of his reading of Tolstoy's novels, or because of the impression made on Howells by the conviction of the Chicago Anarchists in 1887, or because of the loss of his daughter Winifred at the time of his association with the Christian Socialists of Boston and New York, we do not know. We know only that during these crucial six years in Howells' life he reached, with the publication of *A Hazard of New Fortunes* in 1890 and of *Criticism and Fiction* in 1891, the pinnacle of his career both as a novelist and a critic, and that, unsatisfying as he assures us criticism was to him, his vehement belief in realism contributed to his strongest novel. As Hamlin Garland wrote at the time in an essay entitled "Mr. Howells's Latest Novels," by 1890 the novelist-critic had become "an issue."

There is no man in American literature to-day who so challenges discussion as the candid writer of the Editor's Study, which has come to be the expression of Americanism in art and literature. Mr. Howells has become an issue in the literary movement of the day, and his utterances from month to month have the effect of dividing the public into two opposing camps. It is no common man whose name can thus become the synonym for a great literary movement; and those who know him the most intimately feel the greatest admiration for him as he pursues his way calmly through the hail of ignoble personalities which opposing critics have ceaselessly rained upon him. He is writing upon conviction, and convictions are not changed by splenetic assaults, especially if these convictions are begotten and sustained by the spirit of a great social movement.

That Howells himself felt the importance of *Criticism and Fiction* is clearly indicated by the very fact that before he left *Harper's* in 1892, he cut and clipped and rearranged the important paragraphs he had written in "The Editor's Study" during the preceding six years. A glance at Gibson and Arms's *Bibliography of William Dean Howells* will show the reader how Howells sorted out the critical passages, and a further comparison with the reviews as they appeared in *Harper's* will indicate how Howells changed the editorial "we" to "I," omitted the summaries of books, added a transition sentence here and there, sometimes in fact shifted the meaning of a passage by the change of a word or the omission of a reference. As Everett Carter points out in *Howells and the Age of Reason* (1950), the famous passage concerning "the smiling aspects of American life" undergoes an important shift in meaning between its first appearance in a *Harper's* review and its reappearance in *Criticism and Fiction*. Other such shifts in emphasis are readily discoverable. The fact remains, however, that Howells himself made the selections, rewrote the linking sentences, and achieved a wholeness of thought that "The Editor's Study" was not designed to have. No possible selections from these columns could be so important to the reader today as Howells' own.

The edition of *Criticism and Fiction* here printed is that of 1891. It reflects more nearly than the 1911 reprint the views of Howells during his most important period. As indicated in the Textual Note (see p. 379), some of the anti-British passages are toned down in the later edition and some phrases that seemed to him to be in "bad taste" are omitted. As Howells grew older, his sympathetic appreciation of the English increased. No doubt the passage of the copyright law in 1891 helped to moderate Howells' views by 1911. It is clearly the earlier unaltered edition of *Criticism and Fiction* that is of greater interest today. In both the 1891 and the 1911 editions Howells retained from "The Editor's Study" the very paragraphs most interesting to a modern reader, omitting references to dozens of minor works that a monthly columnist must notice.

Criticism and Fiction is, then, a long essay divided into twenty-eight sections, loosely linked together to form what Howells considered a unit. This volume is as complete and significant a statement of Howells' position at the very height of his career as *The Art of Fiction* (1884) was of the critical position of Henry James. Both novelists were, because of the very nature of their fictional realism, emphatically critical; neither of these two friends, who had hammered out their basic beliefs together as young men in Cambridge, was quite systematic in the statement of his views. Would they have been novel writers had they also been metaphysicians? In spite of their obvious philosophical shortcomings, both James and Howells wrote novels that gained in importance because they had something to say about truth in fiction; we, in turn, must consider their critical views of the works of others in order fully to understand their own novels.

Howells' real contribution to the critical thought of his time lay in the fact that he saw the relationship between the critic and the novelist and conceived of them both as seekers after truth in the new light of science. The ultimate value of this truth lay in its power to redeem the lot of the common man. The critic in the new mode must postpone judgment, for it is his duty to "classify and analyse the fruits of the human mind very much as the naturalist classifies the objects of his study, rather than to praise or blame them." Similarly, "the true realist . . . cannot look upon human life and declare this thing or that thing unworthy of notice, any more than the scientist can declare a fact of the material world beneath the dignity of his inquiry." Like the scientist too, the realist cannot report on what he does not find. He must maintain what Howells called "scientific decorum" when attempting to imitate the naturalism of a Dostoevsky or a Flaubert in his account of ordinary life in this country in the last quarter of the nineteenth century. Though Howells cautions both author and critic to accept the wisdom of the scientist and to postpone judgment, it is clear that he believed the moment does finally arrive when both must pass judgment—not by the standard of tradition, nor by popular clamor, but according to an apprehension of truth, which is accessible to ordinary man. The validity of Howells' position rests entirely on the insight with which he dealt with the social scene of his day in his novels and on the critical acumen he displayed in judging the writing of others. The true realist, as well as the true scientist, Howells said, "feels in every nerve the equality of things and the unity of man." It was the urgency of this feeling that impelled him to point out the underlying relationship between criticism and fiction and the importance of both to democratic thought.

Though *Criticism and Fiction* reflects the range of critical ideas that had been forming in his mind for many years, it was also designed by Howells to carry on the international argument for realism. As he himself said in the last essay he wrote for "The Editor's Study":

Not content with the passing result of his monthly ministrations of gall and wormwood, the ill-advised Study-presence thought to bottle a portion of it, and offer it to the public, with the label, "Criticism and Fiction," and a guaranty of its worst effects in any climate, which has been everywhere received with wry faces and retchings; and among the inhabitants of the British Isles has produced truly deplorable consequences.

CRITICISM AND FICTION

Brander Matthews, commenting on "Mr. Howells as a Critic," in the *Forum* of January, 1902, said of the "tiny tome called 'Criticism and Fiction' ":

In this little volume, made up out of earlier articles then first set in order, Mr. Howells said boldly what he thought about certain idols of the market-place; and probably no one was more surprised than he at the turmoil he created. To many placid creatures of habit, the publication of this little book was very like the explosion of a bomb in a reading-room; and the reverberation has not yet died out.

By rereading this critical manifesto, and then by considering it in relation to the influences playing on Howells from abroad, which he in turn was interpreting to American writers, the reader of today should be able to catch reverberations from that distant bomb.

CRITICISM AND FICTION

THE question of a final criterion for the appreciation of art is one that perpetually recurs to those interested in any sort of aesthetic endeavor. Mr. John Addington Symonds, in a chapter of The Renaissance in Italy [1] treating of the Bolognese school of painting, which once had so great cry, and was vaunted the supreme exemplar of the grand style, but which he now believes fallen into lasting contempt for its emptiness and soullessness, seeks to determine whether there can be an enduring criterion or not; and his conclusion is applicable to literature as to the other arts. "Our hope," he says, "with regard to the unity of taste in the future then is, that all sentimental or academical seekings after the ideal having been abandoned, momentary theories founded upon idiosyncratic or temporary partialities exploded, and nothing accepted but what is solid and positive, the scientific spirit shall make men progressively more and more conscious of these bleibende Verhältnisse,[2] more and more capable of living in the whole; also, that in proportion as we gain a firmer hold upon our own place in the world, we shall come to comprehend with more instinctive certitude what is simple, natural, and honest, welcoming with gladness all artistic products that exhibit these qualities. The perception of the enlightened man will then be the task of a healthy person who has made himself acquainted with the laws of evolution in art and in society, and is able to test the excellence of work in any stage from immaturity to decadence by discerning what there is of truth, sincerity, and natural vigor in it."

I

That is to say, as I understand, that moods and tastes and fashions change; people fancy now this and now that; but what is unpretentious and what is true is always beautiful and good, and nothing else is so. This is not saying that fantastic and monstrous and artificial things do not please; everybody knows that they do please immensely for a time, and then, after the lapse of a much longer time, they have the charm of the rococo. Nothing is more curious than the charm that fashion has. Fashion in women's dress, almost every fashion, is somehow delightful, else it would never have been the fashion; but if any one will look through a collection of old fashion plates, he must own that most fashions have been ugly. A few, which could be readily instanced, have been very pretty, and even beautiful, but it is doubtful if these have pleased the greatest number of people. The ugly delights as well as the beautiful, and not merely because the ugly in fashion is associated with the young loveliness of the women who wear the ugly fashions, and wins a grace from them, not because the vast majority of mankind are tasteless, but for some cause that is not perhaps ascertainable. It is quite as likely to return in the fashions of our clothes and houses and furniture, and poetry and fiction and painting, as the beautiful, and it may be from an instinctive or a reasoned sense of this that some of the extreme naturalists have refused to make the old discrimination against it, or to regard the ugly as any less worthy of celebration in art than the beautiful; some of them, in fact, seem to regard it as rather more worthy, if anything. Possibly there is no absolutely ugly, no absolutely beautiful; or possibly the ugly contains always an element of the beautiful better adapted to the general appreciation than the more perfectly beautiful. This is a somewhat discouraging conjecture, but I offer it for no more than it is worth; and I do not pin my faith to the saying of one whom I heard denying, the other day, that a thing of beauty was a joy forever. He contended that Keats's line should have read, "Some things of beauty are sometimes joys forever," and that any assertion beyond this was too hazardous.

II

I should, indeed, prefer another line of Keats's, if I were to profess any formulated creed, and should feel much safer with his "Beauty is Truth, Truth Beauty," than even with my friend's reformation of the more quoted verse. It brings us back to the solid ground taken by Mr. Symonds, which is not essentially different from that taken in the great Mr. Burke's Essay on the Sublime and the Beautiful—a singularly modern book, considering how long ago it was wrote (as the great Mr. Steele would have written the participle a little longer ago), and full of a certain well-mannered and agreeable instruction. In some things it is of that droll little eighteenth-century world, when philosophy had got the neat little universe into the hollow of its hand, and knew just what it was, and what it was for; but it is quite without arrogance. "As for those called critics," the author says, "they have generally sought the rule of the arts in the wrong place; they have sought among poems, pictures, engravings, statues, and buildings; but art can never give the rules that make an art. This is, I believe, the reason why artists in general, and poets principally, have been confined in so narrow a circle; they have been rather imitators of one another than of nature. Critics follow them, and therefore can do little as guides. I can judge but poorly of anything while I measure it by no other standard than itself. The true standard of the arts is in every man's power; and an easy observation of the most common, sometimes of the meanest things, in nature will give the truest lights, where the greatest sagacity and industry that slights such observation must leave us in the dark, or, what is worse, amuse and mislead us by false lights."

If this should happen to be true—and it certainly commends itself to acceptance—it might portend an immediate danger to the vested interests of criticism, only that it was written a hundred years ago; and we shall probably have the "sagacity and industry that slights the observation" of nature long enough yet to allow most critics the time to learn some more useful trade than criticism as they pursue it. Nevertheless, I am in hopes that the communistic era in taste foreshadowed by Burke is approaching, and that it will occur within the lives of men now overawed by the foolish old superstition that literature and art are anything but the expression of life, and are to be judged by any other test than that of their fidelity to it. The time is coming, I hope, when

11

each new author, each new artist, will be considered, not in his proportion to any other author or artist, but in his relation to the human nature, known to us all, which it is his privilege, his high duty, to interpret. "The true standard of the artist is in every man's power" already, as Burke says; Michelangelo's "light of the piazza," the glance of the common eye, is and always was the best light on a statue; Goethe's "boys and blackbirds" have in all ages been the real connoisseurs of berries; [3] but hitherto the mass of common men have been afraid to apply their own simplicity, naturalness, and honesty to the appreciation of the beautiful. They have always cast about for the instruction of some one who professed to know better, and who browbeat wholesome common-sense into the self-distrust that ends in sophistication. They have fallen generally to the worst of this bad species, and have been "amused and misled" (how pretty that quaint old use of amuse is!) "by the false lights" of critical vanity and self-righteousness. They have been taught to compare what they see and what they read, not with the things that they have observed and known, but with the things that some other artist or writer has done. Especially if they have themselves the artistic impulse in any direction they are taught to form themselves, not upon life, but upon the masters who became masters only by forming themselves upon life. The seeds of death are planted in them, and they can produce only the still-born, the academic. They are not told to take their work into the public square and see if it seems true to the chance passer, but to test it by the work of the very men who refused and decried any other test of their own work. The young writer who attempts to report the phrase and carriage of every-day life, who tries to tell just how he has heard men talk and seen them look, is made to feel guilty of something low and unworthy by the stupid people who would like to have him show how Shakespeare's men talked and looked, or Scott's, or Thackeray's, or Balzac's, or Hawthorne's, or Dickens's; he is instructed to idealize his personages, that is, to take the life-likeness out of them, and put the book-likeness into them. He is approached in the spirit of wretched pedantry into which learning, much or little, always decays when it withdraws itself and stands apart from experience in an attitude of imagined superiority, and which

CRITICISM AND FICTION

would say with the same confidence to the scientist: "I see that you are looking at a grasshopper there which you have found in the grass, and I suppose you intend to describe it. Now don't waste your time and sin against culture in that way. I've got a grasshopper here, which has been evolved at considerable pains and expense out of the grasshopper in general; in fact, it's a type. It's made up of wire and card-board, very prettily painted in a conventional tint, and it's perfectly indestructible. It isn't very much like a real grasshopper, but it's a great deal nicer, and it's served to represent the notion of a grasshopper ever since man emerged from barbarism. You may say that it's artificial. Well, it is artificial; but then it's ideal too; and what you want to do is to cultivate the ideal. You'll find the books full of my kind of grasshopper, and scarcely a trace of yours in any of them. The thing that you are proposing to do is commonplace; but if you say that it isn't commonplace, for the very reason that it hasn't been done before, you'll have to admit that it's photographic." [4]

As I said, I hope the time is coming when not only the artist, but the common, average man, who always "has the standard of the arts in his power," will have also the courage to apply it, and will reject the ideal grasshopper wherever he finds it, in science, in literature, in art, because it is not "simple, natural, and honest," because it is not like a real grasshopper. But I will own that I think the time is yet far off, and that the people who have been brought up on the ideal grasshopper, the heroic grasshopper, the impassioned grasshopper, the self-devoted, adventureful, good old romantic card-board grasshopper, must die out before the simple, honest, and natural grasshopper can have a fair field. I am in no haste to compass the end of these good people, whom I find in the mean time very amusing. It is delightful to meet one of them, either in print or out of it—some sweet elderly lady or excellent gentleman whose youth was pastured on the literature of thirty or forty years ago—and to witness the confidence with which they preach their favorite authors as all the law and the prophets. They have commonly read little or nothing since, or, if they have, they have judged it by a standard taken from these authors, and never dreamed of judging it by nature; they are destitute of the documents in the case of the later writers; they suppose that Balzac was the beginning of realism, and that Zola is its wicked end; they are quite ignorant, but they are ready to talk you down, if you differ from them, with an assumption of knowledge sufficient for any occasion. The horror, the resentment, with which they receive any question of their literary saints is genuine; you descend at once very far in the moral and social scale, and anything short of offensive personality is too good for you; it is expressed to you that you are one to be avoided, and put down even a little lower than you have naturally fallen.

These worthy persons are not to blame; it is part of their intellectual mission to represent the petrifaction of taste, and to preserve an image of a smaller and cruder and emptier world than we now live in, a world which was feeling its way towards the simple, the natural, the honest, but was a good deal "amused and misled" by lights now no longer mistakable for heavenly luminaries. They belong to a time, just passing away, when certain authors were considered authorities in certain kinds, when they must be accepted entire and not questioned in any particular. Now we are beginning to see and to say that no author is an authority except in those moments when he held his ear close to Nature's lips and caught her very accent. These moments are not continuous with any authors in the past, and they are rare with all. Therefore I am not afraid to say now that the greatest classics are sometimes not at all great, and that we can profit by them only when we hold them, like our meanest contemporaries, to a strict accounting, and verify their work by the standard of the arts which we all have in our power, the simple, the natural, and the honest.

Those good people, those curious and interesting if somewhat musty back-numbers, must always have a hero, an idol of some sort, and it is droll to find Balzac, who suffered from their sort such bitter scorn and hate for his realism while he was alive, now become a fetich in his turn, to be shaken in the faces of those who will not blindly worship him. But it is no new thing in the history of literature: whatever is established is sacred with those who do not think. At the beginning of the century, when romance was making the same fight against effete classicism which realism is making to-day against effete romanticism, the Italian poet Monti [5]

14

declared that "the romantic was the cold grave of the Beautiful," just as the realistic is now supposed to be. The romantic of that day and the real of this are in certain degree the same. Romanticism then sought, as realism seeks now, to widen the bounds of sympathy, to level every barrier against aesthetic freedom, to escape from the paralysis of tradition. It exhausted itself in this impulse; and it remained for realism to assert that fidelity to experience and probability of motive are essential conditions of a great imaginative literature. It is not a new theory, but it has never before universally characterized literary endeavor. When realism becomes false to itself, when it heaps up facts merely, and maps life instead of picturing it, realism will perish too. Every true realist instinctively knows this, and it is perhaps the reason why he is careful of every fact, and feels himself bound to express or to indicate its meaning at the risk of over-moralizing. In life he finds nothing insignificant; all tells for destiny and character; nothing that God has made is contemptible. He cannot look upon human life and declare this thing or that thing unworthy of notice, any more than the scientist can declare a fact of the material world beneath the dignity of his inquiry. He feels in every nerve the equality of things and the unity of men; his soul is exalted, not by vain shows and shadows and ideals, but by realities, in which alone the truth lives. In criticism it is his business to break the images of false gods and misshapen heroes, to take away the poor silly toys that many grown people would still like to play with. He cannot keep terms with Jack the Giant-killer or Puss in Boots, under any name or in any place, even when they reappear as the convict Vautrec, or the Marquis de Montrivaut, or the Sworn Thirteen Noblemen. He must say to himself that Balzac, when he imagined these monsters, was not Balzac, he was Dumas; he was not realistic, he was romantic.

III

Such a critic will not respect Balzac's good work the less for contemning his bad work. He will easily account for the bad work historically, and when he has recognized it, will trouble himself no further with it. In his view no living man is a type, but a character; now noble, now ignoble; now grand, now little; complex, full of vicissitude. He will not expect Balzac to be always Balzac, and will be perhaps even more attracted to the study of him when he was trying to be Balzac than when he had become so. In César Birotteau, for instance, he will be interested to note how Balzac stood at the beginning of the great things that have followed since in fiction. There is an interesting likeness between his work in this and Nicolas Gogol's in Dead Souls, which serves to illustrate the simultaneity of the literary movement in men of such widely separated civilizations and conditions. Both represent their characters with the touch of exaggeration which typifies; but in bringing his story to a close, Balzac employs a beneficence unknown to the Russian, and almost as universal and as apt as that which smiles upon the fortunes of the good in the Vicar of Wakefield. It is not enough to have rehabilitated Birotteau pecuniarily and socially; he must make him die triumphantly, spectacularly, of an opportune hemorrhage, in the midst of the festivities which celebrate his restoration to his old home. Before this happens, human nature has been laid under contribution right and left for acts of generosity towards the righteous bankrupt; even the king sends him six thousand francs. It is very pretty; it is touching, and brings the lump into the reader's throat; but it is too much, and one perceives that Balzac lived too soon to profit by Balzac. The later men, especially the Russians, have known how to forbear the excesses of analysis, to withhold the weakly recurring descriptive and caressing epithets, to let the characters suffice for themselves. All this does not mean that César Birotteau is not a beautiful and pathetic story, full of shrewdly considered knowledge of men, and of a good art struggling to free itself from self-consciousness. But it does mean that Balzac, when he wrote it, was under the burden of the very traditions which he has helped fiction to throw off. He felt obliged to construct a mechanical plot, to surcharge his characters, to moralize openly and baldly; he permitted himself to "sympathize" with certain of his people, and to point out others for the abhorrence of his readers. This is not so bad in him as it would be in a novelist of our day. It is simply primitive and inevitable, and he is not to be judged by it.

CRITICISM AND FICTION

IV

In the beginning of any art even the most gifted worker must be crude in his methods, and we ought to keep this fact always in mind when we turn, say, from the purblind worshippers of Scott to Scott himself, and recognize that he often wrote a style cumberous and diffuse; that he was tediously analytical where the modern novelist is dramatic, and evolved his characters by means of long-winded explanation and commentary; that, except in the case of his lower-class personages, he made them talk as seldom man and never woman talked; that he was tiresomely descriptive; that on the simplest occasions he went about half a mile to express a thought that could be uttered in ten paces across lots; and that he trusted his readers' intuitions so little that he was apt to rub in his appeals to them. He was probably right: the generation which he wrote for was duller than this; slower-witted, aesthetically untrained, and in maturity not so apprehensive of an artistic intention as the children of today. All this is not saying Scott was not a great man; he was a great man, and a very great novelist as compared with the novelists who went before him. He can still amuse young people, but they ought to be instructed how false and how mistaken he often is, with his mediaeval ideals, his blind Jacobitism, his intense devotion to aristocracy and royalty; his acquiescence in the division of men into noble and ignoble, patrician and plebeian, sovereign and subject, as if it were the law of God; for all which, indeed, he is not to blame as he would be if he were one of our contemporaries. Something of this is true of another master, greater than Scott in being less romantic, and inferior in being more German, namely, the great Goethe himself. He taught us, in novels otherwise now antiquated, and always full of German clumsiness, that it was false to good art—which is never anything but the reflection of life—to pursue and round the career of the persons introduced, whom he often allowed to appear and disappear in our knowledge as people in the actual world do. This is a lesson which the writers able to profit by it can never be too grateful for; and it is equally a benefaction to readers; but there is very little else in the conduct of the Goethean novels which is in advance of their time; this remains almost their sole contribution to the science of fiction. They are very primitive in certain characteristics, and unite with their calm, deep insight, an amusing helplessness in dramatization. "Wilhelm retired to his room, and indulged in the following reflections," is a mode of analysis which would not be practised nowadays; and all that fancifulness of nomenclature in Wilhelm Meister is very drolly sentimental and feeble. The adventures with robbers seem as if dreamed out of books of chivalry, and the tendency to allegorization affects one like an endeavor on the author's part to escape from the unrealities which he must have felt harassingly, German as he was. Mixed up with the shadows and illusions are honest, wholesome, every-day people, who have the air of wandering homelessly about among them, without definite direction; and the mists are full of a luminosity which, in spite of them, we know for common-sense and poetry. What is useful in any review of Goethe's methods is the recognition of the fact, which it must bring, that the greatest master cannot produce a masterpiece in a new kind. The novel was too recently invented in Goethe's day not to be, even in his hands, full of the faults of apprentice work.

v

In fact, a great master may sin against the "modesty of nature" in many ways, and I have felt this painfully in reading Balzac's romance—it is not worthy the name of novel—Le Père Goriot, which is full of a malarial restlessness, wholly alien to healthful art. After that exquisitely careful and truthful setting of his story in the shabby boarding-house, he fills the scene with figures jerked about by the exaggerated passions and motives of the stage. We cannot have a cynic reasonably wicked, disagreeable, egoistic; we must have a lurid villain of melodrama, a disguised convict, with a vast criminal organization at his command, and

"So dyèd double red"

in deed and purpose that he lights up the faces of the horrified spectators with his glare. A father fond of unworthy children, and leading a life of self-denial for their sake, as may probably and pathetically be, is not enough; there must be an imbecile, trembling dotard, willing to promote even the liaisons of his daughters to give them happiness and to teach the sublimity of the paternal instinct. The hero cannot sufficiently be a selfish young fellow, with alternating impulses of greed and generosity; he must superfluously intend a career of iniquitous splendor, and be swerved from it by nothing but the most cataclysmal interpositions. It can be said that without such personages the plot could not be transacted; but so much the worse for the plot. Such a plot had no business to be; and while actions so unnatural are imagined, no mastery can save fiction from contempt with those who really think about it. To Balzac it can be forgiven, not only because in his better mood he gave us such biographies as Eugénie Grandet, but because he wrote at a time when fiction was just beginning to verify the externals of life, to portray faithfully the outside of men and things. It was still held that in order to interest the reader the characters must be moved by the old romantic ideals; we were to be taught that "heroes" and "heroines" existed all around us, and that these abnormal beings needed only to be discovered in their several humble disguises, and then we should see every-day people actuated by the fine frenzy of the creatures of the poets. How false that notion was few but the critics, who are apt to be rather belated, need now be told. Some of these poor fellows, however, still contend that it ought to be done, and that human feelings and motives, as God made them and as men know them, are not good enough for novel-readers.

This is more explicable than would appear at first glance. The critics—and in speaking of them one always modestly leaves one's self out of the count for some reason—when they are not elders ossified in tradition, are apt to be young people, and young people are necessarily conservative in their tastes and theories. They have the tastes and theories of their instructors, who perhaps caught the truth of their day, but whose routine life has been alien to any other truth. There is probably no chair of literature in this country from which the principles now shaping the literary expression of every civilized people are not denounced and confounded with certain objectionable French novels, or which teaches young men anything of the universal impulse which has given us the work, not only of Zola, but of Tourguéneff and Tolstoï in Russia, of Björnson and Ibsen in Norway, of Valdés and Galdós in Spain, of Verga in Italy. Till these younger critics have learned to think as well as to write for themselves they will persist in heaving a sigh, more and more perfunctory, for the truth as it was in Sir Walter, and as it was in Dickens and in Hawthorne. Presently all will have been changed; they will have seen the new truth in larger and larger degree; and when it shall have become the old truth, they will perhaps see it all.

VI

In the mean time the average of criticism is not wholly bad with us. To be sure, the critic sometimes appears in the panoply of the savages whom we have supplanted on this continent; and it is hard to believe that his use of the tomahawk and the scalping-knife is a form of conservative surgery. It is still his conception of his office that he should assail with obloquy those who differ with him in matters of taste or opinion; that he must be rude with those he does not like, and that he ought to do them violence as a proof of his superiority. It is too largely his superstition that because he likes a thing it is good, and because he dislikes a thing it is bad; the reverse is quite possibly the case, but he is yet indefinitely far from knowing that in affairs of taste his personal preference enters very little. Commonly he has no principles, but only an assortment of prepossessions for and against; and this otherwise very perfect character is sometimes uncandid to the verge of dishonesty. He seems not to mind misstating the position of any one he supposes himself to disagree with, and then attacking him for what he never said, or even implied; the critic thinks this is droll, and appears not to suspect that it is immoral. He is not tolerant; he thinks it a virtue to be intolerant; it is hard for him to understand that the same thing may be admirable at one time and deplorable at another; and that it is really his business to classify and analyze the fruits of the human mind very much as the naturalist classifies the objects of his study, rather than to praise or blame them; that there is a measure of the same absurdity in his trampling on a poem, a novel, or an essay that does not please him as in the botanist's grinding a plant underfoot because he does not find it pretty. He does not conceive that it is his business rather to identify the species and then explain how and where the specimen is imperfect and irregular. If he could once acquire this simple idea of his duty he would be much more agreeable company than he now is, and a more useful member of society; though I hope I am not yet saying that he is not extremely delightful as he is, and wholly indispensable. He is certainly more ignorant than malevolent; and considering the hard conditions under which he works, his necessity of writing hurriedly from an imperfect examination of far more books, on a greater variety of subjects, than he can even hope to read, the average American critic—the ordinary critic of commerce, so to speak—is very well indeed. Collectively he is more than this; for the joint effect of our criticism is the pretty thorough appreciation of any book submitted to it.

VII

The misfortune rather than the fault of our individual critic is that he is the heir of the false theory and bad manners of the English school. The theory of that school has apparently been that almost any person of glib and lively expression is competent to write of almost any branch of polite literature; its manners are what we know. The American, whom it has largely formed, is by nature very glib and very lively, and commonly his criticism, viewed as imaginative work, is more agreeable than that of the Englishman; but it is, like the art of both countries, apt to be amateurish. In some degree our authors have freed themselves from English models; they have gained some notion of the more serious work of the Continent; but it is still the ambition of the American critic to write like the English critic, to show his wit if not his learning, to strive to eclipse the author under review rather than illustrate him. He has not yet caught on to the fact that it is really no part of his business to display himself, but that it is altogether his duty to place a book in such a light that the reader shall know its class, its function, its character. The vast good-nature of our people preserves us from the worst effects of this criticism without principles. Our critic, at his lowest, is rarely malignant; and when he is rude or untruthful, it is mostly without truculence; I suspect that he is often offensive without knowing that he is so. If he loves a shining mark because a fair shot with mud shows best on that kind of target, it is for the most part from a boyish mischievousness quite innocent of malice. Now and then he acts simply under instruction from higher authority, and denounces because it is the tradition of his publication to do so. In other cases the critic is obliged to support his journal's repute for severity, or for wit, or for morality, though he may himself be entirely amiable, dull, and wicked; this necessity more or less warps his verdicts.

The worst is that he is personal, perhaps because it is so easy and so natural to be personal, and so instantly attractive. In this respect our criticism has not improved from the accession of numbers of ladies to its ranks, though we still hope so much from women in our politics when they shall come to vote. They have come to write, and with the effect to increase the amount of little-digging, which rather superabounded in our literary criticism before. They "know what they like"—that pernicious maxim of those who do not know what they ought to like—and they pass readily from censuring an author's performance to censuring him. They bring a lively stock of misapprehensions and prejudices to their work; they would rather have heard about than known about a book; and they take kindly to the public wish to be amused rather than edified. But neither have they so much harm in them; they, too, are more ignorant than malevolent.

VIII

Our criticism is disabled by the unwillingness of the critic to learn from an author, and his readiness to mistrust him. A writer passes his whole life in fitting himself for a certain kind of performance; the critic does not ask why, or whether the performance is good or bad, but if he does not like the kind, he instructs the writer to go off and do some other sort of thing—usually the sort that has been done already, and done sufficiently. If he could once understand that a man who has written the book he dislikes, probably knows infinitely more about its kind and his own fitness for doing it than any one else, the critic might learn something, and might help the reader to learn; but by putting himself in a false position, a position of superiority, he is of no use. He ought, in the first place, to cast prayerfully about for humility, and especially to beseech the powers to preserve him from the sterility of arrogance and the deadness of contempt, for out of these nothing can proceed. He is not to suppose that an author has committed an offence against him by writing the kind of book he does not like; he will be far more profitably employed on behalf of the reader in finding out whether they had better not both like it. Let him conceive of an author as not in any wise on trial before him, but as a reflection of this or that aspect of life, and he will not be tempted to browbeat him or bully him.

The critic need not be impolite even to the youngest and weakest author. A little courtesy, or a good deal, a constant perception of the fact that a book is not a misdemeanor, a decent self-respect that must forbid the civilized man the savage pleasure of wounding, are what I would ask for our criticism, as something which will add sensibly to its present lustre.

IX

I would have my fellow-critics consider what they are really in the world for. It is not, apparently, for a great deal, because their only excuse for being is that somebody else has been. The critic exists because the author first existed.[6] If books failed to appear, the critic must disappear, like the poor aphis or the lowly caterpillar in the absence of vegetation. These insects may both suppose that they have something to do with the creation of vegetation; and the critic may suppose that he has something to do with the creation of literature; but a very little reasoning ought to convince alike aphis, caterpillar, and critic that they are mistaken. The critic—to drop the others—must perceive, if he will question himself more carefully, that his office is mainly to ascertain facts and traits of literature, not to invent or denounce them; to discover principles, not to establish them; to report, not to create.

CRITICISM AND FICTION

It is so much easier to say that you like this or dislike that, than to tell why one thing is, or where another thing comes from, that many flourishing critics will have to go out of business altogether if the scientific method comes in, for then the critic will have to know something beside his own mind, which is often but a narrow field. He will have to know something of the laws of that mind, and of its generic history.

The history of all literature shows that even with the youngest and weakest author criticism is quite powerless against his will to do his own work in his own way; and if this is the case in the green wood, how much more in the dry! It has been thought by the sentimentalist that criticism, if it cannot cure, can at least kill, and Keats was long alleged in proof of its efficacy in this sort. But criticism neither cured nor killed Keats, as we all now very well know. It wounded, it cruelly hurt him, no doubt; and it is always in the power of the critic to give pain to the author—the meanest critic to the greatest author—for no one can help feeling a rudeness. But every literary movement has been violently opposed at the start, and yet never stayed in the least, or arrested, by criticism; every author has been condemned for his virtues, but in no wise changed by it. In the beginning he reads the critics; but presently perceiving that he alone makes or mars himself, and that they have no instruction for him, he mostly leaves off reading them, though he is always glad of their kindness or grieved by their harshness when he chances upon it. This, I believe, is the general experience, modified, of course, by exceptions.

Then, are we critics of no use in the world? I should not like to think that, though I am not quite ready to define our use. More than one sober thinker is inclining at present to suspect that aesthetically or specifically we are of no use, and that we are only useful historically; that we may register laws, but not enact them. I am not quite prepared to admit that aesthetic criticism is useless, though in view of its futility in any given instance it is hard to deny that it is so. It certainly seems as useless against a book that strikes the popular fancy, and prospers on in spite of condemnation by the best critics, as it is against a book which does not generally please, and which no critical favor can make acceptable. This is so common a phenomenon that I wonder it has never hitherto suggested to criticism that its point of view was altogether mistaken, and that it was really necessary to judge books not as dead things, but as living things—things which have an influence and a power irrespective of beauty and wisdom, and merely as expressions of actuality in thought and feeling. Perhaps criticism has a cumulative and final effect; perhaps it does some good we do not know of. It apparently does not affect the author directly, but it may reach him through the reader. It may in some cases enlarge or diminish his audience for a while, until he has thoroughly measured and tested his own powers. If criticism is to affect literature at all, it must be through the writers who have newly left the starting-point, and are reasonably uncertain of the race, not with those who have won it again and again in their own way. I doubt if it can do more than that; but if it can do that I will admit that it may be the toad of adversity, ugly and venomous, from whose unpleasant brow he is to snatch the precious jewel of lasting fame.

I employ this figure in all humility, and I conjure our fraternity to ask themselves, without rancor or offence, whether I am right or not. In this quest let us get together all the modesty and candor and impartiality we can; for if we should happen to discover a good reason for continuing to exist, these qualities will be of more use to us than any others in examining the work of people who really produce something.

X

Sometimes it has seemed to me that the crudest expression of any creative art is better than the finest comment upon it. I have sometimes suspected that more thinking, more feeling certainly, goes to the creation of a poor novel than to the production of a brilliant criticism; and if any novel of our time fails to live a hundred years, will any censure of it live? Who can endure to read old reviews? One can hardly read them if they are in praise of one's own books.

The author neglected or overlooked need not despair for that reason, if he will reflect that criticism can neither make nor unmake authors; that there have not been greater books since criticism became an art than were before; that in fact the greatest books seem to have come much earlier.

That which criticism seems most certainly to have done is to have put a literary consciousness into books unfelt in the early masterpieces, but unfelt now only in the books of men whose lives have been passed in activities, who have been used to employing language as they would have employed any implement, to effect an object, who have regarded a thing to be said as in no wise different from a thing to be done. In this sort I have seen no modern book so unconscious as General Grant's Personal Memoirs. The author's one end and aim is to get the facts out in words. He does not cast about for phrases, but takes the word, whatever it is, that will best give his meaning, as if it were a man or a force of men for the accomplishment of a feat of arms. There is not a moment wasted in preening and prettifying, after the fashion of literary men; there is no thought of style, and so the style is good as it is in the Book of Chronicles, as it is in the Pilgrim's Progress, with a peculiar, almost plebeian, plainness at times. There is no more attempt at dramatic effect than there is at ceremonious pose; things happen in that tale of a mighty war as they happened in the mighty war itself, without setting, without artificial reliefs one after another, as if they were all of one quality and degree. Judgments are delivered with the same unimposing quiet; no awe surrounds the tribunal except that which comes from the weight and justice of the opinions; it is always an unaffected, unpretentious man who is talking; and throughout he prefers to wear the uniform of a private, with nothing of the general about him but the shoulder-straps, which he sometimes forgets.

XI

Canon Farrar's opinions of literary criticism [7] are very much to my liking, perhaps because when I read them I found them so like my own, already delivered in print. He tells the critics that ''they are in no sense the legislators of literature, barely even its judges and police''; and he reminds them of Mr. Ruskin's saying that ''a bad critic is probably the most mischievous person in the world,'' [8] though a sense of their relative proportion to the whole of life would perhaps acquit the worst among them of this extreme of culpability. A bad critic is as bad a thing as can be, but, after all, his mischief does not carry very far. Otherwise it would be mainly the conventional books and not the original books which would survive; for the censor who imagines himself a law-giver can give law only to the imitative and never to the creative mind. Criticism has condemned whatever was, from time to time, fresh and vital in literature; it has always fought the new good thing in behalf of the good old thing; it has invariably fostered and encouraged the tame, the trite, the negative. Yet upon the whole it is the native, the novel, the positive that has survived in literature. Whereas, if bad criticism were the most mischievous thing in the world, in the full implication of the words, it must have been the tame, the trite, the negative, that survived.

Bad criticism is mischievous enough, however; and I think that much if not most current criticism as practised among the English and Americans is bad, is falsely principled, and is conditioned in evil. It is falsely principled because it is unprincipled, or without principles; and it is conditioned in evil because it is almost wholly anonymous. At the best its opinions are not conclusions from certain easily verifiable principles, but are effects from the worship of certain models. They are in so far quite worthless, for it is the very nature of things that the original mind cannot conform to models; it has its norm within itself; it can work only in its own way, and by its self-given laws. Criticism does not inquire whether a work is true to life, but tacitly or explicitly compares it with models, and tests it by them. If literary art travelled by any such road as criticism would have it go, it would travel in a vicious circle, and would arrive only at the point of departure. Yet this is the course that criticism must always prescribe when it attempts to give laws. Being itself artificial it cannot conceive of the original except as the abnormal. It must altogether reconceive its office before it can be of use to literature. It must reduce this to the business of observing, recording, and comparing; to analyzing the material before it, and then synthetizing its impressions. Even then, it is not too much to say that literature as an art could get on perfectly well without it.

27

Just as many good novels, poems, plays, essays, sketches, would be written if there were no such thing as criticism in the literary world, and no more bad ones.

But it will be long before criticism ceases to imagine itself a controlling force, to give itself airs of sovereignty, and to issue decrees. As it exists it is mostly a mischief, though not the greatest mischief; but it may be greatly ameliorated in character and softened in manner by the total abolition of anonymity.

I think it would be safe to say that in no other relation of life is so much brutality permitted by civilized society as in the criticism of literature and the arts. Canon Farrar is quite right in reproaching literary criticism with the uncandor of judging an author without reference to his aims; with pursuing certain writers from spite and prejudice, and mere habit; with misrepresenting a book by quoting a phrase or passage apart from the context; with magnifying misprints and careless expressions into important faults; with abusing an author for his opinions; with base and personal motives. Every writer of experience knows that certain critical journals will condemn his work without regard to its quality, even if it has never been his fortune to learn, as one author did from a repentant reviewer, that in a journal pretending to literary taste his books were given out for review with the caution, "Remember that the Clarion is opposed to Soandso's books." Any author is in luck if he escapes without personal abuse; contempt and impertinence as an author no one will escape.

The final conclusion appears to be that the man, or even the young lady, who is given a gun, and told to shoot at some passer from behind a hedge, is placed in circumstances of temptation almost too strong for human nature.

XII

As I have already intimated, I doubt the more lasting effects of unjust criticism. It is no part of my belief that Keats's fame was long delayed by it, or Wordsworth's, or Browning's. Something unwonted, unexpected, in the quality of each delayed his recognition; each was not only a poet, he was a revolution, a new

CRITICISM AND FICTION

order of things, to which the critical perceptions and habitudes had painfully to adjust themselves. But I have no question of the gross and stupid injustice with which these great men were used, and of the barbarization of the public mind by the sight of the wrong inflicted on them with impunity. This savage condition still persists in the toleration of anonymous criticism, an abuse that ought to be as extinct as the torture of witnesses. It is hard enough to treat a fellow-author with respect even when one has to address him, name to name, upon the same level, in plain day; swooping down upon him in the dark, panoplied in the authority of a great journal, it is impossible.

Every now and then some idealist comes forward and declares that you should say nothing in criticism of a man's book which you would not say of it to his face. But I am afraid this is asking too much. I am afraid it would put an end to all criticism; and that if it were practised literature would be left to purify itself. I have no doubt literature would do this; but in such a state of things there would be no provision for the critics. We ought not to destroy critics, we ought to reform them, or rather transform them, or turn them from the assumption of authority to a realization of their true function in the civilized state. They are no worse at heart, probably, than many others, and there are probably good husbands and tender fathers, loving daughters and careful mothers, among them. I venture to suppose this because I have read that Monsieur de Paris [9] is an excellent person in all the relations of private life, and is extremely anxious to conceal his dreadful occupation from those dear to him.

It is evident to any student of human nature that the critic who is obliged to sign his review will be more careful of an author's feelings than he would if he could intangibly and invisibly deal with him as the representative of a great journal. He will be loath to have his name connected with those perversions and misstatements of an author's meaning in which the critic now indulges without danger of being turned out of honest company. He will be in some degree forced to be fair and just with a book he dislikes; he will not wish to misrepresent it when his sin can be traced directly to him in person; he will not be willing to voice the prejudice of a journal which is "opposed to the books"

29

of this or that author; and the journal itself, when it is no longer responsible for the behavior of its critic, may find it interesting and profitable to give to an author his innings when he feels wronged by a reviewer and desires to right himself; it may even be eager to offer him the opportunity. We shall then, perhaps, frequently witness the spectacle of authors turning upon their reviewers, and improving their manners and morals by confronting them in public with the errors they may now commit with impunity. Many an author smarts under injuries and indignities which he might resent to the advantage of literature and civilization, if he were not afraid of being browbeaten by the journal whose nameless critic has outraged him.

The public is now of opinion that it involves loss of dignity to creative talent to try to right itself if wronged, but here we are without the requisite statistics. Creative talent may come off with all the dignity it went in with, and it may accomplish a very good work in demolishing criticism.

In any other relation of life the man who thinks himself wronged tries to right himself, violently, if he is a mistaken man, and lawfully if he is a wise man or a rich one, which is practically the same thing. But the author, dramatist, painter, sculptor, whose book, play, picture, statue, has been unfairly dealt with, as he believes, must make no effort to right himself with the public; he must bear his wrong in silence; he is even expected to grin and bear it, as if it were funny. Everybody understands that it is not funny to him, not in the least funny, but everybody says that he cannot make an effort to get the public to take his point of view without loss of dignity. This is very odd, but it is the fact, and I suppose that it comes from the feeling that the author, dramatist, painter, sculptor, has already said the best he can for his side in his book, play, picture, statue. This is partly true, and yet if he wishes to add something more to prove the critic wrong, we do not see how his attempt to do so should involve loss of dignity. The public, which is so jealous for his dignity, does not otherwise use him as if he were a very great and invaluable creature; if he fails, it lets him starve like any one else. I should say that he lost dignity or not as he behaved, in his effort to right himself, with petulance or with principle. If he betrayed a wounded vanity, if he impugned the motives and accused the lives of his critics, I should certainly feel that he was losing dignity; but if he temperately examined their theories, and tried to show where they were mistaken, I think he would not only gain dignity, but would perform a very useful work.

The temptation for a critic to cut fantastic tricks before high heaven in the full light of day is great enough, and for his own sake he should be stripped of the shelter of the dark. Even then it will be long before the evolution is complete, and we have the gentle, dispassionate, scientific student of current literature who never imagines that he can direct literature, but realizes that it is a plant which springs from the nature of a people, and draws its forces from their life, that its root is in their character, and that it takes form from their will and taste.

XIII

In fine, I would beseech the literary critics of our country to disabuse themselves of the mischievous notion that they are essential to the progress of literature in the way critics have vainly imagined. Canon Farrar confesses that with the best will in the world to profit by the many criticisms of his books, he has never profited in the least by any of them; and this is almost the universal experience of authors. It is not always the fault of the critics. They sometimes deal honestly and fairly by a book, and not so often they deal adequately. But in making a book, if it is at all a good book, the author has learned all that is knowable about it, and every strong point and every weak point in it, far more accurately than any one else can possibly learn them. He has learned to do better than well for the future; but if his book is bad, he cannot be taught anything about it from the outside. It will perish; and if he has not the root of literature in him, he will perish as an author with it.

But what is it that gives tendency in art, then? What is it makes people like this at one time, and that at another? Above all, what makes a better fashion change for a worse; how can the ugly come to be preferred to the beautiful; in other words, how can art decay?

This question came up in my mind lately with regard to English fiction and its form, or rather its formlessness. How, for instance, could people who had once known the simple verity, the refined perfection of Miss Austen, enjoy anything less refined and less perfect?

With her example before them, why should not English novelists have gone on writing simply, honestly, artistically, ever after? One would think it must have been impossible for them to do otherwise, if one did not remember, say, the lamentable behavior of the actors who support Mr. Jefferson, and their theatricality in the very presence of his beautiful naturalness. It is very difficult, that simplicity, and nothing is so hard as to be honest, as the reader, if he has ever happened to try it, must know. "The big bow-wow I can do myself, like any one going," said Scott,[10] but he owned that the exquisite touch of Miss Austen was denied him; and it seems certainly to have been denied in greater or less measure to all her successors. But though reading and writing come by nature, as Dogberry justly said, a taste in them may be cultivated, or once cultivated, it may be preserved; and why was it not so among those poor islanders? One does not ask such things in order to be at the pains of answering them one's self, but with the hope that some one else will take the trouble to do so, and I propose to be rather a silent partner in the enterprise, which I shall leave mainly to Señor Armando Palacio Valdés. This delightful author will, however, only be able to answer my question indirectly from the essay on fiction with which he prefaces one of his novels, the charming story of The Sister of San Sulphizo, and I shall have some little labor in fitting his saws to my instances. It is an essay which I wish every one intending to read, or even to write, a novel, might acquaint himself with; for it contains some of the best and clearest things which have been said of the art of fiction in a time when nearly all who practise it have turned to talk about it.

Señor Valdés is a realist, but a realist according to his own conception of realism; and he has some words of just censure for the French naturalists, whom he finds unnecessarily, and suspects of being sometimes even mercenarily, nasty. He sees the wide difference that passes between this naturalism and the realism of the English and Spanish; and he goes somewhat further than I should go in condemning it. "The French naturalism represents only a moment, and an insignificant part of life. . . . It is characterized by sadness and narrowness. The prototype of this literature is the Madame Bovary of Flaubert. I am an admirer of this novelist, and especially of this novel; but often in thinking of it I have said, How dreary would literature be if it were no more than this! There is something antipathetic and gloomy and limited in it, as there is in modern French life"; but this seems to me exactly the best possible reason for its being. I believe with Señor Valdés that "no literature can live long without joy," not because of its mistaken aesthetics, however, but because no civilization can live long without joy. The expression of French life will change when French life changes; and French naturalism is better at its worst than French unnaturalism at its best. "No one," as Señor Valdés truly says,[11] "can rise from the perusal of a naturalistic book . . . without a vivid desire to escape" from the wretched world depicted in it, "and a purpose, more or less vague, of helping to better the lot and morally elevate the abject beings who figure in it. Naturalistic art, then, is not immoral in itself, for then it would not merit the name of art; for though it is not the business of art to preach morality, still I think that, resting on a divine and spiritual principle, like the idea of the beautiful, it is perforce moral. I hold much more immoral other books which, under a glamour of something spiritual and beautiful and sublime, portray the vices in which we are allied to the beasts. Such, for example, are the works of Octave Feuillet, Arsène Houssaye, Georges Ohnet,[12] and other contemporary novelists much in vogue among the higher classes of society."

But what is this idea of the beautiful which art rests upon, and so becomes moral? "The man of our time," says Señor Valdés, "wishes to know everything and enjoy everything: he turns the objective of a powerful equatorial towards the heavenly spaces where gravitate the infinitude of the stars, just as he applies the microscope to the infinitude of the smallest insects; for their laws are identical. His experience, united with intuition, has convinced him that in nature there is neither great nor small; all is equal. All is equally grand, all is equally just; all is equally beautiful, because all is equally divine." But beauty, Señor Valdés explains, exists in the human spirit, and is the beautiful effect which it receives from the true meaning of things; it does not matter what the things are, and it is the function of the artist who feels this effect to impart it to others. I may add that there is no joy in art except this perception of the meaning of things and its communication; when you have felt it, and portrayed it in a poem, a symphony, a novel, a statue, a picture, an edifice, you have fulfilled the purpose for which you were born an artist.

The reflection of exterior nature in the individual spirit, Señor Valdés believes to be the fundamental of art. "To say, then, that the artist must not copy but create is nonsense, because he can in no wise copy, and in no wise create. He who sets deliberately about modifying nature, shows that he has not felt her beauty, and therefore cannot make others feel it. The puerile desire which some artists without genius manifest to go about selecting in nature, not what seems to them beautiful, but what they think will seem beautiful to others, and rejecting what may displease them, ordinarily produces cold and insipid works. For, instead of exploring the illimitable fields of reality, they cling to the forms invented by other artists who have succeeded, and they make statues of statues, poems of poems, novels of novels. It is entirely false that the great romantic, symbolic, or classic poets modified nature; such as they have expressed her they felt her; and in this view they are as much realists as ourselves. In like manner if in the realistic tide that now bears us on there are some spirits who feel nature in another way, in the romantic way, or the classic way, they would not falsify her in expressing her so. Only those falsify her who, without feeling classic wise or romantic wise, set about being classic or romantic, wearisomely reproducing the models of former ages; and equally those who, without sharing the sentiment of realism, which now prevails, force themselves to be realists merely to follow the fashion."

The pseudo-realists, in fact, are the worse offenders, to my thinking, for they sin against the living; whereas those who continue to celebrate the heroic adventures of Puss in Boots and the hairbreadth escapes of Tom Thumb, under various aliases, only cast disrespect upon the immortals who have passed beyond these noises.

CRITICISM AND FICTION

XIV

"The principal cause," our Spaniard says,[13] "of the decadence of contemporary literature is found, to my thinking, in the vice which has been very graphically called effectism, or the itch of awaking at all cost in the reader vivid and violent emotions, which shall do credit to the invention and originality of the writer. This vice has its roots in human nature itself, and more particularly in that of the artist; he has always something feminine in him, which tempts him to coquet with the reader, and display qualities that he thinks will astonish him, as women laugh for no reason, to show their teeth when they have them white and small and even, or lift their dresses to show their feet when there is no mud in the street. . . . What many writers nowadays wish, is to produce an effect, grand and immediate, to play the part of geniuses. For this they have learned that it is only necessary to write exaggerated works in any sort, since the vulgar do not ask that they shall be quietly made to think and feel, but that they shall be startled; and among the vulgar, of course, I include the great part of those who write literary criticism, and who constitute the worst vulgar, since they teach what they do not know. . . . There are many persons who suppose that the highest proof an artist can give of his fantasy is the invention of a complicated plot, spiced with perils, surprises, and suspenses; and that anything else is the sign of a poor and tepid imagination. And not only people who seem cultivated, but are not so, suppose this, but there are sensible persons, and even sagacious and intelligent critics, who sometimes allow themselves to be hoodwinked by the dramatic mystery and the surprising and fantastic scenes of a novel. They own it is all false; but they admire the imagination, what they call the 'power' of the author. Very well; all I have to say is that the 'power' to dazzle with strange incidents, to entertain with complicated plots and impossible characters, now belongs to some hundreds of writers in Europe; while there are not much above a dozen who know how to interest with the ordinary events of life, and with the portrayal of characters truly human. If the former is a talent, it must be owned that it is much commoner than the latter. . . . If we are to rate novelists according to their

35

fecundity, or the riches of their invention, we must put Alexander Dumas above Cervantes. Cervantes wrote a novel with the simplest plot, without belying much or little the natural and logical course of events. This novel, which was called Don Quixote, is perhaps the greatest work of human wit. Very well; the same Cervantes, mischievously influenced afterwards by the ideas of the vulgar, who were then what they are now and always will be, attempted to please them by a work giving a lively proof of his inventive talent, and wrote the Persiles and Sigismunda, where the strange incidents, the vivid complications, the surprises, the pathetic scenes, succeed one another so rapidly and constantly that it really fatigues you. . . . But in spite of this flood of invention, imagine,'' says Señor Valdés, ''the place that Cervantes would now occupy in the heaven of art, if he had never written Don Quixote,'' but only Persiles and Sigismunda!

From the point of view of modern English criticism, which likes to be melted, and horrified, and astonished, and blood-curdled, and goose-fleshed, no less than to be ''chippered up'' in fiction, Señor Valdés were indeed incorrigible. Not only does he despise the novel of complicated plot, and everywhere prefer Don Quixote to Persiles and Sigismunda, but he has a lively contempt for another class of novels much in favor with the gentilities of all countries. He calls their writers ''novelists of the world,'' and he says that more than any others they have the rage of effectism. ''They do not seek to produce effect by novelty and invention in plot . . . they seek it in character. For this end they begin by deliberately falsifying human feelings, giving them a paradoxical appearance completely inadmissible. . . . Love that disguises itself as hate, incomparable energy under the cloak of weakness, virginal innocence under the aspect of malice and impudence, wit masquerading as folly, etc., etc. By this means they hope to make an effect of which they are incapable through the direct, frank, and conscientious study of character.'' He mentions Octave Feuillet as the greatest offender in this sort among the French, and Bulwer among the English; but Dickens is full of it (Boffin in Our Mutual Friend will suffice for all example), and the present loathsome artistic squalor of the English drama is witness of the result of this effectism when allowed full play.

But what, then, if he is not pleased with Dumas, or with the effectists who delight genteel people at all the theatres, and in most of the romances, what, I ask, will satisfy this extremely difficult Spanish gentleman? He would pretend, very little. Give him simple, life-like character; that is all he wants. "For me, the only condition of character is that it be human, and that is enough. If I wished to know what was human, I should study humanity."

But, Señor Valdés, Señor Valdés! Do not you know that this small condition of yours implies in its fulfilment hardly less than the gift of the whole earth, with a little gold fence round it? You merely ask that the character portrayed in fiction be human; and you suggest that the novelist should study humanity if he would know whether his personages are human. This appears to me the cruelest irony, the most sarcastic affectation of humility. If you had asked that character in fiction be superhuman, or subterhuman, or preterhuman, or intrahuman, and had bidden the novelist go, not to humanity, but the humanities, for the proof of his excellence, it would have been all very easy. The books are full of those "creations," of every pattern, of all ages, of both sexes; and it is so much handier to get at books than to get at men; and when you have portrayed "passion" instead of feeling, and used "power" instead of common-sense, and shown yourself a "genius" instead of an artist, the applause is so prompt and the glory so cheap, that really anything else seems wickedly wasteful of one's time. One may not make one's reader enjoy or suffer nobly, but one may give him the kind of pleasure that arises from conjuring, or from a puppetshow, or a modern stage play, and leave him, if he is an old fool, in the sort of stupor that comes from hitting the pipe; or if he is a young fool, half crazed with the spectacle of qualities and impulses like his own in an apotheosis of achievement and fruition far beyond any earthly experience.

But apparently Señor Valdés would not think this any great artistic result. "Things that appear ugliest in reality to the spectator who is not an artist, are transformed into beauty and poetry when the spirit of the artist possesses itself of them. We all take part every day in a thousand domestic scenes, every day we see a thousand pictures in life, that do not make any impression upon us, or if they make any it is one of repugnance; but let the novelist come, and without betraying the truth, but painting them as they appear to his vision, he produces a most interesting work, whose perusal enchants us. That which in life left us indifferent, or repelled us, in art delight us. Why? Simply because the artist has made us see the idea that resides in it. Let not the novelists, then, endeavor to add anything to reality, to turn it and twist it, to restrict it. Since nature has endowed them with this precious gift of discovering ideas in things, their work will be beautiful if they paint these as they appear. But if the reality does not impress them, in vain will they strive to make their work impress others.''

XV

Which brings us again, after this long way about, to the divine Jane and her novels, and that troublesome question about them. She was great and they were beautiful, because she and they were honest, and dealt with nature nearly a hundred years ago as realism deals with it to-day. Realism is nothing more and nothing less than the truthful treatment of material, and Jane Austen was the first and the last of the English novelists to treat material with entire truthfulness. Because she did this, she remains the most artistic of the English novelists, and alone worthy to be matched with the great Scandinavian and Slavic and Latin artists. It is not a question of intellect, or not wholly that. The English have mind enough; but they have not taste enough; or, rather, their taste has been perverted by their false criticism, which is based upon personal preference, and not upon principle; which instructs a man to think that what he likes is good, instead of teaching him first to distinguish what is good before he likes it. The art of fiction, as Jane Austen knew it, declined from her through Scott, and Bulwer, and Dickens, and Charlotte Brontë, and Thackeray, and even George Eliot, because the mania of romanticism had seized upon all Europe, and these great writers could not escape the taint of their time; but it has shown few signs of recovery in England, because English criticism, in the presence of the Continental masterpieces, has continued provincial and special and personal, and has expressed a love and hate which had to do with the quality of the artist rather than the character of his work. It was inevitable that in their time the English romanticists should treat, as Señor Valdés says, "the barbarous customs of the Middle Ages, softening and disfiguring them, as Walter Scott and his kind did"; that they should "devote themselves to falsifying nature, refining and subtilizing sentiment, and modifying psychology after their own fancy," like Bulwer and Dickens, as well as like Rousseau and Madame de Staël, not to mention Balzac, the worst of all that sort at his worst. This was the natural course of the disease; but it really seems as if it were their criticism that was to blame for the rest: not, indeed, for the performance of this writer or that, for criticism can never affect the actual doing of a thing; but for the esteem in which this writer or that is held through the perpetuation of false ideals. The only observer of English middle-class life since Jane Austen worthy to be named with her was not George Eliot, who was first ethical and then artistic, who transcended her in everything but the form and method most essential to art, and there fell hopelessly below her. It was Anthony Trollope who was most like her in simple honesty and instinctive truth, as unphilosophized as the light of common day; but he was so warped from a wholesome ideal as to wish at times to be like the caricaturist Thackeray, and to stand about in his scene, talking it over with his hands in his pockets, interrupting the action, and spoiling the illusion in which alone the truth of art resides. Mainly, his instinct was too much for his ideal, and with a low view of life in its civic relations and a thoroughly bourgeois soul, he yet produced works whose beauty is surpassed only by the effect of a more poetic writer in the novels of Thomas Hardy. Yet if a vote of English criticism even at this late day, when all continental Europe has the light of aesthetic truth, could be taken, the majority against these artists would be overwhelmingly in favor of a writer who had so little artistic sensibility, that he never hesitated on any occasion, great or small, to make a foray among his characters, and catch them up to show them to the reader and tell him how beautiful or ugly they were; and cry out over their amazing properties.

Doubtless the ideal of those poor islanders will be finally changed. If the truth could become a fad it would be accepted by all their "smart people," but truth is something rather too large for that; and we must await the gradual advance of civilization among them. Then they will see that their criticism has misled them; and that it is to this false guide they owe, not precisely the decline of fiction among them, but its continued debasement as an art.

XVI

"How few materials," says Emerson, "are yet used by our arts! The mass of creatures and of qualities are still hid and expectant," [14] and to break new ground is still one of the uncommonest and most heroic of the virtues. The artists are not alone to blame for the timidity that keeps them in the old furrows of the worn-out fields; most of those whom they live to please, or live by pleasing, prefer to have them remain there; it wants rare virtue to appreciate what is new, as well as to invent it; and the "easy things to understand" are the conventional things. This is why the ordinary English novel, with its hackneyed plot, scenes, and figures, is more comfortable to the ordinary American than an American novel, which deals, at its worst, with comparatively new interests and motives. To adjust one's self to the enjoyment of these costs an intellectual effort, and an intellectual effort is what no ordinary person likes to make. It is only the extraordinary person who can say, with Emerson: "I ask not for the great, the remote, the romantic. . . . I embrace the common; I sit at the feet of the familiar and the low. . . . Man is surprised to find that things near are not less beautiful and wondrous than things remote. . . . The perception of the worth of the vulgar is fruitful in discoveries. . . . The foolish man wonders at the unusual, but the wise man at the usual. . . . To-day always looks mean to the thoughtless; but to-day is a king in disguise. . . . Banks and tariffs, the newspaper and caucus, Methodism and Unitarianism, are flat and dull to dull people, but rest on the same foundations of wonder as the town of Troy and the temple of Delphos." [15]

Perhaps we ought not to deny their town of Troy and their temple of Delphos to the dull people; but if we ought, and if we did, they would still insist upon having them. An English novel, full of titles and rank, is apparently essential to the happiness of such people; their weak and childish imagination is at home in its familiar environment; they know what they are reading; the fact that it is hash many times warmed over reassures them; whereas a story of our own life, honestly studied and faithfully represented, troubles them with varied misgiving. They are not sure that it is literature; they do not feel that it is good society; its characters, so like their own, strike them as commonplace; they say they do not wish to know such people.

Everything in England is appreciable to the literary sense, while the sense of the literary worth of things in America is still faint and weak with most people, with the vast majority who "ask for the great, the remote, the romantic," who cannot "embrace the common," cannot "sit at the feet of the familiar and the low," in the good company of Emerson. We are all, or nearly all, struggling to be distinguished from the mass, and to be set apart in select circles and upper classes like the fine people we have read about. We are really a mixture of the plebeian ingredients of the whole world; but that is not bad; our vulgarity consists in trying to ignore "the worth of the vulgar," in believing that the superfine is better.

XVII

Another Spanish novelist of our day, whose books have given me great pleasure, is so far from being of the same mind of Señor Valdés about fiction that he boldly declares himself, in the preface to his Pepita Ximenez,[16] "an advocate of art for art's sake." I heartily agree with him that it is "in very bad taste, always impertinent and often pedantic, to attempt to prove theses by writing stories," and yet I fancy that no reader whom Señor Valera would care to please could read his Pepita Ximenez without finding himself in possession of a great deal of serious thinking on a very serious subject, which is none the less serious because it is couched in terms of delicate irony. If it is true that "the object of a novel should be to charm through a faithful representation of human actions and human passions, and to create by this fidelity to nature a beautiful work," and if

41

CRITICISM AND FICTION

"the creation of the beautiful" is solely "the object of art," it
never was and never can be solely its effect as long as men are
men and women are women. If ever the race is resolved into
abstract qualities, perhaps this may happen; but till then the
finest effect of the "beautiful" will be ethical and not aesthetic
merely. Morality penetrates all things, it is the soul of all things.
Beauty may clothe it on, whether it is false morality and an evil
soul, or whether it is true and a good soul. In the one case the
beauty will corrupt, and in the other it will edify, and in either
case it will infallibly and inevitably have an ethical effect, now
light, now grave, according as the thing is light or grave. We
cannot escape from this; we are shut up to it by the very conditions of our being. What is it that delights us in this very Pepita
Ximenez, this exquisite masterpiece of Señor Valera's? Not
merely that a certain Luis de Vargas, dedicated to the priesthood, finds a certain Pepita Ximenez lovelier than the priesthood,
and abandons all his sacerdotal hopes and ambitions, all his
poetic dreams of renunciation and devotion, to marry her. That
is very pretty and very true, and it pleases; but what chiefly
appeals to the heart is the assertion, however delicately and
adroitly implied, that their right to each other through their love
was far above his vocation. In spite of himself, without trying,
and therefore without impertinence and without pedantry,
Señor Valera has proved a thesis in his story. They of the Church
will acquiesce with the reservation of Don Luis's uncle the
Dean that his marriage was better than his vocation, because his
vocation was a sentimental and fancied one; we of the Church-
in-error will accept the result without any reservation whatever; and I think we shall have the greater enjoyment of the
delicate irony, the fine humor, the amusing and unfailing subtlety, with which the argument is enforced. In recognizing
these, however, in praising the story for the graphic skill with
which Southern characters and passions are portrayed in the
gay light of an Andalusian sky, for the charm with which a
fresh and unhackneyed life is presented, and the fidelity with
which novel conditions are sketched, I must not fail to add that
the book is one for those who have come to the knowledge of
good and evil, and to confess my regret that it fails of the re-

42

moter truth, "the eternal amenities" which only the avowed advocates of "art for art's sake" seem to forget. It leaves the reader to believe that Vargas can be happy with a woman who wins him in Pepita's way; and that is where it is false both to life and to art. For the moment, it is charming to have the story end happily, as it does, but after one has lived a certain number of years, and read a certain number of novels, it is not the prosperous or adverse fortune of the characters that affects one, but the good or bad faith of the novelist in dealing with them. Will he play us false or will he be true in the operation of this or that principle involved? I cannot hold him to less account than this: he must be true to what life has taught me is the truth, and after that he may let any fate betide his people; the novel ends well that ends faithfully. The greater his power, the greater his responsibility before the human conscience, which is God in us. But men come and go, and what they do in their limited physical lives is of comparatively little moment; it is what they say that really survives to bless or to ban; and it is the evil which Words- worth felt in Goethe, that must long survive him. There is a kind of thing—a kind of metaphysical lie against righteousness and common-sense—which is called the Unmoral, and is sup- posed to be different from the Immoral; and it is this which is supposed to cover many of the faults of Goethe. His Wilhelm Meister, for example, is so far removed within the region of the "ideal" that its unprincipled, its evil-principled, tenor in re- gard to women is pronounced "unmorality," and is therefore inferably harmless. But no study of Goethe is complete with- out some recognition of the qualities which caused Wordsworth to hurl the book across the room with an indignant perception of its sensuality. For the sins of his life Goethe was perhaps suf- ficiently punished in his life by his final marriage with Chris- tiane; for the sins of his literature many others must suffer. I do not despair, however, of the day when the poor honest herd of mankind shall give universal utterance to the universal in- stinct, and shall hold selfish power in politics, in art, in religion, for the devil that it is; when neither its crazy pride nor its amusing vanity shall be flattered by the puissance of the "gen- iuses" who have forgotten their duty to the common weakness, and have abused it to their own glory. In that day we shall shudder at many monsters of passion, of self-indulgence, of heartlessness, whom we still more or less openly adore for their "genius," and shall account no man worshipful whom we do not feel and know to be good. The spectacle of strenuous achievement will then not dazzle or mislead; it will not sanctify or palliate iniquity; it will only render it the more hideous and pitiable.

In fact, the whole belief in "genius" [17] seems to me rather a mischievous superstition, and if not mischievous always, still always a superstition. From the account of those who talk about it, "genius" appears to be the attribute of a sort of very potent and admirable prodigy which God has created out of the common for the astonishment and confusion of the rest of us poor human beings. But do they really believe it? Do they mean anything more or less than the Mastery which comes to any man according to his powers and diligence in any direction? If not, why not have an end of the superstition which has caused our race to go on so long writing and reading of the difference between talent and genius? It is within the memory of middle-aged men that the Maelstrom existed in the belief of the geographers, but we now get on perfectly well without it; and why should we still suffer under the notion of "genius" which keeps so many poor little authorlings trembling in question whether they have it, or have only "talent"?

One of the greatest captains who ever lived—a plain, taciturn, unaffected soul—has told the story of his wonderful life as unconsciously as if it were all an every-day affair, not different from other lives, except as a great exigency of the human race gave it importance. So far as he knew, he had no natural aptitude for arms, and certainly no love for the calling. But he went to West Point because, as he quaintly tells us, his father "rather thought he would go"; and he fought through one war with credit, but without glory. The other war, which was to claim his powers and his science, found him engaged in the most prosaic of peaceful occupations; he obeyed its call because he loved his country, and not because he loved war. All the world knows the rest, and all the world knows that greater military mastery has

CRITICISM AND FICTION

not been shown than his campaigns illustrated. He does not say this in his book, or hint it in any way; he gives you the facts, and leaves them with you. But the Personal Memoirs of U. S. Grant, written as simply and straightforwardly as his battles were fought, couched in the most unpretentious phrase, with never a touch of grandiosity or attitudinizing, familiar, homely in style, form a great piece of literature, because great literature is nothing more nor less than the clear expression of minds that have something great in them, whether religion, or beauty, or deep experience. Probably Grant would have said that he had no more vocation to literature than he had to war. He owns, with something like contrition, that he used to read a great many novels; but we think he would have denied the soft impeachment of literary power. Nevertheless, he shows it, as he showed military power, unexpectedly, almost miraculously. All the conditions here, then, are favorable to supposing a case of "genius." Yet who would trifle with that great heir of fame, that plain, grand, manly soul, by speaking of "genius" and him together? Who calls Washington a genius? or Franklin, or Bismarck, or Cavour, or Columbus, or Luther, or Darwin, or Lincoln? Were these men second-rate in their way? Or is "genius" that indefinable, preternatural quality, sacred to the musicians, the painters, the sculptors, the actors, the poets, and above all, the poets? Or is it that the poets, having most of the say in this world, abuse it to shameless self-flattery, and would persuade the inarticulate classes that they are on peculiar terms of confidence with the deity?

XVIII

In General Grant's confession of novel-reading there is a sort of inference that he had wasted his time, or else the guilty conscience of the novelist in me imagines such an inference. But however this may be, there is certainly no question concerning the intention of a correspondent who once wrote to me after reading some rather bragging claims I had made for fiction as a mental and moral means. "I have very grave doubts," he said, "as to the whole list of magnificent things that you seem to think novels have done for the race, and can witness in myself many evil things which they have done for me. Whatever in my mental make-up is wild and visionary, whatever is untrue, whatever is injurious, I can trace to the perusal of some work of fiction. Worse than that, they beget such high-strung and supersensitive ideas of life that plain industry and plodding perseverance are despised, and matter-of-fact poverty, or every-day, commonplace distress, meets with no sympathy, if indeed noticed at all, by one who has wept over the impossibly accumulated sufferings of some gaudy hero or heroine.''

I am not sure that I had the controversy with this correspondent that he seemed to suppose; but novels are now so fully accepted by every one pretending to cultivated taste— and they really form the whole intellectual life of such immense numbers of people, without question of their influence, good or bad upon the mind—that it is refreshing to have them frankly denounced, and to be invited to revise one's ideas and feelings in regard to them. A little honesty, or a great deal of honesty, in this quest will do the novel, as we hope yet to have it, and as we have already begun to have it, no harm; and for my own part I will confess that I believe fiction in the past to have been largely injurious, as I believe the stage play to be still almost wholly injurious, through its falsehood, its folly, its wantonness, and its aimlessness. It may be safely assumed that most of the novel-reading which people fancy an intellectual pastime is the emptiest dissipation, hardly more related to thought or the wholesome exercise of the mental faculties that opium-eating; in either case the brain is drugged, and left weaker and crazier for the debauch. If this may be called the negative result of the fiction habit, the positive injury that most novels work is by no means so easily to be measured in the case of young men whose character they help so much to form or deform, and the women of all ages whom they keep so much in ignorance of the world they misrepresent. Grown men have little harm from them, but in the other cases, which are the vast majority, they hurt because they are not true—not because they are malevolent, but because they are idle lies about

46

CRITICISM AND FICTION

human nature and the social fabric, which it behooves us to
know and to understand, that we may deal justly with ourselves
and with one another. One need not go so far as our correspondent, and trace to the fiction habit "whatever is wild and
visionary, whatever is untrue, whatever is injurious," in one's
life; bad as the fiction habit is it is probably not responsible
for the whole sum of evil in its victims, and I believe that if
the reader will use care in choosing from this fungus-growth
with which the fields of literature teem every day, he may
nourish himself as with the true mushroom, at no risk from
the poisonous species.

The tests are very plain and simple, and they are perfectly
infallible. If a novel flatters the passions, and exalts them above
the principles, it is poisonous; it may not kill, but it will certainly injure; and this test will alone exclude an entire class
of fiction, of which eminent examples will occur to all. Then
the whole spawn of so-called unmoral romances, which imagine
a world where the sins of sense are unvisited by the penalties
following, swift or slow, but inexorably sure, in the real world,
are deadly poison: these do kill. The novels that merely tickle
our prejudices and lull our judgment, or that coddle our sensibilities or pamper our gross appetite for the marvelous are
not so fatal, but they are innutritious, and clog the soul with unwholesome vapors of all kinds. No doubt they too help to weaken
the moral fibre, and make their readers indifferent to "plodding
perseverance and plain industry," and to "matter-of-fact
poverty and commonplace distress."

Without taking them too seriously, it still must be owned
that the "gaudy hero and heroine" are to blame for a great
deal of harm in the world. That heroine long taught by example, if not precept, that Love, or the passion or fancy she
mistook for it, was the chief interest of a life, which is really
concerned with a great many other things; that it was lasting
in the way she knew it; that it was worthy of every sacrifice,
and was altogether a finer thing than prudence, obedience, reason; that love alone was glorious and beautiful, and these were
mean and ugly in comparison with it. More lately she has begun
to idolize and illustrate Duty, and she is hardly less mischievous

47

in this new role, opposing duty, as she did love, to prudence, obedience, and reason. The stock hero, whom, if we met him, we could not fail to see was a most deplorable person, has undoubtedly imposed himself upon the victims of the fiction habit as admirable. With him, too, love was and is the great affair, whether in its old romantic phase of chivalrous achievement or manifold suffering for love's sake, or its more recent development of the "virile," the bullying, and the brutal, or its still more recent agonies of self-sacrifice, as idle and useless as the moral experiences of the insane asylums. With his vain posturings and his ridiculous splendor he is really a painted barbarian, the prey of his passions and his delusions, full of obsolete ideals, and the motives and ethics of a savage, which the guilty author of his being does his best—or his worst —in spite of his own light and knowledge, to foist upon the reader as something generous and noble. I am not merely bringing this charge against that sort of fiction which is beneath literature and outside of it, "the shoreless lakes of ditch-water," whose miasms fill the air below the empyrean where the great ones sit; but I am accusing the work of some of the most famous, who have, in this instance or in that, sinned against the truth, which can alone exalt and purify men. I do not say that they have constantly done so, or even commonly done so; but that they have done so at all marks them as of the past, to be read with the due historical allowance for their epoch and their conditions. For I believe that, while inferior writers will and must continue to imitate them in their foibles and their errors, no one hereafter will be able to achieve greatness who is false to humanity, either in its facts or its duties. The light of civilization has already broken even upon the novel, and no conscientious man can now set about painting an image of life without perpetual question of the verity of his work, and without feeling bound to distinguish so clearly that no reader of his may be misled between what is right and what is wrong, what is noble and what is base, what is health and what is perdition, in the actions and the characters he portrays.

The fiction that aims merely to entertain—the fiction that is to serious fiction as the opera-bouffe, the ballet, and the pantomime are to the true drama—need not feel the burden of this obligation so deeply; but even such fiction will not be gay or trivial to any reader's hurt, and criticism will hold it to account if it passes from painting to teaching folly.

More and more not only the criticism which prints its opinions, but the infinitely vaster and powerfuler criticism which thinks and feels them merely, will make this demand. I confess that I do not care to judge any work of the imagination without first of all applying this test to it. We must ask ourselves before we ask anything else, Is it true?—true to the motives, the impulses, the principles that shape the life of actual men and women? This truth, which necessarily includes the highest morality and the highest artistry—this truth given, the book cannot be wicked and cannot be weak; and without it all graces of style and feats of invention and cunning of construction are so many superfluities of naughtiness. It is well for the truth to have all these, and shine in them, but for falsehood they are merely meretricious, the bedizenment of the wanton; they atone for nothing, they count for nothing. But in fact they come naturally of truth, and grace it without solicitation; they are added unto it. In the whole range of fiction we know of no true picture of life—that is, of human nature—which is not also a masterpiece of literature, full of divine and natural beauty. It may have no touch or tint of this special civilization or of that; it had better have this local color well ascertained; but the truth is deeper and finer than aspects, and if the book is true to what men and women know of one another's souls it will be true enough, and it will be great and beautiful. It is the conception of literature as something apart from life, superfinely aloof, which makes it really unimportant to the great mass of mankind, without a message or a meaning for them; and it is the notion that a novel may be false in its portrayal of causes and effects that makes literary art contemptible even to those whom it amuses, that forbids them to regard the novelist as a serious or right-minded person. If they do not in some moment of indignation cry out against all novels, as my correspondent does, they remain besotted in the fume of the delusions purveyed to them, with no higher

feeling for the author than such maudlin affection as the habitué
of an opium-joint perhaps knows for the attendant who fills
his pipe with the drug.

Or, as in the case of another correspondent who writes that
in his youth he "read a great many novels, but always regarded
it as an amusement, like horse-racing and card-playing," for
which he had no time when he entered upon the serious business of life, it renders them merely contemptuous. His view
of the matter may be commended to the brotherhood and sister-
hood of novelists as full of wholesome if bitter suggestion; and
we urge them not to dismiss it with high literary scorn as that
of some Bœotian dull to the beauty of art. Refuse it as we may,
it is still the feeling of the vast majority of people for whom
life is earnest, and who find only a distorted and misleading
likeness of it in our books. We may fold ourselves in our
scholars' gowns, and close the doors of our studies, and affect
to despise this rude voice; but we cannot shut it out. It comes
to us from wherever men are at work, from wherever they are
truly living, and accuses us of unfaithfulness, of triviality, of
mere stage-play; and none of us can escape conviction except
he prove himself worthy of his time—a time in which the great
masters have brought literature back to life, and filled its ebbing
veins with the red tides of reality. We cannot all equal them;
we need not copy them; but we can all go to the sources of their
inspiration and their power; and to draw from these no one
need go far—no one need really go out of himself.

Fifty years ago, Carlyle,[18] in whom the truth was always
alive, but in whom it was then unperverted by suffering, by
celebrity, and by despair, wrote in his study of Diderot: "Were
it not reasonable to prophesy that this exceeding great multitude
of novel-writers and such like must, in a new generation, gradually do one of two things: either retire into the nurseries, and
work for children, minors, and semi-fatuous persons of both
sexes, or else, what were far better, sweep their novel-fabric
into the dust-cart, and betake themselves with such faculty
as they have to understand and record what is true, of which
surely there is, and will forever be, a whole infinitude unknown
to us of infinite importance to us? Poetry, it will more and

CRITICISM AND FICTION

more come to be understood, is nothing but higher knowledge;
and the only genuine Romance (for grown persons), Reality.''
If, after half a century, fiction still mainly works for ''children, minors, and semi-fatuous persons of both sexes,'' it is
nevertheless one of the hopefulest signs of the world's progress
that it has begun to work for ''grown persons,'' and if not
exactly in the way that Carlyle might have solely intended in
urging its writers to compile memoirs instead of building the
''novel-fabric,'' still it has, in the highest and widest sense,
already made Reality its Romance. I cannot judge it, I do not
even care for it, except as it has done this; and I can hardly
conceive of a literary self-respect in these days compatible with
the old trade of make-believe, with the production of the kind
of fiction which is too much honored by classification with card-
playing and horse-racing. But let fiction cease to lie about life;
let it portray men and women as they are, actuated by the
motives and the passions in the measure we all know; let it
leave off painting dolls and working them by springs and wires;
let it show the different interests in their true proportions; let
it forbear to preach pride and revenge, folly and insanity,
egotism and prejudice, but frankly own these for what they
are, in whatever figures and occasions they appear; let it not
put on fine literary airs; let it speak the dialect, the language,
that most Americans know—the language of unaffected people
everywhere—and there can be no doubt of an unlimited future,
not only of delightfulness but of usefulness, for it.

XIX

This is what I say in my severer moods, but at other times I
know that, of course, no one is going to hold all fiction to such
strict account. There is a great deal of it which may be very
well left to amuse us, if it can, when we are sick or when we
are silly, and I am not inclined to despise it in the performance
of this office. Or, if people find pleasure in having their blood
curdled for the sake of having it uncurdled again at the end
of the book, I would not interfere with their amusement, though
I do not desire it. There is a certain demand in primitive natures

51

for the kind of fiction that does this, and the author of it is usually very proud of it. The kind of novels he likes, and likes to write, are intended to take his reader's mind, or what that reader would probably call his mind, off himself; they make one forget life and all its cares and duties; they are not in the least like the novels which make you think of these, and shame you into at least wishing to be a helpfuler and wholesomer creature than you are. No sordid details of verity here, if you please; no wretched being humbly and weakly struggling to do right and to be true, suffering for his follies and his sins, tasting joy only through the mortification of self, and in the help of others; nothing of all this, but a great, whirling splendor of peril and achievement, a wild scene of heroic adventure and of emotional ground and lofty tumbling, with a stage "picture" at the fall of the curtain, and all the good characters in a row, their left hands pressed upon their hearts, and kissing their right hands to the audience, in the good old way that has always charmed and always will charm, Heaven bless it!

In a world which loves the spectacular drama and the practically bloodless sports of the modern amphitheatre the author of this sort of fiction has his place, and we must not seek to destroy him because he fancies it the first place. In fact, it is a condition of his doing well the kind of work he does that he should think it important, that he should believe in himself; and I would not take away this faith of his, even if I could. As I say, he has his place. The world often likes to forget itself, and he brings on his heroes, his goblins, his feats, his hairbreadth escapes, his imminent deadly breaches, and the poor, foolish, childish old world renews the excitements of its nonage. Perhaps this is a work of beneficence; and perhaps our brave conjurer in his cabalistic robe is a philanthropist in disguise.

Within the last four or five years there has been throughout the whole English-speaking world what Mr. Grant Allen [19] happily calls the "recrudescence" of taste in fiction. The effect is less noticeable in America than in England, where effete Philistinism, conscious of the dry-rot of its conventionality, is casting about for cure in anything that is wild and strange and unlike itself. But the recrudescence has been evident enough here, too; and a writer in one of our periodicals has put into convenient shape some common errors concerning popularity as a test of merit in a book.[20] He seems to think, for instance, that the love of the marvellous and impossible in fiction, which is shown not only by "the unthinking multitude clamoring about the book counters" for fiction of that sort, but by the "literary elect" also, is proof of some principle in human nature which ought to be respected as well as tolerated. He seems to believe that the ebullition of this passion forms a sufficient answer to those who say that art should represent life, and that the art which misrepresents life is feeble art and false art. But it appears to me that a little carefuler reasoning from a little closer inspection of the facts would not have brought him to these conclusions. In the first place, I doubt very much whether the "literary elect" have been fascinated in great numbers by the fiction in question; but if I supposed them to have really fallen under that spell, I should still be able to account for their fondness and that of the "unthinking multitude" upon the same grounds, without honoring either very much. It is the habit of hasty casuists to regard civilization as inclusive of all the members of a civilized community; but this is a palpable error. Many persons in every civilized community live in a state of more or less evident savagery with respect to their habits, their morals, and their propensities; and they are held in check only by the law. Many more yet are savage in their tastes, as they show by the decoration of their houses and persons, and by their choice of books and pictures; and these are left to the restraints of public opinion. In fact, no man can be said to be thoroughly civilized or always civilized; the most refined, the most enlightened person has his moods, his moments of barbarism, in which the best, or even the second best, shall not please him. At these times the lettered and the unlettered are alike primitive and their gratifications are of the same simple sort; the highly cultivated person may then like melodrama, impossible fiction, and the trapeze as sincerely and thoroughly as a boy of thirteen or a barbarian of any age.

I do not blame him for these moods; I find something instructive and interesting in them; but if they lastingly estab-

lished themselves in him, I could not help deploring the state
of that person. No one can really think that the "literary
elect," who are said to have joined the "unthinking multitude"
in clamoring about the book counters for the romances of no-
man's land, take the same kind of pleasure in them as they do
in a novel of Tolstoi, Tourguéneff, George Eliot, Thackeray,
Balzac, Manzoni, Hawthorne, Henry James, Thomas Hardy,
Palacio Valdés, or even Walter Scott. They have joined the
"unthinking multitude," perhaps because they are tired of
thinking, and expect to find relaxation in feeling—feeling
crudely, grossly, merely. For once in a way there is no great
harm in this; perhaps no harm at all. It is perfectly natural;
let them have their innocent debauch. But let us distinguish,
for our own sake and guidance, between the different kinds
of things that please the same kind of people; between the
things that please them habitually and those that please them
occasionally; between the pleasures that edify them and those
that amuse them. Otherwise we shall be in danger of becoming
permanently part of the "unthinking multitude," and of remaining puerile, primitive, savage. We shall be so in moods
and at moments; but let us not fancy that those are high moods
or fortunate moments. If they are harmless, that is the most
that can be said for them. They are lapses from which we can
perhaps go forward more vigorously; but even this is not certain.

My own philosophy of the matter, however, would not bring
me to prohibition of such literary amusements as the writer
quoted seems to find significant of a growing indifference to
truth and sanity in fiction. Once more, I say, these amusements
have their place, as the circus has, and the burlesque and negro
minstrelsy, and the ballet, and prestidigitation. No one of these
is to be despised in its place; but we had better understand
that it is not the highest place, and that it is hardly an intellectual delight. The lapse of all the "literary elect" in the
world could not dignify unreality; and their present mood,
if it exists, is of no more weight against that beauty in literature which comes from truth alone, and never can come from

anything else, than the permanent state of the "unthinking multitude."

Yet even as regards the "unthinking multitude," I believe I am not able to take the attitude of the writer I have quoted. I am afraid that I respect them more than he would like to have me, though I cannot always respect their taste, any more than that of the "literary elect." I respect them for their good sense in most practical matters; for their laborious, honest lives; for their kindness, their good-will; for that aspiration towards something better than themselves which seems to stir, however dumbly, in every human breast not abandoned to literary pride or other forms of self-righteousness. I find every man interesting, whether he thinks or unthinks, whether he is savage or civilized; for this reason I cannot thank the novelist who teaches us not to know but to unknow our kind. Yet I should by no means hold him to such strict account as Emerson, who felt the absence of the best motive, even in the greatest of the masters, when he said of Shakespeare that, after all, he was only master of the revels.[21] The judgment is so severe, even with the praise which precedes it, that one winces under it; and if one is still young, with the world gay before him, and life full of joyous promise, one is apt to ask, defiantly, Well, what is better than being such a master of the revels as Shakespeare was? Let each judge for himself. To the heart again of serious youth uncontaminate and exigent of ideal good, it must always be a grief that the great masters seem so often to have been willing to amuse the leisure and vacancy of meaner men, and leave their mission to the soul but partially fulfilled. This, perhaps, was what Emerson had in mind; and if he had it in mind of Shakespeare, who gave us, with his histories and comedies and problems, such a searching homily as "Macbeth," one feels that he scarcely recognized the limitations of the dramatist's art. Few consciences, at times, seem so enlightened as that of this personally unknown person, so withdrawn into his work, and so lost to the intensest curiosity of after-time; at other times he seems merely Elizabethan in his coarseness, his courtliness, his imperfect sympathy.

Of the finer kinds of romance, as distinguished from the novel, I would even encourage the writing, though it is one of the hard conditions of romance that its personages starting with a parti pris can rarely be characters with a living growth, but are apt to be types, limited to the expression of one principle, simple, elemental, lacking the God-given complexity of motive which we find in all the human beings we know.

Hawthorne, the great master of the romance, had the insight and the power to create it anew as a kind in fiction; though I am not sure that The Scarlet Letter and the Blithedale Romance are not, strictly speaking, novels rather than romances. They do not play with some old superstition long outgrown, and they do not invent a new superstition to play with, but deal with things vital in every one's pulse. I am not saying that what may be called the fantastic romance—the romance that descends from Frankenstein rather than The Scarlet Letter —ought not to be. On the contrary, I should grieve to lose it, as I should grieve to lose the pantomime or the comic opera, or many other graceful things that amuse the passing hour, and help us to live agreeably in a world where men actually sin, suffer, and die. But it belongs to the decorative arts, and though it has a high place among them, it cannot be ranked with the works of the imagination—the works that represent and body forth human experience. Its ingenuity can always afford a refined pleasure, and it can often, at some risk to itself, convey a valuable truth.

Perhaps the whole region of historical romance might be re-opened with advantage to readers and writers who cannot bear to be brought face to face with human nature, but require the haze of distance or a far perspective, in which all the disagreeable details shall be lost. There is no good reason why these harmless people should not be amused, or their little preferences indulged.

But here, again, I have my modest doubts, some recent instances are so fatuous, as far as the portrayal of character goes, though I find them admirably contrived in some respects.

CRITICISM AND FICTION

When I have owned the excellence of the staging in every respect, and the conscience with which the carpenter (as the theatrical folks say) has done his work, I am at the end of my praises. The people affect me like persons of our generation made up for the parts; well trained, well costumed, but actors, and almost amateurs. They have the quality that makes the histrionics of amateurs endurable; they are ladies and gentlemen; the worst, the wickedest of them, is a lady or gentleman behind the scene.

Yet, no doubt it is well that there should be a reversion to the earlier types of thinking and feeling, to earlier ways of looking at human nature, and I will not altogether refuse the pleasure offered me by the poetic romancer or the historical romancer because I find my pleasure chiefly in Tolstoi and James and Galdós and Valdés and Thomas Hardy and Tourguéneff, and Balzac at his best.

The reversions or counter-currents in the general tendency of a time are very curious, and are worthy tolerant study. They are always to be found; perhaps they form the exception that establishes the rule; at least they distinguish it. They give us performances having an archaic charm by which, by-and-by, things captivate for reasons unconnected with their inherent beauty. They become quaint, and this is reason enough for liking them, for returning to them, and in art for trying to do them again. But I confess that I like better to go forward than to go backward, and it is saying very little to say that I value more such a novel as Mr. James's Tragic Muse than all the romantic attempts since Hawthorne. I call Mr. James a novelist because there is yet no name for the literary kind he has invented, and so none for the inventor. The fatuity of the story merely as a story is something that must early impress the storyteller who does not live in the stone age of fiction and criticism. To spin a yarn for the yarn's sake, that is an ideal worthy of a nineteenth-century Englishman, doting in forgetfulness of the English masters and grovelling in ignorance of the Continental masters; but wholly impossible to an American of Mr. Henry James's modernity. To him it must seem like the lies swapped between men after the ladies have left the table and they are sinking deeper and deeper into their cups and growing dimmer and dimmer behind their cigars. To such a mind as his the story could never have value except as a means; it could not exist for him as an end; it could be used only illustratively; it could be the frame, not possibly the picture. But in the mean time the kind of thing he wished to do, and began to do, and has always done, amid a stupid clamor, which still lasts, that it was not a story, had to be called a novel; and the wretched victim of the novel habit (only a little less intellectually degraded than the still more miserable slave of the theatre habit), who wished neither to perceive nor to reflect, but only to be acted upon by plot and incident, was lost in an endless trouble about it. Here was a thing called a novel, written with extraordinary charm; interesting by the vigor and vivacity with which phases and situations and persons were handled in it; inviting him to the intimacy of characters divined with creative insight; making him witness of motives and emotions and experiences of the finest import; and then suddenly requiring him to be man enough to cope with the question itself; not solving it for him by a marriage or a murder, and not spoon-victualling him with a moral minced small and then thinned with milk and water, and familiarly flavored with sentimentality or religiosity. I can imagine the sort of shame with which such a writer as Mr. James, so original and so clear-sighted, may sometimes have been tempted by the outcry of the nurslings of fable, to give them of the diet on which they had been pampered to imbecility; or to call together his characters for a sort of round-up in the last chapter.

XXI

It is no doubt such work as Mr. James's that an English essayist (Mr. E. Hughes) [22] has chiefly in mind, in a study of the differences of the English and American novel. He defines the English novel as working from within outwardly, and the American novel as working from without inwardly. The definition is very surprisingly accurate; and the critic's discovery of this fundamental difference is carried into particulars with a distinctness which is as unfailing as the courtesy he has in

53

recognizing the present superiority of American work. He seems to think, however, that the English principle is the better, though why he should think so he does not make so clear. It appears a belated and rather voluntary effect of patriotism, disappointing in a philosopher of his degree; but it does not keep him from very explicit justice to the best characteristics of our fiction. "The American novelist is distinguished for the intellectual grip which he has of his characters. . . . He penetrates below the crust, and he recognizes no necessity of the crust to anticipate what is beneath. . . . He utterly discards heroics; he often even discards anything like a plot. . . . His story proper is often no more than a natural predicament. . . . It is no stage view we have of his characters, but one behind the scenes. . . . We are brought into contact with no strained virtues, illumined by strained lights upon strained heights of situation. . . . Whenever he appeals to the emotions it would seem to be with an appeal to the intellect too . . . because he weaves his story of the finer, less self-evident though common threads of human nature, seldom calling into play the grosser and more powerful strain. . . . Everywhere in his pages we come across acquaintances undisguised. . . . The characters in an American novel are never unapproachable to the reader. . . . The naturalness, with the every-day atmosphere which surrounds it, is one great charm of the American novel. . . . It is throughout examinative, discursory, even more—quizzical. Its characters are undergoing, at the hands of the author, calm, interested observation. . . . He is never caught identifying himself with them; he must preserve impartiality at all costs . . . but . . . the touch of nature is always felt, the feeling of kinship always follows. . . . The strength of the American novel is its optimistic faith. . . . If out of this persistent hopefulness it can evolve for men a new order of trustfulness, a tenet that between man and man there should be less suspicion, more confidence, since human nature sanctions it, its mission will have been more than an aesthetic, it will have been a moral one."

Not all of this will be found true of Mr. James, but all that relates to artistic methods and characteristics will, and the rest is true of American novels generally. For the most part in their range and tendency they are admirable. I will not say they are all good, or that any of them is wholly good; but I find in nearly every one of them a disposition to regard our life without the literary glasses so long thought desirable, and to see character, not as it is in other fiction, but as it abounds outside of all fiction. This disposition sometimes goes with poor enough performance, but in some of our novels it goes with performance that is excellent; and at any rate it is for the present more valuable than evenness of performance. It is what relates American fiction to the only living movement in imaginative literature, and distinguishes by a superior freshness and authenticity any group of American novels from a similarly accidental group of English novels, giving them the same good right to be as the like number of recent Russian novels, French novels, Spanish novels, Italian novels, Norwegian novels.

It is the difference of the American novelist's ideals from those of the English novelist that gives him his advantage, and seems to promise him the future. The love of the passionate and the heroic, as the Englishman has it, is such a crude and unwholesome thing, so deaf and blind to all the most delicate and important facts of art and life, so insensible to the subtle values in either that its presence or absence makes the whole difference, and enables one who is not obsessed by it to thank Heaven that he is not as that other man is.

There can be little question that many refinements of thought and spirit which every American is sensible of in the fiction of this continent, are necessarily lost upon our good kin beyond seas, whose thumb-fingered [23] apprehension requires something gross and palpable for its assurance of reality. This is not their fault, and I am not sure that it is wholly their misfortune: they are made so as not to miss what they do not find, and they are simply content without those subtleties of life and character which it gives us so keen a pleasure to have noted in literature. If they perceive them at all it is as something vague and diaphanous, something that filmily wavers before their sense and teases them, much as the beings of an invisible world might mock one of our material frame by intimations of their presence. It is with reason, therefore, on the part of an

Englishman, that Mr. Henley [24] complains of our fiction as a shadow-land, though we find more and more in it the faithful report of our life, its motives and emotions, and all the comparatively etherealized passions and ideals that influence it.

In fact, the American who chooses to enjoy his birthright to the full, lives in a world wholly different from the Englishman's, and speaks (too often through his nose) another language: he breathes a rarefied and nimble air full of shining possibilities and radiant promises which the fog-and-soot-clogged lungs of those less-favored islanders struggle in vain to fill themselves with. But he ought to be modest in his advantage, and patient with the coughing and sputtering of his cousin who complains of finding himself in an exhausted receiver [25] on plunging into one of our novels. To be quite just to the poor fellow, I have had some such experience as that myself in the atmosphere of some of our more attenuated romances.

Yet every now and then I read a book with perfect comfort and much exhilaration, whose scenes the average Englishman would gasp in. Nothing happens; that is, nobody murders or debauches anybody else; there is no arson or pillage of any sort; there is not a ghost, or a ravening beast, or a hair-breadth escape, or a shipwreck, or a monster of self-sacrifice, or a lady five thousand years old in the whole course of the story; "no promenade, no band of music, nossing!" as Mr. Du Maurier's Frenchman said of the meet for a fox-hunt.[26] Yet it is all alive with the keenest interest for those who enjoy the study of individual traits and general conditions as they make themselves known to American experience.

These conditions have been so favorable hitherto (though they are becoming always less so) that they easily account for the optimistic faith of our novel which Mr. Hughes notices. It used to be one of the disadvantages of the practice of romance in America, which Hawthorne [27] more or less whimsically lamented, that there were so few shadows and inequalities in our broad level of prosperity; and it is one of the reflections suggested by Dostoïevsky's novel, The Crime and the Punishment, that whoever struck a note so profoundly tragic in American fiction would do a false and mistaken thing—as false and as mistaken in its way as dealing in American fiction with certain nudities which the Latin peoples seem to find edifying. Whatever their deserts, very few American novelists have been led out to be shot, or finally exiled to the rigors of a winter at Duluth; and in a land where journeymen carpenters and plumbers strike for four dollars a day the sum of hunger and cold is comparatively small, and the wrong from class to class has been almost inappreciable, though all this is changing for the worse. Our novelists, therefore, concern themselves with the more smiling aspects of life, which are the more American, and seek the universal in the individual rather than the social interests. It is worth while, even at the risk of being called commonplace, to be true to our well-to-do actualities; the very passions themselves seem to be softened and modified by conditions which formerly at least could not be said to wrong any one, to cramp endeavor, or to cross lawful desire. Sin and suffering and shame there must always be in the world, I suppose, but I believe that in this new world of ours it is still mainly from one to another one, and oftener still from one to one's self. We have death too in America, and a great deal of disagreeable and painful disease, which the multiplicity of our patent medicines does not seem to cure; but this is tragedy that comes in the very nature of things, and is not peculiarly American, as the large, cheerful average of health and success and happy life is. It will not do to boast, but it is well to be true to the facts, and to see that, apart from these purely mortal troubles, the race here has enjoyed conditions in which most of the ills that have darkened its annals might be averted by honest work and unselfish behavior.

Fine artists we have among us, and right-minded as far as they go; and we must not forget this at evil moments when it seems as if all the women had taken to writing hysterical improprieties, and some of the men were trying to be at least as hysterical in despair of being as improper. If we kept to the complexion of a certain school—which sadly needs a schoolmaster—we might very well be despondent; but, after all, that school is not representative of our conditions or our intentions. Other traits are much more characteristic of our life and our fiction. In most American novels, vivid and graphic as the best of them are, the people are segregated if not sequestered, and the scene is sparsely populated. The effect may be in instinctive response to the vacancy of our social life, and I shall not make haste to blame it. There are few places, few occasions among us, in which a novelist can get a large number of polite people together, or at least keep them together. Unless he carries a snap-camera [28] his picture of them has no probability; they affect one like the figures perfunctorily associated in such deadly old engravings as that of ''Washington Irving and his Friends.'' [29] Perhaps it is for this reason that we excel in small pieces with three or four figures, or in studies of rustic communities, where there is propinquity if not society. Our grasp of more urbane life is feeble; most attempts to assemble it in our pictures are failures, possibly because it is too transitory, too intangible in its nature with us, to be truthfully represented as really existent.

I am not sure that the Americans have not brought the short story nearer perfection in the all-round sense than almost any other people, and for reasons very simple and near at hand. It might be argued from the national hurry and impatience that it was a literary form peculiarly adapted to the American temperament, but I suspect that its extraordinary development among us is owing much more to more tangible facts. The success of American magazines, which is nothing less than prodigious, is only commensurate with their excellence. Their sort of success is not only from the courage to decide what ought to please, but from the knowledge of what does please; and it is probable that, aside from the pictures, it is the short stories which please the readers of our best magazines. The serial novels they must have, of course; but rather more of course they must have short stories, and by operation of the law of supply and demand, the short stories, abundant in quantity and excellent in quality, are forthcoming because they are wanted. By another operation of the same law, which political economists have more recently taken account of, the demand follows the supply, and short stories are sought for because there is a proven ability to furnish them, and people read them willingly because they are usually very good. The art of writing them is now so disciplined and diffused with us that there is no lack either for the magazines or for the newspaper "syndicates" which deal in them almost to the exclusion of the serials. In other countries the feuilleton of the journals is a novel continued from day to day, but with us the papers, whether daily or weekly, now more rarely print novels, whether they get them at first hand from the writers, as a great many do, or through the syndicates, which purvey a vast variety of literary wares, chiefly for the Sunday editions of the city journals. In the country papers the short story takes the place of the chapters of a serial which used to be given.

XXII

An interesting fact in regard to the different varieties of the short story among us is that the sketches and studies by the women seem faithfuler and more realistic than those of the men, in proportion to their number. Their tendency is more distinctly in that direction, and there is a solidity, an honest observation, in the work of such women as Mrs. Cooke, Miss Murfree, Miss Wilkins and Miss Jewett, which often leaves little to be desired. I should, upon the whole, be disposed to rank American short stories only below those of such Russian writers as I have read, and I should praise rather than blame their free use of our different local parlances, or "dialects," as people call them. I like this because I hope that our inherited English may be constantly freshened and revived from the native sources which our literary decentralization will help to keep open, and I will own that as I turn over novels coming from Philadelphia, from New Mexico, from Boston, from Tennessee, from rural New England, from New York, every local flavor of diction gives me courage and pleasure. M. Alphonse Daudet, in a conversation which Mr. H. H. Boyesen has set down in a recently recorded interview with him,[30] said, in speaking of Tourguéneff: "What a luxury it must be to have a great big untrodden barbaric language to wade into! We poor fellows who work in the language of an old civilization,

CRITICISM AND FICTION

we may sit and chisel our little verbal felicities, only to find in the end that it is a borrowed jewel we are polishing. The crown of jewels of our French tongue have passed through the hands of so many generations of monarchs that it seems like presumption on the part of any late-born pretender to attempt to wear them.''

This grief is, of course, a little whimsical, yet it has a certain measure of reason in it, and the same regret has been more seriously expressed by the Italian poet Aleardi: [31]

> "Muse of an aged people, in the eve
> Of fading civilization, I was born.
> . . . . . . Oh, fortunate,
> My sisters, who in the heroic dawn
> Of races sung! To them did destiny give
> The virgin fire and chaste ingenuousness
> Of their land's speech; and, reverenced, their hands
> Ran over potent strings."

It will never do to allow that we are at such a desperate pass in English, but something of this divine despair we may feel too in thinking of ''the spacious times of great Elizabeth,'' when the poets were trying the stops of the young language, and thrilling with the surprises of their own music. We may comfort ourselves, however, unless we prefer a luxury of grief, by remembering that no language is ever old on the lips of those who speak it, no matter how decrepit it drops from the pen. We have only to leave our studies, editorial and other, and go into the shops and fields to find the ''spacious times'' again; and from the beginning Realism, before she had put on her capital letter, had divined this near-at-hand truth along with the rest. Mr. Lowell, almost the greatest and finest realist who ever wrought in verse, showed us that Elizabeth was still Queen where he heard Yankee farmers talk. One need not invite slang into the company of its betters, though perhaps slang has been dropping its ''s'' and becoming language ever since the world began, and is certainly sometimes delightful and forcible beyond the reach of the dictionary. I would not have any one go about for new words, but if one of them came aptly, not to reject its help. For our novelists to try to write Americanly,

65

from any motive, would be a dismal error, but being born Americans, I would have them use "Americanisms" whenever these serve their turn; and when their characters speak, I should like to hear them speak true American, with all the varying Tennesseean, Philadelphian, Bostonian, and New York accents. If we bother ourselves to write what the critics imagine to be "English," we shall be priggish and artificial, and still more so if we make our Americans talk "English." There is also this serious disadvantage about "English," that if we wrote the best "English" in the world, probably the English themselves would not know it, or, if they did, certainly would not own it. It has always been supposed by grammarians and purists that a language can be kept as they find it; but languages, while they live, are perpetually changing. God apparently meant them for the common people—whom Lincoln believed God liked because he had made so many of them; and the common people will use them freely as they use other gifts of God. On their lips our continental English will differ more and more from the insular English, and I believe that this is not deplorable, but desirable.

In fine, I would have our American novelists be as American as they unconsciously can. Matthew Arnold [32] complained that he found no "distinction" in our life, and I would gladly persuade all artists intending greatness in any kind among us that the recognition of the fact pointed out by Mr. Arnold ought to be a source of inspiration to them, and not discouragement. We have been now some hundred years building up a state on the affirmation of the essential equality of men in their rights and duties, and whether we have been right or wrong the gods have taken us at our word, and have responded to us with a civilization in which there is no "distinction" perceptible to the eye that loves and values it. Such beauty and such grandeur as we have is common beauty, common grandeur, or the beauty and grandeur in which the quality of solidarity so prevails that neither distinguishes itself to the disadvantage of anything else. It seems to me that these conditions invite the artist to the study and the appreciation of the common, and to the portrayal in every art of those finer and higher aspects which unite rather than sever humanity, if he would thrive in our new order of things. The talent that is robust enough to front the every-day world and catch the charm of its work-worn, care-worn, brave, kindly face, need not fear the en-counter, though it seems terrible to the sort nurtured in the superstition of the romantic, the bizarre, the heroic, the distinguished, as the things alone worthy of painting or carving or writing. The arts must become democratic, and then we shall have the expression of America in art; and the reproach which Mr. Arnold was half right in making us shall have no justice in it any longer; we shall be ''distinguished.''

XXIII

In the mean time it has been said with a superficial justice that our fiction is narrow; though in the same sense I suppose the present English fiction is as narrow as our own; and most modern fiction is narrow in a certain sense. In Italy the best men are writing novels as brief and restricted in range as ours; in Spain the novels are intense and deep, and not spacious; the French school, with the exception of Zola, is narrow; the Norwegians are narrow; the Russians, except Tolstoi, are nar-row, and the next greatest after him, Tourguéneff, is the narrowest great novelist, as to mere dimensions, that ever lived, dealing nearly always with small groups, isolated and analyzed in the most American fashion. In fact, the charge of narrowness accuses the whole tendency of modern fiction as much as the American school. But I do not by any means allow that this narrowness is a defect, while denying that it is a uni-versal characteristic of our fiction; it is rather, for the present, a virtue. Indeed, I should call the present American work, North and South, thorough rather than narrow. In one sense it is as broad as life, for each man is a microcosm, and the writer who is able to acquaint us intimately with half a dozen people, or the conditions of a neighborhood or a class, has done something which cannot in any bad sense be called narrow; his breadth is vertical instead of lateral, that is all; and this depth is more desirable than horizontal expansion in a civilization like ours, where the differences are not of classes, but of types, and not of types either so much as of characters. A new method was necessary in dealing with the new conditions, and the new method is world-wide, because the whole world is more or less Americanized. Tolstoi is exceptionally voluminous among modern writers, even Russian writers; and it might be said that the forte of Tolstoi himself is not in his breadth sidewise, but in his breadth upward and downward. The Death of Ivan Illitch leaves as vast an impression on the reader's soul as any episode of War and Peace, which, indeed, can be recalled only in episodes, and not as a whole. I think that our writers may be safely counselled to continue their work in the modern way, because it is the best way yet known. If they make it true, it will be large, no matter what its superficies are; and it would be the greatest mistake to try to make it big. A big book is necessarily a group of episodes more or less loosely connected by a thread of narrative, and there seems no reason why this thread must always be supplied. Each episode may be quite distinct, or it may be one of a connected group; the final effect will be from the truth of each episode, not from the size of the group.

The whole field of human experience was never so nearly covered by imaginative literature in any age as in this; and American life especially is getting represented with unexampled fulness. It is true that no one writer, no one book, represents it, for that is not possible; our social and political decentralization forbids this, and may forever forbid it. But a great number of very good writers are instinctively striving to make each part of the country and each phase of our civilization known to all the other parts; and their work is not narrow in any feeble or vicious sense. The world was once very little, and it is now very large. Formerly, all science could be grasped by a single mind; but now the man who hopes to become great or useful in science must devote himself to a single department. It is so in everything —all arts, all trades; and the novelist is not superior to the universal rule against universality. He contributes his share to a thorough knowledge of groups of the human race under conditions which are full of inspiring novelty and interest. He works more fearlessly, frankly, and faithfully than the novelist ever worked before; his work, or much of it, may be destined never to be reprinted from the monthly magazines; but if he turns to his book-shelf and regards the array of the British or other classics, he knows that they too are for the most part dead; he knows that the planet itself is destined to freeze up and drop into the sun at last, with all its surviving literature upon it. The question is merely one of time. He consoles himself, therefore, if he is wise, and works on; and we may all take some comfort from the thought that most things cannot be helped. Especially a movement in literature like that which the world is now witnessing cannot be helped; and we could no more turn back and be of the literary fashions of any age before this than we could turn back and be of its social, economical, or political conditions.

If I were authorized to address any word directly to our novelists I should say, Do not trouble yourselves about standards or ideals; but try to be faithful and natural: remember that there is no greatness, no beauty, which does not come from truth to your own knowledge of things; and keep on working, even if your work is not long remembered.

At least three-fifths of the literature called classic, in all languages, no more lives than the poems and stories that perish monthly in our magazines. It is all printed and reprinted, generation after generation, century after century; but it is not alive; it is as dead as the people who wrote it and read it, and to whom it meant something, perhaps; with whom it was a fashion, a caprice, a passing taste. A superstitious piety preserves it, and pretends that it has aesthetic qualities which can delight or edify; but nobody really enjoys it, except as a reflection of the past moods and humors of the race, or a revelation of the author's character; otherwise it is trash, and often very filthy trash, which the present trash generally is not.

XXIV

One of the great newspapers [33] the other day invited the prominent American authors to speak their minds upon a point in the theory and practice of fiction which had already vexed some of them. It was the question of how much or how little the

American novel ought to deal with certain facts of life which are not usually talked of before young people, and especially young ladies. Of course the question was not decided, and I forget just how far the balance inclined in favor of a larger freedom in the matter. But it certainly inclined that way; one or two writers of the sex which is somehow supposed to have purity in its keeping (as if purity were a thing that did not practically concern the other sex, preoccupied with serious affairs) gave it a rather vigorous tilt to that side. In view of this fact it would not be the part of prudence to make an effort to dress the balance; and indeed I do not know that I was going to make any such effort. But there are some things to say, around and about the subject, which I should like to have some one else say, and which I may myself possibly be safe in suggesting.

One of the first of these is the fact, generally lost sight of by those who censure the Anglo-Saxon novel for its prudishness, that it is really not such a prude after all; and that if it is sometimes apparently anxious to avoid those experiences of life not spoken of before young people, this may be an appearance only. Sometimes a novel which has this shuffling air, this effect of truckling to propriety, might defend itself, if it could speak for itself, by saying that such experiences happened not to come within its scheme, and that, so far from maiming or mutilating itself in ignoring them, it was all the more faithfully representative of the tone of modern life in dealing with love that was chaste, and with passion so honest that it could be openly spoken of before the tenderest society bud at dinner. It might say that the guilty intrigue, the betrayal, the extreme flirtation even, was the exceptional thing in life, and unless the scheme of the story necessarily involved it, that it would be bad art to lug it in, and as bad taste as to introduce such topics in a mixed company. It could say very justly that the novel in our civilization now always addresses a mixed company, and that the vast majority of the company are ladies, and that very many, if not most, of these ladies are young girls. If the novel were written for men and for married women alone, as in continental Europe, it might be altogether different. But the simple fact is that it is not written for them alone among us, and it is a question of writing, under cover of our universal acceptance, things for young girls to read which you would be put out-of-doors for saying to them, or of frankly giving notice of your intention, and so cutting yourself off from the pleasure—and it is a very high and sweet one—of appealing to these vivid, responsive intelligences, which are none the less brilliant and admirable because they are innocent.

One day a novelist who liked, after the manner of other men, to repine at his hard fate, complained to his friend, a critic, that he was tired of the restriction he had put upon himself in this regard; for it is a mistake, as can be readily shown, to suppose that others impose it. "See how free those French fellows are!" he rebelled. "Shall we always be shut up to our tradition of decency?"

"Do you think it's much worse than being shut up to their tradition of indecency?" said his friend.

Then that novelist began to reflect, and he remembered how sick the invariable motive of the French novel made him. He perceived finally that, convention for convention, ours was not only more tolerable, but on the whole was truer to life, not only to its complexion, but also to its texture. No one will pretend that there is not vicious love beneath the surface of our society; if he did, the fetid explosions of the divorce trials would refute him; but if he pretended that it was in any just sense characteristic of our society, he could be still more easily refuted. Yet it exists, and it is unquestionably the material of tragedy, the stuff from which intense effects are wrought. The question, after owning this fact, is whether these intense effects are not rather cheap effects. I incline to think they are, and I will try to say why I think so, if I may do so without offense. The material itself, the mere mention of it, has an instant fascination; it arrests, it detains, till the last word is said, and while there is anything to be hinted. This is what makes a love intrigue of some sort all but essential to the popularity of any fiction. Without such an intrigue the intellectual equipment of the author must be of the highest, and then he will succeed only with the highest class of readers. But any author who will deal with a guilty love intrigue holds all the readers in his hand, the highest with the

71

lowest, as long as he hints the slightest hope of the smallest potential naughtiness. He need not at all be a great author; he may be a very shabby wretch, if he has but the courage or the trick of that sort of thing. The critics will call him ''virile'' and ''passionate''; decent people will be ashamed to have been limned by him; but the low average will only ask another chance of flocking into his net. If he happens to be an able writer, his really fine and costly work will be unheeded, and the lure to the appetite will be chiefly remembered. There may be other qualities which make reputations for other men, but in his case they will count for nothing. He pays this penalty for his success in that kind; and every one pays some such penalty who deals with some such material. It attaches in like manner to the triumphs of the writers who now almost form a school among us, and who may be said to have established themselves in an easy popularity simply by the study of erotic shivers and fervors. They may find their account in the popularity, or they may not; there is no question of the popularity.

But I do not mean to imply that their case covers the whole ground. So far as it goes, though, it ought to stop the mouths of those who complain that fiction is enslaved to propriety among us. It appears that of a certain kind of impropriety it is free to give us all it will, and more. But this is not what serious men and women writing fiction mean when they rebel against the limitations of their art in our civilization. They have no desire to deal with nakedness, as painters and sculptors freely do in the worship of beauty; or with certain facts of life, as the stage does, in the service of sensation. But they ask why, when the conventions of the plastic and histrionic arts liberate their followers to the portrayal of almost any phase of the physical or of the emotional nature, an American novelist may not write a story on the lines of Anna Karenina or Madame Bovary. Sappho [34] they put aside, and from Zola's work they avert their eyes. They do not condemn him or Daudet, necessarily, or accuse their motives; they leave them out of the question; they do not want to do that kind of thing. But they do sometimes wish to do another kind, to touch one of the most serious and sorrowful problems of life in the spirit of Tolstoi and Flaubert, and they ask why they may not. At one time, they remind us, the Anglo-Saxon novelist did deal with such problems—De Foe in his spirit, Richardson in his, Goldsmith in his. At what moment did our fiction lose this privilege? In what fatal hour did the Young Girl arise and seal the lips of Fiction, with a touch of her finger, to some of the most vital interests of life?

Whether I wished to oppose them in their aspiration for greater freedom, or whether I wished to encourage them, I should begin to answer them by saying that the Young Girl had never done anything of the kind. The manners of the novel have been improving with those of its readers; that is all. Gentlemen no longer swear or fall drunk under the table, or abduct young ladies and shut them up in lonely country-houses, or so habitually set about the ruin of their neighbors' wives, as they once did. Generally, people now call a spade an agricultural implement; they have not grown decent without having also grown a little squeamish, but they have grown comparatively decent; there is no doubt about that. They require of a novelist whom they respect unquestionable proof of his seriousness, if he proposes to deal with certain phases of life; they require a sort of scientific decorum. He can no longer expect to be received on the ground of entertainment only; he assumes a higher function, something like that of a physician or a priest, and they expect him to be bound by laws as sacred as those of such professions; they hold him solemnly pledged not to betray them or abuse their confidence. If he will accept the conditions, they give him their confidence, and he may then treat to his greater honor, and not at all to his disadvantage, of such experiences, such relations of men and women as George Eliot treats in Adam Bede, in Daniel Deronda, in Romola, in almost all her books; such as Hawthorne treats in the Scarlet Letter; such as Dickens treats in David Copperfield; such as Thackeray treats in Pendennis, and glances at in every one of his fictions; such as most of the masters of English fiction have at some time treated more or less openly. It is quite false or quite mistaken to suppose that our novels have left untouched these most important realities of life. They have only not made them their stock in trade; they have kept a true perspective in regard to them; they have relegated them in their

73

pictures of life to the space and place they occupy in life itself, as we know it in England and America. They have kept a correct proportion, knowing perfectly well that unless the novel is to be a map, with everything scrupulously laid down in it, a faithful record of life in far the greater extent could be made to the exclusion of guilty love and all its circumstances and consequences.

I justify them in this view not only because I hate what is cheap and meretricious, and hold in peculiar loathing the cant of the critics who require ''passion'' as something in itself admirable and desirable in a novel, but because I prize fidelity in the historian of feeling and character. Most of these critics who demand ''passion'' would seem to have no conception of any passion but one. Yet there are several other passions: the passion of grief, the passion of avarice, the passion of pity, the passion of ambition, the passion of hate, the passion of envy, the passion of devotion, the passion of friendship; and all these have a greater part in the drama of life than the passion of love, and infinitely greater than the passion of guilty love. Wittingly or unwittingly, English fiction and American fiction have recognized this truth, not fully, not in the measure it merits, but in greater degree than most other fiction.

XXV

Who can deny that fiction would be incomparably stronger, incomparably truer, if once it could tear off the habit which enslaves it to the celebration chiefly of a single passion, in one phase or another, and could frankly dedicate itself to the service of all the passions, and all the interests, all the facts? Every novelist who has thought about his art knows that it would, and I think that upon reflection he must doubt whether his sphere would be greatly enlarged if he were allowed to treat freely the darker aspects of the favorite passion. But, as I have shown, the privilege, the right to do this, is already perfectly recognized. This is proved again by the fact that serious criticism recognizes as master-works (I will not push the question of supremacy) the two great novels which above all others have moved the world

74

by their study of guilty love. If by any chance, if by some prodigious miracle, any American should now arise to treat it on the level of Anna Karenina and Madame Bovary, he would be absolutely sure of success, and of fame and gratitude as great as those books have won for their authors.

But what editor of what American magazine would print such a story?

Certainly I do not think any one would; and here our novelist must again submit to conditions. If he wishes to publish such a story (supposing him to have once written it), he must publish it as a book. A book is something by itself, responsible for its character, which becomes quickly known, and it does not necessarily penetrate to every member of the household. The father or the mother may say to the child, "I would rather you wouldn't read that book"; if the child cannot be trusted, the book may be locked up. But with the magazine and its serial the affair is different. Between the editor of a reputable English or American magazine and the families which receive it there is a tacit agreement that he will print nothing which a father may not read to his daughter, or safely leave her to read herself. After all, it is a matter of business; and the insurgent novelist should consider the situation with coolness and common-sense. The editor did not create the situation; but it exists, and he could not even attempt to change it without many sorts of disaster. He respects it, therefore, with the good faith of an honest man. Even when he is himself a novelist, with ardor for his art and impatience of the limitations put upon it, he interposes his veto, as Thackeray did in the case of Trollope when a contributor approaches forbidden ground.[35]

It does not avail to say that the daily papers teem with facts far fouler and deadlier than any which fiction could imagine. That is true, but it is true also that the sex which reads the most novels reads the fewest newspapers; and, besides, the reporter does not command the novelist's skill to fix impressions in a young girl's mind or to suggest conjecture. The magazine is a little despotic, a little arbitrary; but unquestionably its favor is essential to success, and its conditions are not such narrow ones. You cannot deal with Tolstoi's and Flaubert's subjects in the absolute artistic freedom of Tolstoi and Flaubert; since De Foe, that is unknown among us; but if you deal with them in the manner of George Eliot, of Thackeray, of Dickens, of society, you may deal with them even in the magazines. There is no other restriction upon you. All the horrors and miseries and tortures are open to you; your pages may drop blood; sometimes it may happen that the editor will even exact such strong material from you. But probably he will require nothing but the observance of the convention in question; and if you do not yourself prefer bloodshed he will leave you free to use all sweet and peaceable means of interesting his readers.

Believe me, it is no narrow field he throws open to you, with that little sign to keep off the grass up at one point only. Its vastness is still almost unexplored, and whole regions in it are unknown to the fictionist. Dig anywhere, and do but dig deep enough, and you strike riches; or, if you are of the mind to range, the gentler climes, the softer temperatures, the serener skies, are all free to you, and are so little visited that the chance of novelty is greater among them.

XXVI

While the Americans have greatly excelled in the short story generally, they have almost created a species of it in the Thanksgiving story. We have transplanted the Christmas story from England,[36] while the Thanksgiving story is native to our air; but both are of Anglo-Saxon growth. Their difference is from a difference of environment; and the Christmas story when naturalized among us becomes almost identical in motive, incident, and treatment with the Thanksgiving story. If I were to generalize between them, I should say that the one dealt more with marvels and the other more with morals; and yet the critic should beware of speaking too confidently on this point. It is certain, however, that the Christmas season is meteorologically more favorable to the effective return of persons long supposed lost at sea, or from a prodigal life, or from a darkened mind. The longer, denser, and colder nights are better adapted to the apparition of ghosts, and to all manner of signs and portents; while they seem to present a wider field for the active intervention of angels in behalf of orphans and outcasts. The dreams of elderly sleepers at this time are apt to be such as will effect a lasting change in them when they awake, turning them from the hard, cruel, and grasping habits of a life-time, and reconciling them to their sons, daughters, and nephews, who have thwarted them in marriage; or softening them to their meek, uncomplaining wives, whose hearts they have trampled upon in their reckless pursuit of wealth; and generally disposing them to a distribution of hampers among the sick and poor, and to a friendly reception of chubby gentlemen with charity subscription papers. Ships readily drive upon rocks in the early twilight, and offer exciting difficulties of salvage; and the heavy snows gather thickly round the steps of wanderers who lie down to die in them, preparatory to their discovery and rescue by immediate relatives. The midnight weather is also very suitable to encounter with murderers and burglars; and the contrast of its freezing gloom with the light and cheer in-doors promotes the gayeties which merge, at all well-regulated country-houses, in love and marriage. In the region of pure character no moment could be so available for flinging off the mask of frivolity, or imbecility, or savagery, which one has worn for ten or twenty long years, say, for the purpose of foiling some villain, and surprising the reader, and helping the author out with his plot. Persons abroad in the Alps, or Apennines, or Pyrenees, or anywhere seeking shelter in the huts of shepherds or the dens of smugglers, find no time like it for lying in a feigned slumber, and listening to the whispered machinations of their suspicious-looking entertainers, and then suddenly starting up and fighting their way out; or else springing from the real sleep into which they have sunk exhausted, and finding it broad day and the good peasants whom they had so unjustly doubted, waiting breakfast for them. We need not point out the superior advantages of the Christmas season for anything one has a mind to do with the French Revolution, or the Arctic explorations, or the Indian Mutiny, or the horrors of Siberian exile; there is no time so good for the use of this material; and ghosts

77

on shipboard are notoriously fond of Christmas Eve. In our own logging camps the man who has gone into the woods for the winter, after quarrelling with his wife, then hears her sad appealing voice, and is moved to good resolutions as at no other period of the year; and in the mining regions, first in California and later in Colorado, the hardened reprobate, dying in his boots, smells his mother's dough-nuts, and breathes his last in a soliloquized vision of the old home, and the little brother, or sister, or the old father coming to meet him from heaven; while his rude companions listen round him, and dry their eyes on the butts of their revolvers.

It has to be very grim, all that, to be truly effective; and here, already, we have a touch in the Americanized Christmas story of the moralistic quality of the American Thanksgiving story. This was seldom written, at first, for the mere entertainment of the reader; it was meant to entertain him, of course; but it was meant to edify him, too, and to improve him; and some such intention is still present in it. I rather think that it deals more probably with character to this end than its English cousin, the Christmas story, does. It is not so improbable that a man should leave off being a drunkard on Thanksgiving, as that he should leave off being a curmudgeon on Christmas; that he should conquer his appetite as that he should instantly change his nature, by good resolutions. He would be very likely, indeed, to break his resolutions in either case, but not so likely in the one as in the other.

Generically, the Thanksgiving story is cheerfuler in its drama and simpler in its persons than the Christmas story. Rarely has it dealt with the supernatural, either the apparition of ghosts or the intervention of angels. The weather being so much milder at the close of November than it is a month later, very little can be done with the elements; though on the coast a north-easterly storm has been, and can be, very usefully employed. The Thanksgiving story is more restricted in its range; the scene is still mostly in New England, and the characters are of New England extraction, who come home from the West usually, or New York, for the event of the little drama, whatever it may be. It may be the reconciliation of kinsfolk who have quarrelled; or the union of lovers long estranged; or husbands and wives who have had hard words and parted; or mothers who had thought their sons dead in California and find themselves agreeably disappointed in their return; or fathers who for old time's sake receive back their erring and conveniently dying daughters. The notes are not many which this simple music sounds, but they have a Sabbath tone, mostly, and win the listener to kindlier thoughts and better moods. The art is at its highest in some strong sketch of Mrs. Rose Terry Cooke's, or some perfectly satisfying study of Miss Jewett's or some graphic situation of Miss Wilkins's; and then it is a very fine art. But mostly it is poor and rude enough, and makes openly, shamelessly, sickeningly, for the reader's emotions, as well as his morals. It is inclined to be rather descriptive. The turkey, the pumpkin, the cornfield, figure throughout; and the leafless woods are blue and cold against the evening sky behind the low hip-roofed, old-fashioned homestead. The parlance is usually the Yankee dialect and its western modifications.

The Thanksgiving story is mostly confined in scene to the country; it does not seem possible to do much with it in town; and it is a serious question whether with its geographical and topical limitations it can hold its own against the Christmas story; and whether it would not be well for authors to consider a combination with its elder rival.

The two feasts are so near together in point of time that they could be easily covered by the sentiment of even a brief narrative. Under the agglutinated style of A Thanksgiving-Christmas Story, fiction appropriate to both could be produced, and both could be employed naturally and probably in the transaction of its affairs and the development of its characters. The plot for such a story could easily be made to include a total-abstinence pledge and family reunion at Thanksgiving, and an apparition and spiritual regeneration over a bowl of punch at Christmas.

Not all Thanksgiving-Christmas stories need be of this pattern precisely; I wish to suggest merely one way of doing them. Perhaps when our writers really come to the work they will find sufficient inspiration in its novelty to turn to human life and observe how it is really affected on these holidays, and be tempted to present some of its actualities. This would be a great thing to do, and would come home to readers with surprise.

XXVII

It would be interesting to know the far beginnings of holiday literature, and I commend the quest to the scientific spirit which now specializes research in every branch of history. In the mean time, without being too confident of the facts, I venture to suggest that it came in with the romantic movement about the beginning of this century, when mountains ceased to be horrid and became picturesque; when ruins of all sorts, but particularly abbeys and castles, became habitable to the most delicate constitutions; when the despised Gothick of Addison dropped its "k," and arose the chivalrous and religious Gothic of Scott; when ghosts were redeemed from the contempt into which they had fallen, and resumed their place in polite society; in fact, the politer the society, the welcomer the ghosts, and whatever else was out of the common. In that day the Annual flourished, and this artificial flower was probably the first literary blossom on the Christmas Tree which has since borne so much tinsel foliage and painted fruit. But the Annual was extremely Oriental; it was much preoccupied with Haidees and Gulnares and Zuleikas, with Hindas and Nourmahals, owing to the distinction which Byron and Moore had given such ladies; and when it began to concern itself with the actualities of British beauty, the daughters of Albion, though inscribed with the names of real countesses and duchesses, betrayed their descent from the well-known Eastern odalisques. It was possibly through an American that holiday literature became distinctively English in material, and Washington Irving, with his New World love of the past, may have given the impulse to the literary worship of Christmas which has since so widely established itself. A festival revived in popular interest by a New-Yorker to whom Dutch associations with New-year's had endeared the German ideal of Christmas, and whom the robust gayeties of the season in old-fashioned country-houses had charmed, would be one of those roundabout results which destiny likes, and "would at least be Early English." If we cannot claim with all the patriotic confidence we should like to feel that it was Irving who set Christmas in that light in which Dickens saw its aesthetic capabilities, it is perhaps because all origins are obscure. For anything that we positively know to the contrary, the Druidic rites from which English Christmas borrowed the inviting mistletoe, if not the decorative holly, may have been accompanied by the recitations of holiday triads. But it is certain that several plays of Shakespeare were produced, if not written, for the celebration of the holidays, and that then the black tide of Puritanism which swept over men's souls blotted out all such observance of Christmas with the festival itself. It came in again, by a natural reaction, with the returning Stuarts, and throughout the period of the Restoration it enjoyed a perfunctory favor. There is mention of it often enough in the eighteenth century essayists, in the Spectators and Idlers and Tatlers; but the World about the middle of the last century laments the neglect into which it had fallen. Irving seems to have been the first to observe its surviving rites lovingly, and Dickens divined its immense advantage as a literary occasion. He made it in some sort entirely his for a time, and there can be no question but it was he who again endeared it to the whole English-speaking world, and gave it a wider and deeper hold than it had ever had before upon the fancies and affections of our race.

The might of that great talent no one can gainsay, though in the light of the truer work which has since been done his literary principles seem almost as grotesque as his theories of political economy. In no one direction was his erring force more felt than in the creation of holiday literature as we have known it for the last half-century. Creation, of course, is the wrong word; it says too much; but in default of a better word, it may stand. He did not make something out of nothing; the material was there before him; the mood and even the need of his time contributed immensely to his success, as the volition of the subject helps on the mesmerist; but it is within bounds to say that he was the chief agency in the development of holiday literature as we have known it, as he was the chief agency in universalizing the great Christian holiday as we now have it. Other agencies wrought with him and after him; but it was he who rescued Christmas from Puritan distrust, and humanized it and consecrated it to the hearts and homes of all.

Very rough magic, as it now seems, he used in working his miracle, but there is no doubt about his working it. One opens his Christmas stories in this later day—The Carol, The Chimes, The Haunted Man, The Cricket on the Hearth, and all the rest —and with "a heart high-sorrowful and cloyed," asks himself for the preternatural virtue that they once had. The pathos appears false and strained; the humor largely horse-play; the character theatrical; the joviality pumped; the psychology commonplace; the sociology alone funny. It is a world of real clothes, earth, air, water, and the rest; the people often speak the language of life, but their motives are as disproportioned and improbable, and their passions and purposes as overcharged, as those of the worst of Balzac's people. Yet all these monstrosities, as they now appear, seem to have once had symmetry and verity; they moved the most cultivated intelligences of the time; they touched true hearts; they made everybody laugh and cry.

This was perhaps because the imagination, from having been fed mostly upon gross unrealities, always responds readily to fantastic appeals. There has been an amusing sort of awe of it, as if it were the channel of inspired thought, and were somehow sacred. The most preposterous inventions of its activity have been regarded in their time as the greatest feats of the human mind, and in its receptive form it has been nursed into an imbecility to which the truth is repugnant, and the fact that the beautiful resides nowhere else is inconceivable. It has been flattered out of all sufferance in its toyings with the mere elements of character, and its attempts to present these in combinations foreign to experience are still praised by the poorer sort of critics as masterpieces of creative work.

In the day of Dickens's early Christmas stories it was thought admirable for the author to take types of humanity which everybody knew, and to add to them from his imagination till they were as strange as beasts and birds talking. Now we begin to feel that human nature is quite enough, and that the best an author can do is to show it as it is. But in those stories of his Dickens said to his readers, Let us make believe so-and-so; and the result was a joint juggle, a child's-play, in which the wholesome allegiance to life was lost. Artistically, therefore, the scheme was false, and artistically, therefore, it must perish. It did not perish, however, before it had propagated itself in a whole school of unrealities so ghastly that one can hardly recall without a shudder those sentimentalities at second hand to which holiday literature was abandoned long after the original conjurer had wearied of his performance.

Under his own eye and of conscious purpose a circle of imitators grew up in the fabrication of Christmas stories. They obviously formed themselves upon his sobered ideals; they collaborated with him, and it was often hard to know whether it was Dickens or Mr. Sala or Mr. Collins who was writing. The Christmas book had by that time lost its direct application to Christmas. It dealt with shipwrecks a good deal, and with perilous adventures of all kinds, and with unmerited suffering, and with ghosts and mysteries, because human nature, secure from storm and danger in a well-lighted room before a cheerful fire, likes to have these things imaged for it, and its long-puerilized fancy will bear an endless repetition of them. The wizards who wrought their spells with them contented themselves with the lasting efficacy of these simple means; and the apprentice-wizards and journeyman-wizards who have succeeded them practice the same arts at the old stand; but the ethical intention which gave dignity to Dickens's Christmas stories of still earlier date has almost wholly disappeared. It was a quality which could not be worked so long as the phantoms and hair-breadth escapes. People always knew that character is not changed by a dream in a series of tableaux; that a ghost cannot do much towards reforming an inordinately selfish person; that a life cannot be turned white, like a head of hair, in a single night, by the most allegorical apparition; that want and sin and shame cannot be cured by kettles singing on the hob; and gradually they ceased to make believe that there was virtue in these devices and appliances. Yet the ethical intention was not fruitless, crude as it now appears. It was well once a year, if not oftener, to remind men by parable of the old simple truths; to teach them that forgiveness, and charity, and the endeavor for life better and purer than each has lived, are the principles upon which alone the world holds together and gets forward. It was well for the comfortable and the refined to be put in mind of the savagery and suffering all round them, and to be taught, as Dickens was always teaching, that certain feelings which grace human nature, as tenderness for the sick and helpless, self-sacrifice and generosity, self-respect and manliness and womanliness, are the common heritage of the race, the direct gift of Heaven, shared equally by the rich and poor. It did not necessarily detract from the value of the lesson that, with the imperfect art of the time, he made his paupers and porters not only human, but superhuman, and too altogether virtuous; and it remained true that home life may be lovely under the lowliest roof, although he liked to paint it without a shadow on its beauty there. It is still a fact that the sick are very often saintly, although he put no peevishness into their patience with their ills. His ethical intention told for manhood and fraternity and tolerance, and when this intention disappeared from the better holiday literature, that literature was sensibly the poorer for the loss.

It never did disappear wholly from the writings of Dickens, whom it once vitally possessed, and if its action became more and more mechanical, still it always had its effect with the generation which hung charmed upon his lips, till the lips fell dumb and still forever. It imbued subordinate effort, and inspired his myriad imitators throughout the English-scribbling world, especially upon its remoter borders, so that all holiday fiction, which was once set to the tunes of The Carol and The Chimes, still grinds no other through the innumerable pipes of the humbler newspapers and magazines, though these airs are no longer heard in the politer literary centres.

This cannot go on forever, of course, but the Christmas whose use and beauty Dickens divined will remain, though Christmas literature is going the way of so much that was once admired, like the fine language, the beauties of style, and the ornate manners of the past, down through the ranks of the aesthetical poor, whom we have always with us, to the final rag-bag of oblivion.

CRITICISM AND FICTION

It is still manufactured among us in the form of short stories; but the Christmas book, which now seems to be always a number of paste gems threaded upon a strand of tinsel, must be imported from England if we want it. With the constant and romantic public of the British islands it appears that spectres and imminent dangers still have favor enough to inspire their fabrication, while if I may judge from an absence of native phantasms and perils, the industry has no more encouragement among us than ship-building, though no prohibitive tariff has enhanced the cost of the raw materials, or interfered to paralyze the efforts of the American imagination.

XXVIII

But if the humanitarian impulse has mostly disappeared from Christmas fiction, I think it has never so generally characterized all fiction. One may refuse to recognize this impulse; one may deny that it is in any greater degree shaping life than ever before, but no one who has the current of literature under his eye can fail to note it there. People are thinking and feeling generously, if not living justly, in our time; it is a day of anxiety to be saved from the curse that is on selfishness, of eager question how others shall be helped, of bold denial that the conditions in which we would fain have rested are sacred or immutable. Especially in America, where the race has gained a height never reached before, the eminence enables more men than ever before to see how even here vast masses of men are sunk in misery that must grow every day more hopeless, or embroiled in a struggle for mere life that must end in enslaving and imbruting them.[37]

Art, indeed, is beginning to find out that if it does not make friends with Need it must perish. It perceives that to take itself from the many and leave them no joy in their work, and to give itself to the few whom it can bring no joy in their idleness, is an error that kills. This has long been the burden of Ruskin's message: and if we can believe William Morris,[38] the common people have heard him gladly, and have felt the truth of what he says. ''They see the prophet in him rather than the fantastic rhetorician, as more superfine audiences do''; and the men and women who do the hard work of the world have learned from him and from Morris that they have a right to pleasure in their toil, and that when justice is done them they will have it. In all ages poetry has affirmed something of this sort, but it remained for ours to perceive it and express it somehow in every form of literature. But this is only one phase of the devotion of the best literature of our time to the service of humanity. No book written with a low or cynical motive could succeed now, no matter how brilliantly written; and the work done in the past to the glorification of mere passion and power, to the deification of self, appears monstrous and hideous. The romantic spirit worshipped genius, worshipped heroism, but at its best, in such a man as Victor Hugo,[39] this spirit recognized the supreme claim of the lowest humanity. Its error was to idealize the victims of society, to paint them impossibly virtuous and beautiful; but truth, which has succeeded to the highest mission of romance, paints these victims as they are, and bids the world consider them not because they are beautiful and virtuous, but because they are ugly and vicious, cruel, filthy, and only not altogether loathsome because the divine can never wholly die out of the human. The truth does not find these victims among the poor alone, among the hungry, the houseless, the ragged; but it also finds them among the rich, cursed with the aimlessness, the satiety, the despair of wealth, wasting their lives in a fool's paradise of shows and semblances, with nothing real but the misery that comes of insincerity and selfishness.

It is needless for me to say, either to the many whom my opinions on this point incense or to the few who accept them, that I do not think the fiction of our own time even always equal to this work, or perhaps more than seldom so. But as I have before expressed, to the still-reverberating discontent of two continents,[40] fiction is now a finer art than it has ever been hitherto, and more nearly meets the requirements of the infallible standard. I have hopes of real usefulness in it, because it is at last building on the only sure foundation; but I am by no means certain that it will be the ultimate literary form, or will remain as important as we believe it is destined to become. On the contrary, it is quite imaginable that when the great mass of readers, now sunk in the foolish joys of mere fable, shall be lifted to an interest in the meaning of things through the faithful portrayal of life in fiction, then fiction the most faithful may be superseded by a still more faithful form of contemporaneous history.[41] I willingly leave the precise character of this form to the more robust imagination of readers whose minds have been nurtured upon romantic novels, and who really have an imagination worth speaking of, and confine myself, as usual, to the hither side of the regions of conjecture.

The art which in the mean time disdains the office of teacher is one of the last refuges of the aristocratic spirit which is disappearing from politics and society, and is now seeking to shelter itself in aesthetics. The pride of caste is becoming the pride of taste; but as before, it is averse to the mass of men; it consents to know them only in some conventionalized and artificial guise. It seeks to withdraw itself, to stand aloof; to be distinguished, and not to be identified. Democracy in literature is the reverse of all this. It wishes to know and to tell the truth, confident that consolation and delight are there; it does not care to paint the marvellous and impossible for the vulgar many, or to sentimentalize and falsify the actual for the vulgar few. Men are more like than unlike one another: let us make them know one another better, that they may all be humbled and strengthened with a sense of their fraternity. Neither arts, nor letters, nor sciences, except as they somehow, clearly or obscurely, tend to make the race better and kinder, are to be regarded as serious interests; they are all lower than the rudest crafts that feed and house and clothe, for except they do this office they are idle; and they cannot do this except from and through the truth.

PART II

EUROPEAN MASTERS*

INTRODUCTION

IN Part II we have gathered some of Howells' reviews of the European masters. These not only show the working of his singularly clear and sensitive mind, but serve also as examples of how he educated a generation of American readers in the great realistic writers of fiction then appearing in Europe.

Soon after Howells joined the staff of the *Atlantic Monthly* in 1866, he became friendly with an obscure young contributor named Henry James, and through him he met Thomas Sergeant Perry, a Harvard tutor in French and German from 1868 to 1872, and then for two years editor of the *North American Review*. Under Perry's guidance Howells' range of reading and reviewing was widened to include the writers of Italy, Spain, France, Russia, Germany, and the Scandinavian countries. In "Recollections of an Atlantic Editorship," written for the fiftieth anniversary of the *Atlantic* in November, 1907, Howells tells us with his customary candor that "to the reviews of American and English books I added certain pages of notices of French and German literature, and in these I had the very efficient and singularly instructed help of Mr. Sergeant Perry, who knew not only more of current continental literature than any other American, but more than all other Americans." The new department was called "Recent Literature," and Perry was commissioned to contribute to it when Howells assumed the editorship of the *Atlantic* in January, 1871.

Howells' early reviews of European writers in the *Atlantic*

* *The notes to Part II begin on p. 381.*

reflect his response to the winds of realism blowing across Europe at a time when most Americans were still engaged with Scott (who, Howells asserted, built pasteboard castles), and Dickens (who, according to Howells, thought he felt more deeply than he actually did), and Thackeray (who, Howells claimed, was a trickster).

One has only to reread the early chapters of his retrospective book *My Literary Passions* (1895) to realize that Howells, as a hungry reader of the classics in Ohio, had "given his heart" to each of these giants in turn—and to many another in the "Bookcase at Home." That Howells never forgot these early enthusiasms, even after he recognized the limitations of his favorites, is reflected in portions of an essay he wrote for *Munsey's Magazine* (April, 1897), with which Part II begins.

Now, however, these English authors were swept aside in order to give place to the new and dazzling writers from Europe whom Howells read with eager attention, sometimes before their novels were translated, and introduced to his readers first through the *Atlantic Monthly* and later through *Harper's Weekly, Harper's Monthly, Literature,* the *North American Review,* and many other papers and magazines. Not only did the stories of Björnson, Turgenev, Hardy (the only living English novelist whom Howells consistently admired), Verga, Valdés, Galdós, Zola, and Tolstoy affect Howells' own technique as a writer, but they became for him the standard-bearers of the new realistic movement in novel writing. A reading of Howells' appraisals of these writers as they first appeared in leading American magazines helps us to understand that realism was to Howells much more than a literary movement; it was, in fact, a fresh approach to truth itself, and it held for him an important social implication.

Howells' extraordinary grasp of the new fiction which poured across his editorial desk, and which he discussed with the writers and authors who passed through his office, would not have been possible had he not been himself a linguist. *Years of My Youth* (1916) gives the reader a moving account of Howells' boyish "struggle with those alien languages." The importance to the future critic of the knowledge of these languages was the reading of many writers in the original—Cervantes, Ariosto, Dante,

Schiller, Goldoni, and others—that Howells managed to crowd into his early days as a printer and a reporter in Ohio and into his years in Venice.

Howells later regretted the time he had spent in his lonely youth studying these languages and poring over his well-thumbed classics. As an older man, looking back at the literary passions of a self-taught boy, he wished he had seen "more of the actual world" and had learned to know his "brethren in it better." However, it was because of his knowledge of languages that he was able to escape from the drudgery of the family newspaper. His mastery of German led him to apply for a consulship in Munich; when he actually received an appointment to Venice he knew enough Italian to accept it; his understanding of French gave him an early acquaintance with Zola, Flaubert, Maupassant, Daudet, and others; his reading of the Spanish classics helped him to grasp the importance of Armando Palacio Valdés in his own tradition. Most important of all, through first-hand acquaintance with the Continental novelists Howells was moved to question the supremacy of English fiction, to give impetus to the study of European novels in this country, and through his understanding of these writers to encourage the early signs of "the new spirit" in American writers.

For Howells hoped to relate American fiction, which he freely admitted to be very uneven in its performance, to the "only living movement in imaginative literature," that of the Continental novelists. "The disposition to regard life without the literary glasses so long thought desirable," which he saw in the best of our writers, "distinguishes by a superior freshness and authenticity any group of American novels from a similarly accidental group of English novels, giving them the same good right to be as the like number of recent Russian novels, French novels, Spanish novels, Italian novels, Norwegian novels."

In an essay in *Munsey's Magazine* written in 1897 Howells, still encouraging the "new spirit" wherever he discerns it, admits quite candidly that "if you had a vote of the critics in the United States today, it would declare by a large majority for the romantic novel." He is, however, impressed by the growing popularity of such a writer as Henry B. Fuller, whose realistic picture of Chicago in *The Cliff Dwellers* (1893) makes the author "very distinctly part of the future." Fuller and other young writers of his decade give Howells hope that taste is turning away from the crudely romantic in fiction. "A prodigious impulse in every direction . . . in the arts as well as in affairs" was felt in this country after the Civil War, Howells declares, when American writers, like the realistic writers of Europe, began to do "new things." In Part III of this book we shall see which American writers seemed important and what "new things" they were doing. Although "the yoke of England" is still felt in criticism, Howells observes, "American fiction is as free as it can very well be. We do not take the word from anybody." With an optimistic prophecy—"I should say that America was still coming in fiction"—Howells waves us on to the future.

Part II concerns the European masters whom for a quarter of a century Howells had been introducing to American readers. Each in his way reflected the new interest in the inner lives of ordinary people and thus unconsciously added a new dimension to a definition of realism that Howells helped to establish in American fiction.

DICKENS AND THACKERAY

ᗉᘒ

IN *Criticism and Fiction* Howells said it is the critic's business "to break the images of false gods and misshapen heroes, to take away the poor silly toys that many grown people would still like to play with." These toys were, of course, the "heroes" and "heroines," moved by "the old romantic ideals," and the malevolent villains, quite as false to ordinary experience.

To Howells realism was "nothing more and nothing less than the truthful treatment of material"; one is not surprised, then, to read that "the divine Jane" is "alone worthy to be matched with the great Scandinavian and Slavic and Latin artists." Howells wrote: "Because of the mania of romanticism, the art of fiction, as Jane Austen knew it, declined from her through Scott, and Bulwer, and Dickens, and Charlotte Brontë, and Thackeray, and even George Eliot." This mania seized upon all Europe in the nineteenth century; England, however, has shown few signs of recovery, in spite of the example of a subtle use of realism in the Continental masterpieces at her door. George Eliot and Thomas Hardy, to be sure, break through the fog of "those poor islanders," but they avail little since English criticism has continued "provincial, and special and personal."

Howells' choice of adjectives seems to have been vindicated by the storm of comment that *Criticism and Fiction* elicited from the British critics immediately after its appearance in 1891. Andrew Lang in the *Illustrated London News* of April 1, 1891, records:

The friends of romance pray daily, but almost without hope, for the conversion of Mr. W. D. Howells. At this hour he is impenitent, and the best we can hope for is that his is a case of "invincible ignorance." Mr.

Howells is not content with monthly blaspheming against romance in the magazine of Messrs. Harper. He has reproduced a variety of his remarks in a little volume, "Criticism and Fiction."

In the next issue of the *Illustrated London News* William Archer takes Howells to task for "the injudicious vivacity of expression" that leads him to overstate his case for realism in *Criticism and Fiction*, the "main contentions" of which "the unprejudiced observer" is forced to accept. The critic writing in the *Literary World* of June 20, 1891, treats the author of the provocative little volume with less tenderness. Many of Howells' dicta, he commented, "are as entertaining and instructive as the judgments of a Pawnee brave in the galleries of the Louvre would be."

Howells' attack on British critics and British novelists could not have been a complete surprise to the English, for the battle had been joined in 1882 when Howells inserted several telling paragraphs in his essay "Henry James, Jr." written for the November *Century*. Before Howells sailed for England after his resignation from the *Atlantic*, the essay was left with Richard Watson Gilder, the new editor of the *Century*. Howells and his family spent a happy summer in London, seeing many English and American friends, before setting forth for Switzerland in September. The first intimation of the stir that Howells' latest essay caused in London came to him in a letter from Henry James written from London in November, 1882. He too had been out of London when the *Century* arrived, and thus "I missed the little breeze produced, as I am told, by the November Century." Mildred Howells reports in *Life in Letters* that the paragraphs referring to Dickens and Thackeray "brought a storm of abuse upon Howells from people who probably did not understand what he had said." The reader of today understands more fully than the reader of 1882 possibly could the significance of the statement imbedded in Howells' essay, "Henry James, Jr.," for we read it with the light cast upon the whole controversy by *Criticism and Fiction*. Howells reports that the offending sentences, reprinted below, caused much "skull-cracking."

The art of fiction has, in fact, become a finer art in our day than it was with Dickens and Thackeray. We could not suffer the confidential attitude of the latter now, or the mannerism of the former, any more than we could endure the prolixity of Richardson or the coarseness of Fielding. These great men are of the past—they and their methods and interests; even Trollope and Reade are not of the present. The new school derives from Hawthorne and George Eliot rather than any others; but it studies human nature much more in its wonted aspects, and finds its ethical and dramatic examples in the operation of lighter but not really less vital motives. The moving accident is certainly not its trade; and it prefers to avoid all manner of dire catastrophes. It is largely influenced by French fiction in form; but it is the realism of Daudet rather than the realism of Zola that prevails with it, and it has a soul of its own which is above the business of recording the rather brutish pursuit of a woman by a man, which seems to be the chief end of the French novelist. This school, which is so largely of the future as well as the present, finds its chief exemplar in Mr. James; it is he who is shaping and directing American fiction, at least.

Though Howells had not received the November *Century* in Switzerland, he had heard of the excitement his comments had caused among the English. To Roswell Smith, the new owner of the *Century*, he wrote at once:

I suppose you will have seen that I have stirred up the English papers pretty generally by what I wrote of Dickens and Thackeray in my paper on James. I don't remember just what I said, but so far as they have quoted me, I stand by myself, and should only wish to amplify and intensify the opinions that they object to. I knew what I was talking about, and they don't know at all what they are talking about.

To Edmund Gosse he wrote that he would like to "say [his] say of D. & T.," but, he added, "I am far too lazy and too busy to see the hour of doing it." Howells seized his chance to say his say in answer to "the English clamor" when he took over "The Editor's Study" of *Harper's* in 1886. His rejection of the worn-out novel techniques of Dickens and Thackeray became an essential aspect of his espousal of the new and subtler techniques of the European masters to whom he had been turning during his *Atlantic* period. A sense of how an interest in the Continental writers was connected in James's mind as well as in Howells' with a repudiation of the English novels and of "romantic phantoms" in their own aims as novelists is to be found in a letter written February 21, 1884, by James in Paris to his friend Howells in Boston. James, after reporting that "I have been seeing something of Daudet, Goncourt, and Zola," refers to "the floods of tepid soap and water which under the name of novels are being vomited forth in England," and adds: "I say this to you because I regard you as the great American naturalist. I don't think you go far enough, and you are haunted with romantic phantoms and a tendency to factitious glasses; but you are on the right path and I wish you repeated triumphs."

That readers of the period recognized the importance of the attack on the accepted pillars of the English novel, Dickens and Thackeray, is attested by an article by Maurice Thompson in the Philadelphia *Book News* of November, 1887. After an opening paragraph on Howells' early life and his work on the *Atlantic*, Thompson observed that Howells, before the publication of his *Century* essay on James, was "practically unknown in England":

In November, 1882, was published in the *Century Magazine* Mr. Howells' sketch of Henry James, in which he set forth his critical opinion of Charles Dickens, stating in effect that he considered Henry James a greater artist and a better novelist than either Thackeray or Dickens. No doubt Mr. Howells was as much surprised as anybody else when the English critics attacked him and his little essay with a suddenness and acrimony wholly unlooked for. The result was two-fold: at once Mr. Howells and Mr. James, having gained British attention, stepped to the front of American interest. By what the English critics deemed unmitigated audacity, Mr. Howells had set himself and his method of novel-writing over against the personality and the method of the greatest English romancer since Scott. The situation was one that not even Hawthorne's genius had ever commanded. British resentment was quite sufficient to awaken American attention—it always is. Mr. Howells saw his opportunity and threw the whole force of his talent into an effort to profit by it. But here again, as always, he kept himself well in hand. The situation did not change the current of his development, it merely hastened its flow. He began to attack romance and to set himself forward as the spokesman of the realistic "school" in American fiction. If, as a critic, he has fallen far short of greatness, he has succeeded in attracting wide attention, and has made his position an anomalous and interesting one. Chiefly, in this regard, he has chosen to be the enthusiastic, even headstrong, eulogist of Tolstoi, and, recently, of Zola.

That Howells stood firmly by his opinions in his critical reading of his two old favorites, Dickens and Thackeray, is evident not only in his comments on these novelists in *Criticism and Fiction,* but also in the brief excerpt presented below from a long essay he wrote for *Munsey's Magazine* in April, 1897, entitled "My Favorite Novelist and His Best Book." At the request of the editor, Howells as a member of a symposium of writers, here tells of the development of his literary taste. One is not surprised to discover that "the favorite novelist" at that time was Tolstoy, nor is one unprepared to learn that there have been a great many "favorite novelists" in the literary development of this omnivorous reader, then in his sixtieth year. Howells' recovery from the enthusiasms of his youth, so winningly traced in *My Literary Passions* just two years before the publication of the following essay, reflects his "changed point of view" that turned him from the "potent charm" of Dickens and the "worldly pride" of Thackeray to the truer claim of the writers of Europe. These Continental novelists, without any apparent artifice, bring one to an understanding of the inner life of ordinary people. *My Literary Passions,* Howells' autobiography as a reader (abbreviated in "My Favorite Novelist"), contains a still fuller account of his abiding love of the novels of Dickens and Thackeray. But their heroes and heroines, not to mention their villains, were undoubtedly "poor silly toys," to be cherished only in sentimental moments by a responsible critic conscious of the new voices of psychological realism from Europe.

My Favorite Novelist and His Best Book *

TO SAY something concerning novels, and particularly of my favorite among them? That is a difficult thing to do, for one's point of view changes so much from youth to middle age. One's favorite at twenty would not be one's favorite later; but I am

* *Munsey's Magazine,* April, 1897.

pretty sure that throughout my life there has been an increasing preference for what seems to me *real* in fiction as against
what seems to me *factitious;* and whilst I have been very fond,
from time to time, of the pure romance, I have never cared for
the romantic novel, since I was very young.

I used to be extremely fond of what, perhaps, was a pretty
true picture of life in its way—"Handy Andy." It was one of
the first novels I read, and it was an early favorite with me;
and then I read others of Lover and Lever—their names are
so much alike that I confound their novels as well. But before
that I had favorite novels: the Indian and pioneer romances
of Emerson Bennett, and, the very first of all, a story of Lowell's
friend, George F. Briggs [Charles F. Briggs], called "The
Trippings of Tom Pepper"—I fancy still a pretty good story,
though it is fifty years since I read it. It was not necessary,
then, however, that a novel should be good in order to be my
favorite. In fact, I am rather surprised that "Don Quixote"
should have been my favorite about the same time, and that
Poe's tales should have been equally my favorites.

As a boy, I liked Captain Marryatt's novels ever so much. I
have not read any of them since except "Jacob Faithful"; I
read that about ten years ago, and was very much amused to
find what hard reading it was, though as a boy I had found it
so easy. All this may illustrate what I mean by a changed point
of view.

Later, of course, I read Dickens, and with most passionate
liking, for a long time. Within a little while past I have read
a good part of "Our Mutual Friend," "Bleak House," and
"David Copperfield," and liked them still, but not with the
old, or young ardor. You are always aware in Dickens, how he
is "making it up," [1] but he was a great master; and I suppose
that "David Copperfield" is his most representative book,
though there are some of his later novels, like the "Tale of
Two Cities," which are more shapely; but the English custom
of novel publication was always against form, against balance.
Dickens issued his novels, until he started *Household Words,*
in numbers; George Eliot published hers in the same way, and
I believe wrote them from month to month as they appeared,

as Mr. Hardy still writes his. A novel was not completed when its publication began. In fact, from number to number the author hardly knew what was going to happen. In a letter to Forster, Dickens tells that he was once in a stationer's shop when a lady came in and asked whether a certain number of "David Copperfield" was out; it was to be the next, and he hadn't put pen to paper, or even imagined it fully. Such conditions are fatal to symmetry. But they were the economic conditions. That was the way the author could best make his living, and the way an artist can best make his living always tells upon his art. . . .

The novelist who was my favorite all through my early manhood was Thackeray, whom I don't now think the great artist I then did; indeed, I find him very much less an artist than Dickens. The plots of Dickens, to be sure, are not such as come out of his characters. The true plot comes out of the character; that is, the man does not result from the things he does, but the things he does result from the man, and so plot comes out of character; plot aforethought does not characterize. But Dickens believed it did, and all the romantic school of writers believed it did. Bulwer, Charles Reade, and even George Eliot, in some measure, thought so; but for all that—all that faking, that useless and false business of creating a plot and multiplying incidents—Dickens was the greater artist, because he could somehow make the thing transact itself. He got it to stand upon its legs and walk off. Thackeray is always holding his figures up from behind, and commenting upon them, and explaining them. In the midst of his narration he stops and writes little essays about his characters. That is the business of the critic, not the novelist. The business of the novelist is to put certain characters before you, and keep them before you, with as little of the author apparent as possible. In a play the people have no obvious interference from the author at all. Of course he creates them, but there is no comment; there can be none. The characters do it all. The novelist who carried the play method furthest is Tourguénief, and for a long time I preferred him to any other; he was the first Russian novelist I read, and on my revulsion from Thackeray, Tourguénief became my greatest favorite.

The novels of incident, of adventure, do not interest me. But I do not believe their authors write simply for popularity, or for the moment. I believe they do the thing they like to do; but the thing they do is worthless, as far as I am concerned. I am not sure that I am quite logical in not caring for novels of adventure, for I am very fond of the circus, and like to see people flying through the air; and I would go to a fire, any day.

As to what I once said about our not being able to throw off the yoke of England intellectually, although we had long ago done so politically, I did not mean so much our fiction as our criticism. American fiction is as free as it can very well be. We do not take the word from anybody; but English taste influences our criticism. If you had a vote of the critics in the United States today, it would declare by a large majority for the romantic novel, which is distinctly a second rate novel, judging it by the quality of the men who produce it. It would be the same in England, where the novel of that sort continues to be taken seriously, though there is no other country in Europe where it could possibly be taken seriously. But the English are so far behind that they prefer a novel of that sort. They are a very romantic people. . . .

BJÖRNSTJERNE BJÖRNSON
(1832-1910)

HOWELLS tells us in *My Literary Passions* that during a long illness soon after he went to live in Cambridge, he read with delight translations of the first three of Björnstjerne Björnson's novels to appear in this country, *Arne* (1869), *The Happy Boy* (1870), and *The Fisher-Maiden* (1869). The young editor soon included his appraisal of these stories in "Reviews and Literary Notices" for the *Atlantic Monthly* and thus helped to establish Björnson's reputation in the United States. So rapidly did an appreciation of his novels grow that by 1890 all his works had appeared in translation. Well known in his day as novelist, poet, playwright, and essayist, Björnson is now almost forgotten; but between 1870 and his death he was considered the herald of a new school of writing.

When Howells wrote his review of Björnson's three novels for the *Atlantic* he had not met the Norwegian and knew little of him as a political figure in his own country. Howells himself was at that time the author of several slim books of poetry and travel; he was attending the great Longfellow's Dante evenings; he was lecturng on Italian literature at Harvard College; and he was industriously writing reviews for the *Atlantic*. But the recent success of *Italian Journeys,* which was crowded with realistic pictures of Italian streets and Italian characters in the Goldoni tradition, had set Howells' imagination to work on the problems of a fiction writer as well as on those of a critic. It was as both a critic and an aspiring novelist that he read Björnson's stories. To waste no words on elaborate description, to present one's characters briefly, and then to let the plot flow naturally from the characters—that was to achieve the dramatic effect that charmed Howells, first in Björnson and later in Turgenev. Both novelists managed to stay close to the truth, avoiding the style of the French naturalists and of the "blond romances" then flooding the market.

In Björnson's novels Howells found the blend of poetry and realism for which he himself was searching and which he was soon to express in *Their Wedding Journey, A Chance Acquaintance,* and many other novels. In a brief comment on *The Railroad and the Churchyard,* by Björnson, in the *Atlantic* of November, 1870, Howells pointed out with approval that the realistically treated characters are "as exquisitely painted as any ideal figure" because they are "humble but decent folk" seen through the eyes of a poet who at the same time is true to his simple Norwegian background. Though the reader is aware that he is reading romance, Howells said, he feels that the author presents the truth of the real as well as of the ideal in these stories. Howells learned from Björnson that "the finest poetry is not ashamed of the plainest fact," and he found in the Norwegian's novels the romance of real life, which he carried over to his own stories. "He has my love," wrote Howells in *My Literary Passions,* "not only because he is a poet of the most exquisite verity, but because he is a lover of men, with a faith in them such as can move mountains of ignorance, and dullness, and greed."

When Björnson came to the United States on a lecture tour in 1880–1881, Howells lunched with the "poet" (he does not call him novelist) and recognized him again as a "great genius." For almost thirty years Björnson and Howells read each other's novels and corresponded intermittently. Howells tells us that when he saw "the great Norwegian" again in 1908, Björnson knew him at once and met him "with both hands out, and 'My dear, dear Howells!'" Miss Howells adds, in an editorial note to Howells' letter describing the occasion, that "the two saw each other often in Rome, Björnson towering majestically over Howells at their meetings, for he was a giant physically as well as mentally."

Both Howells and Björnson turned to social problems for subjects for their novels in the 1890's. In "The Editor's Study" of *Harper's Monthly* of February, 1887, Howells refers to "that

BJÖRNSTJERNE BJÖRNSON

colossus of the North"; one cannot but speculate as to the indebtedness of Howells' *Rise of Silas Lapham* (1885) to Björnson's play *The Bankrupt* (1874), a translation of which Howells might have read in French or German. In "The Editor's Study" of February, 1889, he points out that the conditions shown in this play are as familiar in the United States as in Norway. He refers to Björnson as "next to Tolstoy in his willingness to give himself for his kind." In his review of Björnson's novel *In God's Way*, in *Harper's*, February, 1891, Howells notes that his "entirely human characters" are seriously concerned with "matters of conscience," and that the reader is not "trifled with or defrauded by any trick of the trade in any part of the action," for Björnson is concerned with the truth and "never fails of reality on the high level his imagination keeps." If one compares Maupassant's *Notre Cœur* with Björnson's novel, says Howells, he will see how "the Frenchman grovels into mere romanticism and is false even to the fashionable filth he studies." Naturalism and romanticism are aspects of the same movement; true realism, as exemplified by Björnson, stays close to the "never-failing springs" of ordinary life and is not afraid to reflect the element of poetry that surrounds the commonplace. Howells summed up Björnson's place in the realistic movement ("The Editor's Study," February, 1889) as "a foremost one, though his realism is of the spiritual type, like that of the Russians, rather than the sensual type, like that of the French, . . . for he is, above all, a poet, . . . one of the chief of those great Norsemen of our time who have led their poetry back not only to the life but to the language of the people."

Reproduced below is the essay on the stories of Björnson that Howells wrote for the *Atlantic* in 1870. His summaries of the stories are omitted. In this review of the recently translated tales Howells is not only actually introducing a new writer to the reader, but he is also suggesting his own evolving ideas on novel writing. Almost all the critical beliefs that he defined more sharply in *Criticism and Fiction* are to be found in this early essay, as well as implied definitions of such terms as romance, naturalism, and realism.

Norwegian Romances *

THE author of that unique essay, "The Glut of the Fiction Market,"[2] who had the good fortune to put more truth about novels into wittier phrase than any other essayist of this time, held that having exhausted all the types and situations and catastrophes of English fiction, we must give it up as a source of literary amusement; and, indeed, there are very few critics who do not now, in their heart of hearts (if they have any), secretly look forward to a time when people shall read nothing but book-notices.

Whilst this millennial period is still somewhat distant, their weariness of our own novelists is attested by nothing so vividly as the extraordinary welcome which has of late been given to translations of the novels of all other races; for, generally speaking, these invaders of our realm of fiction are not better than the novelists they have displaced, but only different. Miss Mühlbach,[3] the author of a vast, and, we believe, increasing horde of blond romances, is the most formidable foe that our sorrier sort of fictionists have had to contend with, and in her train have followed unnumbered others, though none so popular and so poor. Amongst these, indeed, have appeared several of striking merit, and conspicuously Björnstjerne Björnson, the Norwegian whose beautiful romances we wish all our readers to like with us. Concerning the man himself, we know little more than that he is the son of a country clergyman, and that, after a rather unpromising career in school and college, he has risen to the first place in the literature of the North, and has almost invented a new pleasure in the fresh and wonderful tales he writes about Norwegian life. He has been the manager of a theatre, and he has written many plays,

---

* *Arne: A Sketch of Norwegian Country Life*, translated by Augusta Plesner and S. Rugeley Powers, 1866. *The Happy Boy: A Tale of Norwegian Peasant Life*, translated by H. R. G., 1870. *The Fisher-Maiden: A Norwegian Tale.* From the author's German edition, by M. E. Niles, 1869. Reviews in the *Atlantic Monthly*, April, 1870.

BJÖRNSTJERNE BJÖRNSON

but we believe he is known in English only by the three books
of which we have given the titles below, and which form an
addition to literature of as great and certain value as any which
has been otherwise made during the last two years.
There is in the way the tales are told a singular simplicity,
or a reticence and self-control that pass for this virtue, and
that take the æsthetic sense as winningly as their sentiment
touches the heart. The author has entire confidence in his reader's
intelligence. He believes, it seems, that we can be fully satisfied
with a few distinct touches in representing a situation or a
character; he is the reverse, in a word, of all that is Trollopian
in literary art. He does not concern himself with detail, nor
with general statement, but he makes some one expressive particular serve for all introduction and explanation of a fact. The
life he portrays is that, for the most part, of humble but decent
folk; and this choice of subject is also novel and refreshing
in contrast with the subjects of our own fictions, in which there
seems to be no middle ground between magnificent drawing-
rooms and the most unpleasant back-alleys, or between very
refined and well-born company and the worst reprobates of
either sex. How much of our sense of his naturalness would
survive further acquaintance with Björnson we cannot venture
to say; the conventionalities of a literature are but too perilously
apt to be praised as *naïveté* by foreign criticism, and we have
only the internal evidence that peasant-boys like Arne, and
fisher-maidens like Petra, are not as common and tiresome in
Norwegian fiction as we find certain figures in our own novels.
We would willingly celebrate them, therefore, with a wise reserve, and season our delight with doubt, as a critic should;
though we are not at all sure that we can do this. . . .
With people in another rank, Charles Reade would have
managed this as charmingly, though he would have thrown
into it somewhat too much of the brilliancy of the footlights;
and Auerbach would have done it with equal naturalness; but
neither could have cast about it that poetic atmosphere which
is so peculiarly the gift of Björnson and of the Northern mind,
and which is felt in its creations, as if the glamour of the long
summer days of the North had got into literature. It is very

105

noticeable throughout "Arne." The facts are stated with perfect ruggedness and downrightness when necessary, but some dreamy haze seems still to cling about them, subduing their hard outlines and features like the tender light of the slanting Norwegian sun on the craggy Norwegian headlands. The romance is interspersed with little lyrics, pretty and graceful in their form, but of just the quality to show that Björnson is wise to have chosen prose for the expression of his finer and stronger thoughts.

In that region of novel characters, wholesome sympathies, and simple interests to which he transports us, we have not only a blissful sense of escape from the jejune inventions and stock repetitions of what really seems a failing art with us, but are aware of our contact with an excellent and enviable civilization. Of course the reader sees the Norwegians and their surroundings through Björnson's poetic eyes, and is aware that he is reading romance; yet he feels that there must be truth to the real as well as the ideal in these stories.

"Arne" is the most poetical of the three, and the action is principally in a world where the troubles are from within, and inherent in human nature, rather than from any artificial causes, though the idylic sweetness is chiefly owing to the circumstances of the characters as peasant-folk in a "North countree." In "The Happy Boy" the world of conventions and distinctions is more involved by the fortunes of the lovers; for the happy boy Oeyvind is made wretched enough in the good old way by finding out that there is a difference between riches and poverty in the eyes of grandparents, at least, and he is tormented in his love of Marit by his jealousy of a wealthier rival. It is Marit's worldly and ambitious grandfather who forbids their love, and will have only unpleasant things to say to Oeyvind, until the latter comes back from the Agricultural College, and establishes himself in his old home with the repute of the best farmer in the neighborhood. Meantime unremitted love-making goes on between Marit and Oeyvind, abetted by Oeyvind's schoolmaster, through whom indeed all their correspondence was conducted while Oeyvind was away at school. At last the affair is happily concluded when Ole Nordistuen, the grandfather, finds that his farm is going to ruin, and nothing can save it but the skill of Oeyvind.

In this story the peasant life is painted in a more naturalistic spirit, and its customs are more fully described, though here as always in Björnson's work the people are primarily studied as men and women, and secondarily as peasants and citizens; and the descriptions are brief, incidental, and strictly subordinate to the story. We imagine in this an exercise of self-denial, for Björnson must be in love with all that belongs to his characters or surrounds them, to the degree of desiring to dwell longer than he ever does upon their portrayal. His fashion in dealing with scenery and character both is well shown in this account of Marit's party, to which Oeyvind was invited, and at which he ceases with his experience of the world to be the entirely happy boy of the past. . . .

The religious feeling which is a passive quality in ''Arne'' is a positive and controlling influence in ''The Happy Boy,'' where it is chiefly exerted by the old schoolmaster. To him a long and bitter quarrel with an only brother, now dead, has taught lifelong meekness and dread of pride; and he affectingly rebukes Oeyvind's ambition to be first among the candidates for confirmation, in order that he may eclipse all others in Marit's eyes. But Björnson's religious feeling is not pietistic; on the contrary, it teaches, as in ''The Fisher-Maiden,'' that a cheerful life of active goodness is the best interpretation of liberal and hopeful faith, and it becomes at no time a theological abstraction. It is always more or less blended with love of home, and a sense of the sweetness and beauty of natural affections. It is a strengthening property in the tenderness of a sentiment which seems almost distinctively his, or which at least is very clearly distinguished from German sentiment, and in which we Anglo-Saxon readers may indulge our hearts without that recoil of shame which otherwise attends the like surrender. Indeed, we feel a sort of inherent sympathy with most of Björnson's people on this and other accounts, as if we were in spirit, at least, Scandinavians with them, and the Viking blood had not yet died out of us. Some of the traits that he sketches are those now of New England fishermen and farmers and of Western pioneers,—that is, the pioneers of the time before Pacific Railroads. A conscientiousness also exists in them which is like our own,—for we have really a popular conscientiousness, in spite of many shocking appearances to the contrary,—though there seems to be practically more forgiveness in their morality than in ours, especially towards such errors as those by which Arne and Petra came to be. But their incentives and expectations are all as different from ours as their customs are, and in these romances the reader is always sensible of beholding the life of a vigorous and healthful yet innumerous people, restricted by an unfriendly climate and variable seasons, and gaining a hard subsistence from the treacherous sea and grudging soil. Sometimes the sense of nature's reluctant or cruel attitude toward man finds open expression, as in "The Fisher-Maiden," where the pastor says to the "village saints": "Your homes are far up among the mountains, where your grain is cut down more frequently by the frost than by the scythe. Such barren fields and deserted spots should never have been built upon; they might well be given over to pasturage and the spooks. Spiritual life thrives but poorly in your mountain-home, and partakes of the gloom of the surrounding vegetation. Prejudice, like the cliffs themselves, overhangs your life and casts a shadow upon it." Commonly, however, the pathos of this unfriendliness between the elements and man is not sharply uttered, but remains a subtle presence qualifying all impressions of Norwegian life. Perhaps it is this which gives their singular beauty to Björnson's pictures of the scenery amidst which the action of his stories takes place,—pictures notably of Nature in her kindlier moods, as if she were not otherwise to be endured by the imagination.

In "The Fisher-Maiden," which is less perfect as a romance than "Arne," Björnson has given us in Petra his most perfect and surprising creation. The story is not so dreamy, and it has not so much poetic intimacy with external things as "Arne," while it is less naturalistic than "The Happy Boy," and interests us in characters more independently of circumstance.

It is, however, very real, and Petra is a study as successful as daring. . . . In a little space these people's characters are shown in all their individual quaintness, their narrow life is hinted in its gloom and loneliness, and the reader is made to feel at once respect and compassion for them.

There is no room left here to quote from "The Fisher-Maiden"; but the reader has already been given some idea of Björnson's manner in the passages from "Arne" and "The Happy Boy." This manner is always the same in its freedom from what makes the manner of most of our own stories tedious and abominable: it is always direct, unaffected, and dignified, expressing nothing of the author's personality, while fully interpreting his genius, and supplying no intellectual hollowness and poverty with tricks and caprices of phrase.

We hope that his publishers will find it profitable to give us translations of all his works. From him we can learn that fulness exists in brevity rather more than in prolixity; that the finest poetry is not ashamed of the plainest fact; that the lives of men and women, if they be honestly studied, can, without surprising incident or advantageous circumstance, be made as interesting in literature as are the smallest private affairs of the men and women in one's own neighborhood; that telling a thing is enough, and explaining it too much; and that the first condition of pleasing is a generous faith in the reader's capacity to be pleased by natural and simple beauty.

IVAN TURGENEV (1818–1883)

❧

BETWEEN 1867, the date of the first English translation of *Fathers and Children,* and 1873, the date of Howells' review of *Dimitri Roudine,* Turgenev was read, reviewed, and discussed by a group of cultivated young men, such as T. S. Perry, G. P. Lathrop, C. E. Norton, Henry James—and William Dean Howells.

When Howells joined the staff of the *Atlantic Monthly* in 1866 he was still the literary youth from Ohio with a taste for Thackeray and George Eliot. Besides a few poems in the *Atlantic* and a sheaf of travel sketches sent home to the *Boston Daily Advertiser,* the young journalist had published nothing of literary importance. But in his editorial capacity he had come to know Henry James, who, though six years his junior, was ahead of Howells in his knowledge of the new way of writing fiction; moreover, James knew the young men who were discovering Turgenev. In a reminiscent article written for the *North American Review* of July, 1912, Howells tells us that Perry, to whom James had introduced him, first directed his attention to Russian literature and defined for him Turgenev's contribution to realism.

By 1874, when James wrote an essay on Turgenev, Howells had reviewed a number of the Russian's novels in the *Atlantic.* As he tells in *My Literary Passions:* "In those years at Cambridge my most notable literary experience without doubt was the knowledge of Tourgenief's novels, which began to be recognized in all their greatness about the middle of the seventies." By sharing this "notable literary experience" with readers of the *Atlantic,* Howells hoped, as he said in his review of *Smoke* in 1872, to introduce to the American public a worthier type of fiction. Again, in his review of *Dimitri Roudine* he attempted to show the *Atlantic* readers "the kind of novel which can alone keep the art of fiction from being the weariness and derision of mature readers." More than ten years before he consciously argued the cause of realism from "The Editor's Study" of *Harper's Monthly,* Howells expressed his disgust for the romantic pabulum dear to the nineteenth-century fiction reader and his interest in the new realism reflected in Turgenev.

Howells' next review of Turgenev, in the *Atlantic* for February, 1873, showed that he was interested in *Liza* not only as a critic but also as a novelist. One can best explain the extraordinary gain in power that marked Howells' progress from *Suburban Sketches* (1871) through *Their Wedding Journey* (1872) to *A Chance Acquaintance* (1873) by a realization of Howells' debt to Turgenev. In this meditative review of *Liza* Howells remarked on Turgenev's objectivity, which he himself was attempting to achieve.

[He] never calls on you to admire how well he does a thing; he only makes you wonder at the truth and value of the thing when it is done. He seems the most self-forgetful of the story-telling tribe, and he is no more enamoured of his creatures than of himself; he pets none of them; he upbraids none; you like them or hate them for what they are; it does not seem to be his affair.

When in later years Howells looked back at "one of the profoundest literary passions of my life," he still felt that Turgenev's "method is as far as art can go." What Howells meant by the art of Turgenev he defined very clearly in *My Literary Passions:*

His fiction is to the last degree dramatic. The persons are sparely described, and briefly accounted for, and then they are left to transact their affair, whatever it is, with the least possible comment or explanation from the author. The effect flows naturally from their characters, and when they have done or said a thing you conjecture why as unerringly as you would if they were people whom you knew outside of a book. I had already conceived of the possibility of this from Björnson, who practices the same method, but I was still too sunken in the gross darkness of English fiction to rise to full consciousness of its excellence. . . . It was with a joyful astonishment that I realized the great art of Tourgenief.

Though Howells' early biographer and critic, D. G. Cooke, thinks that traces of Dimitri Roudine are to be found in Don Ippolito in *A Foregone Conclusion,* it is not possible to define with exactness Howells' indebtedness to Turgenev. It is enough to say that Howells, at the very time when his critical creed and his technique as a novelist were being formed, had the good fortune to know intimately a group of young men who were eagerly learning the "lesson of the master"—objectivity tempered by a wide humanity. In an interview with Joyce Kilmer in 1914 Howells, then an old man, recalled that in those days on the *Atlantic* all the younger writers were reading Turgenev. This Russian writer, he remembered with appreciation, opened to him "a new world—and it was the only real world."

Howells never met Turgenev, but greetings were exchanged between the two through Henry James, who had come to know the Russian novelist in Paris. Turgenev read and enjoyed Howells' novels and once remarked, "I have spent the night reading *A Chance Acquaintance,* and now I should like to visit a country where there are girls like the heroine."

A Turgenev Novel *

DIMITRI ROUDINE . . . is mainly the study of one man's character, but a character so complex that there is little to ask of the author in the way of a story. In fact Dimitri Roudine is himself sufficient plot; and the reader is occupied from the moment of his introduction with the skillful development of his various traits, to the exclusion of the other incidents and interests. The other persons of the fiction are of a kind which

* *Dimitri Roudine.* A Novel. By Ivan Turgénieff, 1873. Appeared first in Russia in 1855. Translated and published in *Every Saturday* (January–June, 1873). This translation was made by T. S. Perry from French and German texts. Review in the *Atlantic Monthly,* September, 1873.

IVAN TURGENEV

the reader of Turgénieff stories may begin to classify in some
degree, or at least find in a certain measure familiar. The
women are, as usual, very well portrayed, especially the young
girl Natalie, whose ignorant trust, courage, love, and adoration
for Roudine, changing to doubt and scorn,—whose whole maid-
enly being,—are expressed in a few scenes and phrases. Her
mother, Daria Michaëlovna, is also exceedingly well done. She is
of an entirely different type, a woman of mind, as she supposes,
with advanced ideas, but really full of pride of caste, worldly,
and slight of intellect, though not wanting in selfish shrewdness
or a strong will. The reader ought to note with what delicacy,
and yet with what force, Turgénieff indicates, in Alexandra
Paulovna, a sweet, placid, self-contained maturity, alike different
from the wild fragrance of Natalie's young girlhood and the
artificial perfume of Daria's well-preserved middle life; though
he could hardly fail to do this, for nothing is more observable
in Turgénieff than his success in characterizing the different
epochs of womanhood. Volinzoff's conscious intellectual in-
feriority to Natalie, and his simple, manly love for her are
nearly all there is of him; Pigasoff, who peculated in office
when younger and who in provincial retirement is a brutal
censor of the follies of human nature, is rather a study than an
actor in the drama which develops Roudine; and Leschnieff,
who promises something in himself, and does really prove of
firm and generous stuff, is after all hardly more than a relief and
explanation of the principal person. It is he who expresses the
first doubt of Roudine after that philosopher has made his appearance at Daria Michaëlovna's, crushing Pigasoff, bewildering
and charming Natalie, mystifying Alexandra, and provoking
Volinzoff. Leschnieff knew him in his student days, when filial
love, friendship and all real things were lost in his habit of
eloquent phrasing; when Roudine was cruelly ungrateful and
mean in fact, that he might be magnanimous in the abstract;
and the shadow of this dark recollection Leschnieff casts upon
Roudine's new friends. He does not wish him to marry Natalie,
who, he sees, is fascinated with him; but after Roudine's miserable weakness ends their love and all the others despise him,
then Leschnieff does justice to his elevation of ideas and pur-

113

poses. "He may have genius; I won't deny it; but the trouble is he has no character. . . . He is full of enthusiasm; and you can believe a phlegmatic man like me when I say that it is a most precious quality, especially in a time like the present. We are unendurably cold-blooded, indifferent, and apathetic. . . . Once when I was talking of Roudine I accused him of coldness. I was both just and unjust. His coldness is in his blood,—he's not to blame for it,—not in his head. I was wrong in calling him an actor; he is no swindler, no cheat; he does not live on other people like a parasite, but like a child. Yes, he may die in loneliness and misery, but shall we throw stones at him on that account? He will never accomplish anything because he lacks energy and a strong will; but who can say that he has never done, or never will do, any good? That his words have never sown good seed in some young heart, to which nature has not denied the force to carry out what it has conceived?"

It is touchingly related in an epilogue how, after several years, Roudine and Leschnieff came together by chance in the same inn. Leschnieff asks his old comrade to dine with him, and the two elderly men thee and thou each other in the student fashion. Roudine tells of his successive failures since they last met:

" 'Yes, brother,' he began, 'I can now cry with Kolzoff, "Where hast thou brought me, my youth? I have no longer where to lay my head!" ' . . . And was I really good for nothing, and was there nothing for me to do in this world? I have often asked myself this question, and, in spite of all my attempts to set myself lower in my own esteem, I can't help feeling that I have certain abilities which don't fall to the lot of every one. Why must this force remain powerless? Then, too, dost thou remember when we travelled abroad together, how self-confident and blind I was? . . . It is true, I didn't know definitely what I wanted, I revelled in the sound of my own voice, I chased vain phantoms. But now, on the contrary, I can say aloud to the whole world what it is I want; I have nothing to hide; I am, in the fullest sense of the word, a well-meaning man; I have become humble, I am willing to adapt myself to circumstances, I have limited my wishes, I don't strive for any remote object, I confine myself to doing even the slightest service; and

114

yet I do not succeed in anything. What is the reason of this persistent failure? Why can't I live and work like others? I no sooner get a definite position, I no sooner establish myself somewhere, than fate casts me pitilessly out again. . . . I begin to fear my fate. . . . Why is this? Explain this puzzle!'

" 'Puzzle!' repeated Leschnieff. 'It is true, thou has always been a puzzle to me. Even in your youth, when I saw thee acting ill and speaking well in turn, and that time after time, even then I could not understand thee clearly; that was the reason I ceased to love thee. . . . Thou hast so much fire, so earnest a longing for the ideal.' . . .

" 'Words, nothing but words. Where are the deeds?' interrupted Roudine.

" 'Yes; but a good word is a deed too!'

"Roudine looked at Leschnieff without speaking, and shook his head.''

We almost forget, in following this tender yet keen analysis of a pathetic character, that there is really something of a story in the book. Roudine imagines that he loves Natalie, and he wins her brave, inexperienced heart; but when their love is prematurely discovered to her mother, and Natalie comes to him ready to fly with him, to be his at any cost, he is paralyzed at the thought of Daria's opposition. "We must submit," he says. The scene that follows, with Natalie's amazement, wounded faith, and rising contempt and Roudine's shame and anguish, is terrible,—the one intensely dramatic passage in the book, and a masterpiece of literary art which we commend to all students and lovers of that art.

We are not quite sure whether we like or dislike the carefulness with which Roudine's whole character is kept from us, so that we pass from admiration to despite before we come finally to half-respectful compassion; and yet is this not the way it would be in life? Perhaps, also, if we fully understood him at first, his relations to the others would not so much interest us. But do we wholly understand him at last? This may be doubted, though in the mean time we are taught a merciful distrust of our own judgments, and we take Leschnieff's forgiving and remorseful attitude towards him. It may be safely surmised that this was the chief effect that Turgénieff desired to produce in us; certainly he treats the story involved in the portrayal of Roudine's character with almost contemptuous indifference, letting three epilogues limp in after the first rambling narrative has spent itself, and seeming to care for these only as they further reveal the hero's traits. But for all this looseness of construction, it is a very great novel,—as much greater than the novel of incident as Hamlet is greater than Richard III. It is of the kind of novel which can alone keep the art of fiction from being the weariness and derision of mature readers; and if it is most deeply melancholy, it is also as lenient and thoughtful as a just man's experience of men.

GIOVANNI VERGA (1840-1922)

❧❧

HOWELLS, during four years as consul in Venice, learned to love the daily sights and smells of the old city. One is not surprised, then, to find a paragraph of ''The Editor's Study'' for November, 1886, devoted to Verga's novel *I Malavoglia,* which Howells read first in Italian and introduced at once to his American readers. Howells recounts the story, ''simply the history of a poor family trying to pay off an unjust debt and patiently suffering and even perishing in the long struggle.'' He then enlarges upon the misery of these fisherfolk of Sicily—the father lost at sea, a son killed in battle, another turning to crime, the mother dying of cholera. Such are ''the incidents of this simple and beautiful story of these common people whom vulgar people call commonplace. It has an incomparable grasp of Italian actualities, as they present themselves on such a small stage—social, political, domestic and religious.'' The book, Howells adds, ''is eminently worthy of translation.''

The novel was, in fact, translated four years later by Mary A. Craig with the title *The House by the Medlar-Tree.* Howells quite appropriately wrote the introduction, which is printed below. Until a new translation was made by Eric Mosbacher in 1953, this nineteenth-century version remained the only one available in English. The critic who reviewed the current translation in *The New York Times Book Review* glanced briefly back at Howells and expressed surprise that Howells, with ''his usual flair and competence,'' wrote for his introduction ''that rare thing—a sincere panegyric.'' What Howells said about *The House by the Medlar-Tree* was, to his readers of 1890, more than ''a sincere panegyric'': his review was an episode in the critical discussion of realism or—to use Verga's term—*veritism.* The novel was another vindication of Howells' insistence that, without describing extraordinary people engaged in romantic adventure, without departing from the simple truth of the daily lives of simple people, one can hear the sad poetry of ordinary existence. Moreover, the "lesson" of the story is that of life everywhere, that goodness brings not pleasure but peace to the soul. This inescapable conclusion is expressed by Verga in the circumstances of his tale rather than in the comments of the author. For he, like Turgenev, is an impassive observer of his little drama and achieves his effects by means of a subtle reticence.

Howells, in his quarrel with the "great mass" of readers who prefer "to read the Rider Haggards and the Rudyard Kiplings of the day," points to Verga as an example of the "new spirit" on the Continent. Howells recognized at once that Kipling had "a future," but observed that "there is little in the knowingness and swagger of his performance that is not to be deplored with many tears; it is really so far away from the thing that ought to be." However, the reader need not look to the English for light on fiction. "We must turn to the more artistic people for it, to the Continental writers whose superiority in fiction has often been celebrated here." Howells invites the reader to take *The House by the Medlar-Tree* and "examine a little its structure and material." Here nothing is "operated and explained"; "the characters and conditions" are "frankly left to find their own way to the reader's appreciation" of their universal truth.

Though Howells did not meet or correspond with Verga, whose life span very nearly corresponded to his own, he did list the books of this "contemporary Italian" among his "passions" for reasons that the following introduction makes more clear to the reader of today than to the reader of the 1890's. "For my own part," wrote one subscriber to the *Atlantic* (May, 1892), after reading *The House by the Medlar-Tree*, "I think that a preface by Mr. Howells, recommending a book for its realism, will hereafter be enough to guard me against it. Some may agree with him to prize such novels as masterpieces of modern art, but is the depression they produce a wholesome effect to receive from a work of art?"

GIOVANNI VERGA

The House by the Medlar-Tree *

ANY ONE who loves simplicity or respects sincerity, any one
who feels the tie binding us all together in the helplessness of
our common human life, and running from the lowliest as well
as the highest to Mystery immeasurably above the whole earth,
must find a rare and tender pleasure in this simple story of an
Italian fishing village. I cannot promise that it will interest any
other sort of readers, but I do not believe that any other sort are
worth interesting; and so I can praise Signor Verga's book
without reserve as one of the most perfect pieces of literature
that I know.

When we talk of the great modern movement towards reality
we speak without the documents if we leave this book out of the
count, for I can think of no other novel in which the facts have
been more faithfully reproduced, or with a profounder regard
for the poetry that resides in facts and resides nowhere else.
Signor Verga began long ago, in his *Vita dei Campi* ("Life of the
Fields"), to give proof of his fitness to live in our time; and
after some excursions in the region of French naturalism, he here
returns to the original sources of his inspiration, and offers us
a masterpiece of the finest realism.

He is, I believe, a Sicilian, of that meridional race among whom
the Italian language first took form, and who in these latest days
have done some of the best things in Italian literature. It is of
the far South that he writes, and of people whose passions are
elemental and whose natures are simple. The characters, therefore, are types of good and of evil, of good and of generosity, of
truth and of falsehood. They are not the less personal for this
reason, and the life which they embody is none the less veritable.
It will be well for the reader who comes to this book with the
usual prejudices against the Southern Italians to know that such
souls as Padron 'Ntoni and Maruzza La Longa, with their im-

* Translated by Mary A. Craig, with Introduction by W. D. Howells, 1890.

119

passioned conceptions of honor and duty, exist among them; and that such love idyls as that of Mena and Alfio, so sweet, so pure, and the happier but not less charming every-day romance of Alessio and Nunziata, are passages of a life supposed wholly benighted and degraded. This poet, as I must call the author, does again the highest office of poetry, in making us intimate with the hearts of men of another faith, race, and condition, and teaching us how like ourselves they are in all that is truest in them. Padron 'Ntoni and La Longa, Luca, Mena, Alfio, Nunziata, Alessio, if harshlier named, might pass for New England types, which we boast the product of Puritanism, but which are really the product of conscience and order. The children of disorder who move through the story—the selfish, the vicious, the greedy, like Don Sylvestro, and La Vespa, and Goosefoot, and Dumbbell, or the merely weak, like poor 'Ntoni Malavoglia—are not so different from our own images either, when seen in this clear glass, which falsifies and distorts nothing.

Few tales, I think, are more moving, more full of heartbreak, than this; for few are so honest. By this I mean that the effect in it is precisely that which the author aimed at. He meant to let us see just what manner of men and women went to make up the life of a little Italian town of the present day, and he meant to let the people show themselves with the least possible explanation or comment from him. The transaction of the story is in the highest degree dramatic; but events follow one another with the even sequence of hours on the clock. You are not prepared to value them beforehand; they are not advertised to tempt your curiosity like feats promised at the circus, in the fashion of the feebler novels; often it is in the retrospect that you recognize their importance and perceive their full significance. In this most subtly artistic management of his material the author is most a master, and almost more than any other he has the rare gift of trusting the intelligence of his reader. He seems to have no more sense of authority or supremacy concerning the personages than any one of them would have in telling the story, and he has as completely freed himself from literosity as the most unlettered among them. Under his faithful touch life seems mainly sad in Trezza, because life is mainly sad everywhere, and because men there have not yet adjusted themselves to the only terms which can render life tolerable anywhere. They are still rivals, traitors, enemies, and have not learned that in the vast orphanage of nature they have no resource but love and union among themselves and submission to the unfathomable wisdom which was before they were. Yet seen aright this picture of a little bit of the world, very common and low down and far off, has a consolation which no one need miss. There, as in every part of the world, and in the whole world, goodness brings not pleasure, not happiness, but it brings peace and rest to the soul, and lightens all burdens; the trial and the sorrow go on for good and evil alike; only, those who choose the evil have no peace.

ARMANDO PALACIO VALDÉS
(1853–1938)

"THIS time I made the Study mainly about Tolstoy, Gogol, and Valdés," Howells wrote in January, 1886, to his old friend, Thomas Sergeant Perry, and added: "Isn't it strange that in all this vast land there should not be one intelligent voice besides yours on the right side?"

What Howells meant by "the right side" becomes clear as one reads the six reviews of the novels of Armando Palacio Valdés that he wrote for "The Editor's Study" between 1886 and 1891. The first and the last of this significant group are presented below.

But before turning to these reviews and the critical controversy on the meaning of realism to which they contribute, one must remember that Howells' love for Spanish literature began many years earlier when he was a child in Ohio. The elder Howells, his son tells us, used to recount the story of Don Quixote in the large family kitchen of the home in Hamilton, while "we boys were all shelling peas." The ten-year-old boy made such good use of a Spanish-American dictionary given to his father by a soldier of the Mexican War that he taught himself the rudiments of the Spanish language. One is not surprised to discover that he read the novels of Valdés in Spanish before they appeared in English translations and was therefore able to introduce them to American readers almost as soon as they were published abroad.

The first Valdés novel that Howells reviewed for the Study (April, 1886) and referred to in his letter to Perry was *Marta y Maria* (1883). Howells tells us in *My Literary Passions* that he read very little during his year abroad in 1882 and that it was not until he returned to Boston, "in the old atmosphere of work," that he turned again to books. Undertaking "a critical department in one of the magazines" made Howells feel again "the rise of the old enthusiasm for an author"—this time for two contemporary Spanish writers, Valera and Valdés. The latter, hitherto unknown to Howells, delighted him "beyond words by his friendly and abundant humor, his feeling for character and his subtle insight." Howells was so impressed by the story of two sisters, Marta and Maria, who fell in love with the same man, that he called the novel "one of the most truthful and profound I have ever read." Did the story of the rivalry of the two sisters linger in Howells' mind when he wrote of a similar situation in *The Rise of Silas Lapham* two years later? Since his interest in a novel was always that of both novelist and critic, we are tempted to wonder whether he read Valdés' new novel when it appeared in 1883, and whether in Valdés' story he found a hint for his own.

"Of course it is a realistic novel," said Howells in his review of *Marta y Maria,* and he added, "It is even by an author who has written essays upon realism." One of these essays, the Prologue to *Marta y Maria,* was so good, he assured his readers, that he would have been glad to reprint it in full. In it Valdés said:

I have the presumption to believe that, though *Marta y Maria* may not be beautiful, it is a realistic novel. I know that realism—at the present time called naturalism—has many impulsive adepts, who conceive that truth exists only in the vulgar incidents of life, and that these are the only ones worth transferring to art. Fortunately this is not the case. Outside of markets, garrets, and slums, the truth exists no less. The very apostle of naturalism, Émile Zola, confesses this by painting scenes of polished and lofty poetry which assuredly conflict with his exaggerated aesthetic theories.

Valdés was frequently referred to by Howells in "The Editor's Study" during this decade, not only because he enjoyed the natural, direct, humorous, and often poetic novels of the Spaniard, but also because Valdés, within his own limits, reinforced Howells' ideas of realism. In the November, 1886, issue of *Harper's,* Howells announced that *Marta y Maria* could now be read in translation, and he reviewed briefly the next two novels of Valdés, *José* (1885) and *Riverta* (1886). *Maxima* (1888), *El*

Cuarto poder (1888), and *Scum* (1891) Howells commented on in turn as they appeared.

Howells was in fact so impressed by *Scum* that he discussed it in "The Editor's Study" for February and again for April, 1891. It is the second of these two reviews that is printed below, because it reflects Howells' enlarged sense of the social scope of the novel. In the Study for February he remarked that *Scum*

. . . recognizes, once for all, that it is the top of aristocratic and pluto-cratic "society" in all countries which is really the scum, and not those poor plebeian dregs which mostly boil about the bottom of the caldron and never get to the surface at all. . . . The book is important because it is a part of that expression of contemporary thought about contem-porary things now informing fiction in all countries but England.

Valdés was, according to Howells, one of the few writers who knew that all of life is the province of the novelist; that it be-longs to no class; that the realistic novelist reflects the truth that resides in the simple life about him and disdains the tricks of plot and melodrama, called by Valdés "effectism"; that in hold-ing to this program he produces a work of art full of the joy of life, not weighted down with sordidness and sorrow.

In agreeing with Howells that Valdés' novel is a contribution to realism, Perry puts himself on the "right side" of the contro-versy raging, with varying emphasis, in most of the countries of Europe more violently than in the United States. "You're right," says Howells to Perry in the letter quoted above, "no one invented realism; it came. It's perfectly astonishing that it seems to have come everywhere at once."

Howells' hope was that realism would come to this country too, especially in the form represented by the three contemporary Spanish novelists to whom he frequently referred, Galdós, Pardo-Bazán, and Valdés. Of the three, Valdés is the one with whom Howells was the most familiar, and in fact the only one with whom he had personal relations. In a note placed before a letter to Howells from Valdés, Mildred Howells wrote, "Howells greatly admired the work of Valdés and they often wrote to each other, Valdés in Spanish and Howells in Italian." In this letter of November 26, 1887, Valdés expressed his appreciation of the reviews of his novels appearing in *Harper's* and observed, "I believe that a mysterious current of sympathy joins our hearts and minds across the ocean—the same things impress or disgust us.'' Affectionate letters were exchanged between the two novelist-critics, and their books were sent back and forth across the Atlantic. ''I am reading a new book by Valdés, perfectly charming,'' wrote Howells to Perry in July, 1911. Howells was then seventy-four, but still ''charmed'' by the Spanish novelist.

Though Howells felt that he must occasionally warn ''the intending reader'' of the ''Latin frankness'' to be found in a novel by Valdés, and though he felt more than once that ''Valdés helps himself out with a romantic and superfluous bit of self-sacrifice,'' Howells thoroughly enjoyed the good sense, the sweetness, and the humor of the Spaniard's tales. ''This delightful author'' further pleased Howells by the essay on fiction with which he prefaced one of his novels, the charming story of *Sister Saint Sulpice:* ''It is an essay which I wish every one intending to read, or even to write a novel, might acquaint himself with.'' So well indeed did Howells acquaint himself with this Prologue, which appeared in 1889, that his comments on Valdés' critical views fill Sections XIII–XIV of *Criticism and Fiction.*

Marta y Maria *

ONE would not perhaps look first to find [examples of the best in fiction] in Spain, but we have just been reading a Spanish novel which is very nearly one. Of course it is a realistic novel; it is even by an author who has written essays upon realism, and who feels obliged, poor fellow, in choosing a theme which deals with the inside rather than the outside of life, to protest that the truth exists within us as well as without, and is not confined to the market-houses, the dram-shops, the street corners, or the vulgar facts of existence. Don Armando Palacio Valdés believes

* *Marta y Maria*, by Armando Palacio Valdés, 1883. Review in *Harper's Monthly*, April, 1886.

that his *Marta y Maria* is a realistic novel, although it is not founded upon current and common events, and that the beautiful and the noble also lie within the realm of reality. We should ourselves go a little farther, and say that they are to be found nowhere else; but we have not at present to do with our opinions, or even the prologue to Senor Valdés's novel, though we should be glad to reproduce that in full, it is so good. We must speak, however, of the admirable little illustrations of his book, so full of character and spirit and movement. They are badly printed, and the cover of the book, stamped in black and silver, is as ugly as a ''burial casket,'' but our censure must almost wholly end with the mechanical execution of the book. The literature is delightful: full of charming humor, tender pathos, the liveliest sympathy with nature, the keenest knowledge of human nature, and a style whose charm makes itself felt through the shadows of a strange speech. It is the story of two sisters, daughters of the chief family in a Spanish sea-port city: Maria, who passes from the romance of literature to the romance of religion, and abandons home, father, and lover to become the spouse of heaven, and Marta, who remains to console all these for her loss. We do not remember a character more finely studied than that of Maria, who is followed, not satirically or ironically, through all the involutions of a conscious, artificial personality, but with masterly divination, and is shown as essentially cold-hearted and selfish in her religious abnegation, and as sensuous in her spiritual ecstasies as she was in her abandon to the romances on which she fed her egoistic fancy. But Marta—Marta is delicious! We see her first as an awkward girl of thirteen at her mother's *tertulia*, helplessly laughing at some couples who give a few supererogatory hops in the dance after the music suddenly stops; and the note of friendly simplicity, of joyous, frank, sweet naturalness, struck in the beginning, is felt in her character throughout. Nothing could be lovelier than the portrayal of this girl's affection for her father and mother, and of the tenderness that insensibly grows up between her and her sister's lover, left step by step in the lurch by the intending bride of heaven. One of the uses of realism is to make us know people; to make us understand that the Spaniards, for example, are not the remote cloak-

and-sword gentry of opera which romance has painted them, abounding in guitars, poniards, billets, *autos-da-fe,* and confessionals, but are as "like folks" as we are. It seems that there is much of that freedom among young people with them which makes youth a heavenly holiday in these favored States. Maria's lover has "the run of the house," in this Spanish town, quite as he would have in Chicago or Portland, and he follows Marta about in the frequent intervals of Maria's neglect; he makes her give him lunch in the kitchen when he is hungry, this very human young Marquis de Penalta; he helps her to make a pie, the young lady having a passion for all domestic employments, and to put away the clean clothes. Her father, Don Mariano Elorza, has a passion for the smell of freshly ironed linen, much as any well-domesticated American citizen might have, and loves to go and put his nose in the closets where it hangs. His wife has been a tedious, complaining invalid all her married life, but he is heart-broken when she dies; and it is at this moment that Maria— who has compromised him in the Carlist movement because that is the party of the Church, and has tried in the same cause to make her lover turn traitor to the government which he has sworn as citizen and soldier to defend—comes ecstatic from the death-scene to ask his permission to complete her vocation in the convent. He gives it with a sort of disdain for her pitiless and senseless egotism. The story closes with the happy love of Marta and Ricardo, clasped to the old man's breast and mingling their tears with his; and the author cries, "O eternal God, who dwellest in the hearts of the good, can it be that these tears are less grateful to Thee than the mystical colloquies of the Convent of St. Bernard?"

A sketch of the story gives no idea of its situations, or, what is more difficult and important, the atmosphere of reality in which it moves. The whole social life of the quiet town is skillfully suggested, and an abundance of figures pass before us, all graphically drawn, none touched with weakness or exaggeration. It is a book with a sole blemish—a few pages in which the author thinks it necessary to paint the growth of little Marta's passion in too vivid colors. There is no great harm; but it is a lapse of taste and of art that libels a lovely character, and seems a sacrifice to the ugly French fetich which has possessed itself of the good name of Realism to befoul it.

------◆◆------

Scum *

THE whole essay [*The Palpitating Question,* by Emilia Pardo-Bazán] is redolent of the Spanish humor, which is so like our own, and yet has its peculiar perfume. This humor is what forms the atmosphere of Valdés's novels, and keeps his satire kindly even when his contempt is strongest, as in that last novel of his, which his translator calls *Scum,* and which deals with society as Valdés "found it" in Madrid. Certain points of resemblance are to be found in "good" society the world over, nowadays, and one of these is its decorous religiosity. It appears that wherever people so far experience the favor of Heaven as to have nothing to do but to dress handsomely and to fare sumptuously, they are as punctilious in their devotions as they are in any of their social duties. Nothing could be more edifying than the Spanish novelist's study of the "smart set" of Madrid as he pictures them at a select service in the oratory of a devout lady of their number. They seem certainly to be more vicious than any smart set among ourselves, or at least differently vicious, but they vary little in their theory of life. If they worship God they do not forget their duty to Mammon, and money is to the fore among them as it is among us. One of their leaders is Clementina, the heroine, if the book can be said to have a heroine, who is the daughter of the Duke of Raquena, a robber baron of the stock exchange, an adventurer in Cuba, ennobled for his unscrupulous rapacity in accumulating money, after he returns to Spain. He is a great financier, as such people are with us, sometimes; he knows how to get up "corners" and to "squeeze" those he traps into them, quite as if he were an oil or wheat operator. He is the owner of some great quicksilver mines, and one of the most striking pas-

* *Scum,* by Armando Palacio Valdés, 1890. *Harper's Monthly,* April, 1891.

sages of the book is the account of the visit he pays these mines with a party of the "best" people of Madrid in his train of private cars. They are all hanging upon him in the hope that he will somehow make them rich, but some of the women are shocked at the life, or the death in life, of the miners, who are sufferers from mercurial poisoning, and who go shaking about like decrepit paralytics. The duke tells the ladies that the notion of mercurial poisoning is nonsense, and if the men would leave off drinking they would be well enough; just as one of our own millionaires has told us that the great cause of poverty is "intemperance." The duke's assurance comforts the ladies, and they have a banquet in one of the upper levels of the mine, while all round and under them the haggard miners are digging their own graves. Their gayety is a little chilled by the ironies of the young physician of the company, who takes a less optimistic view of the case than the good duke, though his life is spent among the miners and devoted to them. This physician is a socialist; and it is a curious sign of the times that the socialists should be making their way, in fiction at least, as the friends rather than the enemies of the race.

BENITO PÉREZ GALDÓS
(1845-1920)

❧

"THERE is probably no chair of literature in this country . . . which teaches young men anything of the universal impulse which has given us the books not only of Zola, but of Tourguéneff and Tolstoi in Russia, of Björnsen in Norway, of Valera in Spain, of Verga in Italy," Howells complained in "The Editor's Study" of February, 1886. Five years later in *Criticism and Fiction* he added the names of Ibsen, Valdés, and Galdós, for he was always adding to his acquaintance of foreign writers. Before he entered the Study in January, 1886, he had refused professorships at four institutions, Union College and Washington University in 1868, Johns Hopkins University in 1882, and Harvard University in 1886. When later a similar invitation came from Yale, Howells again refused, for he did not consider himself a teacher; he preferred to educate his generation in European fiction through the columns of *Harper's Magazine*.

Introducing the Spanish novelist Benito Pérez Galdós to the American reader in *Harper's*, May, 1888, Howells compared his recently translated romance, *La familia de Leon Roch,* to Valdés' *Marta y Maria:* "In *Leon Roch*, as in *Marta y Maria*, the name of the devotee is Maria, but in this case she is not an exalted sentimentalist seeking the fulfillment of her selfish pietistic dreams in a convent, but a loving wife whom her religious intolerance transforms into a monster of cruelty and folly." Howells thus presented *Leon Roch* to the reader as an example of the bigotry of the Roman Catholic Church; in the opening paragraph, however, he pointed out that "we cannot hug ourselves upon the freedom of the Protestant faith from such forms of bigotry; it is the touch of poor human nature in [the] heroines

130

[of Galdós and Valdés] which makes them universally recognizable as portraits from life," according to Howells, and is far more important in a novel than the social issues involved. Though Maria "is the terrible spirit of bigotry," nevertheless, she and all her family "are really a delightful group, with their several vices." In fact, it is "hard not to give one's heart" to people "drawn with such wonderful truth," scoundrels though they be. But none of the individuals in this novel by Galdós is entirely good or evil; they belong, rather, to "those mixed characters who are beginning to get out of life into fiction. . . . No other sort seems to get into Galdós's book, and perhaps this is the reason why some of his most reprobate people have a hold upon our sympathies" and leave us finally with a sense of personal acquaintance.

These excerpts from the first of the two reviews Howells wrote of Galdós' novels indicate that he perceived at once the critical problem latent in *Leon Roch,* that of relating a social issue to the story of character in such a way as to allow the individual to dominate the background. Galdós, a Spanish liberal, interested in the social conditions of authoritarian Spain of the nineteenth century, recognized the novelist's difficulty early in his writing career. He, like Howells, objected to the historical romance, popular in the 1860's, and determined to concentrate as a novelist, first on social questions and later on the character of the individual, to which he subordinated social conditions. *La Fontana de Ora* (1867–1868) is essentially a historical novel; *Elandez* (1871) is social in intent; *Doña Perfecta* (1876) is the most dramatic example of Galdós' successful presentation of a character caught in a mesh of environmental factors. It is this greatest of all Galdós' novels that was the subject of Howells' second review. Though *Doña Perfecta* appeared two years before *La familia de Leon Roch,* it was not translated until 1895. The introduction to the translation by Mary E. Serrano was written by Howells; it had already appeared in *Harper's Bazar* on November 2, 1895, one week before the publication of the book, and this is the text printed below.

"The very acute and lively Spanish critic who signs himself Clarín," to whom Howells referred in the opening paragraph of his essay, was Leopoldo Alas (1852–1901), a brilliant professor

131

from Oviedo, himself a novelist, critic, and editor, widely read—
and feared—in Spain. He was a friend of the three Spanish authors most frequently referred to by Howells, Palacio Valdés,
Pardo-Bazán, and Pérez Galdós; his admiration for Galdós dated
back to student days, when he predicted that Galdós would re-
generate the novel in Spain. Clarín hailed *Doña Perfecta* for its
frank presentation of the truth about the provincial little town
of Orbajosa, which he considered a microcosm of reactionary
Spain.

Howells reflected Clarín's ideas in his review; one suspects that
many more of Howells' critical concepts are to be found in the
articles Clarín wrote for *El Solfeo*, a liberal journal of Madrid,
from 1875 to the end of the century. The Spanish critic, like
Howells, was convinced of the beauty as well as the truth of Galdós'
novel *Doña Perfecta*, which he reviewed in *El Solfeo*, October 20,
1876. He conceived of literature as one of the chief instruments of
cultural improvement; the novelist might influence social evolution if he put "art" before "reform," and if he followed the road
of realism rather than that of naturalism, which is merely photographic, or of romanticism, which is unrelated to actuality. "The
method of the modern novel," then, is not that of naturalism,
which readily becomes "tendencious" by overstressing the social
issues, nor is it that of romanticism, which aspires to idealism. It is
the method of the "new realism," which presents a psychological
study of character in its environment.

Howells found similar critical ideas discussed in *La Cuestion
Palpitante*, by Emilia Pardo-Bazán, the third of the trio admired
by Clarín and Howells; she was, Howells tells us, a "valiant lady
in the campaign for realism," who wrote "one of the best and
strongest books on the subject" of the "new realism." This long
essay Howells read in Spanish before he published *Criticism and
Fiction*. These are the three Spanish writers whom Howells names
in *My Literary Passions*, published the same year as the review
below. These are the three whom Howells thought of when, in May,
1899, he commented in a rueful mood on the Spanish-American
War, which had just ended: "If by any effect of advancing
civility," he wrote, "we could have treated with Spain for the
cession of her three novelists, Pérez Galdós, Emilia Pardo-Bazán,

BENITO PÉREZ GALDÓS

and Armando Palacio Valdés, I, for one American, should have
been more content than I am with Cuba, Puerto Rico, and the
Philippines.'' For it was with these three that Howells shared
his distaste for the historical novel and his faith in the ''new realism.''

———————◆◆————————

Doña Perfecta, A Great Novel *

THE very acute and lively Spanish critic who signs himself Clarín,
and is known personally as Don Leopoldo Alas, says the present
Spanish novel has no yesterday, but only a day-before-yesterday.
It does not derive from the romantic novel which immediately
preceded it, but it derives from the realistic novel which preceded
that: the novel, large or little, as it was with Cervantes, Hurtado
de Mendoza, Quevedo, and the masters of picaresque fiction.

Clarín dates its renascence from the political revolution of 1868,
which gave Spanish literature the freedom necessary to the fiction
that studies to reflect modern life, actual ideas, and current aspirations; and though its authors were few at first, ''they have
never been adventurous spirits, friends of Utopia, revolutionists,
or impatient progressists and reformers.'' He thinks that the most
daring, the most advanced, of the new Spanish novelists, and the
best by far, is Don Pérez Galdós.

I should myself have made my little exception in favor of Don
Armando Palacio Valdés, but Clarín speaks with infinitely more
authority, and I am certainly ready to submit when he goes on to
say that Galdós is not a social or literary insurgent; that he has
no political or religious prejudices; that he shuns extremes, and
is charmed with prudence; that his novels do not attack the
Catholic dogmas—though they deal so severely with Catholic
bigotry—but the customs and ideas cherished by secular fanaticism to the injury of the Church. Because this is so evident, our

* *Doña Perfecta*, by B. Pérez Galdós. Review in *Harper's Bazar*, November
2, 1895.

133

critic holds, his novels are "found in the bosom of families in every corner of Spain." Their popularity among all classes in Catholic and prejudiced Spain, and not among free-thinking students merely, bears testimony to the fact that his aim and motive are understood and appreciated, although his stories are apparently so often anti-Catholic.

Doña Perfecta is, first of all, a story, and a great story, but it is certainly also a story that must appear at times potently, and even bitterly, anti-Catholic. Yet it would be a pity and an error to read it with the preoccupation that it was an anti-Catholic tract, for really it is not that. If the persons were changed in name and place, and modified in passion to fit a cooler air, it might equally seem an anti-Presbyterian or anti-Baptist tract; for what it shows in the light of their own hatefulness and cruelty are the perversions of any religion, any creed. It is not, however, a tract at all; it deals in artistic largeness with the passion of bigotry, as it deals with the passion of love, the passion of ambition, the passion of revenge. But Galdós is Spanish and Catholic, and for him bigotry wears a Spanish and Catholic face. That is all.

Up to a certain time, I believe, Galdós wrote romantic or idealistic novels, and one of these I have read, and it tired me very much. It was called Marianela, and it surprised me the more because I was already acquainted with his later work, which is all realistic. But one does not turn realist in a single night, and although the change in Galdós was rapid, it was not quite a lightning change; perhaps because it was not merely an outward change, but artistically a change of heart. His acceptance in his quality of realist was much more instant than his conversion, and vastly wider; for we are told by the critic whom I have been quoting that Galdós's earlier efforts, which he called *Episodios Nacionales,* never had the vogue which his realistic novels have enjoyed.

These were, indeed, tendencious, if I may anglicize a very necessary word from the Spanish *tendencioso.* That is, they dealt with very obvious problems, and had very distinct and poignant significations, at least in the case of Doña Perfecta, Leon Roch, and Gloria. In still later novels, Emilia Pardo-Bazán thinks, he has comprehended that "the novel of to-day must take note of the ambient truth, and realize the beautiful with freedom and independence." This valiant lady, in the campaign for realism which she made under the title of La Cuestión Palpitante—one of the best and strongest books on the subject—counts him first among Spanish realists as Clarín counts him first among Spanish novelists. "With a certain fundamental humanity," she says, "a certain magisterial simplicity in his creations, with the natural tendency of his clear intelligence toward the truth, and with the frankness of his observation, the great novelist was always disposed to pass over to realism with arms and munitions; but his aesthetic inclinations were idealistic, and only in his latest works has he adopted the method of the modern novel, fathomed more and more the human heart, and broken once for all with the picturesque and with the typical personages, to embrace the earth we tread."

For her, as I confess for me, Doña Perfecta is not realistic enough—realistic as it is; for realism at its best is not tendencious. It does not seek to grapple with human problems, but is richly content with portraying human experiences; and I think Señora Pardo-Bazán is right in regarding Doña Perfecta as transitional, and of a period when the author had not yet assimilated in its fullest meaning the faith he had imbibed.

Yet it is a great novel, as I said; and perhaps because it is transitional it will please the greater number who never really arrive anywhere, and who like to find themselves in good company en route. It is so far like life that it is full of significations which pass beyond the persons and actions involved, and envelop the reader, as if he too were a character of the book, or rather as if its persons were men and women of this thinking, feeling, and breathing world, and he must recognize their experiences as veritable facts. From the first moment to the last it is like some passage of actual events in which you cannot withhold your compassion, your abhorrence, your admiration, any more than if they took place within your personal knowledge. Where they transcend all facts of your personal knowledge, you do not accuse them of improbability, for you feel them potentially in yourself, and easily account for them in the alien circumstance. I am not saying that the story has no faults; it has several. There are tags of romanticism fluttering about it here and there; and at times the author permits himself certain old-fashioned literary airs and poses and artifices, which you simply wonder at. It is in spite of these, and with all these defects, that it is so great and beautiful a book.

What seems to be so very admirable in the management of the story is the author's success in keeping his own counsel. This may seem a very easy thing; but, if the reader will think over the novelists of his acquaintance, he will find that it is at least very uncommon. They mostly give themselves away almost from the beginning, either by their anxiety to hide what is coming, or their vanity in hinting what great things they have in store for the reader. Galdós does neither the one nor the other. He makes it his business to tell the story as it grows; to let the characters unfold themselves in speech and action; to permit the events to happen unheralded. He does not prophesy their course; he does not forecast the weather even for twenty-four hours; the atmosphere becomes slowly, slowly, but with occasional lifts and reliefs, of such a brooding breathlessness, of such a deepening density, that you feel the wild passion-storm nearer and nearer at hand, till it bursts at last; and then you are astonished that you had not foreseen it yourself from the first moment.

Next to this excellent method which I count the supreme characteristic of the book merely because it represents the whole, and the other facts are in the nature of parts, is the masterly conception of the characters. They are each typical of a certain side of human nature, as most of our personal friends and enemies are; but not exclusively of this side or that. They are each of mixed motives, mixed qualities; none of them is quite a monster; though those who are badly mixed do such monstrous things.

Pepe Rey, who is such a good fellow—so kind, and brave, and upright, and generous, so fine a mind, and so high a soul—is tactless and imprudent; he even condescends to the thought of intrigue; and though he rejects his plots at last, his nature has once harbored deceit. Don Inocencio, the priest, whose control of Doña Perfecta's conscience has vitiated the very springs of goodness in her, is by no means bad, aside from his purposes. He loves his sister and her son tenderly, and wishes to provide for them by the marriage which Pepe's presence threatens to prevent. The nephew, though selfish and little, has moments of almost being a good fellow; the sister, though she is really such a lamb of meekness, becomes a cat, and scratches Don Inocencio dreadfully when he weakens in his design against Pepe.

Rosario, one of the sweetest and purest images of girlhood that I know in fiction, abandons herself with equal passion to the love she feels for her cousin Pepe, and to the love she feels for her mother, Doña Perfecta. She is ready to fly with him, and yet she betrays him to her mother's pitiless hate.

But it is Doña Perfecta herself who is the transcendent figure, the most powerful creation of the book. In her, bigotry and its fellow-vice, hypocrisy, have done their perfect work, until she comes near to being a devil and really does a devil's deeds. Yet even she is not without some extenuating traits. Her bigotry springs from her conscience, and she is truly devoted to her daughter's eternal welfare; she is of such a native frankness that at a certain point she tears aside her mask of dissimulation and lets Pepe see all the ugliness of her perverted soul. She is wonderfully managed. At what moment does she begin to hate him, and to wish to undo her own work in making a match between him and her daughter? I could defy any one to say. All one knows is that at one moment she adores her brother's son, and at another she abhors him, and has already subtly entered upon her efforts to thwart the affection she has invited in him for her daughter.

Caballuco, what shall I say of Caballuco? He seems altogether bad, but the author lets one imagine that this cruel, this ruthless brute must have somewhere about him traits of lovableness, of leniency, though he never lets one see them. His gratitude to Doña Perfecta, even his murderous devotion, is not altogether bad; and he is certainly worse than nature made him, when wrought upon by her fury and the suggestion of Don Inocencio. The scene where they work him up to rebellion and assassination is a compendium of the history of intolerance; as the mean little conceited city of Orbajosa is the microcosm of bigoted and reactionary Spain.

I have called, or half-called, this book tendencious; but in a

137

certain larger view it is not so. It is the eternal interest of passion working upon passion, not the temporary interest of condition antagonizing condition, which renders Doña Perfecta so poignantly interesting, and which makes its tragedy immense. But there is hope as well as despair in such a tragedy. There is the strange support of a bereavement in it, the consolation of feeling that for those who have suffered unto death, nothing can harm them more; that even for those who have inflicted their suffering this peace will soon come.

"Is Pérez Galdós a pessimist?" asks the critic Clarín. "No, certainly; but if he is not, why does he paint us sorrows that seem inconsolable? Is it from love of paradox? Is it to show that his genius, which can do so much, can paint the shadow lovelier than the light? Nothing of this. Nothing that is not serious, honest, and noble is to be found in this novelist. Are they pessimistic, those ballads of the North, that always end with vague resonances of woe? Are they pessimists, those singers of our own land, who surprise us with tears in the midst of laughter? Is Nature pessimistic, who is so sad at nightfall that it seems as if day were dying forever? The sadness of art, like that of nature, is a form of hope. Why is Christianity so artistic? Because it is the religion of sadness."

HENRIK IBSEN (1828-1906)

WHEN in 1895 Howells considered his tastes as a reader, he did not see fit to devote a chapter of *My Literary Passions* to Ibsen. Instead he referred to "the cold fascination" of the Norwegian, in contrast to the "delight" of Björnson, who held for him nothing of Ibsen's "scornful despair, nothing of his anarchistic contempt." However, Howells added, "I should be far from denying [Ibsen's] mighty mastery."

In spite of Howells' lack of temperamental sympathy for Ibsen, he frequently listed him, next to Zola and Tolstoy, among the Continental writers as a chief ally in the defense of realism. Why, he demanded in *Criticism and Fiction*, have not the critics in this country felt this "universal impulse"? In "The Editor's Easy Chair" of May, 1911, he repeated the list of those the Study had "preached" in "the sulphurous past," and again the name of Ibsen appeared, the only dramatist to be included among the novelists. Did not the Study, he asked, "preach Hardy and George Eliot and Jane Austen, Valdés, Galdós and Pardo-Bazán, Verga and Serao, Flaubert and the Goncourts and Zola, Björnson and Ibsen, Tourgénief and Dostoyevsky and Tolstoy, and Tolstoy, and even more Tolstoy, till its hearers slumbered in their pews?"

Though Howells commented on the plays of Shaw, Pinero, Wilde, and many more in "Life and Letters," which he wrote regularly for *Harper's Weekly* from 1895 to 1898, he observed in *My Literary Passions*, "I suppose I have not been a great reader of the drama." However, he tells us that by 1895 he had read all of Ibsen. Perhaps under the influence of the Norwegian, Howells wrote in *Harper's Weekly*, February 29, 1896, a plea for a national theater and argued that drama is "one of the most potent influences for good or evil in our lives . . . only less so than the novel itself . . . which is only a kind of portable theater." Ibsen, then, became for Howells a "canonized realist" who took his place among the Continental novelists in the Study, where Howells insistently thundered at the gates of "Fiction in Error."

The publication in 1889 in English of three of Ibsen's plays, *Ghosts, The Pillars of Society,* and *The Enemy of the People,* brought from the Study the first peal of thunder from Howells in defense of Ibsen. Before Howells' American readers had had an opportunity to see these plays presented on the stage, he seized upon them to prove once more the importance of the realistic movement sweeping across Europe. In the Study of May, 1889, he declared that the effect of Ibsen's plays is "not much less than tremendous," especially the play called *Ghosts,* "where the sins of the fathers are visibly visited upon the son." This play and others by Ibsen are "bitter with the most caustic irony, which is all the more mordant because it is so just." Howells quite clearly recognized that "there is often more of type than of character in his personages," that "the reality of the action is sometimes strained to an allegorical thinness," that the tone of the writing is frequently tame and flat; the plays, however, rise above their faults because of their truth to human experience. These dramas, banned in England, were being played in Europe, Howells assured his readers. We can only imagine, he said, the effect of Ibsen on the "fat optimism" of those who attend our theaters of New York only to be amused. "What our average audience would have to say of them we will not fancy."

The popularity in 1895 of a translation of Max Nordau's *Degeneration,* which "so many people are reading or making believe to read," again caused Howells to rise to the defense of one of Nordau's chief examples of "degeneracy"—Ibsen. In *Harper's Weekly,* April 13, Howells wrote a blistering attack on "the amusing madman," Dr. Max Nordau, "who fancies himself the only sane person in a world of lunatics." By chance Beerbohm Tree's presentation of *The Enemy of the People* was also under discussion in the spring of 1895, and the performance of the play added fuel to the fire already lit by Nordau's violent and ruthless attack on modern thought in general, especially as expressed by Ibsen, Tolstoy, and Zola. Two weeks after the review of Nordau's *Degeneration* Howells came to the defense of Ibsen in commenting on Beerbohm Tree's dramatic presentation. He found "a vast hope, a deep consolation" in the fact that Ibsen had at last been presented on the New York stage, "that haunt of the decrepitudes and imbecilities of the past." The performance gave Howells an experience in "absolute drama," because both actor and dramatist expressed "a most important conviction in ethics and in aesthetics." Just as Tolstoy reached his greatest effectiveness at the moment when ethics and aesthetics—truth and beauty—were perfectly balanced, so also did Ibsen. His drama became for Howells a "great theatrical event, the very greatest I have ever known," because it presented a social problem in terms of objective art. However, said Howells, the New York audience goes to the theater to be amused; there is "no love interest in the play" by Ibsen, no "action." Therefore, he concluded, "I am not thinking of any great acceptance for Ibsen himself on our stage, but for Ibsenism there is already great acceptance." Ibsen is "the master who has more to say to our generation in the theater than any other."

That the message of Ibsen proved too much for the New York audience of the 1890's is indicated by the second selection printed below, a review of a performance of *Ghosts* in 1899. Remembering the impact of this drama on the New York audience of the 1890's, Howells wrote in the *North American Review*, July, 1906, after the death of Ibsen: "The great and dreadful delight of Ibsen is from his power of dispersing the conventional acceptations by which men live on easy terms with themselves, and obliging them to examine the grounds of their social and moral opinions."

A Question of Propriety *

THE latest performance of Ibsen's "Ghosts" in New York has been followed by quite as loud and long an outburst of wounded delicacy in public and private criticism as the earliest provoked.

* *Literature*, July 7, 1899.

Now, as then, the play has been found immoral, pathological, and revolting; and if nothing else in the case is plain, it is plain that we are not yet used to the sort of extremes which it goes to.

We are used to almost every other imaginable sort of extremes in the theatre. There is hardly anything improper or repulsive which the stage has not shown, except the repulsive impropriety of "Ghosts," and the range outside of that play is so great that it is a little odd the author could not have been content with it. He might have deployed troops of women in lascivious dances with nothing between the audience and their nakedness except a thickness or a thinness of silken gauze; he might have left the scene strewn with shapes of mimic murder; he might have had false wives fooling jealous husbands, and coming back for a maudlin forgiveness; he might have had seducers spreading their lures for victims; he might have had repentant prostitutes dying in the last excesses of virtue and bringing reform to their lovers and remorse to their lovers' families; he might have had heroic thieves and highwaymen doing deeds of dazzling self-sacrifice; he might have had a noble and truthful gentleman wearing a mask of crime through four acts, and tearing it off in the fifth, barely in time to baffle villainy and rescue helpless innocence; he might have had a sister devoting herself to infamy, and taking the shame, in order to save a guilty sister's good name, or her husband's honor, or her children's feelings; he might have had a saintly suicide murdering himself, that his rival may marry the girl he loves; he might have had a girl contriving by every manner of lies the union of another with the man who adores her; he might have any or all of these abominable things, and offended no one. People are used to such things, and to any number of things like them, in the theatre, and if they are not disappointed when they do not get them, they certainly expect them.

But if all these traditions or none of them would have sufficed, there is the whole printed drama, from which the author might have chosen horrors freely, and without the least offence. There is no form of lust, adultery, incest, homicide, cruelty, deceit, which was not open to his choice in the Greek, Spanish, English, and French drama. One Elizabethan play, the "Hamlet" of William Shakespeare, is so infinitely rich in all these motives that Ibsen could have drawn upon it alone and had every revolting and depraving circumstance which he could reasonably desire, without the least offence. That is a play which we not only see without disgust, but with the highest intellectual pleasure, and, as we believe, with spiritual edification. It is never denounced by criticism for its loathsome fable, for its bloodshed, for the atrocity with which its hero breaks the heart of a gentle girl, or for the pathological spectacle of her madness and his own. Strangest of all, it is not condemned for leaving the witness in the same sort of uncertainty as to the specific lesson that he finds himself in at the end of "Ghosts."

The present high disdain for "Ghosts," then, must come simply from our unfamiliarity with the sort of means employed in it to strike terror. The means are novel, that is all; when they become stale and hackneyed; when we have them in the form of hash, as we are sure, finally, to have them, no one will object, and we shall be morally nourished by them, just as we are now morally nourished by those of "Hamlet." Then we may think no worse of the problem which a ghost leaves Mrs. Alving with regard to her son than of the problem which a ghost leaves Hamlet with regard to his mother. Possibly we may even come to think Mrs. Alving's problem is more important, as it is certainly more complex and profound. Compared with the question how she shall suffer to the end with the miserable boy whom his father's pleasant vices have doomed to idiocy, it is an easy matter for Hamlet to decide when and how to kill his uncle.

The psychological difference between the two tragedies is the measure of the vast space between the nerves of the seventeenth and the nineteenth centuries. In the nerves of the later time is the agonising consciousness of things unknown to the nerves of the earlier age; and it may be this tacit consciousness which recoils from the anguish of the touch laying it bare. It is not unimaginable that in some century yet to come, say the twenty-first or twenty-second, a like consciousness will recoil from a yet subtler analysis, and cry out for the good old, decent, wholesome, sanative, dramatic means employed in Ibsen's "Ghosts," as our consciousness now prefers to these the adulterous and vindictive motives of Shakespeare's "Hamlet." I can fancy an indignant and

143

public-spirited criticism demanding the "scientific" methods of our then out-dated day as against those of some yet truer dramatist which shall hold the mirror still more unshrinkingly up to nature. That dramatist will, of course, have his party, very much outnumbered and ashamed, as Ibsen has his party in New York today; and I wonder in what form of revolt against the prevailing criticism this devoted little band will wreak its sense of injustice. Now, one can say that compared to the spare, severe sufficiency of "Ghosts," the romantic surplusage of "Hamlet" is as a Wagner opera to a Greek tragedy; but what will the audacious partisan of the future dramatist say in contrasting his work with that of a then out-Ibsened Ibsen?

Ibsenism *

[Howells first comments on "four or five of the most characteristic of Ibsen's plays" presented in New York during the previous five years and continues] :

I am not thinking . . . of any great acceptance for Ibsen himself on our stage, but for 'Ibsenism' there is already great acceptance, and there will be greater and greater, for he is the master who has more to say to our generation in the theatre than any other, and all must learn his language who would be understood hereafter. The chief trait of his speech, as I have intimated, is its simplicity, and this has impressed itself upon the diction of the new playwrights very noticeably already. Of course, that sort of simplicity is a common tendency of our time, but it is Ibsen who has felt it more than any other, and who has, I think, imparted it in some measure to all who have studied him. Both the theatre and the drama have studied Ibsen, and are studying him more and more: dramatic criticism itself is deigning to look at him a little; but not nearly so much as the drama and the theatre, perhaps because it need not; like "genius" it knows without learn-

* *Harper's Weekly*, April 27, 1895.

ing. The drama and the theatre feel his simplicity in every way —his simplicity of thought and sense, as well as his simplicity of speech. So far as I have spoken with actors who have played Ibsen, I find that without exception, almost, they like to play him, because he gives them real emotions, real characters to express, and they feel in him the support of strong intentions. They have to forget a good deal that they have learned in the school of other dramatists. They have to go back, and become men and women again before Ibsen can do anything with them, or they with him; but when they have once done this, their advance toward a truer art than they have ever known is rapid and unerring. It is very interesting to hear a stage-manager, who has helped them remand themselves to this natural condition, talk of their difficulties in reaching it, when they are most willing and anxious to reach it. They have really to put away from them all that they have learned of artificial and conventional for the stage; everything but their technical skill is a loss, but this is an immense advantage, for Ibsen understands the stage, as perhaps no other dramatist has understood it; and in his knowledge and sympathy with the stage the actor feels a support which he can fully trust. He can implicitly believe that whatever he finds in the dialogue or the direction is fully and positively meant, and that he cannot go wrong if he is true to them. It is not possible to play Ibsen so badly as to spoil him if the actor obeys him; if he obeys him intelligently and skilfully the highest effect is unfailing; but if he merely obeys him blindly and ignorantly, a measure of success is sure to follow. For this reason I have never seen a play of Ibsen's which I felt to be a failure; the Réjane performance of the Doll's House was nearer a failure than any other, because the French stage seemed unwilling to obey Ibsen at all.

The influence of Ibsen on the theatre is very interesting, but it is not so important as his influence on the drama. I think the reader of Ibsen will be able to trace his influence in the work of any of the modern English playwrights, or at least I do not think I have deceived myself in imagining that I trace it in the plays of Mr. Pinero, or Mr. Shaw, or Mr. Jones. I do not mean that they have imitated him, or have slavishly followed him, but that they have learned from him a certain way of dealing with material;

and I do not mean that they deal with life altogether as he does, or even largely, but only that each one does so in some degree. I could wish that they dealt with it altogether as he does in their choice of the problems they treat, or that they would treat such problems as concern conduct rather than such as concern action. The problem which a play of Ibsen hinges upon is as wide as the whole of life, and it seeks a solution in the conscience of the spectator for the future rather than the present; it is not an isolated case; it does not demand what he would do, or would have done, in a given event; and this is what makes the difference between him and the modern English playwrights. In morals, a puritanic narrowness cramps all our race, which will not suffer us to get beyond the question of personality; but Ibsen always transcends this, and makes you feel the import of what has happened civically, socially, humanly, universally. In Ghosts, for instance, who is to blame? You feel that nothing but the reconstitution of society will avail with the wrong and the evil involved.

But the new dramatists have learned from Ibsen to deal with questions of vital interest, and to deal with them naturally, and, on the whole, pretty honestly. For the rest, I should say that it would not be safe or just (what is unjust is never quite safe, I suppose) to say at which point you felt his influence. So much in the tendency of any time is a common effect from common causes, that it is not well to attribute this or that thing to this or that man. All the Elizabethan dramatists wrote somewhat like Shakespeare, and Shakespeare is the greatest of them all; and yet it would not be easy to prove that he was otherwise their master. I should not undertake to prove that the modern English drama was of the school of Ibsen, except as Ibsen is the greatest of the moderns. But I find much in the new plays that makes me think of him: situations, questions, treatment, motive, character, diction. They lack his poetry, but they have much of the same art, and it appears that we can get on without poetry in plays, but not without art. But whether they have their common traits in common with him because of their contemporaneity, and are like him because they are of the same century and the same modern circumstance, I am not ready to say; and so if I were really driven to the wall, and had to point out absolute instances of his influence in them or die, I should perhaps withdraw the word influence; and then go away thinking my own thoughts. He is above all a moralist, and they are all, more or less effectually, moralists both in the larger and the lesser sense.

THOMAS HARDY (1840-1928)

❦

HOWELLS says in *My Literary Passions:* "I came rather late, but I came with all the ardor of what seems my perennial literary youth, to the love of Thomas Hardy, whom I first knew in his story, *A Pair of Blue Eyes.*" Since this novel appeared in 1873 and was not read by Howells until 1885 or 1886, we can only conclude that Howells had little hope for any fiction coming from England and therefore that he did not keep up with the current British books.

While Howells was still editor of the *Atlantic Monthly* he missed the opportunity to include Hardy's name among his contributors. On September 6, 1879, Hardy wrote to James R. Osgood, owner of the magazine, suggesting that he write a serial for the *Atlantic.* Osgood showed the letter to Howells, but the editor—totally ignorant of Hardy's writing—made no proposal. Since *Far from the Madding Crowd* had already appeared in *Every Saturday,* edited by Howells' friend T. B. Aldrich, it is difficult to understand Howells' lapse unless one remembers that he then considered Cambridge, Massachusetts, "the Elysian Fields," beyond which "there was very little good writing being done" in the English language.

Fortunately for Howells' own literary growth, he left the *Atlantic* in 1881 and journeyed to England, where he met Hardy through Edmund Gosse. It was after this visit of 1882–1883 and the return to Boston, "when I undertook a critical department in one of the magazines," that Howells read *A Pair of Blue Eyes.*

A letter "To Millicent from America" in *The Critic,* July 3, 1886, by an English traveler, Frederick Wedmore, shows that Howells continued to read and appreciate Hardy as one of the important writers of the day. Wedmore had luncheon with Howells and described him in the interview as a genial, downright, matter of fact, and withal satirical person—just now in the very fullest possession of his means, writing and talking with the utmost neatness, and without the slightest effort. He talked much of books. . . . He agreed with me very much when I praised Thomas Hardy. We spoke particularly of "Under the Greenwood Tree" and "A Pair of Blue Eyes." Still I can never forgive him for underrating Dickens.

Howells' attack on Dickens, one of the "passions" of his childhood, was in fact an attack on romanticism in fiction writing. In an interview reported in the *Critic* the following year, Howells observed that Balzac, Gogol, and Dickens "marked the inauguration of the realistic era by taking realities and placing them in romantic relations," but that all three were essentially romantic. England, said Howells, stands "at the very bottom of the list among the nations that have produced great modern novelists" —though, he added, "Hardy is a great, I may say, a very great novelist. His pictures of life are life itself."

The attitude that Howells had toward Hardy was well known before the storm broke in this country in 1894 at the appearance of *Jude the Obscure* as a serial in *Harper's*. The excitement caused by *Jude* was described by J. Henry Harper forty years later in *I Remember* (1934). Harper made a special trip to London to persuade Hardy to alter his story when, to his editorial eyes, after the first few installments had appeared, "it looked a little squally." Hardy did, in fact, tone down the objectionable sections for *Harper's*. The book, however, appeared in its entirety in November, 1895. Printed below is Howells' enthusiastic review of *Jude the Obscure,* which came out the following month in *Harper's Weekly,* one day before Jeanette L. Gilder's review in the *New York World* of December 8, in which she declared, "Thomas Hardy has scandalized the critics and shocked his friends."

Howells' support of Hardy never flagged. He reviewed the stage version of *Tess of the D'Urbervilles* for *Harper's Weekly* in 1897, sent messages to Hardy by Hamlin Garland in 1899, included two essays on Hardy's women in *Heroines of Fiction* (1901), and contributed several studies of Hardy's poetry to the *North American Review.* Howells called on Hardy when he visited England in 1910 and received a letter of congratulation from the

British novelist on the occasion of his seventy-fifth birthday dinner. The personal relations of these two men remained unblemished for over twenty-five years. "I liked him," Hardy remarked of Howells to their common friend Hamlin Garland, "he was a good fellow."

Though Hardy was laconic on the subject of Howells, Howells has told us in *Heroines of Fiction* exactly what he thought of Hardy, whose very "faults" he grew to love. Hardy, like Björnson and Turgenev, Howells considered "a great poet as well as a great artist"; his plots are often artificial, even fantastic; his characters, especially his women, "wholly pagan," for "his people live very close to the heart of nature." But Hardy's "vision of humanity" was anything but romantic, and it was this that moved Howells to say of *Jude the Obscure*, "No greater or truer book has been written in our time or any."

Pleasure from Tragedy *

IT HAS never been quite decided yet, I believe, just what is the kind and what is the quality of pleasure we get from tragedy. A great many people have said what it is, but they seem not to have said this even to their own satisfaction. It is certain that we do get pleasure from tragedy, and it is commonly allowed that the pleasure we get from tragedy is nobler than the pleasure we get from comedy. An alloy of any such pleasure as we get from comedy is held to debase this finer emotion, but this seems true only as to the whole effect of tragedy. The Greek tragedy kept itself purely tragic; and English tragedy assimilated all elements of comedy and made them tragic; so that in the end Hamlet and Macbeth are as high sorrowful as Orestes and Oedipus.

I should be rather ashamed of lugging the classic and the romantic in here, if it were not for the sense I have of the return of

* *Jude the Obscure*, by Thomas Hardy, 1895. Review in *Harper's Weekly*, December 7, 1895.

an English writer to the Greek motive of tragedy in a book which seems to me one of the most tragical I have read. I have always felt in Mr. Thomas Hardy a charm which I have supposed to be that of the elder pagan world, but this I have found in his lighter moods, for the most part, and chiefly in his study of the eternal-womanly, surviving in certain unconscienced types and characters from a time before Christianity was, and more distinctly before Puritanism was. Now, however, in his latest work he has made me feel our unity with that world in the very essence of his art. He has given me the same pity and despair in view of the blind struggles of his modern English lower-middle-class people that I experience from the destinies of the august figures of Greek fable. I do not know how instinctively or how voluntarily he has appealed to our inherent superstition of Fate, which used to be a religion; but I am sure that in the world where his hapless people have their being, there is not only no Providence, but there is Fate alone; and the environment is such that character itself cannot avail against it. We have back the old conception of an absolutely subject humanity, unguided and unfriended. The gods, careless of mankind, are again over all; only, now, they call themselves conditions.

The story is a tragedy, and tragedy almost unrelieved by the humorous touch which the poet is master of. The grotesque is there abundantly, but not the comic; and at times this ugliness heightens the pathos to almost intolerable effect. But I must say that the figure of Jude himself is, in spite of all his weakness and debasement, one of inviolable dignity. He is the sport of fate, but he is never otherwise than sublime; he suffers more for others than for himself. The wretched Sue who spoils his life and her own, helplessly, inevitably, is the kind of fool who finds the fool in the poet and prophet so often, and brings him to naught. She is not less a fool than Arabella herself; though of such exaltation in her folly that we cannot refuse her a throe of compassion, even when she is most perverse. All the characters, indeed, have the appealing quality of human creatures really doing what they must while seeming to do what they will. It is not a question of blaming them or praising them; they are in the necessity of what they do and what they suffer. One may indeed blame the author for presenting such a conception of life; one may say that it is demoralizing if not immoral; but as to his dealing with his creations in the circumstance which he has imagined, one can only praise him for his truth.

The story has to do with some things not hitherto touched in fiction, or Anglo-Saxon fiction at least; and there cannot be any doubt of the duty of criticism to warn the reader that it is not for all readers. But not to affirm the entire purity of the book in these matters would be to fail of another duty of which there can be as little doubt. I do not believe any one can get the slightest harm from any passage of it; only one would rather that innocence were not acquainted with all that virtue may know. Vice can feel nothing but self-abhorrence in the presence of its facts.

The old conventional personifications seem drolly factitious in their reference to the vital reality of this strange book. I suppose it can be called morbid, and I do not deny that it is. But I have not been able to find it untrue, while I know that the world is full of truth that contradicts it. The common experience, or perhaps I had better say the common knowledge of life contradicts it. Commonly, the boy of Jude's strong aspiration and steadfast ambition succeeds and becomes in some measure the sort of man he dreamed of being. Commonly, a girl like Sue flutters through the anguish of her harassed and doubting youth and settles into acquiescence with the ordinary life of women, if not acceptance of it. Commonly, a boy like the son of Jude, oppressed from birth with the sense of being neither loved nor wanted, hardens himself against his misery, fights for the standing denied him, and achieves it. The average Arabella has no reversion to her first love when she has freed herself from it. The average Phillotson does not give up his wife to the man she says she loves, and he does not take her back knowing her loathing for himself. I grant all these things; and yet the author makes me believe that all he says to the contrary inevitably happened.

I allow that there are many displeasing things in the book, and few pleasing. Arabella's dimple-making, the pig-killing, the boy suicide and homicide; Jude's drunken second marriage; Sue's wilful self-surrender to Phillotson: these and other incidents are revolting. They make us shiver with horror and grovel with shame, but we know that they are deeply founded in the condition, if not in the nature of humanity. There are besides these abhorrent facts certain accusations against some accepted formalities of civilization, which I suppose most readers will find hardly less shocking. But I think it is very well for us to ask from time to time the reasons of things, and to satisfy ourselves, if we can, what the reasons are. If the experience of Jude with Arabella seems to arraign marriage, and it is made to appear not only ridiculous but impious that two young, ignorant, impassioned creatures should promise lifelong fealty and constancy when they can have no real sense of what they are doing, and that then they should be held to their rash vow by all the forces of society, it is surely not the lesson of the story that any other relation than marriage is tolerable for the man and woman who live together. Rather it enforces the conviction that marriage is the sole solution of the question of sex, while it shows how atrocious and heinous marriage may sometimes be.

I find myself defending the book on the ethical side when I meant chiefly to praise it for what seems to me its artistic excellence. It has not only the solemn and lofty effect of a great tragedy; a work far faultier might impart this; but it has unity very uncommon in the novel, and especially the English novel. So far as I can recall its incidents there are none but such as seem necessary from the circumstances and the characters. Certain little tricks which the author sometimes uses to help himself out, and which give the sense of insincerity or debility, are absent here. He does not invoke the playful humor which he employs elsewhere. Such humor as there is tastes bitter, and is grim if not sardonic. This tragedy of fate suggests the classic singleness of means as well as the classic singleness of motive.

ÉMILE ZOLA (1840–1902)

ON MARCH 18, 1882, Howells wrote to John Hay, "I am a great admirer of French workmanship, and I read everything of Zola's that I can lay hands on." When thirty years later Howells addressed the distinguished guests gathered to celebrate his seventy-fifth birthday, he said: "Some of you may not know this, but I know it, for I am of the generation that lived it and I would fain help to have it remembered that we studied from the French masters . . . to imitate nature, and gave American fiction the bent which it still keeps wherever it is vital."

Between these two dates, 1882 and 1912, Howells' admiration for Zola was frequently repeated in reviews, interviews, and letters. It is surprising, then, to note that though Howells had read *Page d'Amour* (1878) and *L'Assommoir* (1879) in French when they were first published, we find no reference in Howells' writing to Zola's *Rougon-Macquart* novels, which began to appear in France in 1871. Nor have we any indication that Howells ever read Zola's *Roman experimental* (1880). It is difficult to believe that this important essay could have been overlooked by Howells, especially since it was discussed by Melchior de Vogüé, Valdés, Pardo-Bazán, Brander Matthews, and others in the decade before the appearance of *Criticism and Fiction*.

The next sentence in the letter to Hay—"But I have to hide the books from the children!"—suggests something of Howells' attitude toward Zola. It is well to remind ourselves that the critics mentioned above shuddered with Howells over Zola's naturalism, as did also Henry James, who visited Daudet, Goncourt, and Zola in Paris in 1884. "There is nothing more interesting to me now than the effort and experiment of this little group," James wrote to Howells in Boston, ". . . in spite of their ferocious pessimism

154

and their handling of unclean things, they are at least serious and honest.''

A similar hesitation on Howells' part about Zola is reflected in a letter ''To Millicent from America,'' by Frederick Wedmore, who wrote that when he had luncheon with Howells in 1886,

> We spoke of Zola, and when I extolled the "Page d'amour," he said it was certainly immense as a piece of pathos; though he sometimes doubted the motive a little—thought it a little forced—questioned whether the woman would have been quite so much in love with the doctor; whether the contest between her love for her child and the doctor would really have been quite so stubborn. "But in the matter of love, one can never say," and anyway it was immense as pathos.

Though Zola was under attack at this time both in Europe and America on moral grounds, Howells from the beginning recognized him as one of the great writers of the new school. Section XXIV of *Criticism and Fiction* indicates clearly the reservations Howells felt for ''certain objectionable French novels.'' But from this censure Howells always made an exception of Zola, whom he placed by the side of Tolstoy and Ibsen. He perceived, however, that Zola was essentially a ''romanticist,'' not a realist. Though Zola was distinctly not to be read by children, the real critical reservation to his naturalism was not moral but aesthetic—he was a romantic.

A year after the luncheon conversation with Wedmore, an enterprising young reporter from the *Tribune* followed Howells to his summer home in the Adirondacks and secured from him a long and interesting interview that appeared July 10, 1887. ''Of course we all know the character of modern French writers,'' Howells said, but

> Zola is a great writer. I may regret that he has concerned himself with the disagreeable and unhappy things of life, but I do not base my objection to him on that ground. Strange as it may seem, if I objected to him at all it would be that he was a romanticist. He is natural and true but he might better be more so. He has not quite escaped the influence of Balzac, who, with Dickens and Gogol, marked the inauguration of the realistic era by taking realities and placing them in romantic relations.

Later in the same interview Howells outlined what he called ''a true arrangement of literature, in which realism has obtained the

155

supremacy over romance,'' and placed Russia first and ''the French, by virtue of Zola's strength, second.''

Early in the following year, in ''The Editor's Study'' of March, 1888, Howells addressed himself ''to the reader of Zola's latest and perhaps awfulest book, *La Terre*,'' which had just appeared. Though Howells was disgusted by ''the naked realities of lust and crime'' that he found in the book, he insisted—in spite of the objections of the editor of *Harper's*—on printing the notice of *La Terre* that is reproduced below. Howells argued, at a time when French scholars such as Brunetière, Schérer, and Anatole France were attacking Zola, that *La Terre* should not be avoided by the student of civilization, but should instead be seriously considered, for ''this tremendous charge against humanity,'' he said, must be faced.

Howells' insight into the essentially romantic character of the new naturalism tempered his appreciation of Zola's ''epic greatness'' in the single page he devoted to Zola in *My Literary Passions*. He had just read *L'Argent* (1891) with the same fascinated attention he had felt for *L'Assommoir* several years earlier and with the same abhorrence for the material of the novel. But ''the critics know now,'' he wrote, ''that Zola is not the realist he used to fancy himself, and he is full of the best qualities of the romanticism he has hated so much; but for what he is, there is but one novelist of our time, or of any, that outmasters him, and that is Tolstoy.''

The names of Ibsen, Zola, and Tolstoy were linked in Howells' mind; though each of these literary figures was to him a unique genius, together they reflected the vigor of the century then drawing to a close.

Following Howells' review of *La Terre*, is part of his review of Max Nordau's *Degeneration*. In these paragraphs Howells, with insight heightened by indignation, defines the individual gifts of Ibsen, Tolstoy, and Zola, and the importance to modern civilization of their united attack on the shams and evasions of the period.

A few weeks after the death of Zola in 1902, Howells' essay ''Émile Zola,'' appeared in the *North American Review*. In it Howells observed that ''a poet of such great epical imagination, such great ethical force, as Émile Zola may be seen as clearly and judged as fairly immediately after his death as he will be by posterity.'' Having passed beyond the sound of the furor over realism in the 1890's, he reiterated the critical creed achieved in his years in the Study and concluded that Zola ''conceived of reality poetically'' (that is to say, romantically) ; that he was ''an artist, and one of the greatest, but even before and beyond that he was intensely a moralist.'' ''The ethics of his work, like that of Tolstoy's, were always carrying over into his life,'' and when ''an act of public and official atrocity,'' such as the Dreyfus case, ''disturbed the working of his mind and revolted his nature, he could not rest again till he had done his best to right it.'' Though Zola's literary success ''has its imperfections,'' inasmuch as he was bred and nourished a romanticist, ''his success as a humanist is without flaw.''

Zola's Naturalism *

THERE is in the course of history something more than the suggestion that evil dies of the mortal sting which it inflicts, and that it defeats those who employ it, in accomplishing itself. . . .

In the mean time some of the questions involved will present themselves to the reader of Zola's latest and perhaps awfulest book, *La Terre*. Filthy and repulsive as it is in its facts, it is a book not to be avoided by the student of civilization, but rather to be sought and seriously considered. It is certainly not a book for young people, and it is not a book for any one who cares merely for a story, or who finds himself by experience the worse for witnessing in literature the naked realities of lust and crime. This said, it is but fair to add that it legitimately addresses itself to scientific curiosity and humane interest. The scene passes in that France where the first stirring of a personal conscience once promised a brilliant race the spiritual good which triumphant persecution finally denied it; and it is not wholly gratuitous to suppose

* *La Terre*, by Émile Zola, 1888. Review in *Harper's Monthly*, March, 1888.

that we see in the peasants of *La Terre* effects of the old repressions which stifled religious thought among them, and bound all their hopes, desires, and ambitions to the fields they tilled. When the Revolution came, it came too late to undo the evil accomplished, and the immediate good that it did included another evil. It justly gave to the peasant the ownership of the land, but it implanted in him the most insatiable earth-hunger ever known in the world. This creature, this earth-fiend whom Zola paints, is superstitious, but cynically indifferent to religion, and apparently altogether unmoral; lustful and unchaste, but mostly saved from the prodigal vices by avarice that spares nothing, relents to no appeal, stops at no wrong, and aspires only to the possession of land, and more land, and ever more land. This is the prevailing type, varied and relieved by phases of simple, natural good in a few of the characters; and the Church, so potent against the ancestral heresy, struggles in vain against the modern obduracy, in the character of the excellent priest, who is the only virtuous person in the book. The story is a long riot of satyr-lewdness and satyr-violence, of infernal greed that ends in murder, of sordid jealousies and cruel hates; and since with all its literary power, its wonderful force of realization, it cannot remain valuable as literature, but must have other interest as a scientific study of a phase of French life under the Second Empire, it seems a great pity it should not have been fully documented. What are the sources, the proofs, of this tremendous charge against humanity, in those simple conditions, long fabled the most friendly to the simple virtues? This is the question which the reader, impatient if not incredulous of all this horror, asks himself when he has passed through it.

He must ask it also at the end of that curious narrative drama of Tolstoi's known to us as yet only in the French version of *La Puissance des Ténèbres*. This too deals with peasant life, and with much the same hideous shames and crimes as *La Terre*. The main difference—but it is a very great one—is that the Russian peasant, wicked as he is, is not so depraved as the French peasant; he has a conscience; he is capable of remorse, of repentance, of expiation. . . . We should again, however, like to have the

documentary proofs in the case, and should feel more hopeful of
the good to be done among the muzhiks by the play if we felt
sure that they would recognize it as a true picture. In the mean
time they are not likely to know much about it; the censorship
has forbidden its representation in Russia, and it remains for the
consideration of such people of other countries as know how to
read.

Whether much is done to help those whose life is depicted in
fiction is a question which no one is yet qualified to answer, fiction
has only so very recently assumed to paint life faithfully, and
most critics claim that it is best for it not to do so.

Degeneration *

[In the first two sections of Howells' review of *Degeneration*,
by Max Nordau, he points out that the author is neither profound
nor original. Howells denies that the civilization of the West is,
at the end of the century, declining. Sections III, IV, and V
follow.]

The world, in its thinking and feeling, was never so sound and
sane before. There is a great deal of fevered and foolish thinking
and feeling about thinking and feeling, as there always has been
and will be, but there is no more of it than ever. It is no part of
my business to defend the nineteenth century, and if I thought
the noble mood of its last years merely a death-bed repentance,
and not an effect of all the former events of the ages, I should not
rejoice in it. Dr. Nordau himself is able to see that there really
is no such thing as a *fin de siècle* spirit; but the race is in a certain
mood, and the century is near its end, and so the phrase serves as
well as another. The only question is whether the mood is a good
one, and I have already expressed my sense of it.

I believe it is extremely well to have the underpinning of senti-

* *Degeneration*, by Max Nordau, translated, 1895. Review in *Harper's
Weekly*, April 13, 1895.

ment and opinion examined, from time to time, and this is what our age above all others has done. It is not a constructive or a reconstructive age, as compared with some other epochs, but it is eminently critical, and whatever is creative in it, is critically creative. It is very conscious, it not only knows, but it keenly feels, what it is about. It is not for nothing, it is not blindly or helplessly that it has tried this or that, that it has gone forward to new things or reverted to old things. It experiments perpetually, but not empirically; knowledge and greater knowledge are the cause and the effect of all that it has done in the arts as well as in the sciences.

If we stand at the end of things, we also stand at the beginning; we are the new era as well as the old. It is not at all important that certain things have fulfilled themselves and passed away; but it is very important that certain others have just begun their fulfillment, and it is these that we are to judge our time by. Our condition is that of a youth and health unknown to human thought before, and it is an excellent thing that with these we have so much courage; if it were only the courage of youth and health it would be well; but it is in fact the courage of a soul that is as old as the world.

A great many good, elderly minded people think it dreadful Ibsen should show us that the house we have lived in so long is full of vermin, that its drainage is bad, that the roof leaks and the chimney smokes abominably; but if it is true, is it not well for us to know it? It is dreadful because it is so, not because he shows it so; and the house is no better because our fathers got on in it as it is. He has not done his work without showing his weakness as well as his strength, and as I do not believe in genius in the miraculous sense, I am not at all troubled by his occasional weakness. It is really no concern of mine whether he solves his problems or not; generally, I see that he does not solve them, and I see that life does not; the longer I live the more I am persuaded that the problems of this life are to be solved elsewhere, or never. It is not by the solution of problems that the moralist teaches, but by the question that his handling of them suggests to us respecting ourselves. Artistically he is bound, Ibsen as a dramatist is bound, to give an aesthetic completeness to his works, and I do not find that he ever fails to do this; to my thinking they have a high beauty and propriety; but ethically he is bound not to be final; for if he forces himself to be final in things that do not and cannot end here, he becomes dishonest, he becomes a Nordau. What he can and must do ethically, is to make us take thought of ourselves, and look to it whether we have in us the making of this or that wrong, whether we are hypocrites, tyrants, pretenders, shams conscious or unconscious; whether our most unselfish motives are not really secret shapes of egotism; whether our convictions are not mere brute acceptations; whether we believe what we profess; whether when we force good to a logical end we are not doing evil. This is what Ibsen does; he gives us pause; and in that bitter muse he leaves us thinking not of his plays, but of our own lives; not of his fictitious people, but of ourselves. If we find ourselves all right we can go ahead with a good conscience, but never quite so cocksure afterwards.

He does in the region of motive pretty much the same work that Tolstoi does in the region of conduct. If he makes you question yourself before God, Tolstoi makes you question yourself before man. With the one you ask yourself, Am I true? With the other you ask yourself, Am I just? You cannot release yourself from them on any other terms. They will neither of them let you go away, feeling smoothly self-satisfied, patronizingly grateful, smugly delighted, quite charmed. If you want that feeling, you must go to some other shop for it, and there are shops a plenty where you can get it. Both of these great writers now and then overrun each other's province, for their provinces are not very separable, except by a feat of the fancy, though if the reader wishes a distinction between them, I have offered one. I should say, however, that Ibsen dealt with conduct in the ideal, and Tolstoi in the real. How shall I behave with regard to myself? How shall I behave with regard to my neighbor? I imagine that in either case the answer would be the same. It is only the point of view that is different.

As far as any finality is concerned, Tolstoi is no more satisfactory than Ibsen; that is to say, he is quite as honest. He does not attempt to go beyond Christ, who bade us love the neighbor, and cease to do evil; but I suppose this is what Dr. Nordau means by his mysticism, his sentimentality. In fact, Tolstoi has done nothing more than bring us back to the gospels as the fountain of righteousness. Those who denounce him cannot or will not see this, but that does not affect the fact. He asks us to be as the first Christians were, but this is difficult, and it has been so difficult ever since the times of the first Christians, that very few of the later Christians have been at all like them. Even in his most recent crusade, his crusade against the chauvinism which we miscall patriotism, he only continues that warfare against the spirit of provinciality which Christianity began. He preaches no new doctrine, he practices no new life. It is all as old as Calvary; it is the law and life of self-sacrifice. This was and always will be to the Jews a stumbling-block, and to the Greeks foolishness; but it is nothing mystical. There is nothing mystical in Tolstoi's books; as far as they are fictions they are the closest and clearest transcripts of the outer and inner life of man; as far as they are lessons in the form of allegory or essay, they are of the simplest and plainest meaning. His office in the world has been like Ibsen's, to make us look where we are standing, and see whether our feet are solidly planted or not. What is our religion, what is our society, what is our country, what is our civilization? You cannot read him without asking yourself these questions, and the result is left with you. Tolstoi's solution of the problem in his own life is not the final answer, and as things stand it is not the possible answer. We cannot all go dig in the fields, we cannot all cobble peasants' shoes. But we can all do something to lift diggers and cobblers to the same level with ourselves, to see that their work is equally rewarded, and that they share fully with the wisest and the strongest in the good of life. We can get off their backs, or try to get off, and this, after all, is what Tolstoi means us to do.

There is the same mixture of weakness in his power that qualifies the power of Ibsen, and makes his power the more admirable. There are flaws enough in his reasoning; he is not himself the best exponent of his own belief; there is no finality in his precept or his practice. On the other hand, his work has the same aesthetic perfection as Ibsen's, and as an intellect dealing imaginatively with life, he is without a rival. There is the like measure of weakness in Zola, whom Dr. Nordau chooses as the type of realist, with much the same blundering wilfulness that he chooses Ibsen as the type of egomaniac, and Tolstoi as the type of mystic. Zola never was a realist in the right sense, and no one has known this better, or has said it more frankly than Zola himself. He is always showing, as he has often owned that he came too early to be a realist; but it was he who imagined realism, in all its sublime, its impossible beauty, as Ibsen imagined truth, as Tolstoi imagined justice. One has to deal with words that hint rather than say what one means, but the meaning will be clear enough to any one capable of giving the matter thought. What Zola has done has been to set before us an ideal of realism, to recall the wandering mind of the world to that ideal, which was always in the world, and to make the reader feel it by what he has tried to do, rather than by what he has done. He has said, in effect, You must not aim in art to be less than perfectly faithful; and you must not lie about the fact any more than you can help. Go to life; see what it is like, and then tell it as honestly as possible. Above all he has shown us what rotten foundations the most of fiction rested on, and how full of malaria the whole region was. He did not escape the infection himself; he was born in that region; the fever of romanticism was in his blood; the taint is in his work. But he has written great epics, and the time will come when it will be seen that he was the greatest poet of his day, and perhaps the greatest poet that France has produced.

LEO TOLSTOY (1828–1910)

≫⚹≪

WE HAVE already seen that Tolstoy was in a sense the hero of *Criticism and Fiction;* since he remained to Howells the master among all his European masters, the selections for Part II will conclude with Howells' matured judgment of Tolstoy rather than with his early reviews. The essay chosen was written in 1897 for *A Library of the World's Best Literature,* under the editorship of Howells' friend Charles Dudley Warner. Howells' early enthusiasm for the Russian novelist, whom he read for the first time in 1885, began more than a decade before the writing of the essay. "As much as one merely human being can help another I believe that he has helped me," is Howells' simple statement in *My Literary Passions* of the effect on him of Tolstoy's writings. He then adds the significant comment, "He has not influenced me in esthetics only, but in ethics, too, so that I can never again see life in the way I saw it before I knew him." It is for the reader to determine, if he can, the part played by Tolstoy in the formulation of Howells' literary criticism after 1885, when the tone of his reviews was deepened by ethical and social considerations.

In an essay on Tolstoy in the *North American Review* (December, 1908), Howells tells that he first saw *My Religion* and *War and Peace* in a French translation when visiting "two valued friends" in Cambridge. "Seven or eight years" later Howells, at the age of fifty, began the reading of *The Cossacks,* which had been in his possession, though unread, for "four or five years." To T. S. Perry, on October 30, 1885, Howells wrote, *"Anna Karénine* is a wonderful book." Though English translations of Tolstoy began to appear in this country between 1885 and 1887, Howells read *Anna Karénine* in French, and he reviewed the novel, together with *My Religion* and *Scenes of the Siege of Sebastopol,* in "The Editor's Study" of April, 1886. The following February he reviewed in the same magazine the French translations of Tolstoy's *Deux Générations* and *La Mort d'Ivan Illitch,* the effects of which, he told his readers, are "as deep and broad, as far-reaching as in a tragedy of Shakespeare."

Two books from which Howells derived much of his knowledge of Tolstoy, and which he reviewed for *Harper's Weekly,* April 23, 1897, are *The Great Masters of Russian Literature* (1887), by Ernest Dupuy, and *The Russian Novelists* (1887), by Eugène-Melchior de Vogüé. Both books had appeared in France several years earlier and had played an important part in the "Russomania" of that country. M. Dupuy's study contains long biographical essays on Gogol, Turgenev, and Tolstoy; M. de Vogüé's more brilliant essays, which had previously appeared between 1883 and 1886 in the *Revue des Deux Mondes,* added Dostoevski to the list and also included a comparison of Russian realism and French naturalism. Through his review of these two books Howells made his espousal of Tolstoy part of the larger critical argument of the decade. As he was urging a redefinition of realism against the defenders of the falsely romantic in this country, so the French critics presented the Russian novelist to their readers in opposition to exaggerated naturalism as defined by Zola's *Roman experimental* (1880), which seemed to them coarse and materialistic.

By April, 1887, when Howells wrote for *Harper's Weekly* the essay on Tolstoy's critics, he had become an avowed Tolstoyan. The Russian was to Howells at that time "precisely the human being" with whom he found himself "in greatest intimacy," not, he added, through personal contact, but because he knew himself through Tolstoy. Howells freely acknowledged the influence on him at this time of *The Cooperative Commonwealth,* by Laurence Gronlund; of the *Fabian Essays;* of William Morris' tracts; of Bellamy's *Looking Backward;* but, he concluded, "the greatest influence . . . came to me through reading Tolstoy." This influence was deepened by Howells' contact with the Christian Socialists of Boston, who were also followers of the Russian novelist.

Howells' many comments, reviews, and essays on Tolstoy that appeared in magazines and newspapers during the last decades of the nineteenth century and the first of the twentieth show that his devotion to this "master" never wavered. In 1890 John Wana-maker, the Postmaster General, prohibited the mailing of Tol-stoy's *Kreutzer Sonata*. Replying to the discussion aroused by this action, Howells pointed out in "The Editor's Study," October, 1890, "the inexorable truth" of Tolstoy's story, given the char-acter of the hero. He repudiated, however, Tolstoy's "After-word," in which the author admitted that the hero's views were his own. The reading of Tolstoy remained to Howells a "religious experience," in spite of Tolstoy's views on marriage expressed in this pamphlet. In 1914, in a conversation with Joyce Kilmer, Howells remarked: "I never met Tolstoy. But I once sent him a message of appreciation after he had sent a message to me. Tolstoy's force is a moral force. His great art is as simple as nature."

The lesson Howells seems to have derived from Tolstoy, then, is that the moral force of such a writer is greater than any rules of art. It is for this reason that Howells placed Tolstoy above Turgenev, as he tells us in *My Literary Passions:* "I thought the last word in literary art had been said to me by the novels of Tourguenif, but it seemed like the first, merely, when I began to acquaint myself with the simpler method of Tolstoy." Turgenev taught Howells the art of novel writing; Tolstoy taught him to be impatient "even of the artifice that hides itself" and to seek only "the incomparable truth" beneath the tale.

Exactly what this Tolstoyan truth was to Howells he tells us, as nearly as he can, when he says that Tolstoy taught him to see life not as the pursuit of personal happiness but as "a field for endeavor toward the happiness of the whole human family." Through Tolstoy, and the Christian Socialists, Howells recognized the meaning of the life of Christ with "a rapture such as I have known in no other reading." How Howells equated the new real-ism with the truth of Christianity, on which he felt that democ-racy in the true sense was based, can be traced in his essay "Lyof Tolstoi." He wrote this essay at a time in his own development when his enthusiasm for Tolstoy had in no way abated, and the place Tolstoy was to occupy in his own hierarchy of values was most finely felt. Tolstoy for Howells became the basis not only of the literary, but also of the social and religious, dreams for this country, which underlies the thought of *Criticism and Fiction*.

Both ethically and aesthetically, Howells tells us, Tolstoy showed him a greatness that the Russian could never teach his American admirer. Though Howells disclaimed any effect of "the giant strides" of Tolstoy in the "pace" of his own writing—"I think that I had determined what I had to do before I read any Russian novels"—one cannot fail to observe that his concept of "complicity," which he first expressed in *The Minister's Charge* (1887), then in *Annie Kilburn* (1889), and later in *A Hazard of New Fortunes* (1890), reflects his understanding of the interrelation of the "whole human family," upon which he was led to meditate more deeply by his reading of Tolstoy. These ideas Howells had discussed with a group of like-minded men and women during his two years in Boston, 1889–1891, and had expressed again in *A Traveler from Altruria* and *A World of Chance*. In the following essay Howells gives full expression to what at the turn of the century Tolstoy finally meant to him.

The Philosophy of Tolstoy [*]

THERE is a certain unsatisfactory meagreness in the facts of Lyof Tolstoy's life, as they are given outside of his own works. In these he has imparted himself with a fullness which has an air almost of anxiety to leave nothing unsaid,—as if any reticence would rest like a sense of insincerity on his conscience. But such truth as relates to dates and places, and seems the basis of our knowledge concerning other men, is with him hardly at all structural: we do not try to build his moral or intellectual figure upon it or about it.

He is of an aristocratic lineage, which may be traced back to Count Piotr Tolstoy, a friend and comrade of Peter the Great; and he was born in 1828 at Yasnaya Polyana near Tula, where he still lives. His parents died during his childhood, and he was

[*] From *The Library of the World's Best Literature*, ed. R. S. Peale and J. A. Hill, 1897.

left with their other children to the care of one of his mother's relatives at Kazan, where he entered the university. He did not stay to take a degree, but returned to Yasnaya Polyana, where he lived in retirement till 1851; when he went into the army, and served in the Caucasus and the Crimea, seeing both the big wars and the little. He quitted the service with the rank of division commander, and gave himself up to literary work at St. Petersburg, where his success was in every sort most brilliant; but when the serfs were set free, he retired to his estates, and took his part in fitting them for freedom by teaching them, personally and through books which he wrote for them.

He learned from these poor people far more than he taught them; and his real life dates from his efforts to make it one with their lives. He had married the daughter of a German physician in Moscow,—the admirable woman who has remained constant to the idealist through all his changing ideals,—and a family of children was growing up about him; but neither the cares nor the joys of his home sufficed to keep him from the despair which all his military and literary and social success had deepened upon him, and which had begun to oppress him from the earliest moments of moral consciousness.

The wisdom that he learned from toil and poverty was, that life has no meaning and no happiness except as it is spent for others; and it did not matter that the toiling poor themselves illustrated the lesson unwittingly and unwillingly. Tolstoy perceived that they had the true way often in spite of themselves; but that their reluctance or their ignorance could not keep the blessing from them which had been withheld from him, and from all the men of his kind and quality. He found that they took sickness and misfortune simply and patiently, and that when their time came to die, they took death simply and patiently. To them life was not a problem or a puzzle; it was often heavy and hard, but it did not mock or deride them; it was not malign, it was not ironical. He believed that the happiness he saw in them came first of all from their labor.

So he began to work out his salvation with his own hands. He put labor before everything else in his philosophy, and through

168

LEO TOLSTOY

all his changes and his seeming changes he has kept it there. There
had been a time when he thought he must destroy himself, after
glory in arms and in letters had failed to suffice him, after the
love of wife and children had failed to console him, and nothing
would ease the intolerable burden of being. But labor gave him
rest; and he tasted the happiness of those whose existence is a
continual sacrifice through service to others.

He must work hard every day, or else he must begin to die at
heart; and so he believes must every man. But then, for the life
which labor renders tolerable and significant, some sort of formulated faith was essential; and Tolstoy began to search the Scrip-
tures.[4] He learned from the teachings of Jesus Christ that he must
not only not kill, but he must not hate or despise other men; he
must not only keep himself chaste, but he must keep his thoughts
from unchastity; he must not only not forswear himself, but he
must not swear at all; he must not only not do evil, but he must
not *resist* evil. If his own practice had been the negation of these
principles, he could not therefore deny their righteousness; if all
civilization, as we see it now, was the negation of these principles,
civilization—in so far as it was founded upon war, and pride, and
luxury, and oaths, and judgments, and punishments—was wrong
and false. The sciences, so far as they failed to better the lot of
common men, seemed to him futile; the fine arts, so far as they
appealed to the passions, seemed worse than futile; the mechanic
arts, with their manifold inventions, were senseless things in the
sight of this seer, who sought the kingdom of God. Titles, honors,
riches; courts, judges, executioners; nationalities, armies, battles;
culture, pleasure, amusement,—he counted these all evil or vain.

The philosophy of Tolstoy is neither more nor less than the doctrine of the gospels, chiefly as he found it in the words of Jesus.
Some of us whose lives it accused, have accused him of going beyond Christ in his practice of Christ's precepts. We say that having himself led a worldly, sensual, and violent life, he naturally
wished to atone for it by making every one also lead a poor, dull,
and ugly life. It is no part of my business to defend him, or to
justify him; but as against this anger against him, I cannot do
less than remind the reader that Tolstoy, in confessing himself

so freely and fully to the world, and preaching the truth as he feels it, claims nothing like infallibility. He compels no man's conscience, he shapes no man's conduct. If the truth which he has learned from the teachings of Jesus, and those other saviors and sages whom he follows less devotedly, compels the conscience and shapes the conduct of the reader, that is because this reader's soul cannot deny it. If the soul rejects it, that is no more than men have been doing ever since saviors and sages came into the world; and Tolstoy is neither to praise nor to blame.

No sincere person, I believe, will deny his sincerity, which is his authority outside of the gospel's: if any man will speak simply and truly to us, he masters us; and this and nothing else is what makes us helpless before the spirit of such books as "My Confession," "My Religion," "Life," "What to Do," and before the ethical quality of Tolstoy's fictions. We can remind ourselves that he is no more final than he pretends to be; that on so vital a point as the question of a life hereafter, he seems of late to incline to a belief in it, though at first he held such a belief to be a barbarous superstition. We can justly say that he does not lead a life of true poverty if his wife holds the means of keeping him from want, and from that fear of want which is the sorest burden of poverty. We can point out that his labor in making shoes is a worse than useless travesty, since it may deprive some wretched cobbler of his chance to earn his living by making and selling the shoes which Count Tolstoy makes and gives away. In these things we should have a certain truth on our side; though we should have to own that it was not his fault that he had not really declassed himself, and was constrained to the economic safety in which he dwells. We should have to confess that in this the great matter is the will; and that if benevolence stopped to take account of the harm it might work, there could be no such thing as charity in the world. We should have to ask ourselves whether Tolstoy's conversion to a belief in immortality is not an effect of his unselfish labor; whether his former doubt of immortality was not a lingering effect of the ambition, vanity, and luxury he has renounced. It had not indeed remained for him to discover that whenever we love, the truth is added unto us; but possibly it had remained for him to live the fact, to realize that unselfish labor gives so much meaning to human life that its significance cannot be limited to mortality.

However this may be, Tolstoy's purpose is mainly to make others realize that religion, that Christ, is for this actual world here, and not for some potential world elsewhere. If this is what renders him so hateful to those who postpone the Divine justice to another state of being, they may console themselves with the reflection that his counsel to unselfish labor is almost universally despised. There is so small danger that the kingdom of heaven will come by virtue of his example, that none of all who pray for it need be the least afraid of its coming. In any event his endeavor for a right life cannot be forgotten. Even as a pose, if we are to think so meanly of it as that, it is by far the most impressive spectacle of the century. All that he has said has been the law of Christianity open to any who would read, from the beginning; and he has not differed from most other Christians except in the attempt literally to do the will of Christ. Yet even in this he is not the first. Others have lived the life of labor voluntarily, and have abhorred war, and have suffered evil. But no man so gloriously gifted and so splendidly placed has bowed his neck and taken the yoke upon it. We must recognize Tolstoy as one of the greatest men of all time, before we can measure the extent of his renunciation. He was gifted, noble, rich, famous, honored, courted; and he has done his utmost to become plebeian, poor, obscure, neglected. He has truly endeavored to cast his lot with the lowliest, and he has counted it all joy so far as he has succeeded. His scruple against constraining the will of others suffers their will to make his self-sacrifice finally histrionic; but this seems to me not the least part of his self-sacrifice, which it gives a supreme touch of pathos. It is something that in fiction he alone could have imagined, and is akin to the experience of his own Karénin, who in a crucial moment forgives when he perceives that he cannot forget without being ridiculous. Tolstoy, in allowing his family to keep his wealth, for fear of compelling them to the righteousness which they do not choose, becomes absurd in his inalienable safety and superiority; but we cannot say that he ought not to suffer this indignity. There is perhaps a lesson in his fate which we ought not to refuse, if we can learn from it that in our time men are bound together so indissolubly that every advance must include the whole of society, and that even self-renunciation must not accomplish itself at the cost of others' free choice.

It is usual to speak of the ethical and the aesthetical principles as if they were something separable; but they are hardly even divergent in any artist, and in Tolstoy they have converged from the first. He began to write at a time when realistic fiction was so thoroughly established in Russia that there was no question there of any other. Gogol had found the way out of the mists of romanticism into the open day, and Turguénief had so perfected the realistic methods that the subtlest analysis of character had become the essence of drama. Then Tolstoy arrived, and it was no longer a question of methods. In Turguénief, when the effect sought and produced is most ethical, the process is so splendidly aesthetical that the sense of its perfection is uppermost. In Tolstoy the meaning of the thing is so supreme that the delight imparted by the truth is qualified by no consciousness of the art. Up to his time fiction had been part of the pride of life, and had been governed by the criterions of the world which it amused. But he replaced the artistic conscience by the human conscience. Great as my wonder was at the truth in Tolstoy's work, my wonder at the love in it was greater yet. Here for the first time, I found the most faithful pictures of life set in the light of that human conscience which I had falsely taught myself was to be ignored in questions of art, as something inadequate and inappropriate. In the august presence of the masterpieces, I had been afraid and ashamed of the highest instincts of my nature as something philistine and provincial. But here I stood in the presence of a master, who told me not to be afraid or ashamed of them, but to judge his work by them, since he had himself wrought in honor of them. I found the tests of conduct which I had used in secret with myself, applied as the rules of universal justice, condemning and acquitting in motive and action, and admitting none of those lawyers' pleas which baffle our own consciousness of right and wrong. Often in Tolstoy's ethics I feel a hardness, almost an arrogance (the word says too much); but in his aesthetics I have never felt this. He has transmuted the atmosphere of a realm hitherto supposed unmoral into the very air of heaven. I found nowhere in his work those base and cruel lies which cheat us into the belief that wrong may sometimes be right through passion, or genius, or heroism. There was everywhere the grave noble face of the truth that had looked me in the eyes all my life, and that I knew I must confront when I came to die. But there was something more than this,—infinitely more. There was that love which is before even the truth, without which there is no truth, and which, if there is any last day, must appear the Divine justice.

It is Tolstoy's humanity which is the grace beyond the reach of art in his imaginative work. It does not reach merely the poor and the suffering: it extends to the prosperous and the proud, and does not deny itself to the guilty. There had been many stories of adultery before "Anna Karénina,"—nearly all the great novels outside of English are framed upon that argument,—but in "Anna Karénina" for the first time the whole truth was told about it. Tolstoy has said of the fiction of Maupassant that the truth can never be immoral; and in his own work I have felt that it could never be anything but moral. In the "Kreutzer Sonata," [5] which gave a bad conscience to Christendom, there was not a moment of indecency or horror that was not purifying and wholesome. It was not the logic of that tremendous drama that marriage was wrong,—though Tolstoy himself pushed on to some such conclusion,—but only that lustful marriage, provoked through appetite and fostered in idleness and luxury, was wrong. We may not have had the last word from him concerning the matter: he may yet see marriage, as he has seen immortality, to be the inevitable deduction from the human postulate. But whatever his mind about it may finally be, his comment [6] on that novel seems to me his one great mistake, and a discord in the harmony of his philosophy.

It jars the more because what you feel most in Tolstoy is this harmony,—this sense of unity. He cannot admit in his arraignment of civilization the plea of a divided responsibility: he will not suffer the prince, or the judge, or the soldier, personally to shirk the consequences of what he officially does; and he refuses to allow in himself the division of the artist from the man. As I have already more than once said, his ethics and aesthetics are inseparably at one; and this is what gives a vital warmth to all his art. It is never that heartless skill which exists for its own sake, and is content to dazzle with the brilliancy of its triumphs. It seeks always the truth in the love to which alone the truth unveils itself. If Tolstoy is the greatest imaginative writer who ever lived, it is because, beyond all others, he has written in the spirit of kindness, and not denied his own personal complicity with his art.

As for the scope of his work, it would not be easy to measure it; for it seems to include all motives and actions, in good and bad, in high and low, and not to leave life untouched at any point as it shows itself in his vast Russian world. Its chief themes are the old themes of art always,—they are love, passion, death; but they are treated with such a sincerity, such a simplicity, that they seem almost new to art, and as effectively his as if they had not been touched before.

Until we read "The Cossacks," and witness the impulses of kindness in Olenin, we do not realize how much love has been despised by fiction, and neglected for passion. It is with a sort of fear and trembling that we find ourselves in the presence of this wish to do good to others, as if it might be some sort of mawkish sentimentality. But it appears again and again in the cycle of Tolstoy's work: in the vague aspirations recorded in "Childhood, Boyhood, and Youth"; in the abnegation and shame of the husband in "Anna Karénina," when he wishes to forgive his wife's paramour; in the goodness of the *muzhik* to the loathsome sick man in "The Death of Ivan Ilyitch"; in the pitying patience of Prince Andreí Bolkonsky with Anatol Kuragin in "War and Peace," where amidst his own anguish he realizes that the man next him under the surgeon's knife is the wretch who robbed him of the innocent love of his betrothed; in the devotion of the master, even to the mergence of conscious identity, to the servant in "Master and Man";—and at no time does it justify our first skeptical shrinking. It is as far as possible from the dramatic *tours de force* in Hugoesque fiction; it is not a conclusion that is urged or an effect that is solicited: it is the motive to which all beauty of action refers itself; it is human nature,—and it is as frankly treated as if there could be no question of it.

This love—the wish to do good and to be good, which is at the bottom of all our hearts, however we try to exclude it or deny it—is always contrasting itself in Tolstoy's work with passion, and proving the latter mortal and temporal in itself, and enduring only in its union with love. In most other novelists, passion is treated as if it were something important in itself,—as if its intensity were a merit and its abandon were a virtue,—its fruition Paradise, its defeat perdition. But in Tolstoy, almost for the first time, we are shown that passion is merely a condition; and that it has almost nothing to do with happiness. Other novelists represent lovers as forced by their passion to an ecstasy of selfish joy, or an ecstasy of selfish misery; but he shows us that they are only the more bound by it to the rest of the world. It is in fact, so far as it eventuates in marriage, the beginning of subjection to humanity, and nothing in it concerns the lovers alone.

It is not the less but the more mystical for this; and Tolstoy does full justice to all its mystical beauty, its mystical power. Its power upon Natacha,—that pure, good, wise girl,—whom it suddenly blinds and bewilders till she must be saved from ruin in spite of herself, and almost by violence; and upon Anna Karénina, —that loving mother, true friend, and obedient wife,—are illustrated with a vividness which I know not where to match. Dolly's wretchedness with her faithless husband, Kitty's happiness in the constancy of Levine, are neither unalloyed; and in all the instances and examples of passion, we are aware of the author's sense of its merely provisional character. This appears perhaps most impressively in the scenes of Prince Andreí Bolkonsky's long dying, where Natacha, when restored and forgiven for her aberration, becomes as little to him at last as if she had succeeded in giving herself to Anatol Kuragin. The theory of such matters is, that the passion which unites them in life must bring them closer still in death; but we are shown that it is not so.

Passion, we have to learn from the great master, who here as everywhere humbles himself to the truth, has in it life and death; but of itself it is something only as a condition precedent to these: without it neither can be; but it is lost in their importance, and is strictly subordinate to their laws. It has never been more charmingly and reverently studied in its beautiful and noble phases than it is in Tolstoy's fiction; though he has always dealt with it so sincerely, so seriously. As to its obscure and ugly and selfish

175

phases, he is so far above all others who have written of it, that he alone seems truly to have divined it, or portrayed it as experience knows it. He never tries to lift it out of nature in either case, but leaves it more visibly and palpably a part of the lowest as well as the highest humanity.

He is apt to study both aspects of it in relation to death; so apt that I had almost said he is fond of doing it. He often does this in "War and Peace"; and in "Anna Karénina" the unity of passion and death might be said to be the principle and argument of the story. In "The Death of Ivan Ilyitch" the unworthy passion of the marriage is a part of the spiritual squalor in which the wretched worldling goes down to his grave. In the "Kreutzer Sonata" it is the very essence of the murder; and in the "Powers of Darkness" it is the spring of the blackest evil. I suppose that one thing which has made Tolstoy most distasteful to man-made society is, that in all sins from passion he holds men chiefly accountable. It is their luxury which is so much to blame for the perversion. I can recall, at the moment, only one woman—the Princess Helena—in whom he censures the same evils; and even in her he lets you feel that her evil is almost passive, and such as man-made society chiefly forced upon her. Tolstoy has always done justice to women's nature; he has nowhere mocked or satirized them without some touch of pity or extenuation: and he brings Anna Karénina through her passion to her death, with that tender lenity for her sex which recognizes womanhood as indestructibly pure and good.

He comes nearer unriddling life for us than any other writer. He persuades us that it cannot possibly give us any personal happiness; that there is no room for the selfish joy of any one except as it displaces the joy of some other, but that for unselfish joy there is infinite place and occasion. With the same key he unlocks the mystery of death; and he imagines so strenuously that death is neither more nor less than a transport of self-surrender, that he convinces the reason where there can be no proof. The reader will not have forgotten how in those last moments of earth which he has depicted, it is this utter giving up which is made to appear the first moment of heaven. Nothing in his mastery is so wonderful as his power upon us in the scenes of the borderland where

LEO TOLSTOY

his vision seems to pierce the confines of another world. He comes again and again to it, as if this exercise of his seership had for him the same fascination that we feel in it: the closing hours of Prince Andreí, the last sorrowful instants of Anna Karénina, the triumphal abnegation of the philistine Ivan Ilyitch, the illusions and disillusions of the dying soldier in "Scenes of the Siege of Sebastopol," the transport of the sordid merchant giving his life for his servant's in "Master and Man,"—all these, with perhaps others that fail to occur to me, are qualified by the same conviction, imparting itself so strongly that it is like a proven fact.

Of a man who can be so great in the treatment of great things, we can ask ourselves only after a certain reflection whether he is as great as some lesser men in some lesser things; and I have a certain diffidence in inquiring whether Tolstoy is a humorist. But I incline to think that he is, though the humor of his facts seeks him rather than he it. One who feels life so keenly cannot help feeling its grotesqueness through its perversions, or help smiling at it, with whatever pang in his heart. I should say that his books rather abounded in characters helplessly comic. Oblensky in "Anna Karénina," the futile and amiably unworthy husband of Dolly, is delicious; and in "War and Peace," old Count Rostof, perpetually insolvent, is pathetically ridiculous,—as Levine in the first novel often is, and Pierre Bezukhof often is in the second. His irony, without harshness or unkindness, often pursues human nature in its vain twistings and turnings, with effects equally fresh and true; as where Nikolai Rostof, flying before the French, whom he had just been trying his worst to kill, finds it incredible that they should be seeking to harm one whom he knew to be so kind and good as himself. In Polikoushka, where the two *muzhiks* watching by the peasant's dead body try to shrink into themselves when some polite people come in, and to make themselves small because they are aware of smelling of the barn-yard, there is the play of such humor as we find only now and then in the supreme humorists. As for pathos, the supposed corollary of humor, I felt that I had scarcely known what it might be till I read Tolstoy. In literature, so far as I know it, there is nothing to match with the passage describing Anna Karénina's stolen visit to her little son after she has deserted her husband.

177

I touch this instance and that, in illustration of one thing and another; but I feel after all as if I had touched almost nothing in Tolstoy, so much remains untouched; though I am aware that I should have some such feeling if I multiplied the instances indefinitely. Much is said of the love of nature in writers, who are supposed to love it as they catalogue or celebrate its facts; but in Tolstoy's work the nature is there just as the human nature is: simple, naked, unconscious. There is the sky that is really over our heads; there is the green earth, the open air; the seasons come and go: it is all actual, palpable,—and the joy of it as uncontrived apparently as the story which it environs, and which gives no more the sense of invention than the history of some veritable passage of human events. In "War and Peace" the fortunes of the fictitious personages are treated in precisely the same spirit, and in the same manner, as the fortunes of the real personages: Bezukhof and Napoleon are alike real.

Of methods in Tolstoy, then, there can scarcely be any talk. He has apparently no method: he has no purpose but to get what he thinks, simply and clearly before us. Of style there seems as little to say; though here, since I know him only in translation, I cannot speak confidently. He may have a very marked style in Russian; but if this was so, I do not see how it could be kept out of the versions. In any case, it is only when you come to ask yourself what it is, that you realize its absence. His books are full of Tolstoy,—his conviction, his experience,—and yet he does not impart his personal quality to the diction as other masters do. It would indeed be as hard to imitate the literature as the life of Tolstoy, which will probably find only a millennial succession.

PART III

AMERICAN WRITERS *

INTRODUCTION

NINE years after the appearance of *Criticism and Fiction*
in 1891, Howells published another collection of critical
essays, *Literary Friends and Acquaintance, A Personal Retrospect of American Authorship.* In this delightful book we walk
the shaded streets of Cambridge with the youthful Howells, share
his trepidation at conversing with Lowell in his study, visit Hawthorne and Emerson with him in Concord. There is no ''sound of
battle'' in these quiet, faintly humorous chapters on the early
encounter of the young poet-reporter from the Middle West with
literary deities of Boston, Cambridge, and Concord. Yet one feels
between the lines the importance of this trip to New England
not only because Howells was in a deep sense nourished on the
American tradition, nor because Howells ''thought it a favorable
moment to propose himself as the assistant editor of the *Atlantic
Monthly,*'' but also because the journey gave him ''the intimacy
of the New England country'' as he could have had it in no other
way. Howells not only sat at the feet of the writers he had been
reading in his lonely Ohio days, but he also steeped his soul in
''the summer sweetness'' of old farmhouses, gray stone walls,
orchards, and ''thick-brackened valleys.'' But all this retrospective
reappraisal of writers and countryside that charms the reader of
Literary Friends and Acquaintance, this personal account of a
sensitive young writer in the studies, drawing rooms, and offices
of an established literary circle, we cannot, for want of space, include in our selections below.

* *The notes to Part III begin on p. 381.*

AMERICAN WRITERS

We have chosen, instead, as the opening essay for Part III, "Recollections of an Atlantic Editorship," written by Howells in 1907, when he was seventy years of age. Here with extraordinary accuracy he recalls the scenes of almost fifty years earlier, the personalities of former editors and contributors, the names of writers now forgotten, the literary and business customs of the *Atlantic Monthly*—then "in some sort a critical authority in a country where criticism is rare." This essay is the autobiography of an editor, eagerly following the realistic movement in Europe and personally welcoming young writers from remote parts of the United States. By thus encouraging talent from all corners of the country, Howells extended the borders of our national literature beyond the confines of New England. "The fact is," he observed, "we were growing, whether we liked it or not, more and more American. Without ceasing to be New England, without ceasing to be Bostonian, at heart, we had become southern, mid-western and far-western in our sympathies." With one eye on European novelists, whom he constantly reviewed, Howells was scanning the horizon for signs of "regionalism" in his own country. Henry James, weighing the merits of Europe and America as habitats for writers, recognized Howells' shrewd insight as an editor in encouraging all hopeful signs of the American novel, which, James pointed out, "had its first seeds . . . sown very exactly in Atlantic soil, . . . where Howells soon began editorially to cultivate them."

"Recollections" is followed by some of Howells' reviews of books by some of his contemporaries—such as John W. De Forest, Mark Twain, Edward Eggleston—whose reputations Howells' early reviews in the *Atlantic* helped to establish. For the most part, the reviews chosen reflect Howells' initial contact with unestablished writers, rather than his later, more "literary" appraisals of these authors, because these brief essays prove that Howells was a critic and editor of extraordinary acumen, boldness, and generosity. Furthermore, they make it evident that Howells knew from the beginning what he wanted of a writer—an honest reflection of the life of our country, whether it were "commonplace," or as in the case of James, "romantic," in a very special sense. The lesson Howells was learning from Europe—that

INTRODUCTION

the truly observed carries its own sufficient beauty—he taught by
example and precept to the American writers of his day. This
lesson was to Howells the meaning of realism.

The implications of this much-discussed word realism are suggested in an essay "William Dean Howells," by Thomas Sergeant Perry, published in the *Century Magazine* of March, 1882,
several months before Howells resigned from the *Atlantic* and
sailed for Europe. Perry understood that what Howells had
attempted as a contributor to the magazine threw light on what
he had been seeking as its editor. *A Chance Acquaintance, The
Lady of the Aroostook,* and *Dr. Breen's Practice* were to this
critic not merely pleasant diversions; they reflected an important
break with the English novel, directing the way to the sort of
fiction that catches "a truly national spirit." Wrote Perry:

In so many formless English novels we see the frank acceptance of conventional rewards, the bride and the money-bags awaiting the young
man who has artificially prolonged a tepid courtship, that the reader
grows weary of the implied compliment to wealth and position. There
is a truly national spirit in the way Mr. Howells shows the other side—
the emptiness of convention and the dignity of native worth. . . . After
all, what can realism produce but the downfall of conventionality? Just
as the scientific spirit digs the ground from beneath superstition, so
does its fellow worker, realism, tend to prick the bubble of abstract
types. Realism is the tool of the democratic spirit, the modern spirit,
by means of which the truth is elicited, and Mr. Howells's realism is tireless. It is, too, unceasingly good natured. We feel that Mr. Howells is
scrutinizing the person he is writing about with undisturbed calmness,
and that no name and no person can impose upon him by its conventional
value.

The concept of realism, as an aspect of the modern spirit, is
essentially the interpretation Howells enlarged upon in "The
Editor's Study." The reviews written for *Harper's* merely indicate how in the 1880's and 1890's Howells' understanding of
the term was deepened by the circumstances of his life in New
York, where he came into contact with a larger, more cosmopolitan circle of men and women.

HOWELLS AND THE ATLANTIC

☙❧

IN THE *Atlantic Monthly* of November, 1907, W. D. Howells, the third editor of that magazine, wrote the memoirs of his editorship to celebrate the fiftieth birthday of a publication that had occupied a unique position in the cultural pattern of this country. Howells' "Recollections of an Atlantic Editorship" is not only a mine of information on the publishing conditions of a hundred years ago and a roll call of writers of the day, but it is also the most intimate picture we have of Howells functioning in the Tremont Street office of the *Atlantic* in his dual capacity of editor and contributor to its pages. What other editor ever corrected so painstakingly both manuscript and proof; who but Howells ever welcomed so cordially literary aspirants from all parts of the country; who but he ever formed so many permanent friendships from such an extraordinary variety of contacts? The fact that Howells himself was moving rapidly through his apprentice years as a novelist at the same time that he was establishing himself as an editor made all the difference in the critical and personal advice he gave to writers. For he was a fellow craftsman, venturing into the new and wide-open field of realistic fiction, a field so rich and promising that he generously encouraged others to follow. The names of some of those who accepted the invitation are found in the headings of the reviews below; the "Recollections of an Atlantic Editorship" lists dozens more, of lesser fame today, who in their way contributed to what soon became a movement of enormous importance in American culture. The meaning of realism, which Howells learned in part through his "European Masters," he translated into native terms, and as editor of the *Atlantic,* he interpreted these ideas to his readers through publication of the work of unknown young American writers.

HOWELLS AND THE ATLANTIC

Literary Friends and Acquaintance tells how Howells, recently returned from a consulship in Venice and not yet thirty years old, became in 1866 assistant to James T. Fields, then editor of the *Atlantic*. In those pages too one goes back still farther and participates in the dinner at the Parker House, when Howells made his famous pilgrimage to Boston in 1860. At that time the first editor of the *Atlantic*, James Russell Lowell, together with James T. Fields, the second editor, and Oliver Wendell Holmes, accepted the young Ohioan into their charmed circle, partly on the strength of several poems published in the *Atlantic*, but more especially because of the winning personality of this entirely literary young man of twenty-three, who carried with him a peculiar air of determination. Before the meal was over Holmes turned to Lowell, with the laughing remark, "Well, James, this is something like the apostolic succession; this is the laying on of hands."

In his "Recollections" at the age of seventy, Howells continued the story begun in *Literary Friends and Acquaintance*, from the moment of the official parting with his "kindly chief," James T. Fields, and his assumption of the editorship of the *Atlantic* in 1871. Howells tells us modestly: "The Magazine was already established in its traditions when I came to it, and when I left it fifteen years later it seemed to me that if I had done any good it was little more than to fix it more firmly in them." A reading of the "Recollections" and the volumes of the *Atlantic* during this period convinces one that Howells in fact slowly and tactfully extended the confines of this New England publication. When he says, "To the reviews of American and English books I added certain pages of notices of French and German literature," we realize that by doing so, the new editor thereby placed the magazine in the stream of European thought, where realism was already a strong movement. When Howells tells us that he himself "read all the manuscripts which claimed critical attention," that he personally and in longhand "wrote to contributors who merited more than a printed circular," we realize that this tireless editor was actually sowing the seeds of the new movement in this country. When we are told further that Howells "was writing not only criticism, but sketches, stories, and poems for the body of the magazine, and, in the course of time, a novel each year," we are

convinced that the third editor of the *Atlantic* did indeed lay the
basis of the magazine that in 1957 marked its centennial. "I
found it by no means drudgery," said Howells, referring to his
long hours in the Tremont Street office; he admitted, however,
that he never liked writing criticism and never satisfied himself
in his reviews. His increasing occupation with fiction left him too
little time for the book notices for the magazine, and these he
turned over to younger men.

Howells' welcome to Miss Murfree, Miss Sarah Orne Jewett,
Bret Harte, S. Weir Mitchell, described below, is typical of the
cordial reception he accorded many authors now almost forgotten.
Would that we could rummage with Howells in "that half-barrel
of accepted manuscripts" that came down to him from his predecessors, Lowell and Fields; Howells passed on to the next editor,
Thomas Bailey Aldrich, "a half-peck" of these yellowing sheets,
and Aldrich promptly returned them to their authors. So busy
was Howells with his "fictioning," he tells us, that he kept many
"a poor contributor" of "the patient tribe" waiting at his door,
his unread manuscript lying in one of "the darkling drawers" of
his desk, while the harassed young editor polished off his own contribution. Howells' double role of editor and contributor proved
finally too much even for his energy, and ill health forced him to
resign from the *Atlantic* in 1881. After some time spent in European travel, he returned to the United States and in 1885 signed
a contract with Harper's, the publishing house with which he
remained, with a brief interruption, until his death.

From the offices of various publications of Harper's, Howells'
"open editorial hand" was extended from 1886 to 1920, with
unflagging cordiality, to the promising young writers who joined
forces with him in what Stephen Crane called "the beautiful
war" for truth in literature. Howells greeted Frank Norris as a
new recruit in the battle; the younger novelist, under the influence of Zola, was transforming realism into something called
"naturalism," a term not new to Howells.

Norris' thinly disguised portrait of Howells in "The Lost
Story," quoted below, is a reminder of how the younger generation (Crane and Norris were infants when Howells became editor
of the *Atlantic* in 1871) regarded the short, stocky "Dean of

American Literature'' at the turn of the century. His stamp of approval was ''sterling''; his style seemed by 1900 somewhat tame. He was, Norris tells us:

. . . a short, rotund man, rubicund as to face, bourgeois as to clothes and surroundings . . . jovial in manner, indulging even in slang. One might easily set him down as a retired groceryman—wholesale, perhaps, but none the less a groceryman. Yet touch him upon the subject of his profession, and the *bonhomie* lapsed away from him at once. . . . Then he became serious. . . . This elderly man of letters, who had seen the rise and fall of a dozen schools, was above the influence of fads, and he whose books were among the classics even before his death, was infallible in his judgments on the work of the younger writers. All the stages of their evolution were known to him—all their mistakes, all their successes. He understood; and a story by one of them, a poem, a novel, that bore the stamp of his approval, was "sterling."

''Bourgeois'' though Howells appeared to the young Norris, recently returned from a year in Paris, one must also observe that ''in his judgment of the works of the younger writers,'' the occupant of ''The Easy Chair'' seemed to one of them ''infallible.'' But more arresting to the ''new critics'' of Norris' day than his words of appreciation was the image of ''a retired groceryman'' caught by his pen. Soon Gertrude Atherton was asking in the *North American Review*, May, 1904, pointing her finger at Howells: ''Why is American Literature Bourgeois?'' Since this ''elderly man of letters'' had, as Norris observed, ''seen the rise and fall of a dozen schools,'' he happily disregarded his detractors when he compiled ''The Recollections of an Atlantic Editorship'' three years later.

Recollections of an Atlantic Editorship *

IN ANOTHER place I have told how I came to be the assistant of Mr. Fields in the editorship of the Atlantic Monthly. That was in 1866, and in 1872 [1] he gave up to me the control which he had

* *Atlantic Monthly*, November, 1907.

held rather more in form than in fact from the time I joined him. He had left the reading of manuscripts to me, and almost always approved my choice in them, only reserving to himself the supreme right of accepting things I had not seen, and of inviting contributions. It was a suzerainty rather than a sovereignty which he exercised, and I might well have fancied myself independent under it. I never thought of questioning his easy over-lordship, and my assistant editorship ended with far more regret to me than my editorship, when in 1881 I resigned it to Mr. Aldrich.

I recall very distinctly the official parting with my kindly chief in his little room looking into the corner of the Common at 124 Tremont Street, for it was impressed upon me by something that had its pathos then, and has it now. In the emotion I felt at his willingness to give up his high place (it seemed to me one of the highest), I asked him why he wished to do it, with a wonder at which he smiled from his fifty-six years down upon my thirty-five. He answered, what I very well knew, that he was tired of it, and wanted time and a free mind to do some literary work of his own. "Besides," he added, with a cheerfulness that not only touched but dismayed me, "I think people generally have some fore-knowledge of their going; I am past fifty, and I do not expect to live long." He did not cease smiling as he said this, and I cannot recall that in my amaze I answered with any of the usual protests we make against the expression of far less frank and open prescience. He lived much longer than he expected, after he had felt himself a stricken man; but still it was not many years before he died, when a relation marred by scarcely a moment of displeasure, and certainly without one unkindness from him, had altogether ceased.

The magazine was already established in its traditions when I came to it, and when I left it fifteen years later it seemed to me that if I had done any good it was little more than to fix it more firmly in them. During the nine years of its existence before my time it had the best that the greatest writers of New England could give it. First of these were, of course, Longfellow, Emerson, Hawthorne, Whittier, Holmes, Lowell, Mrs. Stowe, and Bryant, and after them followed a long line of gifted people, whom but to number will recall many names of the second brilliancy, with some faded or fading beyond recall. I will not attempt a full list, but my memories of the Atlantic would be very faulty if they did not include the excellence in verse or prose of such favorites [2] as Agassiz, Mrs. Paul Akers, Mr. Alden, Aldrich, Boker, Mr. Burroughs, Alice Cary, Caroline Chesebro', Lydia Maria Child, James Freeman Clarke, Conway, Rose Terry Cooke, Cranch, Curtis, J. W. De Forest, Mrs. Diaz, Rebecca Harding Davis, Mrs. Fields, J. T. Fields, Henry Giles, Annie Douglas Greene, Dr. E. E. Hale, Lucretia Hale, Gail Hamilton, Colonel Higginson, G. S. Hillard, J. G. Holland, Mrs. Howe, Henry James, father and son, Lucy Larcom, Fitz Hugh Ludlow, Donald G. Mitchell, Walter Mitchell, Fitz-James O'Brien, J. W. Palmer, Francis Parkman, T. W. Parsons, Norah Perry, Mr. and Mrs. J. J. Piatt, Buchanan Read, Epes Sargent, Mrs. Prescott Spofford, W. J. Stillman, R. H. Stoddard, Elizabeth Stoddard, W. W. Story, Bayard Taylor, Celia Thaxter, Thoreau, Mr. J. T. Trowbridge, Mrs. Stuart Phelps Ward, David A. Wasson, E. P. Whipple, Richard Grant White, Adeline D. T. Whitney, Forceythe Wilson, Theodore Winthrop.

The tale is very long, but it might be lengthened a third without naming other names which could accuse me of having forgotten many delightful authors remembered by my older readers, and in some instances known to my younger readers. In the alphabetical course there is here no intimation of the writers' respective order or degree, and their quantity is as little suggested. Many of them were frequent contributors of very even excellence; others wrote one thing, or one or two or three things, that caught the public fancy with as potent appeal as the best of the many things that others did. Some of those who were conspicuous in 1866 lost their foremost place, and others then of no wider celebrity grew in fame that would rank them with those greatest ones whom I have mentioned first.

Beginning myself to contribute to the magazine in its third year, I held all its contributors in a devout regard and did not presume to distinguish between the larger and lesser luminaries, though I knew very well which I liked best. I was one of four singularly favored youths beyond the Alleghanies suffered more than once in the company of those gods and half-gods and quarter-

187

gods of New England; the other two lonely Westerners I met in those gleaming halls of morn being my room-mate in Columbus, A. T. Fullerton, and another, my friend and fellow-poet Piatt in Louisville. Leonard Case [3] dwelt in a lettered and moneyed seclusion (as we heard) at Cleveland, but Alice Cary had lived so long in the East that she was less an Ohioan than one of those few New Yorkers admitted with the overwhelming majority of New Englanders, whom I figured standing aloof from all us outsiders.

It was with a sort of incredulous gasping that I realized myself in authority with these when it came to that, and I should not now be able to say how or why it came to that, without allowing merits in myself which I should be the last to assert. These things are always much better attributed to Fortune, or at the furthest to Providence. What I know is that it was wonderful to me to go through the editorial record (which with my want of method I presently disused) and find my own name among the Accepted and the Rejected. It was far oftenest among the rejected; but there was a keener pleasure in those rejections, which could not now be repeated, than in the acceptances which stretched indefinitely before me.

Otherwise the record, where the disappointments so heavily outnumbered the fruitions, had its pathos; and at first I could not return a manuscript without a pang. But in a surprisingly little time that melting mood congealed into an icy indifference, if it did not pass into the sort of inhuman complacency of the judge who sentences a series of proven offenders. We are so made that we quickly turn the enemies of those who give us trouble; the hunter feels himself the foe of the game that leads him a long and difficult chase; and in like manner the editor wreaks a sort of revenge in rejecting the contributor who has bothered him to read a manuscript quite through before it yields itself unfit for publication. Perhaps I am painting the case in rather blacker colors than the fact would justify, though there is truth in what I say. Yet, for the most part, the affair did not come to this. It was at first surprising, and when no longer surprising it was gratifying, to find that the vast mass of the contributions fixed their own fate, almost at a glance. They were of subjects treated before, or subjects not to be treated at all, or they were self-condemned by their uncouth and slovenly style, or were written in a hand so crude and ignorant that it was at once apparent that they had not the root of literature in them. The hardest of all to manage were those which had some savor of acceptance in them; which had promise, or which failed so near the point of success that it was a real grief to refuse them. Conscience then laid it upon me to write to the authors and give hopes, or reasons, or tender excuses, and not dismiss any of them with the printed circular that carried insult and despair in the smooth uncandor of its assurance that the contribution in question was not declined necessarily because of a want of merit in it.

The poor fellows, and still more the poor dears, were apt in the means by which they tried to find a royal road to the public through the magazine. Claims of acquaintance with friends of the editors, distressful domestic circumstances, adverse fortune, irresistible impulse to literature, mortal sickness in which the last hours of the writer would be brightened by seeing the poem or story in print, were the commonest of the appeals. These must have been much alike, or else I should remember more distinctive cases. One which I do remember was that of a woman in the West who sent the manuscript of a serial story with a letter, very simply and touchingly confiding that in her youth she had an ardent longing to be an author. She had married, instead, and now at fifty, with her large family of children grown up about her, prosperous and happy, she felt again the impulse of her girlhood. She enclosed a ten-dollar note to pay the editor for the trouble of reading her story, and she wished his true opinion of it. I should have been hard-hearted indeed if I had not answered this letter at length, with a carefully considered criticism which I sincerely grieved that I could not make favorable, and returned the sum of my hire with every good wish. I could not feel it a bribe, and I could not quite believe that it was with the design of corrupting me, that a very unliterary author came one day with two dollars to pay me for noticing his book. He said he had been told that this was the way to get it noticed.

In those days, and for seven or eight years afterwards, I wrote nearly all the "Literary Notices" in the magazine. When I began to share the work with others, and at last to leave it almost wholly to them, they and I wrote so very much alike that I could not always be sure which notices I had done. That is a very common psychological event in journalism, when one prevalent will has fixed the tone, and I was willful, if not strong, in my direction after I came into full control. I never liked writing criticism, and never pleased myself in it; but I should probably have kept writing most of the Atlantic notices to the end, if my increasing occupation with fiction had not left me too few hours out of the twenty-four for them. The editorial salary I received covered the pay for my contributions, but I represented to the publishers that I could not write everything in the magazine, and they saw the reason of my delegating the notices. I had the help of the best young critics whom I knew, and who abounded in Boston and Cambridge; and after I succeeded Mr. Fields, I enlarged the editorial departments at the end of the magazine so as to include comment on politics, art, and music, as well as literature. For a while, I think for a year, I indulged the fancy of printing each month a piece of original music, with original songs; but though both the music and the songs were good, or at least from our best younger composers and poets, the feature did not please,—I do not know why,—and it was presently omitted.

To the reviews of American and English books I added certain pages of notices of French and German literature, and in these I had the very efficient and singularly instructed help of Mr. Thomas Sergeant Perry, who knew not only more of current continental literature than any other American, but more than all the other Americans. He wrote cleverly and facilely, and I felt that his work had unique value too little recognized by the public, and to which I should feel it a duty, if it were not so entirely a pleasure, to bear witness here. He was one of the many new contributors with whom I had the good fortune to work forward in the magazine. I could not exaggerate his rare qualifications for the work he undertook; his taste, and his temperament, at once just and humane, were equal to his unrivaled knowledge. It is not too much to say that literally he read every important French and German book which appeared, not only in fiction, but in history, biography, criticism, and metaphysics, as well as those exact sciences which are nearest allied to the humanities.

I grouped the books according to their kinds, in the critical department, but eventually I broke from the departmental form altogether, and began to print the different groups and the longer reviews as separate articles. It was a way of adding to the apparent as well as real variety of the table of contents which has approved itself to succeeding editors.

In the course of time, but a very long time, the magazine felt the need of a more informal expression than it found in the stated articles, and the Contributors' Club took the place of all the different departments, those of politics, music, and art having been dropped before that of literature. The new idea was talked over with the late George Parsons Lathrop, who had become my assistant, and we found no way to realize it but by writing the first paragraphs ourselves, and so tempting others to write for the Club. In the course of a very few months we had more than help enough, and could easily drop out of the coöperation.

Except for the brief period of a year or eighteen months, I had no assistance during my editorship. During the greater part of the time I had clerkly help, most efficient, most intelligent; but I read all the manuscripts which claimed critical attention; I wrote to contributors who merited more than a printed circular; I revised all the proofs, verifying every quotation and foreign word, and correcting slovenly style and syntax, and then I revised the author's and my own corrections. Meantime I was writing not only criticisms, but sketches, stories, and poems for the body of the magazine; and in the course of time, a novel each year. It seems like rather full work, but I had always leisure, and I made a long summer away from Cambridge in the country. The secret, if there was any secret, lay in my doing every day two or three hours' work, and letting no day pass idly. The work of reading manuscripts and writing letters could be pushed into a corner, and taken out for some interval of larger leisure; and this happened oftener and oftener as I grew more and more a novelist, and needed every morning for fiction. The proof-reading, which was seldom other than a pleasure, with its tasks of revision and research, I kept for the later afternoons and evenings; though sometimes it well-nigh took the character of original work, in that liberal Atlantic tradition of bettering the authors by editorial transposition and paraphrase, either in the form of suggestion or of absolute correction. This proof-reading was a school of verbal exactness and rhetorical simplicity and clearness, and in it I had succeeded others, my superiors, who were without their equals. It is still my belief that the best proof-reading in the world is done in Cambridge, Massachusetts, and it is probably none the worse for my having a part in it no longer.

As I have intimated, I found it by no means drudgery; though as for drudgery, I think that this is for the most part in the doer of it, and it is always a very wholesome thing, even when it is real, objective drudgery. It would be a much decenter, honester, and juster world if we each took his share of it, and I base my best hopes of the future in some such eventuality. Not only the proofs were a pleasing and profitable drudgery, but the poor manu-scripts, except in the most forbidding and hopeless instances, yielded their little crumbs of comfort; they supported while they fatigued. Very often they startled the drooping intelligence with something good and new amidst their impossibility; very often, when they treated of some serious matter, some strange theme, some unvisited country, some question of unimagined import, they instructed and delighted the judge who knew himself inex-orably averse to their acceptance, for editorial reasons; they, con-demned to darkness and oblivion, enlightened and edified him with some indelible thought, some fresh, or some freshly related, fact. My information is not of so great density yet but I can still distinguish points in its nebulous mass, from time to time, which I cannot follow to their luminous source in the chapter or verse of any book I have read. These, I suspect, derive from some far-forgotten source in the thousands of manuscripts which in my fifteen editorial years I read and rejected.

The rejection of a manuscript often left a pang, but the accept-able manuscript, especially from an unknown hand, brought a glow of joy which richly compensated me for all I suffered from the others.[4] To feel the touch never felt before, to be the first to find the planet unimagined in the illimitable heaven of art, to be in at the dawn of a new talent, with the light that seems to mantle the written page: who would not be an editor, for such a privilege? I do not know how it is with other editors who are also authors, but I can truly say for myself that nothing of my own which I thought fresh and true ever gave me more pleasure than that I got from the like qualities in the work of some young writer revealing his power.

It was quite as often *her* power, for in our beloved republic of letters the citizenship is not reserved solely to males of twenty-one and over. I have not counted up the writers who came forward in these pages during my time, and I do not know which sex prevails in their number, but if any one were to prove that there were more women than men, I should not be surprised. I do not remember any man who feigned himself a woman, but now and then a woman liked to masquerade as a man, though the disguise never deceived the editor, even when it deceived the reader, except in the very signal and very noted instance of Miss Mary N. Murfree, whom, till I met her face to face, I never suspected for any but Charles Egbert Craddock. The severely simple, the robust, the athletic, hand which she wrote would have sufficed to carry conviction of her manhood against any doubt. But I had no doubts. I believe I took the first story she sent, and for three or four years I addressed my letters of acceptance, or criticism, to Charles Egbert Craddock, Murfreesboro', Tennessee, without the slightest misgiving. Then she came to Boston, and Aldrich, who had succeeded me, and who had already suffered the disillusion awaiting me, asked me to meet Craddock at dinner. He had asked Dr. Holmes and Lawrence Barrett, too; and I should not attempt to say whose astonishment he enjoyed most. But I wish I could recall word for word the exquisite terms in which Dr. Holmes turned his discomfiture into triumph in that most delicately feminine presence.

The proof of identity, if any were needed, came with the rich, full pipe of a voice in which she answered our words and gasps of amaze. In literary history I fancy there has been no such perfect masquerade; but masquerade was the least part of Miss Murfree's success. There seems in the dust and smoke of the recent literary explosions an eclipse of that fine talent, as strong as it is fine, and as native as it is rare; but I hope that when the vaporous reputations blow away, her clear light will show the stronger for its momentary obscuration. She was the first to express a true

Southern quality in fiction, and it was not the less Southern because it rendered the strange, rude, wild life of a small section
of the greater section which still unhappily remains a section.
One might have said, looking back from the acknowledged fact
of her personality, that a woman of the Rosa Bonheur type could
well have caught the look of that half-savagery in her men; but
that only a man could have touched in the wilding, flower-like,
pathetic loveliness of the sort of heroine she gave to art.

She was far from the first, and by no means the last of those
women, not less dear than great, whose work carried forward the
early traditions of studied beauty in the magazine with something newer and racier in the flavor and fragrance of their fiction.
I must name at the head of these that immediate classic Miss Sarah
Orne Jewett, whose incomparable sketches of New England character began to appear well within my assistant-editorship, with
whatever credit to me I may not rob my chief of. The truth is,
probably, that he liked them as well as I, and it was merely my
good luck to be the means of encouraging them in the free movement, unfettered by the limits of plot, and keeping only to the
reality, which no other eye than hers has seen so subtly, so humorously, so touchingly. It is the foible of editors, if it is not rather
their forte, to flatter themselves that though they may not have
invented their contributions, they have at least invented their
contributors; and if any long-memoried reader chooses to hail
me an inspired genius because of my instant and constant appreciation of Miss Jewett's writing, I shall be the last to snub him
down.

Without greatly fearing my frown, he may attribute a like
merit to me for having so promptly and unremittingly recognized the unique artistry and beauty of Mr. Henry James's
work. My desert in valuing him is so great that I can freely confess the fact that two of his stories and one of his criticisms appeared in the magazine some years before my time, though perhaps not with the band of music with which I welcomed every
one afterwards. I do not know whether it was to try me on the
story, or the story on me, that my dear chief (who was capable
of either subtlety) gave me the fourth of Mr. James's contributions to read in the manuscript; but I was equal to either test, and

returned it with the jubilant verdict, "Yes, and as many more as you can get from the author." He was then writing also for other magazines; after that I did my best to keep him for the Atlantic, and there was but one of his many and many contributions about which we differed.[5] This was promptly printed elsewhere; but though I remember it very well, I will not name it, for we might differ about it still, and I would not make the reader privy to a quarrel where all should be peace.

I feel a danger to the general peace in mentioning certain favorite contributors without mentioning others who have an equal right; but if it is understood that some are mentioned with a bad conscience for those passed in silence (I was not asked to write this whole number of the magazine) I hope I shall be forgiven. There was now and then a single contribution, or two contributions, which gave me high hopes of the author, but which were followed by no others, or no others so acceptable. Among such was "Captain Ben's Choice," a sketch of New England shore-character by Mrs. Frances L. Pratt, done with an authentic touch, and as finely and firmly as something of Miss Jewett's or Mrs. Wilkins Freeman's. There were two stories, the only ones sent me, by Mrs. Sarah Butler Wister,[6] which had a distinction in the handling, and a penetrating quality in the imagining, far beyond that of most of the stories I was editorially proud of. Other contributors who began in Atlantic air were acclimated in another. In one volume I printed four poems, which I thought and still think admirable, by Miss Edith Jones, who needs only to be named as Mrs. Edith Wharton to testify to that prophetic instinct in me which every editor likes to think himself endowed with; it does not matter if the prophecy fulfills itself a little circuitously.

My liking for Dr. Weir Mitchell and his work was a taste likewise inherited from my chief, though, strictly speaking, we began contributor and assistant editor together. From the first there was something equally attractive to me in his mystic, his realistic, and his scientific things, perhaps because they were all alike scientific. "The Case of George Dedlock" and "Was He Dead?" gave me a scarcely different delight from that I took in "The Autobiography of a Quack." I have since followed the writer far in other fields, especially where he made his poetic ventures, but I keep a steadfast preference for those earlier things of his; I do not pretend it is a reasoned preference.

In another place (there are now so many other places!) I have told of my pleasure in the acquaintance, which instantly became friendship, with Hjalmar Hjorth Boyesen and his poetry; whether he wrote it in verse or prose, it was always poetry. I need not dwell here upon that pleasure which his too early death has tinged with a lasting grief; but surely the reader who shared the first joy of his "Gunnar" with me, would not like me to leave it unnamed among these memories. That romance was from the rapture of his own Norse youth and the youth of the Norse literature then so richly and fully adolescent in Björnson, and Lie,[7] and Kielland,[8] and hardening to its sombre senescence in Ibsen. Boyesen never surpassed "Gunnar" in the idyllic charm which in him was never at odds with reality; but he went forward from it, irregularly enough, as a novelist and critic and poet, till he arrived at his farthest reach in "The Mammon of Unrighteousness," a great picture of the American life which he painted with a mastery few born to it have equaled, and fewer yet surpassed.

There was long a superstition, which each of the editors before me had tried to enlighten, that the Atlantic was unfriendly to all literature outside of Boston or New England, or at the farthest, New York or Philadelphia. The fact was that there was elsewhere little writing worth printing in it; but that little it had cordially welcomed. When the little became a good deal the welcome was not more cordial, for it could not have been; and in seeking a further expansion, I was only following the tradition of the magazine. I cannot claim that there was anything original in my passion for the common, for "the familiar and the low," which Emerson held the strange and high.[9] Lowell had the same passion for it in the intervals of his "toryism of the nerves," and nobody could have tasted its raciness with a keener gusto than my chief. But perhaps it was my sense not only of the quaint, the comic, but of the ever-poetic in the common, that made it dear to me. It was with a tingling delight that I hailed any verification of my faith in it, and among the confirmations which I received there was none stronger than that in the "Adirondack Sketches" of Mr. Philip [Philander] Deming. They were, whether instinctively or consciously, in the right manner, and of simplicity in motive, material, and imagination as fine as something Norse, or Slavic, or Italian, or Spanish. No doubt, "Lida Ann," "Lost," "John's Trial," and "Willie" are distinguishable among the multitude of ghosts that haunt the memory of elder readers, but would only come to trouble joy in the younger sort, who delight in the human-nature fakirs of our latter-day fiction. Surely, in some brighter and clearer future, such dear, and true, and rare creatures of the sympathetic mind must have their welcome palingenesis for all.

Mr. Deming was only of the West which is as near Boston as Albany, but as I have said, there were four trans-Alleghanian poets, who had penetrated to the mournful and misty Atlantic (as they had feared it) from their native lakes and rivers. Even in the sixth year of the magazine, Bret Harte of California had appeared in it; and others of the San Francisco school, notably Charles Warren Stoddard, had won an easy entrance after him. Where, indeed, would Mr. Stoddard have been denied, if he had come with something so utterly fresh and delicious as "A Prodigal in Tahiti"? Branches he bore of that and many another enchanted stem, which won his literature my love, and keep it to this day, so that a tender indignation rises in my heart when I find it is not known to every one. John Hay, so great in such different kinds, came also with verse and fiction, studies of the West, and studies of the lingering East in Spain as he found it in his "Castilian Days." Later came Mark Twain, originally of Missouri, but then provisionally of Hartford, and now ultimately of the Solar System, not to say the Universe. He came first with "A True Story," one of those noble pieces of humanity with which the South has atoned chiefly if not solely through him for all its despite to the negro. Then he came with other things, but preeminently with "Old Times on the Mississippi," which I hope I am not too fondly mistaken in thinking I suggested his writing for the magazine. "A True Story" was but three pages long, and I remember the anxiety with which the business side of the magazine tried to compute its pecuniary value. It was finally decided to give the author twenty dollars a page, a rate unexampled in our modest history. I believe Mr. Clemens has since been offered a thousand dollars a thousand words, but I have never regretted that we paid him so handsomely for his first contribution. I myself felt that we were throwing in the highest recognition of his writing as literature, along with a sum we could ill afford; but the late Mr. Houghton, who had then become owner and paymaster, had no such reflection to please him in the headlong outlay. He had always believed that Mark Twain was literature, and it was his zeal and courage which justified me in asking for more and more contributions from him, though at a lower rate. We counted largely on his popularity to increase our circulation when we began to print the piloting papers; but with one leading journal in New York republishing them as quickly as they appeared, and another in St. Louis supplying the demand of the Mississippi Valley, and another off in San Francisco offering them to his old public on the Pacific slope, the sales of the Atlantic Monthly were not advanced a single copy, so far as we could make out. Those were the simple days when the magazines did not guard their copyright as they do now; advance copies were sent to the great newspapers, which helped their readers to the plums, poetic and prosaic, before the magazine could reach the news-stands, and so relieved them of the necessity of buying it.

Among other contributors to whom we looked for prosperity and by whom we looked for prosperity and by whom we were disappointed of it, was Charles Reade, whose star has now declined so far that it is hard to believe that at the time we printed his "Griffith Gaunt" it outshone or presently outflashed any other light of English fiction. We had also a short serial story from Charles Dickens, eked out into three numbers for which we paid (I remember gasping at the monstrous sum) a thousand dollars; and one poem by Tennyson, and several by Browning, without sensible pecuniary advantage. But this was in the earlier rather than the later part of my term, that the transatlantic muse was more invited; I thought either she did not give us of her best, or that she had not anything so acceptable to give us as our own muse.

The fact is we were growing, whether we liked it or not, more and more American. Without ceasing to be New England, without ceasing to be Bostonian, at heart, we had become southern, mid-western and far-western in our sympathies. It seemed to me that the new good things were coming from those regions rather than from our own coasts and hills, but it may have been that the things were newer oftener than better. A careful count of heads might still show that a majority of the good heads in the magazine were New England heads. In my time, when I began to have it quite to myself, our greatest writers continued to contribute, with the seconding which was scarcely to be distinguished in quality. As if from the grave, Hawthorne rose in the first number I made up, with ''Septimius Felton'' in his wizard hand, amidst a company of his living contemporaries who are mostly now his fellow-ghosts. Dr. Holmes printed ''The Poet at the Breakfast-Table'' in my earliest volumes, and thereafter with touching fealty to the magazine responded to every appeal of the young editor. Longfellow was constant, as before; Lowell was even hurt when once, to spare him the tiresome repetition, I had not put his name in the prospectus; Emerson sent some of his most Emersonian poems; Whittier was forgivingly true to the flag, after its mistaken bearer had once refused his following. Among the younger poets (I will call none of them minor) Aldrich was as constant as Holmes, and Stedman as responsive as Longfellow; Bayard Taylor was generous of his best, as he had always been. Mrs. Stuart Phelps, Mrs. Thaxter, Mrs. Prescott Spofford, Mrs. L. C. Moulton, Mrs. Fields, Lucy Larcom, Mr. Trowbridge, wrote characteristic verse which I cannot believe any one more valued than the new host who welcomed it.

If he welcomed from Indiana the note of Maurice Thompson with a glad sense of its freshness, he accepted every one of the twelve pieces offered him by Hiram Rich[10] of Gloucester, Massachusetts, with as deep a pleasure in their new touch; and he printed as eagerly the richly fancied, richly pictorial poems of that sadly unvalued true poet, Edgar Fawcett. Helen Hunt Jackson of Massachusetts and Paul H. Hayne of South Carolina had always the same hospitality if not always the same esteem. They were poets both, though one is scarcely more remembered than the other. Constance Fenimore Woolson of Cleveland sent stories and studies of life in the Great Lake lands; and Mr. William

Henry Bishop [11] of Milwaukee contributed a romance which those who have not forgotten "Detmold" must remember for the restraint and delicacy with which a new motive in fiction was managed, and the truth with which the daring situation was imagined. George Parsons Lathrop, Hawaiian-born and German-bred, came to my help in the editorship about the time that the most American of Scotchmen, Robert Dale Owen, was writing his charming autobiography in separable chapters, after the fashion adopted by that most American of Englishmen, James Parton, in printing his biography of Jefferson. John Fiske, one of the most autochthonic of New Englanders, pursued at my suggestion the same method with the papers forming his "Myths and Myth-Makers," [12] and began with them his long line of popular contributions to the magazine, though some minor articles had preceded them. Another New Englander, quite as autochthonic, began contributor with a series of brilliant sketches, and ended with a series of papers on "Sanitary Drainage" which were equally characteristic of his various talent. This was George E. Waring, who had been the soldier he always looked, and who had afterwards the boldness to dream of cleaning New York, and when he had realized his dream, went to Cuba and died a hero of humanity in the cause of sanitary science. Yet another New Englander of almost equal date, as absolutely New England in his difference from the others as either, was that gentle and fine and quaint Charles Dudley Warner; his studies of travel shed a light on these pages as from a clear lamp of knowledge, which every now and then emitted a flash of the tricksy gayety, the will-o'-the-wisp humor, pervading his playful essays.

It is in vain that I try to separate my editorial achievements from those of my immediate predecessor. I had certainly the indisputable credit of suggesting, if not instigating, the publication of Mrs. Frances Kemble's autobiography by asking why she did not write it, when I already knew she was writing it, and so perhaps taking her fancy. But shall I claim the honor of being Aldrich's editor, because I published all his romances and many of his best poems? Many others yet of his best had appeared in the Atlantic during my own literary nonage, when I classed him with Longfellow and Lowell in his precocious majority; and the reader may be sure there were none of his pieces in that half-barrel of accepted manuscripts which came down to me from the first as well as the second editor of the magazine.

I say half-barrel, but if that seems too much I will compromise on a bushel, on condition that it shall be full measure, pressed down and running over. From the beginning up to my time and all through it, the custom of the magazine had been to pay for contributions on publication, and such inhibition as fear of the publisher's check had not been laid upon Lowell's literary tenderness or Fields's generous hopefulness when it came to the question of keeping some passable sketch, or article, or story, or poem. These were now there, in all their sad variety, in that half-barrel, or call it bushel, which loomed a hogshead in my view, when my chief left it to me. But I was young and strong, and comparatively bold, and I grappled with these manuscripts at once. I will not pretend that I read them; for me the fact that they were accepted was enough, if they still had any life in them. The test was very simple. If the author was still living, then his contribution was alive; if he was dead, then it was dead too; and I will never confess with what ghoulish glee I exulted in finding a manuscript exanimate. With the living I struggled through a long half-score of years, printing them as I could, and if any author dropped by the way, laying his unpublished manuscript like a laurel crown upon his tomb. When Aldrich came to my relief, I placed a pathetic remnant of the bushel, say a half-peck, in his hands, and it was with a shock that I learned later of his acting upon a wholly different conception of his duty to these heirlooms; he sent them all back, dead or alive, and so made an end of an intolerable burden.

I do not blame him for this short and easy method with them; I am not sure but it would be well for mankind if we could use some such method with all the heirlooms of the past. But now that I am no longer an editor, and am without the reasonable hope of ever being one again, I am going to free my mind with regard to the sin I once shared. I think an editor has no right to accept a contribution unless he has some clear expectation of printing it within a reasonable time. His obligation toward the author is not discharged when he pays him; he is still bound to him in the debt of that publicity which the author was seeking from him and to which he has a right, as forming by far, especially if he is young and unknown, the greater part of his reward. In my time I was guilty of wrong in this sort to so many authors that if there is really going to be a Last Day I shall not know where to hide myself from them. In vain shall I plead a misplaced tenderness for their feelings; in vain a love for their work. I ought to have shielded them from both, and given them their contributions back with tears of praise, and hopes for them with other editors able to publish them soon, mingling with my fond regrets. Instead of that, I often kept them waiting a year, two years, three, five, when I had already kept them waiting months for a reading. The image of my desk is before me as I write, with unread manuscripts cumbering a corner of it, and I busy with my fictioning, and pretending that I was only seeking to get the mood and the moment together for reading them. These were selected manuscripts which I had dug out of darkling drawers where I had thrown them indiscriminately, good, bad, and indifferent, as they came, and now and then visited them, to satisfy my bad conscience, and pluck forth a possibility or two, and add it to the heap at the corner of my desk. There, if I had been as honest with myself as I am now trying to be with the reader, I should not have let them lie so long, how long! before I got the mood and moment together for them. That was a favorite phrase of mine, in those days; I remember using it with many contributors whom I cannot remember.

They are a patient tribe, these poor contributors, and they seldom turned upon me. Now and then they did, though, and wreaked a just resentment. This I took meekly when I had some excuse; when I had none, I returned it with a high professional scorn, tacit or explicit, which I am afraid editors still practice toward injured contributors; for if I, a very good man, as editors go, could carry myself so to their indignation, what must be the behavior of the average wicked editor of this degenerate day? I hate still to think of their vengeance, but how much more of their pardon, patient, silent, saintly?

But it was not to indulge these fond pleasures of autobiography that I began by speaking of the essential unity of editorial tradition. Fields had continued Lowell, and perforce I infrangibly continued Fields, coloring the web a little, it seems a very little, from my own tastes and opinions. Certain writers besides those I have already named wrote on from him to me. Prime among these was Harriet Beecher Stowe, and next her was our honored and revered Dr. Hale, whose charmingly ingenious work came to me first in "My Visit to Sybaris," and last in "Life in the Brick Moon": work not only charming and ingenious, but of a penetration, a presage, not yet fully realized through the play of humor and fancy. His peer and contemporary, Colonel Thomas Wentworth Higginson, who had written so much, and always in the interest of art and humanity, honored my page as he had that of my predecessors; but I came to my place too late to welcome a contemporary of both, the friend whom I cannot trust myself to praise except in naming him, Charles Eliot Norton. His scholarship, his taste, his skill were already dedicated to other tasks; he was, with Lowell, editor of the North American Review; and I never edited anything of his except one brief critical notice, though the tale of his earlier contributions to the magazine continued from the first number, in criticisms and essays, to the last number of Mr. Lowell's time. I was proud to edit the brilliant chapters which Francis Parkman continued to give the magazine from the forthcoming volumes of history, ranking him at the head of American historians, and with the great historians of our time. The natural-historian, Mr. John Burroughs, who lives to instruct our day in the modest and beautiful truth of the life so near and yet so far from ours, was a guest of Fields's long before he was mine; and Clarence King, worthy to be named with him for the charm of his science, came distinctly within the time of my suzerain. I read his proofs, though, and acclaimed the literature which King was always humorously ready to disclaim. Among the first serials which I printed was that story of Caroline Chesebro's, "The Foe in the Household," which I still think of a singular excellence. Later, quite within my time, were a novel and several short stories by William M. Baker, so racy of the South, and so good of their kind, that I remember them yet with satisfaction. Of the South, racy and excellent too, were the "Rebel's Recollections" of Mr. George Cary Eggleston, which it is pleasant to think that I asked him to set down for the magazine. I have often testified my esteem for the novels of J. W. De Forest, which I was so willing to print, and I need not repeat the witness here. But

I should wrong myself if I did not record my strong belief that I was among the first editors to recognize the admirable talent of Octave Thanet.

I should like to speak of them all, those contemporaries and contributors of mine, whom naming a few of brings me my old joy in, with a grief for leaving any unnamed. Their successes could not have been dearer to them than they were to me. As each new talent revealed itself to me I exulted in it with a transport which I was sure the public would share with me, and which, whether it fell out so or not, it was an unselfish and unalloyed delight to edit, such as few things in life can give. It was all very, very intimate, that relation of editor and contributor. I do not mean as to personal acquaintance, for in the vast, the overwhelming majority of cases, it never came to that; but I mean the sort of metempsychosis by which I was put so entirely in their place, became so more than one with them, that any slight or wrong done them hurt me more than if it were done to me. Each number of the magazine was an ever new and ever dear surprise for me, at every advance of its being, from the time I put it together in manuscript and gave the copy to the printers until it came into my hands a finished product from the bindery, smelling so intoxicatingly of the ink and paper. At the end of the editor's month, which was a full month before the reader's, there was a struggle with the physical limitations of the magazine which tasked all my powers. I went to have it out, first to the University Press, and then to the Riverside Press; and there I cut and hewed and pared at the quivering members of the closing pages till they came into bounds and the new number was ready to orb about in the space that was perhaps finally too large for it. For the publishers, the corrections, especially the excisions, were expensive pangs, like those of all surgery; but often I wished to avoid them by the yet more expensive enlargement of the magazine, entreating the publishers for eight pages more, or even for four, though I knew they must lose money by it.

There go with these more material memories flitting remembrances, psychical to ineffability, of winter days, and laborious trudges to the printers' through the deep Cambridge snow, when the overwrought horse-car faltered in its track; and of Cambridge summer nights spent far toward their starry noons over obdurate proofs, while the crickets and the grasshoppers rasped together under the open window, and the mad moth beat against the chimney of the lamp. What sounds long silent, what scents fallen odorless, renew themselves in the content of these records! They are parts of the universal death, which, unless we call it the universal life, we are forever dying into. They who equally with myself composed the Atlantic, the beloved, the admired contributors, outdied me, so many of them, years and years ago. The great Agassiz, who wept to think he should not finish his book, stayed to give the magazine only a few first chapters. It was but the other year that the wise, the good Shaler, whose writing in it began almost with mine, ceased from it; and now Aldrich, my time-mate, my work-mate, my play-mate, is gone, he who should have died hereafter, how long hereafter! For the greater great, they who were still living presences when the enterprise which their genius had stamped with ineffaceable beauty and dignity was safe in its strong maturity, the tears were dried years ago. If one outlives, one loses, one sorrows and ceases to sorrow. That is the law. I cannot wish that these intimates in the ideal and the real had outlived the least of their friends, but I wish they had not died till the work which they, far more than any editor, or all the editors, created, was crowned with the end of its half-hundredth year.

I did not well know how to begin these wandering lucubrations —I believe I never used the word before, but it is not too late— and I do not know better how to end them. But the reader may care to learn how it was with one when he parted with the task which had so intensely occupied him for fifteen years. When the burden dropped from me, it was instantly as if I had never felt it. I did not think of it enough to miss it, to rejoice that it was gone. After another fifteen years I began to dream of resuming it. I would dream that I was on the train from New York to Boston, going back to be editor of the Atlantic again. The dream went on, fitfully or frequently, for five or six years. Then at last I found myself on the train with one of my successors, not the least of my friends, and I said, ''Well, Scudder, I have often dreamed of going back to be editor of the Atlantic, and here, now, I am really going.'' But that was a dream, too.

JOHN WILLIAM DE FOREST
(1826–1906)

❧

WHEN in 1867 the assistant editor of the *Atlantic Monthly* wrote a review of *Miss Ravenel's Conversion,* he himself had published no novel. John William De Forest, some eleven years Howells' senior, was already known for his study of Connecticut Indians, for several travel books on Europe and the Orient, and for two or three novels; moreover, he had recently published in *Harper's Monthly* some vivid descriptions of the battles of the Civil War based on his own experience. At the outbreak of the war, when Howells sailed for Italy as United States consul in Venice, De Forest returned from Europe to recruit a company of volunteers in New Haven, with whom he served for the next four years. The letters De Forest wrote home to his family during these campaigns in Louisiana and the Shenandoah were the basis for his first important novel, *Miss Ravenel's Conversion from Secession to Loyalty.*

Among the books that came to his hand after his return from Italy, Howells tells us, was *Miss Ravenel's Conversion,* which he recognized at once as "the best novel suggested by the civil war"—indeed, one of the best American novels he had known. Though Howells at once conceived a "passion" for the book and for all the books that De Forest was to write, he was never able to make the public care for them as much as he did, a fact he considered more discreditable to the taste of the times than to the talent of the author. It is to Howells' credit, certainly, that in *My Literary Passions* he hailed De Forest as "one of our foremost novelists, for his keen and accurate touch in character, his wide scope, and his unerring rendition of whatever he has attempted to report of American life." *Kate Beaumont* (1872), *The Weth-*

erel Affair (1873), *Honest John Vane* (1875), and others, Howells reviewed without ever persuading ''either critics or readers to think with me.'' In *Harper's Bazar*, October, 1901, Howells attributed De Forest's lack of popular success to a ''sort of disdainful honesty'' and a ''certain scornful bluntness'' which, he said, was not appreciated by women, who formed the larger portion of the novel readers of the nineteenth century.

So strong was the public feeling against the realism of De Forest's description of war that Harper's, having published *Miss Ravenel's Conversion* for $1,250 for serial publication in 1865, decided not to risk it in the magazine; instead, Harper's published the novel in 1867 in book form. As Gordon Haight points out in his 1939 edition of the story, De Forest was writing a ''realism not generally acceptable in America until after World War I.'' Howells, however, recognized at once that the ''inexorable veracity'' of this firsthand report of the Civil War made De Forest ''really the only American novelist'' so far to appear.

Howells' review of *Miss Ravenel's Conversion,* printed below, makes the reader perceive that in admiring De Forest's realism, Howells was learning how he himself might make use of this new, more direct approach to real people in actual situations. The shock of meeting recognizable people in novels—''his soldiers are the soldiers we actually know''—far outweighed in Howells' mind any interest in plot, which he passed over with a glance. Haight suggests, indeed, that Howells was sufficiently impressed with the character of Colonel Carter to convert him, minus a uniform, into the Bartley Hubbard of *A Modern Instance* (1882), and remarks that ''Howells borrowed De Forest's theme of a fine young girl, who, against her father's advice, married a man of weak character and lived to regret it; but he refined it to the taste of genteel readers.'' Whether one agrees with Haight as to the refinement of Bartley Hubbard, one can certainly see in Colonel Carter, ''with his brown eyes at once audacious and mirthful,'' more than a suggestion of Hubbard. It is not impossible that an early reading of De Forest deepened Howells' concept of what realism in character might imply.

The writer who affected most profoundly Howells' sense of the importance of truth in novel writing was Tolstoy, whom, Howells tells us, he read for the first time in 1886. A letter from De Forest to Howells, published in *Harper's*, May, 1887, shows us that Howells' enthusiasm for Tolstoy was caught by De Forest. Howells quoted from the letter of De Forest, naming him "a writer who is one of our chief novelists, and who was one of our bravest soldiers": "You do right to praise Tolstoy," wrote De Forest in this significant letter. "Something that you wrote a while ago sent me to his *Peace and War* [sic]. . . . Let me tell you that nobody but he has written the whole truth about war and battle." In "The Editor's Study" of the following September, Howells compared De Forest with Tolstoy, "the incomparable," "as presenting an image of American life" in *Miss Ravenel's Conversion* that might be placed beside Tolstoy's *War and Peace*, without shrinking it to "pitiful dimensions." "It is an admirable novel," Howells remarked, "and spacious enough for the vast drama glimpsed in it."

Howells again spoke of De Forest's "Tolstoyan fidelity" in his review of De Forest's *Lover's Revolt* in *Literature* for December, 1898. It is, Howells writes, "in infinitely smaller compass, a story akin to 'War and Peace' through the moral quality of truth to universal and eternal human experience." His comments on De Forest in "The New Historical Romances," in the *North American Review*, December, 1900, show that Howells, as a mature and experienced critic, found in De Forest "the artistic conscience of a true novelist"; this he had sensed when, as a young reviewer on the *Atlantic*, he first read *Miss Ravenel's Conversion*. De Forest's novels remained for him a "passion," for he read them not only to fill his column, but also to catch from the author the new "strong" realistic approach to novel writing. In *Heroines of Fiction*, written the year after his essay in the *North American Review*, Howells expressed the hope that "in some future moment" De Forest's "belated turn" would come. Howells himself had long recognized De Forest as "a novelist whose work has in some respects not only not been surpassed, but not approached, among us—a realist before realism was named."

JOHN WILLIAM DE FOREST

The Stamp of Verity *

THE light, strong way in which our author goes forward in this
story from the first, and does not leave difficulty to his readers, is
pleasing to those accustomed to find an American novel a good
deal like the now extinct American stage-coach, whose passengers
not only walked over bad pieces of road, but carried fence-rails
on their shoulders to pry the vehicle out of the sloughs and miry
places. It was partly the fault of the imperfect roads, no doubt,
and it may be that our social ways have only just now settled into
such a state as makes smooth going for the novelist; nevertheless, the old stage-coach was hard to travel in, and what with
drafts upon one's good nature for assistance, it must be confessed that our novelists have been rather trying to their readers.
It is well enough with us all while the road is good,—a study of
individual character, a bit of landscape, a stretch of well-worn
plot, gentle slopes of incident; but somewhere on the way the
passengers are pretty sure to be asked to step out,—the ladies
to walk on ahead, and the gentlemen to fetch fence-rails.

Our author imagines a Southern loyalist and his daughter so-
journing in New Boston, Barataria, during the first months of
the war. Dr. Ravenel has escaped from New Orleans just before
the Rebellion began, and has brought away with him the most
sarcastic and humorous contempt and abhorrence of his late
fellow-citizens, while his daughter, an ardent and charming little
blonde Rebel, remembers Louisiana with longing and blind admiration. The Doctor, born in South Carolina, and living all his
days among slaveholders and slavery, has not learned to love
either; but Lillie differs from him so widely as to scream with
joy when she hears of Bull Run. Naturally she cannot fall in love
with Mr. Colburne, the young New Boston lawyer, who goes into
the war conscientiously for his country's sake, and resolved for

* *Miss Ravenel's Conversion from Secession to Loyalty*, by J. W. De Forrest,
1867. Review in the *Atlantic Monthly*, July, 1867. (In the edition reviewed
the author's name was spelled De Forrest.)

his own to make himself worthy and lovable in Lillie's blue eyes
by destroying and desolating all that she holds dear. It requires
her marriage with Colonel Carter—a Virginia gentleman, a
good-natured drunkard and *roué* and soldier of fortune on our
side—to make her see Colburne's worth, as it requires some
comparative study of New Orleans and New Boston, on her return to her own city, to make her love the North. Bereft of her
husband by his own wicked weakness, and then widowed, she
can at last wisely love and marry Colburne; and, cured of Secession by experiencing on her father's account the treatment received by Unionists in New Orleans, her conversion to loyalty is a
question of time duly settled before the story ends.

We sketch the plot without compunction, for these people of
Mr. De Forrest's are so unlike characters in novels as to be like
people in life, and none will wish the less to see them because he
knows the outline of their history. Not only is the plot good and
very well managed, but there is scarcely a feebly painted character or scene in the book. As to the style, it is so praiseworthy
that we will not specifically censure occasional defects,—for the
most part, slight turgidities notable chiefly from their contrast to
the prevailing simplicity of the narrative.

Our war has not only left us the burden of a tremendous national debt, but has laid upon our literature a charge under which
it has hitherto staggered very lamely. Every author who deals in
fiction feels it to be his duty to contribute towards the payment
of the accumulated interest in the events of the war, by relating
his work to them; and the heroes of young-lady writers in the
magazines have been everywhere fighting the late campaigns
over again, as young ladies would have fought them. We do not
say that this is not well, but we suspect that Mr. De Forrest is
the first to treat the war really and artistically. His campaigns do
not try the reader's constitution, his battles are not bores. His
soldiers are the soldiers we actually know,—the green wood of
the volunteers, the warped stuff of men torn from civilization and
cast suddenly into the barbarism of camps, the hard, dry, tough,
true fibre of the veterans that came out of the struggle. There
could hardly be a better type of the conscientious and patriotic
soldier than Captain Colburne; and if Colonel Carter must not

stand as type of the officers of the old army, he must be acknowledged as true to the semi-civilization of the South. On the whole he is more entertaining than Colburne, as immoral people are apt to be to those who suffer nothing from them. ''His contrasts of slanginess and gentility, his mingled audacity and *insouciance* of character, and all the picturesque ins and outs of his moral architecture, so different from the severe plainness of the spiritual temples common in New Boston,'' do take the eye of peace-bred Northerners, though never their sympathy. Throughout, we admire, as the author intends, Carter's thorough and enthusiastic soldiership, and we perceive the ruins of a generous nature in his aristocratic Virginian pride, his Virginian profusion, his imperfect Virginian sense of honor. When he comes to be shot, fighting bravely at the head of his column, after having swindled his government, and half unwillingly done his worst to break his wife's heart, we feel that our side has lost a good soldier, but that the world is on the whole something better for our loss. The reader must go to the novel itself for a perfect conception of this character, and preferably to those dialogues in which Colonel Carter so freely takes part; for in his development of Carter, at least, Mr. De Forrest is mainly dramatic. Indeed, all the talk in the book is free and natural, and, even without the hard swearing which distinguishes the speech of some, it would be difficult to mistake one speaker for another, as often happens in novels.

The character of Dr. Ravenel, though so simple, is treated in a manner invariably delightful and engaging. His native purity, amiability, and generosity, which a life-long contact with slavery could not taint; his cordial scorn of Southern ideas; his fine and flawless instinct of honor; his warm-hearted courtesy and gentleness, and his gayety and wit; his love of his daughter and of mineralogy; his courage, modesty, and humanity,—these are the traits which recur in the differing situations with constant pleasure to the reader.

Miss Lillie Ravenel is as charming as her adored papa, and is never less nor more than a bright, lovable, good, constant, inconsequent woman. It is to her that the book owes its few scenes of tenderness and sentiment; but she is by no means the most prominent character in the novel, as the infelicitous title would imply, and she serves chiefly to bring into stronger relief the traits of Colonel Carter and Doctor Ravenel. The author seems not even to make so much study of her as of Mrs. Larue, a lady whose peculiar character is skilfully drawn, and who will be quite probable and explicable to any who have studied the traits of the noble Latin race, and a little puzzling to those acquainted only with people of Northern civilization. Yet in Mrs. Larue the author comes near making his failure. There is a little too much of her,—it is as if the wily enchantress had cast her glamour upon the author himself,—and there is too much anxiety that the nature of her intrigue with Carter shall not be misunderstood. Nevertheless, she bears that stamp of verity which marks all Mr. De Forrest's creatures, and which commends to our forbearance rather more of the highly colored and strongly-flavored parlance of the camps than could otherwise have demanded reproduction in literature. The bold strokes with which such an amusing and heroic reprobate as Van Zandt and such a pitiful poltroon as Gazaway are painted, are no less admirable than the nice touches which portray the Governor of Barataria, and some phases of the aristocratic, conscientious, truthful, angular, professorial society of New Boston, with its young college beaux and old college belles, and its life pure, colorless, and cold to the eye as celery, yet full of rich and wholesome juices. It is the goodness of New Boston, and of New England, which, however unbeautiful, has elevated and saved our whole national character; and in his book there is sufficient evidence of our author's appreciation of this fact, as well as of sympathy only and always with what is brave and true in life.

MARK TWAIN (1835–1910)

∾≮

AMONG "the good things" that "began to come out of the West" in the 1860's and 1870's were the manuscripts of a certain Mark Twain, known to Howells as Clemens. As assistant editor of the *Atlantic Monthly*, Howells had eagerly welcomed and reviewed *Innocents Abroad* before its redheaded author strolled into the Boston office late in the winter of 1869 to thank the editor in person. This meeting marked the beginning of a friendship that lasted until Clemens' death in 1910.

Innocents Abroad was based on the reports Clemens had sent back to the *Alta-California* and the New York *Herald* and *Tribune* of a trip he had taken in 1867 with a party of excursionists to the Mediterranean and the Holy Land. The only other book he had published was *The Celebrated Frog of Calaveras County and Other Sketches* (1867). Howells, who took boundless delight in both books, did not hesitate to announce in the last sentence of his review of *Innocents Abroad:* "It is no business of ours to fix his rank among the humorists California has given us, but we think he is, in an entirely different way from all the others, quite worthy of the company of the best."

Clemens and Howells have both left us descriptions of their notable meeting. More to our purpose here is the account of the interview by Clemens' biographer, Albert Bigelow Paine, for in this paragraph is suggested something of the literary relationship immediately established by the two men.

[Mark Twain's] manner, his humor, his quaint colloquial forms all delighted Howells—more, in fact, than the opulent sealskin overcoat which he affected at this period . . . startling enough, we may believe, in the conservative atmosphere of the *Atlantic* rooms. And Howells—gentle, genial, sincere—filled with the early happiness of his calling, won the heart of Mark Twain and never lost it, and what is still more notable, won his absolute and unvarying confidence in all literary affairs. It was always Mark Twain's habit to rely on somebody, and in matters pertaining to literature and to literary people in general he laid his burden on William Dean Howells from that day.

In a letter to T. B. Aldrich in 1871, Clemens tells us that it was Bret Harte on whom he relied before he met Howells: "Bret Harte trimmed and trained and schooled me patiently until he changed me from an awkward utterer of coarse grotesqueness to a writer of paragraphs and chapters that have found a certain favor in the eyes of even some of the very decentest people in the land." We know, moreover, that Olivia Langdon, whom Clemens married in 1870, helped him edit the proof sheets of *Innocents Abroad* before Howells saw the book, and she continued to "edit" her husband until her death in 1905. What part Howells played in the curbing of his friend's "bold fancy" and "breadth of parlance" no one, not even Howells himself, could say. In *My Mark Twain*, Howells attempted to define their difference of character, and hence of style:

Throughout my long acquaintance with him his graphic touch was always allowing a freedom which I cannot bring my fainter pencil to illustrate. He had the Southwestern, the Lincolnian, the Elizabethan breadth of parlance, which I suppose one ought not to call coarse without calling one's self prudish; and I was often hiding away in discreet holes and corners the letters in which he had loosed his bold fancy.

That Howells' "fainter pencil" was an effective editorial weapon against Clemens' extravagances, is quite evident from Howells' remark in *My Mark Twain* on Clemens' association with him as a contributor to the *Atlantic:*

When Clemens began to write for it he came willingly under its rules, for with all of his wilfulness there never was a more biddable man in things you could show him reason for. . . . If you wanted a thing changed, very good, he changed it; if you suggested that a word or a sentence or a paragraph had better be struck out, very good, he struck it out.

Clemens relied on Howells completely, and in 1875 he took the manuscript of *Tom Sawyer* to him to read, "as a friend and critic, and not as an editor." For Clemens counted on Howells' unfailing appreciation of his humor, his realism, his naturalness of style, his common sense. Clemens soon learned the importance of a favorable review from the editor of the *Atlantic*. *Roughing It* (1872), *Sketches Old and New* (1875), *The Adventures of Tom Sawyer* (1876), *A Tramp Abroad* (1880), and all the others, were reviewed by Howells, one by one, as they came off the press. So powerful was Howells' criticism, even while he was still on the *Atlantic*, that, as Clemens tells us in his *Autobiography*:

More than once I took the precaution of sending my book, in manuscript, to Mr. Howells, when he was editor of the *Atlantic Monthly* so that he could prepare a review of it at leisure. I knew that he would find more merit than demerit in it, because I already knew that that was the condition of the book. I allowed no copy of that book to go out to the press until after Mr. Howells's notice of it had appeared. That book was always safe. There wasn't a man behind a pen in America that had spirit enough to say a brave and original thing about the book on his own responsibility.

Amusingly practical as the above paragraph shows Clemens to have been, we know that his literary relationship with Howells was far more complex. He depended on Howells not merely for favorable book reviews, but even more for his deep understanding of the inner intent of his humorous-tragic, realistic-romantic, exuberant-commonsense, and altogether individual way of writing.

Because Howells shows in his essay in the *North American Review* of February, 1901, his appreciation of the whole range of contradictory characteristics that mark Clemens' manner and style, we have selected a portion of this essay rather than one of his earlier *Atlantic* reviews. The occasion for the article "Mark Twain: An Inquiry" was the publication of a "uniform edition" of his writings, and also, Howells adds, "his return to his own country after an absence so long as to form a psychological perspective in which his characteristics make a new appeal." Clemens had, in fact, recently brought to a close the famous round-the-world lecture tour that had enabled him to recover from bankruptcy. The "psychological perspective" through which Howells tells us he viewed the characteristics of Clemens in 1901 gives us a portrait perhaps more finely shaded than critics in our generation remember.

Howells himself included this essay in *My Mark Twain,* with the brief introductory remark that the reviews in the book, arranged chronologically, begin ''rather stiffly, pedantically, and patronizingly, but that they grow suppler, wiser, and more diffident as they go on.'' We realize, as we read this essay, that the perspective Howells had gained extended beyond Clemens to the ''characteristics'' of the colloquial, native, honest realism, closely related to romance, for which Howells fought for so many years. Clemens summed up the movement, but with a difference that was genius, and this Howells recognized.

Mark Twain: An Inquiry *

[Mark Twain's] great charm is his absolute freedom in a region where most of us are fettered and shackled by immemorial convention. He saunters out into the trim world of letters, and lounges across its neatly kept paths, and walks about on the grass at will, in spite of all the signs that have been put up from the beginning of literature, warning people of dangers and penalties for the slightest trespass.

One of the characteristics I observe in him is his singleminded use of words, which he employs as Grant did to express the plain, straight meaning their common acceptance has given them with no regard to their structural significance or their philological implications. He writes English as if it were a primitive and not a derivative language, without Gothic or Latin or Greek behind it, or German and French beside it. The result is the English in which the most vital works of English literature are cast, rather than the English of Milton, and Thackeray, and Mr. Henry James. I do not say that the English of the authors last named

* *North American Review,* February, 1901.

MARK TWAIN

is less than vital, but only that it is not the most vital. It is
scholarly and conscious; it knows who its grandfather was; it
has the refinement and subtlety of an old patriciate. You will
not have with it the widest suggestion, the largest human feeling, or perhaps the loftiest reach of imagination, but you will
have the keen joy that exquisite artistry in words can alone impart, and that you will not have in Mark Twain. What you will
have in him is a style which is as personal, as biographical as the
style of any one who has written, and expresses a civilization
whose courage of the chances, the preferences, the duties, is not
the measure of its essential modesty. It has a thing to say, and it
says it in the word that may be the first or second, or third choice,
but will not be the instrument of the most fastidious ear, the
most delicate and exacting sense, though it will be the word that
surely and strongly conveys intention from the author's mind
to the reader's. It is the Abraham Lincolnian word, not the
Charles Sumnerian; it is American, Western.

Now that Mark Twain has become a fame so world-wide, we
should be in some danger of forgetting, but for his help, how
entirely American he is, and we have already forgotten, perhaps,
how truly Western he is, though his work, from first to last, is
always reminding us of the fact. But here I should like to distinguish. It is not alone in its generous humor, with more honest
laughter in it than humor ever had in the world till now, that
his work is so Western. Any one who has really known the West
(and really to know it one must have lived it), is aware of the
profoundly serious, the almost tragical strain which is the fundamental tone in the movement of such music as it has. Up to a
certain point, in the presence of the mystery which we call life,
it trusts and hopes and laughs; beyond that it doubts and fears,
but it does not cry. It is more likely to laugh again, and in the
work of Mark Twain there is little of the pathos which is supposed to be the ally of humor, little suffusion of apt tears from
the smiling eyes. It is too sincere for that sort of play; and if
after the doubting and the fearing it laughs again, it is with a
suggestion of that resentment which youth feels when the disillusion from its trust and hope comes, and which is the grim
second-mind of the West in the presence of the mystery. It is

217

not so much the race-effect as the region-effect; it is not the Anglo-American finding expression, it is the Westerner, who is not more thoroughly the creature of circumstances, of conditions, but far more dramatically their creature, than any prior man. He found himself placed in them and under them, so near to a world in which the natural and primitive was obsolete, that while he could not escape them, neither could he help challenging them. The inventions, the appliances, the improvements of the modern world invaded the hoary eld of his rivers and forests and prairies, and while he was still a pioneer, a hunter, a trapper, he found himself confronted with the financier, the scholar, the gentleman. They seemed to him, with the world they represented, at first very droll, and he laughed. Then they set him thinking, and as he never was afraid of anything, he thought over the whole field, and demanded explanations of all his prepossessions, of equality, of humanity, of representative government and re-vealed religion. When they had not their answers ready, with-out accepting the conventions of the modern world as solutions or in any manner final, he laughed again, not mockingly, but patiently, compassionately. Such, or somewhat like this, was the genesis and evolution of Mark Twain.

Missouri was Western, but it was also Southern, not only in the institution of slavery, to the custom and acceptance of which Mark Twain was born and bred without any applied doubt of its divinity, but in the peculiar social civilization of the older South from which his native State was settled. It would be reaching too far out to claim that American humor, of the now prevailing Western type, is of Southern origin, but without staying to attempt it I will say that I think the fact could be established; and I think one of the most notably Southern traits of Mark Twain's humor is its power of seeing the fun of South-ern seriousness, but this vision did not come to him till after his liberation from neighborhood in the vaster far West. He was the first, if not the only man of his section, to betray a consciousness of the grotesque absurdities in the Southern inversion of the civilized ideals in behalf of slavery, which must have them up-side down in order to walk over them safely. No American of Northern birth or breeding could have imagined the spiritual struggle of Huck Finn in deciding to help the negro Jim to his freedom, even though he should be forever despised as a negro thief in his native town, and perhaps eternally lost through the blackness of his sin. No Northerner could have come so close to the heart of a Kentucky feud, and revealed it so perfectly, with the whimsicality playing through its carnage, or could have so brought us into the presence of the sardonic comi-tragedy of the squalid little river town where the store-keeping magnate shoots down his drunken tormentor in the arms of the drunkard's daughter, and then cows with bitter mockery the mob that comes to lynch him. The strict religiosity compatible in the Southwest with savage precepts of conduct is something that could make itself known in its amusing contrast only to the native Southwesterner, and the revolt against it is as constant in Mark Twain as the enmity to New England orthodoxy is in Dr. Holmes. But he does not take it with such serious resentment as Dr. Holmes is apt to take his inherited Puritanism, and it may be therefore that he is able to do it more perfect justice, and impart it more absolutely. At any rate there are no more vital passages in his fiction than those which embody character as it is affected for good as well as evil by the severity of the local Sunday-schooling and church-going. . . .

Slavery in a small Missouri river town could not have been the dignified and patriarchal institution which Southerners of the older South are fond of remembering or imagining. In the second generation from Virginia ancestry of this sort, Mark Twain was born to the common necessity of looking out for himself, and while making himself practically of another order of things he felt whatever was fine in the old and could regard whatever was ugly and absurd more tolerantly, more humorously than those who bequeathed him their enmity to it. Fortunately for him, and for us who were to enjoy his humor, he came to his intellectual consciousness in a world so large and free and safe that he could be fair to any wrong while seeing the right so unfailingly; and nothing is finer in him than his gentleness with the error which is simply passive and negative. He gets fun out of it, of course, but he deals almost tenderly with it, and hoards his violence for the superstitions and traditions which are arrogant and active. His pictures of that old river-town, South-western life, with its faded and tattered aristocratic ideals and its squalid democratic realities, are pathetic, while they are so unsparingly true and so inapologetically and unaffectedly faithful.

The West, when it began to put itself into literature, could do so without the sense, or the apparent sense, of any older or politer world outside of it; whereas the East was always looking fearfully over its shoulder at Europe, and anxious to account for itself as well as represent itself. No such anxiety as this entered Mark Twain's mind, and it is not claiming too much for the Western influence upon American literature to say that the final liberation of the East from this anxiety is due to the West, and to its ignorant courage or its indifference to its difference from the rest of the world. It would not claim to be superior, as the South did, but it could claim to be humanly equal, or rather it would make no claim at all, but would simply be, and what it was, show itself without holding itself responsible for not being something else.

The Western boy of forty or fifty years ago grew up so close to the primeval woods or fields that their inarticulate poetry became part of his being, and he was apt to deal simply and uncritically with literature when he turned to it, as he dealt with nature. He took what he wanted, and left what he did not like; he used it for the playground, not the workshop of his spirit. Something like this I find true of Mark Twain in peculiar and uncommon measure. I do not see any proof in his books that he wished at any time to produce literature, or that he wished to reproduce life. When filled up with an experience that deeply interested him, or when provoked by some injustice or absurdity that intensely moved him, he burst forth, and the outbreak might be altogether humorous, but it was more likely to be humorous with a groundswell of seriousness carrying it profoundly forward. In all there is something curiously, not very definably, elemental, which again seems to me Western. He behaves himself as if he were the first man who was ever up against the proposition in hand.

EDWARD EGGLESTON
(1837-1902)

∌≪

IN THE *Atlantic Monthly* of March, 1872, Howells reviewed a best seller by an obscure Methodist circuit rider from Indiana who had begun his literary career as a writer of Sunday-school stories. *The Hoosier Schoolmaster,* by Edward Eggleston, had appeared the previous December in book form after having been serialized in fourteen issues of *Hearth and Home.* The little volume achieved an immediate and unexpected success; 10,000 copies were sold in this country in the first six months after publication. Howells hailed the book as "a picture of manners hitherto strange to literature," reflecting "the rudeness and ugliness of the intermediate West." The story, he said, is well told in "a plain fashion," though the reader does foresee the "fortunate ending." Other reviews of *The Hoosier Schoolmaster* appeared in the same month, both in *Harper's* and in *Scribner's,* but the editor of the *Atlantic* was the only critic to point out the false pathos of some of Eggleston's characterizations, as well as to commend him for his village types and local dialect.

Before the appearance of *The Hoosier Schoolmaster,* Howells had written to Eggleston congratulating him on his story "Huldah, the Help" and pronouncing it "a very unaffected bit of good work." As though in reply, Eggleston had cited Howells in the July 6, 1871, issue of the *Independent* as among those men "who will do justice to the customs and speech of the West." When Eggleston made a hurried visit to Boston the following December, he called on Howells and wrote home to his wife, "Saw Mr. Howells to-day and am to dine in his beautiful cottage to-morrow." No doubt the recently appointed editor of the *Atlantic* and the supervising editor of the *Inde-*

pendent had much to talk about, for they had many things in common besides the fact that they were ambitious young journalists from the "intermediate West" who had escaped from the limitations of their small towns by means of writing.

Both Howells and Eggleston were then venturing into the writing of sketches based on their own experiences. At the time when Eggleston's account of his younger brother's experiences in teaching were appearing in *Hearth and Home,* Howells was making literary copy for the *Atlantic* of his own daily observations (published in 1871 as *Suburban Sketches*). But there the similarity between the two writers ended, for Howells, after all, was the author of *Italian Journeys,* a lecturer at Harvard, and editor of the *Atlantic.* Eggleston, a Methodist preacher by training and a writer by chance, had scarcely read a novel before he happened to write a best seller in an attempt to rescue an expiring magazine.

Howells greeted Eggleston's next novel, *The End of the World,* in his review for the *Atlantic* of December, 1872, with the same blend of praise and blame he had accorded *The Hoosier Schoolmaster.* This "natural story teller," Howells remarked, made use of materials that were "simple and even common," but by his sincerity in observing the scene around him, presented the reader with new characters and threw "the shadow of a grand dramatic element" across the ordinary plot. A cursory glance at the *Independent,* for which Eggleston was writing at this period, indicates that he was conscious of a wide range of social and political issues of the day but that his literary interests did not go beyond the roster of well-known American names, Irving, Poe, Hawthorne, Emerson, Lowell, and Holmes.

Howells' own appreciation of the value of "everyday experience and common homespun," on the other hand, came not only from his early Ohio experience, but also from the reading at this time of the novels of Björnson and Turgenev. As we have seen in Part II, Howells, between 1869 and 1870, reviewed Björnson as the herald of "the new way of writing" and in 1872 praised Turgenev's *Smoke* in similar terms. What Howells admired in the technique of the Europeans was that they reflected the life about them, that they wasted no words

in explaining their characters, and that they never senti-
mentalized. When Howells reviewed Eggleston's third novel,
The Circuit Rider, in the *Atlantic* of June, 1874, he took him
to task, with Björnson as his authority, for pausing to comment
on his characters. "This is bad art, as Mr. Eggleston himself
must feel," Howells wrote, bringing home the lesson of Björnson
to this "natural story teller" with an instinct for Indiana
dialect and frontier incident, but with no knowledge of the
European writers engaged in similar quests. The review of
The Circuit Rider, printed below, shows better than any other
how Howells grafted critical ideas from abroad on native stock.

Though Eggleston was unaware of the European realist from
whom Howells was gathering hints both as critic and writer,
he had read Hippolyte Taine, whose *Philosophy of Art in the
Netherlands* he reviewed briefly in the *Independent* of December
8, 1870. His younger brother tells us that Eggleston "set forth
his theory of art—that the artist, whether with pen or brush,
who would do his best work, must choose his subjects from the
life he knows. He cited the Dutch painters." Interestingly
enough, Howells reviewed the same Taine book in the *Atlantic*
of March, 1871, but, imbued as he was with the writings of
Björnson and Turgenev, he found Taine's work, though entertaining, "of no great original value." He remarked, "The considerations of race are not new nor striking; perhaps they are
rather conventional." In February, 1872, Howells reviewed
Taine's *History of English Literature,* which he found disappointing, especially Taine's concept of the study of art, about
which Howells himself had ideas. In the August issue of the
Atlantic for the same year Howells commented on Taine's
Notes on the English, pointing out that Emerson and Hawthorne
had done the same thing better. Since Howells as a novelist
found Taine's descriptions of English types amusing, he laid
aside the book with "penitential distrust"; Taine's "distorted
philosophy" seemed to Howells only "lucky thrusts in the dark."

Though the reading of Taine's *Philosophy of Art in the
Netherlands* might have contributed to Eggleston's resolve to
write of his own countryside, it was Björnson and Turgenev
whose literary techniques enabled Howells both to criticize and

to praise the novelist from Indiana. In *Harper's* of February, 1889, he reviewed one of Eggleston's later novels, *The Graysons*, which he considered one of his best works, for "the story deals with elements that lie about us like earth and water." In this review, written in the thick of the battle for realism, Howells was reminded again of his "literary passion" of former days, especially for Björnson, who not only influenced Howells' own style, but, through Howells, helped to establish a basis for commenting on the "new way of writing," of which *The Hoosier Schoolmaster* is a humble example.

Flat Creek *

IN MR. EGGLESTON's "Hoosier Schoolmaster" we are made acquainted with the rudeness and ugliness of the intermediate West, after the days of pioneering, and before the days of civilization,—the West of horse-thief gangs and of mobs, of protracted meetings and of extended sprees, of ignorance drawn slowly through religious fervors towards the desire of knowledge and decency in this world. The scene of the story is in Hoopole County, Indiana, a locality which we hope the traveller would now have some difficulty in finding, and in a neighborhood settled, apparently, by poor whites from Virginia and Kentucky, sordid Pennsylvania Dutchmen, and a sprinkling of 'cute dishonest Yankees. The plot is very simple and of easy prevision from the first, being the struggles of Ralph Hartsook with the young idea in the district school on Flat Creek, where the twig was early bent to thrash the schoolmaster. He boards round among the farmers, starting with "old Jack Means," the school trustee, whose son Bud, the most formidable bully among his pupils, he wins over to his own side, and whose daughter, with her mother's connivance, falls in love with

* *The Hoosier Schoolmaster*, by Edward Eggleston, 1871. Review in the *Atlantic Monthly*, March, 1872.

him and resolves to marry him. But the schoolmaster loves their bound girl Hannah, and makes enemies of the mother and daughter; and they are not slow to aid in the persecution which rises against him, and ends in his arrest for a burglary committed by the gang of the neighborhood, including some of the principal citizens of Flat Creek. Of course it comes out all right, though the reader is none the less eager because he foresees the fortunate end. The story is very well told in a plain fashion, without finely studied points. It is chiefly noticeable, however, as a picture of manners hitherto strange to literature, and the characters are interesting as part of the picture of manners, rather than as persons whose fate greatly concerns us; yet they all have a movement of their own, too, and are easily known from each other,—which is much for characters. One of the best is old Mrs. Means, who is also one of the worst in another sense. Her talk is the talk of all Flat Creek; and we cannot suggest the dialect in which the conversation of the story is chiefly written better than by giving a speech of hers:—

"Here Mrs. Means stopped to rake a live coal out of the fire with her skinny finger, and then to carry it in her skinny palm to the bowl—or to the *hole*—of her cobpipe. When she got the smoke agoing she proceeded:

" 'You see this ere bottom land was all Congress land in them there days, and it sold for a dollar and a quarter, and I says to my ole man, "Jack," says I, "Jack, do you git a plenty while you're a gittin'. Git a plenty while you're a gittin'," says I, "fer 'twon't never be no cheaper'n 'tis now," and it ha'nt been, I knowed 'twouldn't,' and Mrs. Means took the pipe from her mouth to indulge in a good chuckle at the thought of her financial shrewdness. " 'Git a plenty while you're a gittin',' says I. I could see, you know, they was a powerful sight of money in Congress land. That's what made me say, "Git a plenty while you're a gittin'." And Jack, he's wuth lots and gobs of money, all made out of Congress land. Jack didn't git rich by hard work. Bless you, no! Not him. That a'n't his way. Hard work a'n't, you know. 'Twas that air six hundred dollars he got along of me, all salted down into Flat Crick bottoms at a dollar and a quarter a acre, and 'twas my sayin', "Git a plenty while you're a gittin'," as done it.' And here the old ogre laughed, or grinned horribly, at Ralph, showing her few straggling, discolored teeth.

"Then she got up and knocked the ashes out of her pipe, and laid the pipe away and walked round in front of Ralph. After adjusting the 'chunks' so that the fire would burn, she turned her yellow face toward Ralph, and scanning him closely came out with the climax of her speech in the remark, 'You see as how, Mr. Hartsook, the man what gits my Mirandy'll do well. Flat Crick land's worth nigh upon a hundred a acre.' "

We should say the weak side of Mr. Eggleston's story was the pathos that gets into it through some of Little Shocky's talk, and the piety that gets into it through Bud Means; and we mean merely that these are not so well managed as the unregeneracy, and not at all that they are not good things to have in a story. The facts about Shocky are touching enough, and the facts about Bud most respectable.

Mr. Eggleston is the first to touch in fiction the kind of life he has represented, and we imagine that future observers will hardly touch it in more points. Its traits seem to be all here, both the good and the bad; but that it is a past or passing state of things is sufficiently testified by the fact, to which Mr. Eggleston alludes in his Preface, that the story, as it appeared serially, was nowhere more popular than in Southern Indiana. Flat Creek, Hoopole County, would not, we imagine, have been so well pleased thirty years ago with a portrait which, at any rate, is not flattered.

A Tale of the Heroic Age *

NO AMERICAN story-teller has of late years had greater success, of a good kind, than Mr. Eggleston, who in four years

* *The Circuit Rider: A Tale of the Heroic Age*, by Edward Eggleston, 1874. Review in the *Atlantic Monthly*, June, 1874.

has given us consecutively, The Hoosier Schoolmaster, The End of the World, The Mystery of Metropolisville, and now The Circuit Rider. His books have been read by the hundred thousands; they have been respectfully considered by the most difficult criticism amongst us, they have been translated, we believe, and misunderstood in the *Revue des Deux Mondes*,[13] they have enjoyed the immortality of English republication. They merited as much. They were exceedingly well theorized. Mr. Eggleston considered the vast fields of fiction lying untouched in the region of his birth and the home of his early manhood, and for his plots, scenes, and characters, he acted on Mr. Greeley's famous advice, and went West. It must have been that he truthfully painted the conditions and people whom he aimed to portray, for it was in the West that his popularity began, and it is there doubtless that it is now the greatest. He does not deal with the contemporary West, but with the West of forty or fifty years ago; and except in The Mystery of Metropolisville he does not leave the familiar ground of the Ohio Valley. The scene of his first two stories is in Southern Indiana, that of the last is in Southern Ohio. On this ground he was at home, yet he was able to view all the people and situations from the outside, and in the light of subsequent life in the East. Some disadvantages came from this advantage. He was too conscious of the oddity of his material, and he placed an inartistic stress upon unimportant details of dialect, customs, and character. Even in The Circuit Rider, he stops from time to time, in the description of some rude or grotesque scene, to make the reader an ironical or defiant apology for treating of such unrefined matters; or, if he has some wild incident or trait to handle, pauses to expatiate upon it and caress its singularity. This is bad art, as Mr. Eggleston must himself feel, and he ought not to indulge it. The novelist's business is to paint such facts of character and custom as he finds so strongly that their relative value in his picture will be at once apparent to the reader without a word of comment: otherwise his historical picture falls to the level of the panorama with a showman lecturing upon the striking points and picking them out for observance with a long stick. It is not in this way that the masters of the art which Mr. Eggleston reveres accomplish their results. Björnson does not add a word to impress on our imaginations the Norwegian incidents and characters he sets before us in *Arne;* and Turgénieff, in such a Russian tale as The Lear of the Steppes, leaves all comment to the reader. Everything necessary to the reader's intelligence should be quietly and artfully supplied, and nothing else should be added.

We speak the more frankly of this blemish in Mr. Eggleston's last work because we find The Circuit Rider such a vast advance upon his former stories. The Mystery of Metropolisville was disappointing; for though it showed a good sense of character and the story was interesting, it was not so fresh as The Hoosier Schoolmaster, and it had not such poetic elements as The End of the World. It was not an advance; it was something of a retrogression. But in our pleasure with The Circuit Rider we have been willing to forget this, and we are glad to recognize the author in his most fortunate effort. The story is of backwoods life in Ohio at the time when the Methodists began to establish the foundations of their church in the new land, among the children of the Indian-fighters and pioneers, and the hero of the story is one of those ardent young preachers who throughout the Southwest were known as circuit riders. They were each given a certain field of labor by the Conference, and they traveled on horseback from point to point in this field, preaching, praying, and turning sinners to repentance, and at due seasons assembling their forces in mighty camp-meetings, and gathering whole neighborhoods into the capacious bosom of their church at once. No history is more picturesque or dramatic than theirs, and Mr. Eggleston has well called their time the heroic age.

HENRY JAMES (1843-1916)

"TALKING of talks: young Henry James and I had a famous one last evening, two or three hours long, in which we settled the true principles of literary art," Howells wrote to Edmund Clarence Stedman on December 5, 1866. Though James was at that time only twenty-three years old, Howells, the recently appointed assistant editor of the *Atlantic Monthly*, recognized at once the quality of the young man, six years his junior, about whom he was writing to his New York friend. "He is a very earnest fellow," the letter continued, "and I think extremely gifted—gifted enough to do better than any one has yet done toward making us a real American novel." Surely a remarkable prediction concerning James, who, in December, 1866, had to his credit only a scattering of reviews and stories published in three or four magazines.

The famous talks between Howells and James took place in the course of "nocturnal rambles," which began in the summer of 1866 and "followed one another into the mild autumnal weather." The Jameses had arrived in Cambridge six months after the Howellses had settled into "Cottage Quiet" on Sacramento Street. Though the aimless strolls of the two young writers were frequent enough, they met more often in Howells' small house, for James liked to talk over his stories with Howells and his wife and to read aloud from his manuscript by the light of a kerosene lamp. Even more important to the young James, Howells was eager to accept from him all the stories he could supply, in spite of the misgivings of his "senior editor, Mr. Fields."

Beginning with James's review of Howells' *Italian Journeys*, for the January, 1868, issue of the *North American Review*, and ending with Howells' discussion of James's *Hawthorne* in the *Atlantic Monthly* for February, 1880, James and Howells continued to exchange critical views in a series of seven articles in the *Atlantic,* the *North American Review,* the *Independent,* and the *Nation* before Howells resigned from the *Atlantic* and before James took up his permanent residence in London. Through these reviews, three by Howells and four by James, one can trace some of the "principles of literary art" that the two writers explored together in the days when both were experimenting in the novel form. The difference between romanticism and romance; the symbolism of Hawthorne; the realism of Balzac; the psychological insight of George Eliot; the technique of Turgenev; the richness of the European scene as contrasted with the provincialism of Concord and Boston; "the great American novel" and who should write it—all these questions and many more were raised by Howells and James in the reviews of each other's books as they were published. Were not the same questions discussed in the strolls around Fresh Pond in the summer of 1866 and by the side of the air-tight stove in Howells' parlor in the following winter? Before Howells himself went to Europe in 1882, he wrote "Henry James, Jr." for *Century Magazine,* which one may read as a conclusion to the talks begun more than fifteen years earlier.

The most important of these seven essays, Howells' review of Henry James's small book on Hawthorne, is given below. Since it was Howells who, in the course of their Cambridge rambles, had directed James's attention to Hawthorne, he must have studied with particular interest James's presentation of this New England author to the British public in Morley's "English Men of Letters" series in 1879.

Howells' review of James's essay is in a sense a continuation of the earlier conversations that must frequently have touched on the general question of the provincial tone of the American scene and the position of the writer in such a society. Howells' review begins with a discussion of James's remarks on the exquisite provinciality of Hawthorne. Is it provincial for an Englishman to be English, a Frenchman to be French, or an American to be American? Howells' question no doubt reflects not only his argument with James as to the narrowness of Hawthorne's experience, but also the prolonged discussions between Howells and James themselves as to whether the American soil was sufficiently rich to nourish an American novelist. By the time James wrote his essay on Hawthorne he had definitely decided to abandon his American roots and to establish himself in England; Howells had come to the opposite decision and some of his reasons are reflected in the review. Though Howells and James continued to correspond for the remainder of their lives, though they exchanged their latest books and visited one another in London, Cambridge, and New York, the significant period of their relationship came to a close at the time when each one made his basic decision as to his relation to his native land.

Not only does Howells take issue with James on the subject of Hawthorne's provinciality but he also points out to him "the confusion which, for some reason not made clear, he permits himself" in his discussion of Hawthorne's definition of romance, to be found in the preface to *The House of the Seven Gables*. The romance and the novel, Howells pointed out with some impatience, are as distinct as the poem and the novel. Since Howells, as James's critic and editor, had urged him to correct the exaggerated analytical realism of his early stories by a touch of romance as defined by Hawthorne, and since James in several stories he had submitted to the *Atlantic* followed Howells' advice, one can understand the asperity of Howells in his remarks on James's apparent confusion.

James's unwillingness to accept the sharp distinction between romance and realism, the romance and the novel, is attributable to the fact that at the time when Howells was urging upon James a reconsideration of the romances of Hawthorne, James was introducing to Howells the realistic novels of Balzac. These studies of the Comédie Humaine Howells discussed in his review of James's *French Poets and Novelists* in the *Atlantic* of July, 1878, a discussion which he continued in Sections III and V of *Criticism and Fiction*. Immense as Balzac undoubtedly was as a realist, Balzac unfortunately was not always Balzac, and when he erred it was in terms of romantic exaggeration. Reading his romance *Le Père Goriot*—"it is not worthy the name of novel"— is to discover that Balzac's realism, like that of Dickens, is profoundly romantic, "full of malarial restlessness, wholly alien to healthful art." On the other hand, Hawthorne's romance is merely the poetic atmosphere cast over his essentially realistic probing of the human heart and is truer to experience than Balzac's "realistic" overstatement. So, at least, ran Howells' part in the dialogue, a portion of which is found in the essay below.

Thus the dialogue continued between these two novelists bent on discovering the "true principles of literary art." Howells' review of James's *Hawthorne* is but one speech in this conversation, which began in 1866 and ended for a time in 1882, when both authors were prepared to write their greatest novels. Here we are concerned with the first and more inseminating chapter of this friendship, which in fact lasted until James's death in 1916, or, more truly, until Howells' death in 1920, for he left unfinished an essay to be called "The American James."

James's Hawthorne *

MR. JAMES'S book on Hawthorne, in Morley's English Men of Letters series, merits far closer examination and carefuller notice than we can give it here, alike for the interest of its subject, the peculiarity of its point of view, and the charm and distinction of its literature. An American author writing of an American author for an English public incurs risks with his fellow-countrymen which Mr. James must have faced, and is much more likely to possess the foreigner whom he addresses with a clear idea of our conditions than to please the civilization whose portrait is taken. Forty-six, fifty, sixty-four, are not dates so remote, nor are Salem and Concord societies so extinct, that the people of those periods and places can be safely described as

* *Hawthorne*, by Henry James, 1879. Review in the *Atlantic Monthly*, February, 1880.

provincial, not once, but a dozen times; and we foresee, without any very powerful prophetic lens, that Mr. James will be in some quarters attainted of high treason. For ourselves, we will be content with saying that the provinciality strikes us as somewhat over-insisted upon, and that, speaking from the point of not being at all provincial ourselves, we think the epithet is sometimes mistaken. If it is not provincial for an Englishman to be English, or a Frenchman French, then it is not so for an American to be American; and if Hawthorne was "exquisitely provincial," one had better take one's chance of universality with him than with almost any Londoner or Parisian of his time. Provinciality, we understand it, is a thing of the mind or the soul; but if it is a thing of the experiences, then that is another matter, and there is no quarrel. Hawthorne undoubtedly saw less of the world in New England than one sees in Europe, but he was no cockney, as Europeans are apt to be.

At the same time we must not be thought to deny the value and delightfulness of those chapters on Salem and Brook Farm and Concord. They are not very close in description, and the places seem deliciously divined· rather than studied. But where they are used unjustly, there will doubtless be abundant defense; and if Salem or Brook Farm be mute, the welkin will probably respond to the cries of certain critics who lie in wait to make life sorrowful to any one dealing lightly with the memory of Thoreau or the presence of the poet Channing. What will happen to a writer who says of the former that he was "worse than provincial, he was parochial," and of the latter that he resembles the former in "having produced literary compositions more esteemed by the few than by the many," we wait with the patience and security of a spectator at an *auto da fé,* to see. But even an unimbattled outsider may suggest that the essential large-mindedness of Concord, as expressed in literature, is not sufficiently recognized, although it is thoroughly felt. The treatment of the culture foible and of the colorless æsthetic joys, the attribution of "a great deal of Concord five and thirty years ago" to the remark of a visitor of Hawthorne that Margaret Fuller "had risen perceptibly into a higher state of being since their last meeting," are exquisite,—too exquisite, we fear, for the sense of most Englishmen, and not too fine only for the rarefied local consciousness which they may sting. Emerson is indeed devoutly and amply honored, and there is something particularly sweet and tender in the characterization of such surviving Brook Farmers as the author remembers to have met; but even in speaking of Emerson, Mr. James has the real misfortune to call his grand poem for the dedication of the monument to Concord Fight a "little hymn." It is little as Milton's sonnet on Shakespeare is little.

We think, too, that in his conscience against brag and *chauvinism* Mr. James puts too slight a value upon some of Hawthorne's work. It is not enough to say of a book so wholly unexampled and unrivaled as The Scarlet Letter that it was "the finest piece of imaginative writing put forth in" America; as if it had its parallel in any literature. When he comes to speak of the romances in detail, he repairs this defect of estimation in some degree; but here again his strictures seem somewhat mistaken. No one better than Mr. James knows the radical difference between a romance and a novel, but he speaks now of Hawthorne's novels, and now of his romances, throughout, as if the terms were convertible; whereas the romance and the novel are as distinct as the poem and the novel. Mr. James excepts to the people in The Scarlet Letter, because they are rather types than persons, rather conditions of the mind than characters; as if it were not almost precisely the business of the romance to deal with types and mental conditions. Hawthorne's fictions being always and essentially, in conception and performance, romances, and not novels, something of all Mr. James's special criticism is invalidated by the confusion which, for some reason not made clear, he permits himself. Nevertheless, his analysis of the several books and of the shorter tales is most interesting; and though we should ourselves place The Blithedale Romance before The House of Seven Gables, and should rank it much higher than Mr. James seems to do, we find ourselves consenting oftener than dissenting as we read his judgments. An admirably clear and just piece of criticism, we think, is that in which he pronounces upon the slighter and cheaper *motif* of Septimius Felton. But here there are not grounds for final sentence; it is possible, if that book had received the author's last touches, it might have been, after all, a playful and gentle piece of irony rather than a tragedy. What gives us entire satisfaction, however, is Mr. James's characterization, or illustrations of Hawthorne's own nature. He finds him an innocent, affectionate heart, extremely domestic, a life of definite, high purposes singularly unbaffled, and an "unperplexed intellect." The black problem of evil, with which his Puritan ancestors wrestled concretely, in groans and despair, and which darkens with its portentous shadow nearly everything that Hawthorne wrote, has become his literary material; or, in Mr. James's finer and more luminous phrase, he "transmutes this heavy moral burden into the very substance of the imagination." This strikes us as beautifully reasonable and true, and we will not cloud it with comment of ours. But satisfactorily as Mr. James declares Hawthorne's personality in large, we do not find him sufficient as to minor details and facts. His defect, or his error, appears oftenest in his discussion of the note-books, where he makes plain to himself the simple, domestic, democratic qualities in Hawthorne, and yet maintains that he sets down slight and little aspects of nature because his world is small and vacant. Hawthorne noted these because he loved them, and as a great painter, however full and vast his world is, continues to jot down whatever strikes him as picturesque and characteristic. The disposition to allege this inadequate reason comes partly from that confusion of the novelist's and the romancer's work of which we have spoken, and partly from a theory, boldly propounded, that it needs a long history and "a complex social machinery to set a writer in motion." Hawthorne himself shared, or seemed to share, this illusion, and wrote The Marble Faun, so inferior, with its foreign scene, to the New England romances, to prove the absurdity of it. As a romancer, the twelve years of boyhood which he spent in the wild solitudes of Maine were probably of greater advantage to him than if they had been passed at Eton and Oxford. At least, until some other civilization has produced a romantic genius at all comparable to his, we must believe this. After leaving out all those novelistic "properties," as sovereigns, courts, aristocracy, gentry, castles, cottages, cathedrals, abbeys, universities, museums, political class, Epsoms, and Ascots, by the absence of which Mr. James suggests our poverty to the English conception, we have the whole of human life remaining, and a social structure presenting the only fresh and novel opportunities left to fiction, opportunities manifold and inexhaustible. No man would have known less what to do with that dreary and worn-out paraphernalia than Hawthorne.

We can only speak of the excellent comment upon Hawthorne's Old Home, and the skillful and manly way in which Mr. James treats of that delicate subject to his English audience. Skillful and manly the whole book is,—a miracle of tact and of self-respect, which the author need not fear to trust to the best of either of his publics. There is nothing to regret in the attitude of the book; and its literature is always a high pleasure, scarcely marred by some evidences of hurry, and such *writerish* passages as that in which *sin* is spoken of as "this baleful substantive with its attendant adjective."

It is a delightful and excellent essay, refined and delicate in perception, generous in feeling, and a worthy study of the unique romancer whom its closing words present with justice so subtle and expression so rich:—

"He was a beautiful, natural, original genius, and his life had been singularly exempt from worldly preoccupations and vulgar efforts. It had been as pure, as simple, as unsophisticated, as his work. He had lived primarily in his domestic affections, which were of the tenderest kind; and then—without eagerness, without pretension, but with a great deal of quiet devotion—in his charming art. His work will remain; it is too original and exquisite to pass away; among the men of imagination he will always have his niche. No one has had just that vision of life, and no one has had a literary form that more successfully expressed his vision. He was not a moralist, and he was not simply a poet. The moralists are weightier, denser, richer, in a sense; the poets are more purely inconclusive and irresponsible. He combined in a singular degree the spontaneity of the imagination with a haunting care for moral problems. Man's conscience was his theme, but he saw it in the light of a creative fancy which added, out of its own substance, an interest, and, I may almost say, an importance."

236

JOHN HAY (1838-1905)

≫≪

The Bread-Winners: A Social Study appeared serially in *Century Magazine*—where it "did not lack comment more or less impassioned"—from August, 1883, to January, 1884, when it was issued by Harper's in book form. John Hay, biographer of Lincoln, ambassador to Great Britain, and twice Secretary of State, did not during his life admit that he was also the author of this much-discussed novel. Nor did Howells ever acknowledge that he wrote the review of *The Bread-Winners,* signed "W," for the May, 1884, issue of *Century.* However, the authorship of this early review can hardly be doubted after a consideration of "John Hay in Literature," written for the *North American Review,* September, 1905, soon after the death of Hay. In this essay Howells looked back over his long friendship with Hay, which had begun twenty-five years before the publication of *The Bread-Winners,* and referred to their meeting in London while Hay was writing the book. Almost unconsciously, Howells threw light on the anonymity of his earlier review in his later essay.

John Hay wrote his "social study" in about four months' time in the summer of 1882 and asked Howells to read it while he and his family were in London, enjoying association with Henry James, Bret Harte, Thomas Bailey Aldrich, James Osgood, and others. Howells hoped to persuade Aldrich to accept the manuscript for the *Atlantic,* since he himself had recently written *The Stillwater Tragedy,* another antilabor novel. Aldrich refused it, however, because Hay insisted on anonymity, perhaps following the lead of his friend Henry Adams, who, four years earlier, had not acknowledged his authorship of *Democracy.* After the serializing of *The Bread-Winners* in the *Century,* Hay explained, in an unsigned letter to that magazine, why it seemed important to him not to declare his name: "a working man" himself, he was also a businessman, he pointed out, and could not afford to endanger his relationship with either group. Howells, in the 1905 essay cited above, continued to guard Hay's secret, referring only to "a piece of fiction" that he had found Hay writing in London in 1882, and which Hay asked him to read. Though many guessed the authorship of Hay's novel, it was not officially disclosed until 1907.

When Hay and Howells met in London during the summer of 1882, both men had reached an important milestone in their careers, as they probably realized. Howells had resigned his editorship of the *Atlantic* and had recently published his most important novel up to that time, *A Modern Instance;* Hay, having started his career as poet, essayist, and journalist, had become a successful businessman and, in 1877, Assistant Secretary of State under President Hayes. To understand why Hay turned from writing to business, then to politics, and why in 1882 he wrote *The Bread-Winners* from a violently antilabor angle, one must know something of the personal life of the author.

In 1875 Hay moved to Cleveland as a young newspaper man and married the daughter of the railroad millionaire Amasa Stone. Hay soon gave up journalism, entered his father-in-law's business, and proved himself a very capable man of affairs at a time when Amasa Stone stood in need of help. Stone, who began life as a simple carpenter interested in building bridges for westward-moving pioneers, was estimated to have lost over a million and a half dollars in the depression of 1873, which followed the great industrialization and capital expansion of the post-Civil War period. The plight of labor, caught between inflated prices and depreciated currency, brought on the wave of strikes, especially at railroad centers such as St. Louis, Pittsburgh, and Cleveland, that made many think the "Revolution" had arrived in this country. John Hay, as an associate of Stone, was deeply concerned with these railroad strikes; in two long anonymous letters to the *Century* in answer to the critics of *The Bread-Winners,* Hay explained how he had gathered all the material for the novel from the daily

238

newspapers of Cleveland, St. Louis, and elsewhere at the time of the strikes of 1877. "I contend," he wrote, "that the book is true, and was written with an honest purpose"—which was to warn the public against the "foreign" labor agitators, who, he said, exploited the industrious and contented workers of Anglo-Saxon origin. Hay insisted that he was not opposed to trade unions, which seemed to many a threat to the country, but to the self-interested labor leaders, the new villain of American fiction proposed by the anonymous writer. Moreover, Hay felt, it was the duty of the novelist to utter public warnings when he clearly perceived danger.

Howells, in his review of *The Bread-Winners* for the *Century*, applauded this interpretation of the novelist's responsibility. If the author of *The Bread-Winners* means only to tell the truth about his characters, if he refuses to flatter either the employer or the workingman, "he has done the cause of labor and the cause of art both a service." Critical realism meant, at this time as well as later, that morality, truth, and art are all one and the same. Howells' only objection to Hay's novel, from the point of view of realism, had to do with the happy ending, which seemed to him untrue and therefore artistically false.

When "W" admitted that "we should have been well content to see the strike of the telegraphers succeed," he spoke as a citizen rather than as a critic, and expressed views that diverged from those of the author of *The Bread-Winners*. The strike to which Howells referred took place in July, 1883, just one month before the serializing of Hay's novel in the *Century*. Since Amasa Stone was at that time on the board of directors of Western Union, a position that John Hay filled after the death of his father-in-law the following May, we may be sure that Hay was not among those who would have been content to see the strikers win. The strikers did in fact lose, and Hay continued to sit on the board until he resigned to become ambassador to Great Britain.

Again in his essay "John Hay in Literature," Howells touched on his essential disagreement with Hay on labor questions, as well as on the realistic treatment of character in novels. In this essay he looked back to the publication of *The Bread-*

Winners, and observed: "It dealt with the labor question in the old persuasion concerning united labor, and it cannot be found a modern criticism of economic conditions." Howells' social thinking was so at variance with that of Hay that the very platform of the Society of Bread-Winners—"The downfall of the money power, the rehabilitation of labor, the organization for mutual profit"—which is satirized by Hay, is accepted by Howells as the basis of life in Altruria. What Howells appreciated in *The Bread-Winners* was the range of new characters set before the reader of fiction, rather than the antiunion attitude of the author—"the sketches of the local politicians, the leaders who can swing their wards." Hay's genius turned us from "our provisional gentility" toward our "crude potentialities," just as Howells' was to do in the social novels that came soon after *The Bread-Winners.* For the notable books Howells reviewed not only helped him define his critical beliefs but also inspired him to further fictional experiments of his own, such as *A Hazard of New Fortunes.* On Hay's strikers Howells commented: "It is quite time we were invited to consider some of them in fiction as we saw some of them in fact during the great railroad strike"; and as a novelist he followed the suggestion.

———————◆———————

A Social Study *

THIS story did not lack comment, more or less impassioned, during the course of its publication in THE CENTURY, and its characteristics will probably have been canvassed still more thoroughly before these pages meet the eye of the reader. From the first it was noticeable that the criticism it received concerned the morality of the story, and even the morality of the writer, rather than the art of either; and, on the whole,

* The Bread-Winners: A Social Study, 1884. Review in the *Century Magazine,* May, 1884.

we do not see why this was not well enough. It was, we think, a wholesome way of regarding the performance, and, even in those who most disliked it, implied a sense of conscience and of thinking in the book, however warped, however mistaken. It was a better way of looking at it than a mere survey of its literary qualities would have been, and it marked an advance in popular criticism. The newspapers did not inquire so much whether this or that character was well drawn, this or that incident or situation vividly reported, as whether the writer, dealing forcibly with some living interests of our civilization, meant one thing or another by what he was doing; though they did not fail to touch upon its literature at the same time. The discussion evolved an interesting fact, which we recommend to all intending novelists, that among us at least the novelist is hereafter to be held to account as a public teacher, that he must expect to be taken seriously, and must do his work with the fear of a community before his eyes which will be jealous of his ethical soundness, if nothing else. What did the author of ''The Bread-winners'' mean by making his rich and well-to-do people happy, and leaving all the suffering to the poor? Does he believe that it is wrong for the starving laborer and operative to strike? Are his sympathies with the rich against the poor? Does he think workingmen are all vicious? Does he mean that it was right for Captain Farnham to kiss Maud Matchin when she had offered herself to him in marriage and dropped herself into his arms, unless he meant to marry her? Was he at all better than she if he could do such a thing? Was it nice of Mrs. Belding to tell her daughter of this incident? Ought Alice Belding to have accepted him after such a thing as that?

Some of these voices—which still agitate the air—are unmistakably soprano and contralto; some, for which we have less respect, are falsetto. We do not know whether it would be possible, or whether it would be profitable, to answer them conclusively. At any rate, we shall not attempt it; but we would like to call attention to the very important fact that the author of ''The Bread-winners'' shows no strong antipathy to strikers till they begin to burn and rob and propose to kill; and we will ask the abstract sympathizer to recall his own sensations in regard to the great railroad strike in 1877, after the riots began. In our own mind there is no question that any laborer, or any multiple of him, not being content with his hire, has the right to leave his work; and we should have been well content to see the strike of the telegraphers succeed, and not ill pleased to see those who thought them paid enough put to live awhile on their wages. But if the striking telegraphers, like the striking railroad men, had begun to threaten life and destroy property, we should have wanted the troops called out against them. We cannot see that the author of "The Bread-winners" has gone beyond this point in his treatment of the question of strikes.

We cannot see, either, that he has in any sort a prejudice against the workingman as a workingman. We are all working-men in America, or the sons of workingmen, and few of us are willing to hear them traduced; but, for our own part, they do not seem to us preeminent for wisdom or goodness, and we cannot perceive that they derive any virtue whatever from being workingmen. If they were lawyers, doctors, or clergymen, they would be equally respectable, and not more so. They are certainly better than the idle rich, as they are better than the idle poor—the two classes which we have chiefly, if not solely, to dread; and it is the idle poor whom our author does not like, whom he finds mischievous, as other writers of romance have long found the idle rich. It is the Offitts and the Botts and the Bowersoxes whom he detests, not the Matchins, nor even the Sleenys. These are treated with respect, and Sleeny, at least in the end, is rather more lavishly rewarded than any of the millionaires, if his luck in escaping the gallows is not more than neutralized by the gift of Miss Maud Matchin as a wife. But there is no doubt the author meant well by him; and we think there is no doubt that he means well by all honest, hard-working people. He has not made them very brilliant, for still "the hand of little employment hath the nicer sense''; he has not heaped them with worldly prosperity, and it must be owned that Divine Providence has done no better by them. Let us be just before we are generous, even to the workingman. Let us

JOHN HAY

recognize his admirable qualities in full measure; but let us not make a fetich of him, impeccable, immaculate, infallible. We suspect that in portraying a certain group of people as he has done, the author of "The Bread-winners" meant no more nor less than to tell the truth about them; and if he has not flattered the likeness of his workingmen, he has done the cause of labor and the cause of art both a service. Workingmen are in no bad way among us. They have to practice self-denial and to work hard, but both of these things used to be thought good for human nature. When they will not work, they are as bad as club men and ladies of fashion, and perhaps more dangerous. It is quite time we were invited to consider some of them in fiction as we saw some of them in fact during the great railroad strike.

When we come to the question whether Captain Farnham ought to have kissed Maud Matchin, or turned from her with loathing, we confess that we feel the delicacy of the point. Being civilians, we will venture to say that we fear it was quite in character for an ex-army man to kiss her, and so far the author was right. Whether it was in character for a perfect gentleman to do so, we cannot decide; something must be conceded to human nature and a sense of the girl's impudence, even in a perfect gentleman. But, having dodged this point, we feel all the more courage to deal with another, namely, whether he was not quite as bad as she. We think not, for reasons which his accusers seem to forget. Miss Matchin did not offer herself to him because she loved him, but because she loved his wealth and splendor, and wished to enjoy them, and though she was careful to tell him that she would only be his wife, it is not clear to our minds that if she could have been equally secure of his wealth and splendor in another way, there was anything in her character to make her refuse. He did behave with forbearance and real kindness to that foolish and sordid spirit; he did use her with magnanimity and do what he could to help her, though she had forfeited all claim upon his respect. He may not have been a perfect gentleman, but he was certainly a very good sort of man, in spite of that questionable kiss.

We might wish to have Miss Matchin other than she was for her own sake; but if she were different, she would not be so useful nor so interesting. She is the great invention, the great discovery, of the book; and she is another vivid and successful study of American girlhood, such as it seems to be largely the ambition of our novelists to make. She is thoroughly alive, caught by an instantaneous process, in which she almost visibly breathes and pulsates. One has a sense of her personal presence throughout, though it is in the introductory passages that we realize most distinctly her mental and spiritual qualities, and the wonderful degree in which she is characterized by American conditions—by the novels of the public library, by the ambitious and inadequate training of the high school, by the unbounded freedom of our social life. These conditions did not produce her; with other girls they are the agencies of inestimable good. But, given the nature of Miss Maud Matchin, we see the effect upon her at every point. We can see the effect, also, of the daily newspaper and of the display of Algonquin Avenue, with its histories in brick and stone of swift, and recent, and immeasurable riches. The girl's poetry is money, her romantic dream is to marry a millionaire. She has as solid and sheer a contempt for the girl who dreams of an old-fashioned hero and love in a cottage as she has for her hard-working father and mother. There are no influences in her home to counteract the influences from without. She grows up a beautiful, egotistic, rapacious, unscrupulous fool. But take the novels and the high school away, and she would still have been some kind of fool. The art of the author consists in having painted her as she exists through them. The novelist can do no more. He shows us this creature, who is both type and character, and fitly leaves the moralist to say what shall be done about her. Probably nothing can be done about her at once; but if she is definitely ascertained as a fact of our civilization, it is a desirable step in self-knowledge for us.

At the end the author's strong hand seems to falter a little in the treatment of Miss Matchin. We read of her ''rosy and happy face'' when the man she has driven to murder is acquitted, and the chief weakness of the book here betrays itself. Something should have been done to show that those people had entered hand in hand into their hell, and that thenceforth there could be no hope for them.

There are some admirable passages of casual or subordinate interest in the book, and a great many figures drawn with a force that leaves a permanent impression. The episode of Maud's canvass for the place in the public library, and her triumph through the "freeze-out" that leaves Pennybaker "kickin' like a Texas steer"; the behavior of the rascal mayor during the strike; all the politicians' parlance; the struggle of Alice Belding with herself after her good-natured but not very wise mother has told her of Maud's offer to Farnham; her feeling that this has somehow stained or "spoiled" him;—these are traits vigorously or delicately treated, that may be set against an account of less interesting handling of some society pictures. The scenes of the riot and the attack on Farnham's house are stirringly done; that of the murderous attack on Farnham by Offitt less so; and it appears to us rather precipitate in Alice to fall asleep as soon as she hears that her lover is not fatally hurt. But these are very minor points. Generally speaking, we think the author has done what he meant to do. We believe that he has been faithful to his observation of facts. If the result is not flattering, or even pleasing, that is not his fault, and neither his art nor his morality is to blame for it.

EDWARD BELLAMY (1850–1898)

⁂

"I DO not think it by any means a despicable thing to have hit the popular fancy of our enormous commonplace average," Howells wrote in an essay for the *North American Review* of December, 1900, commenting on the popularity of "The New Historical Romances." In this essay he looked back sadly at "the welter of overwhelming romance" that had inundated the book market during the very period when "the natural tendency" in fiction prevailed. It was not, Howells insisted, that these historical romances "hit the popular fancy" that made them "despicable." "Some of the best and truest books have done this"—*Pilgrim's Progress,* for instance, *Uncle Tom's Cabin,* and *Roughing It;*—"Edward Bellamy's gospel of justice in *Looking Backward* did it." What was really lamentable was "to have hit the popular fancy and not to have done anything to change it, but everything to fix it." Romance that "flatters with false dreams of splendor" is false romance.

Bellamy's posthumous romance, *The Duke of Stockbridge* (written in part by Bellamy in 1879 and finished by his cousin, the Rev. Francis Bellamy, in 1900) is an example of the kind of romance Howells admired. For this historical romance is concerned with "the short and simple annals of the poor" in "that squalid period immediately following the Revolution" and reflects the real feelings of the common man. For the same reason Howells considered *Dr. Heidenhoff's Process* (1880) one of "the finest feats in the region of romance" that he had ever read; here the author's imagination worked on "the level of average life, and built the fabric of its dreams out of common clay."

Howells wrote the memorial essay reprinted below for the *Atlantic Monthly* soon after the early death of Bellamy in 1898, and it was reprinted in October of the same year as a preface to the posthumous collection of Bellamy's short stories, *The Blindman's World and Other Stories.* The essay not only tells us of the life and work of this modest, retiring man from Chicopee Falls, Massachusetts, but also reflects Howells' idea that romance is justified only if the feelings of "the average man" are woven into "the webs of fancy." The action of Bellamy's romances, Howells pointed out, always took place in the atmosphere of the American village. Bellamy spent most of his life in the village of Chicopee Falls, except for a year in Germany as a youth and a brief period in Boston, where he studied for the law before becoming, in 1880, a journalist in New York City and in Springfield, Massachusetts. Always more interested in his romances than in journalism, he soon returned to live and write in his native village.

Bellamy's full-length romance, *Miss Ludington's Sister* (1884), Howells reviewed in *Century Magazine* for August, 1884, commenting on the air of reality that marked it. Possibly this review served to introduce Howells to Bellamy, for shortly after its appearance Bellamy wrote to Howells elaborating his idea of the relationship between romance and realism. "Whether I belong to the school of realists or not I do not know," he wrote.

It is the business of the author to write as the spirit moves, and of the critic to classify him. But my own belief is that while the warp, that is the framework and main lines of the story, should be the author's own invention, the woof and filling should be supplied from his observations of the real life about him. It is the undertaking of the romancer to give an air of reality even to the unreal.

Perhaps Howells had this letter of 1884 in mind when he observed in his essay that Bellamy "does not so much transmute our every day reality to the substance of romance as make the airy stuff of dreams one in quality with veritable experience." This is the secret of Bellamy's "singular art," and also of the art of Hawthorne, the other "great romancer" admired by Howells.

Howells presided at the Bellamy memorial meeting held in the Social Reform Club of New York, June 7, 1898. On that occasion he remarked: "We know him best as a social agitator, and we do not value him enough as a literary man.'' The following essay is important primarily as a just appraisal of the imaginative literary power of Bellamy; it should also be read as a comment on Bellamy's social ideas by the man who wrote *A Traveler from Altruria* (1894). Since the novelist Mr. Twelvemouth in Howells' utopian romance is undoubtedly a satiric partial portrait of the author himself, and since the traveler, Mr. Homos, cites Bellamy as the source of his information, we can assume that their conversation is a reflection of the lively exchange of ideas that took place between Bellamy and Howells from 1884 to 1894.

"I know him not only in his books, but also in his life, and it is there that I grew to love him,'' Howells told the Social Reform Club. Whether he was also familiar with a curious little essay, *The Religion of Solidarity,* written by Bellamy in 1874 but not published until 1940, one does not know; certainly the thought of the essay was familiar to him. "We are a part of all'' and are saved from "self-hood'' only by recognizing that fact, wrote Bellamy, expressing the basic philosophy of Howells' "complicity,'' first suggested in 1887 in *The Minister's Charge* and fully explored in *A Traveler from Altruria.* Bellamy and Howells were both aware of the waves of Comtian positivism that stressed the religion of brotherhood in the new age of science (the very word "altruism'' was first used by Comte), but Bellamy seems to have supplied the practical thought that Howells needed for his less clearly formulated social feeling.

In 1886, when Howells' life was changed, he tells us, by his reading of Tolstoy, Bellamy was in search of a program for the reform of society. Bellamy wrote:

According to my best recollections, it was in the fall or winter of 1886 that I sat down to my desk with the definite purpose of trying to reason out a method of economic organization by which the republic might guarantee the livelihood and material welfare of its citizens on the basis of equality corresponding to and supplanting their political equality.

The public stand that Howells took in 1887 against the execution of the Chicago Anarchists, when he risked his position as editor and novelist by a letter of protest to the New York *Trib-*

une, indicates that his social concern was then sufficiently strong to make him anxious to learn all he could of practical schemes for the reform of society. Howells eagerly read and reviewed *Looking Backward* (*Harper's,* June, 1888), noting its kinship with Gronlund's *Cooperative Commonwealth,* which he had reviewed two years earlier. He "was at that time deeply moved by the social injustice which we had all recently discovered," Garland reports in "Meetings with Howells." He added, "Often as we walked and talked he spoke of Bellamy's delineation of the growing contrast between rich and poor." Howells, Bellamy, Gronlund, Garland, and others were meeting during the winters of 1889–1891 to discuss these new ideas at the Church of the Carpenter, in Boston, of which W. D. P. Bliss, the well-known Christian Socialist, was minister.

Bellamy's picture of the social inequalities of modern American society influenced Howells' scenes in *A Hazard of New Fortunes,* on which he was working when Bellamy's *Looking Backward* was making the best-seller list and Bellamy Clubs (later called Nationalist Clubs) were being formed all over the country. "I cannot refrain from congratulating you upon *The Hazard of New Fortunes,*" Bellamy wrote Howells when the serial began to appear in *Harper's Weekly* in March, 1889. "I have read the last number with enthusiasm. You are writing what everyone is thinking and all the rest will have to follow or lose their readers."

The enthusiasm with which Bellamy read Howells' novel was deepened by the fact that Howells and Bellamy frequently met in Boston during the winters of 1889, 1890, and 1891. Howells was present at the organization meeting of the first Nationalist Club of Boston, December 1, 1888. Both men were interested in the Society of Christian Socialists, inaugurated in 1889 in the same city under the leadership of the liberal Episcopal priest, the Rev. W. D. P. Bliss, and Howells also attended the opening by Bliss of the Church of the Carpenter, April 3, 1890. Not only Bellamy and Howells but also Edward Everett Hale, Laurence Gronlund, Hamlin Garland, and other reformers met and discussed the new economic and social ideas in the light of Christianity. Though the Nationalist Club retained its essentially economic outlook and the Society of Christian Socialists its religious orientation, the membership of both groups overlapped and their ideas, as reflected in their publications, *The Nationalist* and *The Dawn,* were closely related. *A Traveler From Altruria* contains many of Bellamy's economic ideas, but the Christian thought suffusing it may be traced to Howells' association with the Society of Christian Socialists in Boston.

Bellamy was so enthusiastic about Howells' utopia that he wrote a special article about it in *The New Nation,* November 26, 1892, and reviewed it again in the October 14, 1893, issue, when *A Traveler* was completed. In a congratulatory letter to Howells, Bellamy signed himself, "Yours in the sympathy of a common aspiration." Both men had been drawn into the discussions of Boston liberal thinkers, who "revived throughout Christendom the faith in a millennium," as Howells said in the following essay, and both men hoped through their utopian romances to affect the thinking of "our enormous commonplace average."

The Romantic Imagination *

THE first book of Edward Bellamy's which I read was Dr. Heidenhoff's Process, and I thought it one of the finest feats in the region of romance which I had known. It seemed to me all the greater because the author's imagination wrought in it on the level of average life, and built the fabric of its dream out of common clay. The simple people and their circumstance were treated as if they were persons whose pathetic story he had witnessed himself, and he was merely telling it. He wove into the texture of their sufferings and their sorrows the magic thread of invention so aptly and skillfully that the reader felt nothing improbable in it. One even felt a sort of moral necessity for it, as if such a clue not only could be, but must be given for their escape. It became not merely probable, but imperative, that there should

* Essay in the *Atlantic Monthly,* August, 1898.

be some means of extirpating the memory which fixed a sin in lasting remorse, and of thus saving the soul from the depravity of despair. When it finally appeared that there was no such means, one reader, at least, was inconsolable. Nothing from romance remains to me more poignant than the pang that this plain, sad tale imparted.

The art employed to accomplish its effect was the art which Bellamy had in degree so singular that one might call it supremely his. He does not so much transmute our every-day reality to the substance of romance as make the airy stuff of dreams one in quality with veritable experience. Every one remembers from Looking Backward the allegory which figures the pitiless prosperity of the present conditions as a coach drawn by slaves under the lash of those on its top, who have themselves no firm hold upon their places, and sometimes fall, and then, to save themselves from being ground under the wheels, spring to join the slaves at the traces. But it is not this, vivid and terrible as it is, which most wrings the heart; it is that moment of anguish at the close, when Julian West trembles with the nightmare fear that he has been only dreaming of the just and equal future, before he truly wakes and finds that it is real. That is quite as it would happen in life, and the power to make the reader feel this like something he has known himself is the distinctive virtue of that imagination which revived throughout Christendom the faith in a millennium.[14]

A good deal has been said against the material character of the happiness which West's story promises men when they shall begin to do justice, and to share equally in the fruits of the toil which operates life; and I confess that this did not attract me. I should have preferred, if I had been chooser, to have the millennium much simpler, much more independent of modern inventions, modern conveniences, modern facilities. It seemed to me that in any ideal condition (the only condition finally worth having) we should get on without most of these things, which are but sorry patches on the rags of our outworn civilization, or only toys to amuse our greed and vacancy. Aesthetically, I sympathized with those select spirits who were shocked that nothing better than the futile luxury of their own selfish lives could be imagined for the lives which overwork and underpay had forbidden all pleasures; I acquired considerable merit with myself by asking whether the hope of these formed the highest appeal to human nature. But I overlooked an important condition which the other critics overlooked; I did not reflect that such things were shown as merely added unto those who had first sought the kingdom of God and his righteousness, and that they were no longer vicious or even so foolish when they were harmlessly come by. I have since had to own that the joys I thought trivial and sordid did rightly, as they did most strenuously, appeal to the lives hitherto starved of them. In depicting them as the common reward of the common endeavor Edward Bellamy builded better than we knew, whether he knew better or not, and he builded from a thorough sense of that level of humanity which he was destined so potently to influence,—that American level which his book found in every Christian land.

I am not sure whether this sense was ever a full consciousness with him; very possibly it was not; but in any case it was the spring of all his work, from the earliest to the latest. Somehow, whether he *knew* or not, he unerringly *felt* how the average man would feel; and all the webs of fancy that he wove were essentially of one texture through his sympathy. His imagination was intensely democratic, it was inalienably plebeian, even,—that is to say, humane. It did not seek distinction of expression; it never put the simplest and plainest reader to shame by the assumption of those fine-gentleman airs which abash and dishearten more than the mere literary swell can think. He would use a phrase or a word that was common to vulgarity, if it said what he meant; sometimes he sets one's teeth on edge, in his earlier stories, by his public school diction. But the nobility of the heart is never absent from his work; and he has always the distinction of self-forgetfulness in his art.

I have been interested, in recurring to his earlier work, to note how almost entirely the action passes in the American village atmosphere. It is like the greater part of his own life in this. He was not a man ignorant of other keeping. He was partly educated abroad, and he knew cities both in Europe and in America. He was a lawyer by profession, and he was sometime editor of a daily newspaper in a large town. But I remember how, in one of our meetings, he spoke with distrust and dislike of the environment of cities as unwholesome and distracting, if not demoralizing (very much to the effect of Tolstoy's philosophy in the matter), and in his short stories his types are village types. They are often such when he finds them in the city, but for much the greater part he finds them in the village; and they are always, therefore, distinctively American; for we are village people far more than we are country people or city people. In this as in everything else we are a medium race, and it was in his sense, if not in his knowledge of this fact, that Bellamy wrote so that there is never a word or a look to the reader implying that he and the writer are of a different sort of folk from the people in the story.

Looking Backward, with its material delights, its communized facilities and luxuries, could not appeal to people on lonely farms who scarcely knew of them, or to people in cities who were tired of them, so much as to that immense average of villagers, of small-town-dwellers, who had read much and seen something of them, and desired to have them. This average, whose intelligence forms the prosperity of our literature, and whose virtue forms the strength of our nation, is the environment which Bellamy rarely travels out of in his airiest romance. He has its curiosity, its principles, its aspirations. He can tell what it wishes to know, what problem will hold it, what situation it can enter into, what mystery will fascinate it, and what noble pain it will bear. It is by far the widest field of American fiction; most of our finest artists work preferably in it, but he works in it to different effect from any other. He takes that life on its mystical side, and deals with types rather than with characters; for it is one of the prime conditions of the romancer that he shall do this. His people are less objectively than subjectively present; their import is greater in what happens to them than in what they are. But he never falsifies them or their circumstance. He ascertains them with a fidelity that seems almost helpless, almost ignorant of different people, different circumstance; you would think at times that he had never known, never seen, any others; but of course this is only the effect of his art.

When it comes to something else, however, it is still with the same fidelity that he keeps to the small-town average,—the American average. He does not address himself more intelligently to the mystical side of this average in Dr. Heidenhoff's Process, or Miss Ludington's Sister, or any of his briefer romances, than to its ethical side in Equality. That book disappointed me, to be frank. I thought it artistically inferior to anything else he had done. I thought it was a mistake to have any story at all in it, or not to have vastly more. I felt that it was not enough to clothe the dry bones of its sociology with paper garments out of Looking Backward. Except for that one sublime moment when the workers of all sorts cry to the Lords of the Bread to take them and use them at their own price, there was no thrill or throb in the book. But I think now that any believer in its economics may be well content to let them take their chance with the American average, here and elsewhere, in the form that the author has given them. He felt that average so wittingly that he could not have been wrong in approaching it with all that public school exegesis which wearies such dilettanti as myself.

Our average is practical as well as mystical; it is first the dust of the earth, and then it is a living soul; it likes great questions simply and familiarly presented, before it puts its faith in them and makes its faith a life. It likes to start to heaven from home, and in all this Bellamy was of it, voluntarily and involuntarily. I recall how, when we first met, he told me that he had come to think of our hopeless conditions suddenly, one day, in looking at his own children, and reflecting that he could not place them beyond the chance of want by any industry or forecast or providence; and that the status meant the same impossibility for others which it meant for him. I understood then that I was in the presence of a man too single, too sincere, to pretend that he had begun by thinking of others, and I trusted him the more for his confession of a selfish premise. He never went back to himself in his endeavor, but when he had once felt his power in the world, he dedicated his life to his work. He wore himself out in thinking and feeling about it, with a belief in the good time to come that penetrated his whole being and animated his whole purpose, but apparently with no manner of fanaticism. In fact, no one could see him, or look into his quiet, gentle face, so full of goodness, so full of common sense, without perceiving that he had reasoned to his hope for justice in the frame of things. He was indeed a most practical, a most American man, without a touch of sentimentalism in his humanity. He believed that some now living should see his dream—the dream of Plato, the dream of the first Christians, the dream of Bacon, the dream of More—come true in a really civilized society; but he had the patience and courage which could support any delay.

These qualities were equal to the suffering and the death which came to him in the midst of his work, and cut him off from writing that *one more book* with which every author hopes to round his career. He suffered greatly, but he bore his suffering greatly; and as for his death, it is told that when, toward the last, those who loved him were loath to leave him at night alone, as he preferred to be left, he asked, "What can happen to me? I can only die."

I am glad that he lived to die at home in Chicopee,—in the village environment by which he interpreted the heart of the American nation, and knew how to move it more than any other American author who has lived. The theory of those who think differently is that he simply moved the popular fancy; and this may suffice to explain the state of some people, but it will not account for the love and honor in which his name is passionately held by the vast average, East and West. His fame is safe with them, and his faith is an animating force concerning whose effect at this time or some other time it would not be wise to prophesy. Whether his ethics will keep his aesthetics in remembrance I do not know; but I am sure that one cannot acquaint one's self with his merely artistic work, and not be sensible that in Edward Bellamy we were rich in a romantic imagination surpassed only by that of Hawthorne.

HAMLIN GARLAND (1860-1940)

HAMLIN GARLAND describes for us, in the *Bookman* of March, 1917, his introduction to Howells. One afternoon in the spring of 1881 his eye fell on "a small volume labelled *The Undiscovered Country*, by W. D. Howells," lying on the counter of a bookstand in the post office of Osage, Iowa, and, having half an hour to wait for the mail, he picked up the book and began to read. From the very first page he "dimly perceived something new in fiction." But when the letters were distributed, he laid the book aside; and he did not finish reading the story until he moved to Boston five years later. There he heard again the name of W. D. Howells.

In 1884 Garland left his father's Wisconsin farm and traveled east to prepare himself to be a teacher; in Boston he read in the public library and earned a precarious living by lecturing and reviewing. When he arrived, poor and friendless, Howells had recently returned to this country after a year in Europe. His reviews of new books by John Hay, Edward Bellamy, and others, appearing in the current issues of the *Century*, announced to his readers that Howells was again interested in untried talent. The first chapter of *Silas Lapham*, published in the November, 1884, *Century*, brought Howells, according to Garland, to "the full tide of his powers" and made him the subject of conversation on all sides. In fact, Garland soon discovered that Howells had become something like "a literary issue" in the clubs, newspaper offices, and drawing rooms Garland himself had begun to frequent. "All literary Boston was divided into three parts," Garland reported—those who read Howells and liked him, those who read Howells and disliked him, and those who hated Howells without reading him.

Garland found himself in the third group and did not hesitate to attack "this fictional iconoclast" in his public lectures because of Howells' reputation as an antiromantic. However, after Garland "studied to improve [his] case" and actually read *A Lady of the Aroostook, A Modern Instance, A Woman's Reason, Silas Lapham,* and all the other volumes on the lengthening shelf of Howells fiction, he became not only a convert to the cause of realism but Howells' devoted disciple and "public advocate." This attitude of enthusiastic admiration marked Garland's many comments on Howells for the rest of his life. It was Garland, indeed, who proposed the toast at Howells' eightieth birthday dinner in 1917, "To William Dean Howells, dean of us all!"

Garland did not exaggerate when in his *Bookman* article he called his meeting with Howells in June, 1887,[15] "the most important literary event" of his life, for it was a long and sympathetic conversation held with Howells at this time that led to the writing of Garland's most important work, *Main-Travelled Roads,* in 1891. Before his visit with Howells in Auburndale, near Boston, Garland had published only a few poems and descriptive sketches. Howells listened to the younger man's literary dreams and encouraged him to give up his lecturing. He advised him to go back to South Dakota, where his parents were then living, and write stories of his own life. "Whatever you do, keep to the West," Howells admonished.

Though as a boy Garland had read Eggleston's *Hoosier Schoolmaster* with eager delight, he had not thought of himself as a chronicler of his own drab Western surroundings. Soon after his talk with Howells, however, he returned to South Dakota, helped on his father's farm, and began to write of the treeless plains, the boxlike houses, and the barbed-wire fences, which he saw with a new clarity. "The ugliness, the endless drudgery, and the loneliness of the farmer's lot smote me with stern insistence. I was the militant reformer." The result of Garland's indignation was a collection of stories that has become a classic in our literature, *Main-Travelled Roads.*

The book was instantly recognized by Howells and acclaimed from "The Editor's Study" of September, 1891. In his review of this "robust and terribly serious" book, Howells declared that these stories are full of the bitter and burning dust, the foul and trampled slush of the common avenues of life: the life of the men who hopelessly and cheerlessly make the wealth that enriches the alien and the idler, and impoverishes the producer. . . . The stories are full of those gaunt, grim, sordid, pathetic, ferocious figures . . . whose blind groping for fairer conditions is so grotesque to the newspapers and so menacing to the politicians.

Main-Travelled Roads marked the high standard that Garland set for himself and never again attained, for he was incapable of keeping to his chosen path. He tells us that after his first visit with Howells, he called on him as often as he dared, to discuss his social ideas and his literary plans. After one such meeting Howells stood with his visitor at the garden gate and, with a wave of the hand, said, ''There lies your path.'' ''Alas!'' added Garland in his retelling of the episode in 1917, ''how far I have fallen short of the aspirations which filled my heart at that moment!'' Garland the farm boy, self-educated too late, was unable to sort out the eagerly seized ideas that he had discovered in the Boston Public Library, and hence lost the way marked out for him by his first book.

Howells remembered, in his 1912 essay on Garland, here reprinted, that Garland, when he first called on him in 1887, was ''preaching Georgism equally with veritism in the same generous self-forgetfulness.'' Howells, who had already found his own path amid conflicting literary and economic ideologies, did not fall into step with Garland in his views of ''veritism,'' a word that Garland borrowed, he tells us, from Eugène Véron's *Aesthetics*. The two men continued to discuss economic as well as literary questions during the two years, 1889–1891, that Howells and Garland were both in Boston. Their discussions were enlarged by their association during those years with Bellamy's Nationalist Club and the Christian Socialists.

How far Garland was influenced by his older, more experienced monitor, how far he departed from him and discerned a new dimension in the word ''realism,'' can be determined by comparing Howells' *Criticism and Fiction* (1891) with Garland's *Crumbling Idols* (1894), which, we discover, differ from one another more in emotional tone than in critical ideas. Garland does not define veritism, for example, with any exactness: instead, he casts around realism a romantic aura and calls it veritism. "The veritist," he says, "is really an optimist, a dreamer. He sees life in terms of what it might be, as well as in terms of what it is; but he writes of what is, and, at his best, suggests what is to be by contrast."

An "optimist" and "a dreamer" who adopts economic cure-all theories becomes a preacher in spite of his belief, shared with the more sober realist, that a novelist's duty is to present the concrete incident, not to moralize it. Garland's "fine courage to leave a fact with the reader, ungarnished and unvarnished," Howells recognized and applauded in his 1891 review of *Main-Travelled Roads;* when Garland seemed to have lost this adherence to "the fact" in his later novels full of partially assimilated economic theory, Howells merely refrained from reviewing them, even though *A Spoil of Office* (1891) was dedicated to him as "The Foremost Historian of Our Common Lives and the Most Vital Figure in Our Literature."

That Garland was able to resist preaching in his stories as well as he did was due, he tells us, "in large measure to Howells, who taught me to exemplify, not to preach." In letters, conversations, and reviews Howells also attempted to curb Garland's romantic tendency—always dangerously associated with his didactic impulse—but without success. In his introduction to Garland's novel *They of the High Trails* (1908), Howells mildly remarked that "we own we enjoyed the level footing more and got our breath better in the lower altitudes of *Main-Travelled Roads,*" where Howells and Garland first met. "Be true to the dream of thy youth—the dream of an absolute and unsparing veritism," Howells cautioned Garland in 1910. Whether Howells felt that his younger friend did in fact remain constant to "his old young ideal of veritism" may be studied in Howells' 1912 account of "Mr. Garland's Books."

Mr. Garland's Books *

THE life of any man of letters who has lived long with strong convictions becomes part of the literary history of his time, though the history may never acknowledge it. Or, if the reader will not allow so much as this, then we may agree that inevitably such an author's life becomes bound up with that of his literary contemporaries, especially his younger contemporaries. He must have been friends or foes with nearly all of them; in the wireless of print, whether he ever met them otherwise or not, he must have exchanged with them flashes of reciprocity or repulsion, electrical thrills, which remain memories after they have ceased to be actual experiences. Shall I own at once that in this abstract case some such relation was concrete in me and the author of these admirable books; that he is the younger contemporary and I the man of letters who has lived long with strong convictions?

I suppose we were friends in the beginning, and never foes, because he had strong convictions too, and they were flatteringly like mine. When first we met, twenty years ago or more, in a pleasant suburb of Boston, there was nothing but common ground between us, and our convictions played over it together as freely and affectionately as if they had been fancies. He was a realist to the point of idealism, and he was perhaps none the less, but much the more, realist because he had not yet had time to show his faith by his works. I mean his inventive works, for he was already writing radiant criticism in behalf of what he called veritism,[16] a word he had borrowed, with due thanks, from a French critic whom he was reading with generous devotion and talking into any body who would hear him. There were as yet only a few years between him and the Wisconsin farm which grew him as genuinely as if he had been a product of its soil. He was as poor as he was young, but he was so rich in purpose of

* From the *North American Review*, October, 1912.

high economic and social import that he did not know he was poor. Some day, perhaps, he will himself tell the tale of that struggle to make both ends meet, the artistic and the economic ends, in those Boston days, and by teaching and lecturing to earn the time that he wished to spend in literature. He gladly wrote in the Boston newspapers for nothing, and in the best of them he was given the free hand which was far better for his future than a conditioned salary could have been. As to his present, he was such an ardent believer in Henry George's plan for abolishing poverty that with his heart and hopes fixed on a glorious tomorrow for all men he took no thought of his own narrow day.

He seems at that time to have gone about preaching Georgism equally with veritism in the same generous self-forgetfulness. A large public, much more intelligent than the public which reads novels instead of listening to lectures, already knew him, but I was never of this worthier public so far as hearing him speak was concerned, while we continued of the same thinking about fiction. When we both left Boston and came to New York, neither of us experienced that mental expansion, not to call it distension, which is supposed to await the provincial arriving in the metropolis; we still remained narrow-mindedly veritistic. This possibly was because we were both doubly provincial, being firstly Middle Westerners, and secondarily Bostonians, but for whatever reason it was he had already begun to show his faith by his works, in those severely conscientious studies of Wisconsin life, which I should not blame the reader for finding the best of his doing in fiction. But it is not necessary to make any such restriction in one's liking in order to vouch one's high sense of the art and the fact in *Main-Travelled Roads* and *Other Main-Travelled Roads*. The volumes are happily named: these highways are truly the paths that the sore feet of common men and women have trodden to and fro in the rude new country; they are thick with the dust and the snow of fierce summers and savage winters. I do not say but they lead now and then through beautiful springtimes and mellow autumns; they mostly seek the lonely farmers, but sometimes they tarry in sociable villages where youth and love have their dances. I do not think that I am wrong in taking "The Return of the Private" and "Up the Coolly" for types of the bare reality prevailing with the hot pity which comes from the painter's heart for the conditions he depicts.

At the time he was telling these grim stories of farm life in the West—that is, in the later years of his Boston sojourn—our author was much in contact with that great and sincere talent James A. Hearne, whom it was a dramatic education to know.[17] So far as one influenced the other I do not think Mr. Garland owed more to Hearne than Hearne to him in practising in their art the veritism which they both preached. If I may confess a dreadful secret, I suspected them both at that time of being unconsciously romantic at heart, and only kept to reality because they did not know unreality. Hearne, in spite of such cunningest pieces of excelling nature as "Margaret Fleming" and "Drifting Apart," was often tempted to do the thing that was not—beautifully not, as Mr. James might say—in his other plays,[18] and was willing to please his public with it, for of course the thing that is not will mainly please any public. I have no doubt the author of these books did very greatly help to stay the dramatist in his allegiance to the thing that was, while on his part Hearne doubtless helped his younger friend to clarify his native dramatic perception. At any rate, some plays relating to the nearer and farther West which Mr. Garland wrote in the heyday of his Hearne friendship (it lasted to the end of the great player's life) may have been inspired by his association with a man who was to the heart of his true humanity essentially representative. As both were secretly romantic a little, so both were openly idyllic a good deal. Of course Mr. Garland's treatment of country life is more direct, more authentic, more instructive, and there is pretty sure always to be a thrill or a throe of indignant compassion in it which the milder poet did not impart to his hearers. Some plays which the novelist wrote at this time (notably "Under the Lion's Paw," a tragedy of Far Western farming) expressed this compassion, still more directly and explicitly than the stories of *Main-Travelled Roads,* and I believe it the loss of our theatre that they have never got upon the stage.

But no doubt fortune that kept him to the story written to

HAMLIN GARLAND

be read was not so unintelligent as her enemies might like to imagine. In the invention of such a group of novels as *Rose of Dutcher's Coolly, The Eagle's Heart, Hesper, The Captain of the Gray-Horse Troop, Money Magic,* and *Cavanagh* he has justified the constancy of purpose which the fickle goddess has shown in his case. She seems to have known what she was about in guiding his talent from West to Farther West, from the farms to the wilds, and liberating it to the freer and bolder adventure which he must always have loved.

If the work seems to lose at times in closeness of texture on its westering way, it gains in breadth. The workman does not change in it; he is always what he was: mindful of his own past, and tenderly loyal to the simplest life, as embracing not only the potentialities but the actualities of beauty, of sublimity.

Mr. Garland's books seem to me as indigenous, in the true sense, as any our country has produced. They are western American, it is true, but America is mostly western now. But that is a question apart from the question of the author's literature. I for my part find this wholesome and edifying: I like being in the company of a man who believes so cordially in man's perfectibility; who believes that wrongs can really be righted, and that even in our depraved conditions, which imply selfishness as the greatest personal good, teaches that generosity and honesty and duty are wiser and better things. I like stirring adventure without bloodshed, as I find it so often in these pages; I like love which is sweet and pure, chivalry which is in its senses, honor for women which recognizes that while all women ultimately are good and beautiful some women are better and beautifuler than others, and some are more foolish and potentially vile enough to keep the balance of the virtues even between the sexes.

This brings me to the question of something in the author's work which I suppose has given question of its advantage to other readers as well as myself. It is something which deals with character rather than incident, and has nothing of that bad allure of so much modern fiction in its dances of the seven veils. It puts the gross passions, the propensities to shame, rather than flatters or entices them; but it doesn't recognize the beast in the

263

man's desire of the woman, the satyr leer which is the complement of the lover's worship. In *Rose of Dutcher's Coolly,* in *Hesper,* in *Money Magic,* measurably in them all, you find the refusal, when it comes to the fact, to ignore what cannot be denied. I am old-fashioned, and I have moments when I could wish that the author had not been of such unsparing conscience. That is all, and with this wish noted I can give myself to the entire pleasure which the purity and wholesomeness of his fiction offers me.

There is an apparent want cf continuity in his work. He has ventured from the open day at times into the mystical regions of old night, but the books here are an unbroken series in which the average West and Far West may behold itself as in a mirror. There is throughout, and in spite of everything, a manly and hopeful belief in the perfectibility of man and things. Indians, soldiers, woods, water, he teaches me that they may all be considered to the national advantage. He does not allow me to despair of the hero, even of the heroine; he finds me new sorts of these in every sort of people and persuades me that they may still be naturally and charmingly in love with one another. He paints me a West in which the physiognomy of the East has put on new expression, kindlier, gentler, truer, he makes me imagine a life out there which has been somehow pacified and humbled and exalted as an escape from death and restored in gratitude to new usefulness in that new air on that new earth. He holds me with his story and he will not let me go till he has taught me something more than he has told me. Greater than this I do not think we ought to ask of any, and if we do I am sure we shall not get it.

At the end of my praise I feel that I should leave it largely unspoken if I did not specify the power with which certain characters and characteristics are enforced in this book and in that. With some hesitancy I choose *Money Magic* as possibly the most masterly of the author's books. More than any other since the stories of *The Main-Travelled Roads,* it expresses constancy to his old young ideal of veritism. He has not hesitated to take clay from the "rude breast of the unexhausted West," and he has molded it in shapes which breathe as with a life of their own like Bertha and Mart Haney (Marshall Haney); she the young, beautiful wife and he an old broken gambler, are heroine and hero on their own plane, where they may stand with the creations of great modern fiction. The make as well as the manner of the uneducated girl, derived from New England and bred on the frontier, but not with all her slang and Far Western freedom underbred, is not more credibly portrayed than the rough Irishman who has outlived the saloon-keeper and desperado and has re-entered as it were into the primitive goodness of his generous nature. In both the power and the meaning of vast wealth is studied, what it can and what it cannot do, as I do not remember to have found it studied before. They seem the witnesses of its magic, rather than sorcerers who work it. The situation is most interesting, and the situation in Mr. Garland's book is what interests me more than the action; if I can know what people are, rather than what they do, I am the more content; and I have noted with the satisfaction which I should like to have others feel the clear conditioning of his people. In fact, his people mainly derive their importance from that. A given book of his does not present a problem for this or that character to solve it; it describes a condition which shall test him. Sometimes it is an unfriendly condition, sometimes not; but the business is to show how he copes with it. In *Money Magic*, in *The Captain of the Gray-Horse Troop*, in *Cavanagh*, in *Hesper*, in *The Eagle's Heart*, it is always a sense of the conditions which remains with me. I remember the persons from them as I learned to recognize the persons from them in their full meaning. Perhaps this is so in the novels of others, but I do not think it is, and I consider Mr. Garland's novels for this reason particularly valuable as materials of social history, no less than as very entertaining personal history. One cannot read them (and if you begin on them you *must* read them) without becoming more and more convinced that it is our conditioning which determines our characters, even though it does not always determine our actions. The strong man, the good woman, grows stronger and better for the struggle with them, though I am not sure that this is what Mr. Garland is conscious of seeking to show. I dare say that he paints them and cannot help painting them, because in his own career he has been passionately sensible of their stress even when he has not mastered all their meaning. As a singularly American artist, too, he instinctively devotes himself to the portrayal of conditions because America itself is all a novel condition.

STEPHEN CRANE (1871–1900)

≫≪

The one thing that deeply pleases me in my literary life—brief and inglorious as it is—is the fact that men of sense believe me to be sincere. "Maggie," published in paper covers, made me the friendship of Hamlin Garland and W. D. Howells, and the one thing that makes my life worth living in the midst of all this abuse and ridicule is the consciousness that never for an instant have those friendships at all diminished.

THUS wrote Stephen Crane to Joseph O'Connor, literary editor of the Rochester *Post-Express*, on April 18, 1900, from England where he had gone to escape the outcry against *Maggie*. Early in the following June, Crane died of tuberculosis in the Black Forest, Germany.

In *Roadside Meetings* Garland tells the story of his introduction to Crane in the summer of 1891, when he was lecturing on "The Local Novel" at a summer hotel in Avon-by-the-Sea, New Jersey. After the lecture, Crane, a young reporter for the Philadelphia *Record*, asked to see the speaker's manuscript. Though Garland was not particularly impressed by the "slim boyish" reporter, "with sallow complexion, and light hair," he was struck by the correctness of the report that appeared the next day. The two met several times later, but more "to pass ball" and to discuss pitching than to talk about literature. Garland had all but forgotten his younger friend when, in March, 1892, he received through the mail a yellow paperbound volume called *Maggie, A Girl of the Streets*, by "Johnstone Smith." Across the cover, in Crane's clear script, was written: "The reader of this book must inevitably be shocked, but let him keep on till the end, for in it the writer has put something which is important."

Needless to say, Garland was not shocked; instead he secured Crane's address—he was then living in New York at The Art

Students' League on East Twenty-third Street—and invited him to dinner. Crane, "pale and thin," soon appeared on Garland's doorstep, confessed his authorship of *Maggie*, and told him the story of the unsold copies of the small book, which had been privately printed with money borrowed from Crane's older brother. Garland urged Crane to mail a copy to Howells, who in the stress of his own writing and editing was not able to read the story for several weeks. Howells recalled the incident in a letter to Crane's wife, written to her after the death of her husband:

Hamlin Garland first told me of "Maggie," which your husband then sent me. I was slow in getting at it, and he wrote me a heartbreaking note to the effect that he saw that I did not care for his book. On this I read it, and found that I did care for it immensely. I asked him to come and see me, and he came to tea and stayed far into the evening, talking about his work, and the stress that was on him to put in the profanities which I thought would shock the public from him, and about the semi-savage poor, whose type he had studied in that book.

No doubt Crane told Howells of the miserable evening he had spent the year before with Richard Watson Gilder, editor of the *Century*, who had turned down the manuscript of *Maggie* because of the "damns and the curse yehs." Howells, for his part, encouraged Crane to publish his work. In an essay on Frank Norris in the *North American Review* of December, 1902, Howells recalls these conversations with Crane. "It was interesting to hear him defend what he had written, in obedience to his experience of things, against any charge of convention. 'No,' he would contend, in behalf of the profanities of his people, 'that is the way they *talk*. I have thought of that, and whether I ought to leave such things out, but if I do I am not giving the thing as I *know* it.'"

Mildred Howells, in *Life in Letters,* tells us that her father continued to do all that he could to help launch Crane, himself taking *Maggie* from publisher to publisher. Equally important to the younger man were the conversations he held with Howells in his apartment overlooking Central Park. "William Dean Howells leaned his cheek upon the two outstretched fingers of his right hand and gazed thoughtfully at the window—the panes black from the night without—although studded once or twice with little electric stars far up on the west side of the Park.'' Thus Crane begins his report of a discursive talk with Howells for the October 28, 1894, issue of *The New York Times*. On one occasion Howells read Emily Dickinson's poetry aloud to his visitor. On another evening he presented Crane to dinner guests at his home with the remark, ''Here is a writer who has sprung into life fully armed.'' Later in the evening, when Mark Twain was under discussion, Howells observed, ''Mr. Crane can do things that Clemens can't.''

The things that Crane could do that struck Howells as of immense importance are analyzed by Howells in his comment on *Maggie* for ''Life and Letters'' in *Harper's Weekly*, June 8, 1895, and in his review of *The Red Badge of Courage* for the same column soon after its publication the following October. In spite of Howells' practical acumen as an editor, what he particularly commended in *Maggie* was that ''it embodied perhaps the best tough dialect which has yet found its way into print.'' This ''parlance,'' impossible ''to cultured ears,'' may be heard, Howells remarked, ''by any listener in the streets of certain quarters of the city'' where Howells himself often strolled. Howells liked *The Red Badge* less than *Maggie*, because ''the dialect does not so much convince.'' But here it is ''the divinations of motive and experience . . . decidedly on the psychological side'' which make the book worth-while, ''as an earnest of the greater things that we may hope from a new talent working upon a high level, not quite clearly as yet, but strenuously.''

On the strength of the success of *The Red Badge of Courage* both in England and in the United States, *Maggie*, together with *George's Mother*, at last appeared in both countries in June, 1896. ''An Appreciation by W. D. Howells'' was added to the London edition; this ''Appreciation'' was expanded for the New York *World* of July 26, 1896, and published under the rather journalistic title, ''New York Low Life in Fiction,'' the first and second sections of which are reproduced below.

On July 30, before Crane went to report the Greco-Turkish War for the New York *Journal* and the *Westminster Gazette*, Howells sent him ''this notice of your last book.'' Howells saw no more of Crane, for the next year he was in Cuba, reporting the Spanish-American War for the New York *World*. He returned to New York in 1899 to meet the meaningless "abuse and ridicule" that made him decide to leave the country permanently in December, 1899. Crane lived in England until he went to Germany in a futile attempt to regain his health.

In a presentation copy of *The Red Badge of Courage* dated August 17, 1896, is the following inscription in Crane's hand: "To W. D. Howells this small and belated work as a token of veneration and gratitude of Stephen Crane for the many things he has learned of the common man and, above all, for a certain re-adjustment of his point of view victoriously concluded some time in 1892."

We know that Crane was familiar with Howells' little volume, *Criticism and Fiction*, published in May, 1891, since from this book Garland quoted his definition of realism in the lecture that Crane reported the following summer. Howells' repeated insistence on "truth" as the basis of "art," expressed so fully in *Criticism and Fiction*, is restated by Crane in these words: "To keep close to my honesty is my supreme ambition." Referring back to this period in his life, Crane wrote in 1896:

I developed all alone a little creed of art which I thought was a good one. Later I discovered that my creed was identical with the one of Howells and Garland and in this way I became involved in the beautiful war between those who say that art is men's substitute for nature and we are most successful in art when we approach the nearest to nature and truth, and those who say—well, I don't know what they say . . . they fight villainously and keep Garland and I [sic] out of the big magazines. Howells, of course, is too powerful for them.

The "re-adjustment" of his point of view surely had something to do with Crane's discovery, in the summer of 1891, that his quest for truth was not such a bitterly lonely one as he had supposed. Howells frequently announced that he was fighting for realism, and Garland insisted that he believed in veritism; Crane might have preferred the word naturalism, made familiar by Zola's *Experimental Novel* (1880). All three were engaged in "the beautiful war" and did not quarrel over terminology. "I decided," wrote Crane, "that the nearer a writer gets to life, the greater he becomes as an artist, and most of my prose writings have been towards the goal partially described by that misunderstood and abused word, realism.'' When Howells asserted in *Criticism and Fiction* that ''in the whole range of fiction'' he knew of ''no true picture of life— that is, of human nature—which is not also a masterpiece of literature,'' he made room for ''the little tragedy,'' *Maggie*, which came to him in the mail the following year from an unknown young journalist.

New York Low Life in Fiction *

IT IS a long time since I have seen the once famous and popular play ''A Glance at New York,'' [19] but I distinctly recall through the misty substance of some forty-five very faded years the heroic figures of the volunteer fireman and his friends, who were the chief persons of the piece. I do not remember the others at all, but I remember Mose, and Sikesy, and Lize. Good and once precious fragments of the literature linger in my memory, as: '' 'Mose,' says he, 'git off o' dem hose, or I'll swat you over der head wid der trumpet.' And I didn't get off o' der hose, and he did swat me over der head wid der trumpet.'' Other things have gone, things of Shakespeare, of Alfieri, of Cervantes, but these golden words of a forgotten dramatist poet remain with me.

It is interesting to note that the first successful attempt to represent the life of our streets was in dramatic form. Some actor saw and heard things spoken with the peculiar swagger and whopper-jaw [20] utterance of the b'hoy of those dreadful old days, when the blood-tubs and the plug-uglies reigned over us, and Tammany was still almost purely American, and he put them on the stage and spread the poison of them all over the land, so that there was hardly anywhere a little blackguard boy who did not wish to act and talk like Mose.

* The *New York World*, July 26, 1896.

The whole piece was painted with the large brush and the vivid pigments of romanticism, and yet the features were real. So it was many long years later when Mr. Harrigan came to the study of our low life in his delightful series of plays. He studied it in the heyday of Irish supremacy, when Tammany had become almost purely Celtic, and he naturally made his heroes and heroines Irish. The old American b'hoy [21] lingered among them in the accent and twist of an occasional barkeeper, but the brogue prevailed, and the high-shouldered sidelong carriage of the Americanized bouncer of Hibernian blood.

The treatment, however, was still romanticistic, though Mr. Harrigan is too much of a humorist not to return suddenly to nature, at times from the most exalted regions of "imagination." He loves laughing and making laugh, and that always saved him when he was in danger of becoming too grand, or fine, or heroic. He had moments when he was exactly true, but he allowed himself a good many friendly freedoms with the fact, and the effect was not always that of reality.

It seemed to me that so far as I could get the drift of a local drama in German which flourished at one of the East Side theatres a winter ago, that the author kept no more faithfully to life than Mr. Harrigan, and had not his sublime moments of absolute fidelity. In fact, the stage is almost as slow as criticism to perceive that there is no other standard for the arts but life, and it keeps on with the conventional in motive even when the matter is honest, apparently in the hope that by doing the stale falsehood often enough it will finally affect the witness like a fresh verity. It is to the honor of the stage, however, that it was first to recognize the value of our New York low life as material; and I shall always say that Mr. Harrigan, when he was not overpowered by a tradition or a theory, was exquisitely artistic in his treatment of it. He was then true, and, as Tolstoy has lately told us, to be true is to be moral.

The fiction meant to be read, as distinguishable from the fiction meant to be represented, has been much later in dealing with the same material, and it is only just beginning to deal with it in the spirit of the great modern masters. I cannot find that such clever and amusing writers as Mr. Townsend, or Mr. Ralph, or Mr. Ford have had it on their consciences to report in the regions of the imagination the very effect of the life which they all seem at times to have seen so clearly. There is apparently nothing but the will that is wanting in either of them, but perhaps the want of the will is the want of an essential factor, though I should like very much to have them try for a constant reality in their studies; and I am far from wishing to count them out in an estimate of what has been done in that direction. It is only just to Mr. Stephen Crane, however, to say that he was first in the field where they made themselves known earlier. His story of "Maggie, a Girl of the Streets," which has been recently published by the Appletons, was in the hands of a few in an edition which the author could not even give away three years ago; and I think it is two years, now, since I saw "George's Mother," which Edward Arnold has brought out, in the manuscript.

Their present publication is imaginably due to the success of "The Red Badge of Courage"; but I do not think that they will owe their critical acceptance to the obstreperous favor which that has won. As pieces of art they are altogether superior to it, and as representations of life their greater fidelity cannot be questioned. In "The Red Badge of Courage" there is a good deal of floundering, it seems to me. The narration repeats itself; the effort to imagine, to divine, and then to express ends often in a huddled and confused effect; there is no repose, such as agony itself assumes in the finest art, and there is no forward movement. But in these other books the advance is relentless; the atmosphere is transparent; the texture is a continuous web where all the facts are wrought with the unerring mastery of absolute knowledge. I should say that "The Red Badge of Courage" owed its excellence to the training the author had given himself in setting forth the life he knew in these earlier books of later publication. He learned to imagine vividly from seeing clearly.

There is a curious unity in the spirit of the arts; and I think that what strikes me most in the story of "Maggie" is that quality of fatal necessity which dominates Greek tragedy. From the conditions it all had to be, and there were the conditions. I felt this in Mr. Hardy's "Jude," where the principle seems to become conscious in the writer; but there is apparently no consciousness of any such motive in the author of "Maggie." Another effect is that

273

of an ideal of artistic beauty which is as present in the working out of this poor girl's squalid romance as in any classic fable. This will be foolishness, I know, to the foolish people who cannot discriminate between the material and the treatment in art, and who think that beauty is inseparable from daintiness and prettiness, but I do not speak of them. I appeal rather to such as feel themselves akin with every kind of human creature, and find neither high nor low when it is a question of inevitable suffering, or of a soul struggling vainly with an inexorable fate.

My rhetoric scarcely suggests the simple terms the author uses to produce the effect which I am trying to report again. They are simple, but always most graphic, especially when it comes to the personalities of the story: the girl herself, with her bewildered wish to be right and good; with her distorted perspective; her clinging and generous affections; her hopeless environments; the horrible old drunken mother, a cyclone of violence and volcano of vulgarity; the mean and selfish lover, a dandy tough, with his gross ideals and ambitions; her brother, an Ishmaelite from the cradle, who, with his warlike instincts beaten back into cunning, is what the b'hoy of former times has become in our more strenuously policed days. He is indeed a wonderful figure in a group which betrays no faltering in the artist's hand. He, with his dull hates, his warped good-will, his cowed ferocity, is almost as fine artistically as Maggie, but he could not have been so hard to do, for all the pathos of her fate is rendered without one maudlin touch.

So is that of the simple-minded and devoted and tedious old woman who is George's mother in the book of that name. This is scarcely a study at all, while Maggie is really and fully so. It is the study of a situation merely: a poor, inadequate woman, of a commonplace religiosity, whose son goes to the bad. The wonder of it is the courage which deals with persons so absolutely average, and the art that graces them with the beauty of the author's compassion for everything that errs and suffers. Without this feeling the effects of his mastery would be impossible, and if it went further or put itself into the pitying phrases it would annul the effects. But it never does this; it is notable how in all respects the author keeps himself well in hand. He is quite honest with his reader. He never shows his characters or his situations in any sort of sentimental glamour; if you will be moved by the sadness of common fates you will feel his intention, but he does not flatter his portraits of people or conditions to take your fancy.

In George and his mother he has to do with folk of country origin as the city affects them, and the son's decadence is admirably studied; he scarcely struggles against temptation, and his mother's only art is to cry and to scold. Yet he loves her, in a way, and she is devotedly proud of him. These simple country folk are contrasted with simple city folk of varying degrees of badness. Mr. Crane has the skill to show how evil is greatly the effect of ignorance and imperfect civilization. The club of friends, older men than George, whom he is asked to join, is portrayed with extraordinary insight, and the group of young toughs whom he finally consorts with is done with even greater mastery. The bulldog motive of one of them, who is willing to fight to the death, is most impressively rendered.

The student of dialect ought to be interested in the parlance of the class Mr. Crane draws upon for his characters. They are almost inarticulate; not merely the grammar, but the language itself, decays in their speech. The Theta sound, so characteristic of English, disappears altogether, and the vowels tend to lose themselves in the obscure note heard in *fur* and *stir*. What will be the final language spoken by the New Yorker? We shall always write and print a sort of literary English, I suppose, but with the mixture of races the spoken tongue may be a thing composite and strange beyond our present knowledge.

FRANK NORRIS (1870-1902)

୬୬୬

FRANK NORRIS spent the spring of 1898 in New York as a reader for the publishing house of *McClure's Magazine,* having been invited to join the staff on the strength of the first few installments of *Moran,* which appeared in the San Francisco *Wave* between January and April, 1898. In a small back bedroom on West Thirty-third Street, Norris was lonely, homesick, and often ill. Through Gelett Burgess he met Howells soon after his arrival and discussed with him the manuscript of his new novel, *McTeague,* on which he had been working under Lewis Edwards Gates at Harvard. On March 12, 1898, Norris wrote to a friend in San Francisco: "By the way, Mr. Burgess took me to call on Howells last Monday evening. We had a most charming visit. I find him one of the most delightful men imaginable and, as you told me, especially fond of good talk."

Howells reviewed the completed novel, *Moran of the Lady Letty,* the following December for *Literature,* commending it—in spite of its "romanticistic" atmosphere—for "being so boldly circumstanced in the light of common day, and in a time and place of our own." He reviewed *McTeague* for the March 24, 1899, issue of the same magazine, claiming for himself a "weather-wise eye," for in his earlier review he had suggested that one might expect a change in Norris' writing from the romantic to the realistic. He recognized, however, the influence of Zola, whose novels Norris had been eagerly reading at the University of California after his return from a year in Paris. In his adherence to Zola, Howells pointed out, Norris had stressed the brutal side of his story: therefore his "true picture of life is not true, because it leaves beauty out." A mild reproof, indeed, amid the flood of reviews that stamped *McTeague* as "repulsive," "sordid," and "brutal." In an undated letter of thanks for Howells' kind no-

FRANK NORRIS

tice Norris showed that he agreed—within limits—with his strictures and that he was "buzzing" with new ideas for a trilogy of
far wider scope. This letter is the only one we have from Norris
to his older friend and adviser; it indicates the confidence and the
respectful appreciation this vigorous exponent of the new school
of naturalism felt for his elderly critic.

61 Washington Sq. S.
Tuesday

MY DEAR MR. HOWELLS:

Need I say how pleased and delighted I am over your review of
McTeague in this last number of *Literature*. It has encouraged me
more than anything that has ever been said of my work. I believe, too,
you were quite right in saying that it was not the whole truth, and that
the novel that is true to life cannot afford to ignore the finer things. I
agree in every one of your criticisms always excepting the anticlimax,
the "death in the desert" business. I am sure that has its place. I have
the idea of another novel or rather series of novels buzzing in my head
these days. I think there is a chance for somebody to do some great
work with the West and California as a background, and which will be
at the same time thoroughly American. My idea is to write three novels
around the one subject of *Wheat*. First, a story of California (the producer), second, a story of Chicago (the distributor), third, a story of
Europe (the consumer) and in each to keep up the idea of this huge
Niagara of wheat rolling from West to East. I think a big epic trilogy
could be made out of such a subject, that at the same time would be
modern and distinctly American. The idea is so big that it frightens me
at times but I have about made up my mind to have a try at it.

Thanking you again, Mr. Howells, for your very kind interest in my
work, believe me

Very sincerely,
FRANK NORRIS

By April, Norris had gone to California to gather his material
for *The Octopus;* before leaving he discussed the plan for the
trilogy with Howells "in one of those few meetings which seem,
too late, as if they might have been so many," which Howells
recalled a few weeks after the death of the younger man in the
essay on Norris written for the *North American Review*, December, 1902. Norris' plan must have been particularly interesting
to Howells, for the enormous concept was an illustration of Howells' own idea of social "complicity."

In his essay "The Novel With a Purpose" (1901) Norris explained his technique for the sociological novel, which "draws conclusions from a whole congeries of forces, social tendencies, race impulses" and devotes itself "not to a study of men, but of man," a technique that Norris had discovered in Zola's *Experimental Novel* (1880). *The Octopus*, a milestone in American naturalistic fiction, was finally published in April, 1901; Howells reviewed it for "The Editor's Easy Chair" the following October, and welcomed "this poet among the California wheat-fields," who had written "an epic of Zolaesque largeness." Norris, said Howells, owed to the great romantic realist "nothing but the conception of treating a modern theme epically. That is what he did, as to the place, in his *McTeague*, and that is what he has done, as to the action, in *The Octopus*." The tricks of Norris' character portrayal, the melodrama of his plot, Howells deplored in his, on the whole laudatory, appraisal of "a great book, simple, sombre, large, and of a final authority as the record of a tragical passage of American, of human events." The justice of Howells' final appraisal of Norris' books may be seen in an article by Howells on Arnold Bennett, which is included in this volume (see p. 345).

Norris died one year after Howells' review of *The Octopus*. Howells, looking back over the astonishing career of the first genuine American naturalistic writer, remarked, "I never met him but he made me feel that he could do it, the thing he meant to do, and do it robustly and quietly." The thing he meant to do was "the great American novel." *The Pit*, published posthumously in March, 1903, and reviewed the same month by Howells in *Harper's Weekly*, became at once a best seller, almost fulfilling this hope for the readers of that decade. It is interesting to notice that the rough and powerful hero of the novel, Curtis Jadwin, considered Howells his favorite novelist when he was introduced to Howells' stories by his culture-seeking wife. "Lapham he loved as a brother," wrote Norris.

A year before his death Norris hastily composed several essays on the novel, later gathered together under the title *The Responsibilities of the Novelist*. In one, entitled "An American School of Fiction?" Norris discussed Howells. Though Norris referred to Howells' realism as "the drama of the broken teacup, the adventure of an invitation to dinner," he also observed:

Of all producers of American fiction he has had the broadest vision, at once a New Englander and a New Yorker, an Easterner and—in the Eastern sense—a Westerner. But one swallow does not make a summer, nor does one writer constitute a "school." Mr. Howells has had no successors. Instead, just as we had with *Lapham* and *The Modern Instance* laid the foundation of fine, hardy literature, that promised to be our very, very own, we commence to build upon it a whole confused congeries of borrowed, faked, pilfered romanticisms.

Romantic follower of Zola though he was, Norris was also the successor of Howells and an admirer of *Silas Lapham* and *A Modern Instance*. *The Responsibilities of the Novelist* drew from Howells' *Criticism and Fiction* as well as from Zola's *Experimental Novel*. In one of the essays in his collection, "A Plea for Romantic Fiction," Norris carried on the familiar argument with Howells as to the meaning of realism and romance, giving his own twist to the definition of romance, to which, as a follower of Zola, he was partial:

Now, let us understand at once what is meant by Romance and what by Realism. Romance, I take it, is the kind of fiction that takes cognizance of variations from the type of normal life. Realism is the kind of fiction that confines itself to the type of normal life. According to this definition, then, Romance may even treat of the sordid, the unlovely—as, for instance, the novels of M. Zola. (Zola has been dubbed a Realist, but he is, on the contrary, the very head of the Romanticists.) Also, Realism, used as it sometimes is as a term of reproach, need not be in the remotest sense or degree offensive, but on the other hand respectable as a church and proper as a deacon—as, for instance, the novels of Mr. Howells.

A Case in Point *

THE question of expansion in American fiction lately agitated by a lady novelist of Chicago [22] with more vehemence than power, and more courage than coherence, seems to me again palpitant in the case of a new book by a young writer, which I feel obliged at once to recognise as altogether a remarkable book. Whether we

* *Literature*, March 24, 1899.

shall abandon the old-fashioned American ideal of a novel as something which may be read by all ages and sexes, for the European notion of it as something fit only for age and experience, and for men rather than women; whether we shall keep to the bounds of the provincial proprieties, or shall include within the imperial territory of our fiction the passions and the motives of the savage world which underlies as well as environs civilisation, are points which this book sums up and puts concretely; and it is for the reader, not for the author, to make answer. There is no denying the force with which he makes the demand, and there is no denying the hypocrisies which the old-fashioned ideal of the novel involved. But society, as we have it, is a tissue of hypocrisies, beginning with the clothes in which we hide our nakedness, and we have to ask ourselves how far we shall part with them at his demand. The hypocrisies are the proprieties, the decencies, the morals; they are by no means altogether bad; they are, perhaps, the beginning of civilisation; but whether they should be the end of it is another affair. That is what we are to consider in entering upon a career of imperial expansion in a region where the Monroe Doctrine was never valid. From the very first Europe invaded and controlled in our literary world. The time may have come at last when we are to invade and control Europe in literature. I do not say that it has come, but if it has we may have to employ European means and methods.

It ought not to be strange that the impulse in this direction should have come from California, where, as I am always affirming rather than proving, a continental American fiction began. I felt, or fancied I felt, the impulse in Mr. Frank Norris' "Moran of the Lady Letty," and now in his "McTeague" I am so sure of it that I am tempted to claim the prophetic instinct of it. In the earlier book there were, at least, indications that forecast to any weather-wise eye a change from the romantic to the realistic temperature, and in the later we have it suddenly, and with the overwhelming effect of a blizzard. It is saying both too much and too little to say that Mr. Norris has built his book on Zolaesque lines, yet Zola is the master of whom he reminds you in a certain epical conception of life. He reminds you of Zola also in the lingering love of the romantic, which indulges itself at the end

FRANK NORRIS

in an anticlimax worthy of Dickens. He ignores as simply and
sublimely as Zola any sort of nature or character beyond or above
those of Polk Street in San Francisco, but within the ascertained
limits he convinces you, two-thirds of the time, of his absolute
truth to them. He does not, of course, go to Zola's lengths,
breadths, and depths; but he goes far enough to difference his
work from the old-fashioned American novel.

Polite readers of the sort who do not like to meet in fiction people of the sort they never meet in society will not have a good
time in "McTeague," for there is really not a society person in
the book. They might, indeed, console themselves a little with an
elderly pair of lovers on whom Mr. Norris wreaks all the sentimentality he denies himself in the rest of the story; and as readers of that sort do not mind murders as much as vulgarity, they
may like to find three of them, not much varying in atrocity. Another sort of readers will not mind the hero's being a massive
blond animal, not necessarily bad, though brutal, who has just wit
enough to pick up a practical knowledge of dentistry and follow
it as a trade; or the heroine's being a little, pretty, delicate daughter of German-Swiss emigrants, perfectly common in her experiences and ideals, but devotedly industrious, patient, and
loyal. In the chemistry of their marriage McTeague becomes a
prepotent ruffian, with always a base of bestial innocence; and
Trina becomes a pitiless miser without altogether losing her
housewifely virtues or ceasing to feel a woman's rapture in giving up everything but her money to the man who maltreats her
more and more, and, finally, murders her.

This is rendering in coarse outline the shape of a story realized
with a fulness which the outline imparts no sense of. It abounds in
touches of character at once fine and free, in little miracles of
observation, in vivid insight, in simple and subtle expression.
Its strong movement carries with it a multiplicity of detail which
never clogs it; the subordinate persons are never shabbed or
faked; in the equality of their treatment their dramatic inferior-
ity is lost; their number is great enough to give the feeling of a
world revolving round the central figures without distracting the
interest from these. Among the minor persons, Maria Macapa,
the Mexican chorewoman, whose fable of a treasure of gold turns

the head of the Polish Jew Zerkow, is done with rare imaginative force. But all these lesser people are well done; and there are passages throughout the book that live strongly in the memory, as only masterly work can live. The one folly is the insistence on the love-making of those silly elders, which is apparently introduced as an offset to the misery of the other love-making; the anti-climax is McTeague's abandonment in the alkali desert, handcuffed to the dead body of his enemy.

Mr. Norris has, in fact, learned his lesson well, but he has not learned it all. His true picture of life is not true, because it leaves beauty out. Life is squalid and cruel and vile and hateful, but it is noble and tender and pure and lovely, too. By and by he will put these traits in, and then his powerful scene will be a reflection of reality; by and by he will achieve something of the impartial fidelity of the photograph. In the mean time he has done a picture of life which has form, which has texture, which has color, which has what great original power and ardent study of Zola can give, but which lacks the spiritual light and air, the consecration which the larger art of Tolstoy gives. It is a little inhuman, and it is distinctly not for the walls of living-rooms, where the ladies of the family sit and the children go in and out. This may not be a penalty, but it is the inevitable consequence of expansion in fiction.

PART IV

FURTHER CRITICAL ISSUES*

INTRODUCTION

THEODORE DREISER thus described his first sight of W. D. Howells "one January day in Fifth Avenue" at the turn of the century:

Some one who knew him said, "Here comes Howells," and I saw a stout, thick-set, middle-aged man trudging solemnly forward. He was enveloped in a great fur ulster, and peered, rather ferociously, upon the odds and ends of street life that passed. He turned out again and again for this person and that, and I wondered why a stout man with so fierce a mien did not proceed resolutely forward, unswerving for the least or the greatest.

Because Howells did not "proceed resolutely forward" but always turned out for "the least or the greatest," glancing at the odds and ends of life, Part IV contains some of his views on subjects that perhaps lie just outside the range of the critic of fiction, but nevertheless seemed to Howells, as he peered shrewdly to either side of the street, very near to the problems of the novel writer.

Howells' lack of a formal education, his early plunge into journalism, his absorbingly busy days as an editor and contributor to magazines, and the extraordinary diversity of his literary output have made many readers conclude that he had no sustained beliefs. As Dreiser observed in the essay quoted above, Howells' "sympathies are right, but he is not primarily a deep reasoner; . . . he is inclined to let the great analysis of things go by the board." He added, however, after considering Howells' drawbacks as a logical thinker, "the man has the speculative philo-

* The notes to Part IV begin on p. 383.

sophic make-up.'' It is this quality in Howells' temperament that invites us to stray beyond the bounds of his strictly literary reviews and essays. We shall limit ourselves to what contributes to the concept of Howells as a *writer* of novels and of Howells as a *critic* of novels, in the last decade of the nineteenth century and the first of the twentieth, and shall refuse to be tempted by his essays on, for example, the copyright law, the Spanish-American War, or woman suffrage, New York apartments, interesting and important as these topics are.

Portions of two companion essays, ''The Country Printer'' and ''The Man of Letters as a Man of Business,'' both of which appeared in *Scribner's* in 1893, are in the first section, ''The Writer as Worker.'' In these essays Howells coped with the question of literature in a democracy, from the pre-Civil War days of the small-town paper interested in poetry and stories as well as in politics, to the era of great magazine corporations, such as Harper Brothers, serializing the novelist's work and then publishing it in book form. Where does the writer fit into a moneymaking society? A critic who does not know what he thinks of the baffling problems of the publisher-editor-contributor relationship in an acquisitive society is a critic who is astray in Altruria. Though Howells often strolled about this noncompetitive land during these years, he was found most frequently behind a large desk piled high with manuscripts, his own or others'. Howells helped many aspirants to place their writing; he seldom failed to do well by his own.

The section ''The Teacher, the Critic, and 'the Vital Word' '' contains two selections that suggest why Howells remained a critic-novelist and did not become a teacher, in spite of the several offers of professorships he received and the numerous honorary degrees bestowed upon him. He became, by popular acclaim rather than by university appointment, ''the Dean of American Writers.'' The first selection is a letter of 1882 from Switzerland to President Daniel Coit Gilman of Johns Hopkins University, who had urged upon Howells a professorship. In his reply Howells not only described his qualifications—and limitations—as a teacher and the democratic methods he would like to use in his classroom, but also unconsciously, described himself as a critic.

Tempted as he was by the flattering offer, he did not accept it though the teacher-critic relationship always remained in his mind an important one.

Almost twenty years later Howells again had occasion to consider the critical problem involved in teaching literature in an American university. The second selection is a review of Barrett Wendell's *Literary History of America*, written by Howells for the *North American Review* of April, 1901. Howells' essay reflects his impatience with the aristocratic view of literature, then exemplified by the popular Harvard professor. In tearing to shreds the basic assumptions of this book, Howells restated not only his own reading of Lowell, Holmes, Emerson, and in fact of most of the great names of a past day in Boston, but also expressed with vehemence his appreciation of the new writers from all sections of the country, quite unknown to Wendell. Behind Howells' indignation lay his belief in a democratic literature, which was bound up with his faith in the United States.

What particular ''hopes for the great American novel'' did Howells see in our rapidly growing business civilization, where, as he observed to Dreiser, ''the struggle really does grow more bitter''? Are our ''opportunities'' different from those of the English or the European novelist? Are our ''poor,'' for instance, as dramatic, when put in a novel, as the ''poor people'' of Dostoevsky? Do writers on social and economic questions suggest new material to the fictionist? Can the American writer no longer find an ''opportunity'' in his own locality as differences in regions fade? And is ''the great American novel'' about to appear? In these essays, and in hundreds more contributed by Howells to magazines of the 1890's and early 1900's, one can discover the outlines at least of Howells' mature views on novel writing.

The next section, ''Poetry or Prose?'' suggests to the reader the fact that Howells' brooding mind recognized no neat boundaries of thought and feeling between poetry and prose. Not only did Howells try every form of writing, but he also welded together the personality of the small boy in Ohio imitating Pope's verses, the poetizing consul in Venice, the magazine editor pleading for realism, the writer of popular—and often poetic—novels and plays illustrating his theory of realism, the observer traveling in England, Spain, and other lands. Nothing by way of experience was ever lost on him; all flowed together in "one continuous whole," as he admitted. In "The Turning Point of My Life" Howells at seventy-three looked back at the "continuous whole" of his developing literary powers and reflected upon the "turn" he had taken many years before from poetry to prose. A further thought brought him to the reflection that no turn was taken at all, for poetry and prose are essentially one. Not only does this conclusion affect Howells' peculiarly prosaic way of judging poetry, but it also throws light on his poetic feeling for prose.

Howells' speech at his seventy-fifth anniversary dinner is reprinted in the last section; his backward and forward glance in this address indicates that he grew steadily in his understanding of himself in his dual role of novelist and critic in American society. His views on literature underwent no violent change; they developed with the changing circumstances of his personal fortunes and of those of the country, and they continued to grow until his death in 1920. In this speech by the aging Dean the reader is invited to share the pleasure of familiar Howellsian ideas, that carry him back to the great days of *Criticism and Fiction* and still farther back into the *Atlantic* and *Harper's,* when "European masters" were being discovered by Howells and introduced to "American writers." Recognizing "the new conditioning of our lives," Howells did not acknowledge that he felt bewildered by changes of style in writing and shifts in modes of thought. The essential difference in the present from the past was to him, he asserted, that "all of human life" was turning "more to the light of democracy, of equality."

Was Howells, in his ramified relations with three generations of American writers, "greater than his literary volumes make him out to be," as Dreiser said? Was he "even greater than his reputation"? If Dreiser's judgment is correct, the explanation perhaps lies in the fact that Howells' critical sensibilities never slept, whether he himself was writing a novel, composing a review, or conversing with a young author—or with the person sitting next to him on a train. The same critical eye observed a streetcar strike, watched children playing in a city park, studied the paintings in an art exhibit, or read the manuscript of an unknown contributor. Since what Howells was seeking was the "truth" of these various experiences, since he believed that a democratic society depends on the articulate communication of these truths, his personal manner was always direct and clear, both in writing and in speaking. He never subscribed to a dogma, creed, or cause; though he sympathized with many, he maintained a certain aloofness. Dreiser's description of Howells after an interview brings the older man directly before us:

His manner is so simple, his wonder at life so fresh and unsatisfied, that he appeals to the student and observer as something truly rare—a wholly honest man. He is evidently so honest at heart that he is everywhere at home with himself, and will contribute that quiet, home-like atmosphere to everything and everybody around. He will compel sincerity in you, when you talk with him, not by any suggestion from him, but by the wholesome atmosphere which he exhales, and which steals over all, and makes plain that forms and slight conventionalities are not necessary.

Howells' manner, no doubt, contributed to the notable success of the anniversary dinner at Sherry's given by the House of Harper to the occupant of "The Easy Chair." But the gala occasion called for a speech, not for a detailed account of Howells' long and—as he then thought—futile battle for serious standards in fiction.

Several weeks before the dinner, on February 17, 1912, J. Henry Harper's history, *The House of Harper,* had appeared, giving the first full account of that establishment. "Mr. Howells's Paper" was Howells' response to Harper's request for his memories of the early days of their relationship. The paper, offered to Harper as a personal reminiscence, and not considered by Howells in any sense an essay, seemed to Harper, because of its modesty and charm, to be worth printing in its entirety.

Howells' speech and Howells' paper, different as they are in tone, together bring to a conclusion the long history of *Criticism and Fiction.*

THE WRITER AS WORKER

⊱⊰

INTRODUCTION

IN "The Country Printer" we are introduced to Howells setting type at his father's printing press in Jefferson, Ohio, occasionally slipping into the column of print his own poem or story. At the same time the boy is listening intently to the political or literary conversation of his elders, rejoicing over the arrival of a new press, or pondering the problem of subscribers who do not pay. In "The Man of Letters as a Man of Business" we meet the same practical and literary temperament more than forty years later, reflecting on the difficulties that beset the young writer attempting to break into literature without ceasing to be a journalist. We recognize Howells also in the shrewd but sensitively responsive editor scanning his pile of manuscripts, on the lookout for the fresh and the honest. Just as Howells was a "writer" at the age of seven, and also a hardworking typesetter, so he is at fifty-six primarily a writer and only secondarily a practical editor.

Howells' earliest memories "concern a country newspaper, or, rather, a country printing-press," owned and directed by his father, William Cooper Howells. Behind all his later thoughts on journalism, literature, and society lies his memory of the family newspaper in which politics and poetry were mingled and problems of taste and questions of finance were faced every day. *The Sentinel*, the Howells' family paper, was ardently Free-soil in the troubled days before the Civil War; it reached between fifteen and sixteen thousand subscribers, all of whom the Howellses hoped to convert to antislavery even though many of them failed to pay their two-dollar annual subscription fee. The press was "domiciled in an old dwelling house," which was wintry cold during long months when fierce winds blew across the lakes. However, the printing office, though unheated, "was the center of civic and social interests; it was frequented by visitors at all times," especially on publication day, "when the school girls and young ladies of the village flocked in, and made it like a scene of comic opera, with their pretty dresses and faces and their eager chatter, and lively energy in folding and addressing the paper to the subscribers."

We have chosen the portions of this account of a country paper of the 1850's in which Howells described the make-up of the paper, divided among poems, political diatribes, and letters to the editor; the unending struggle with advertisers, those "live business men" who threatened editorial integrity; and, perhaps most important of all, the conversations of the journeymen who produced *The Sentinel*.

"The Country Printer" became, three years after its appearance in *Scribner's*, the first essay in *Impressions and Experiences* (1896). In like manner "The Man of Letters as the Man of Business," also published in *Scribner's* in 1893, became the lead essay in *Literature and Life* (1902). Together they form a unit that pushes back Howells' peculiar blend of practical, social, and literary thinking to his early experiences in a family printing office in the Western Reserve and brings it forward to the crowded offices of New York newspapers and magazines of the 1890's. Howells' realism is closely related to the fact that he always had to put his talents to work in the world-as-it-is; his critical editorial decisions are circumstanced by his shrewd knowledge of the public, which he understood and frequently led.

When Howells wrote these two essays for *Scribner's* he had left the Study and had ventured forth on an extensive program of free lancing before he rejoined *Harper's* in 1900 as the occupant of "The Easy Chair." He had been briefly coeditor of the *Cosmopolitan,* and for this magazine he had begun to write "Letters of an Altrurian Traveller" one month after the second of the two essays for *Scribner's* had appeared. In these "Letters," gathered in book form the following year, Howells pondered the question of the artist in an acquisitive society in the light of his conversations with Bellamy, Hale, Garland, Bliss, and others connected with the Nationalists and the Society of Christian Socialists in Boston, from 1889 to 1891. "I think that every man ought to work for his living, without exception, and that, when he has once avouched his willingness to work, society should provide him with work and warrant him a living. I do not think any man ought to live by an art."

In "The Man of Letters as a Man of Business" one finds the ideas later to be used in "Letters of an Altrurian Traveller"; soon, however, Howells turned to practical questions of author-editor-publisher relations, closing with the remark, though the artist is "*apparently* of the classes," he is "*really* of the masses." He is, in fact, "in a transition state"; "perhaps the artist of the future will see in the flesh the accomplishment of that human quality of which the instinct has been divinely planted in the human soul." Portions of this long essay will be found below.

Thoughts on brotherhood, equality, liberty, and the nature of American democracy were expressed in the *North American Review,* the *Century,* and the *Forum* during the two years immediately following Howells' essays for *Scribner's.* Important as these abstract questions were to Howells, especially during the 1890's, he never lost sight of the actual world of editors, publishers, advertisers, journalists, and—occasionally—gifted writers with manuscripts to sell. Howells, as a man of letters as well as a man of business, offered the wisdom and experience of forty years to the struggling writers in a business civilization, for his understanding of the practical problems of the creative artist may be traced to the mind of a small boy setting type for his father.

The Country Printer *

ON THE first page of *The Sentinel* was a poem, which I suppose I must have selected, and then a story, filling all the rest of the page, which my brother more probably chose; for he had a decided fancy in fiction, and had a scrap-book of inexhaustible

* *Scribner's,* May, 1893.

riches, which he could draw upon indefinitely for old personal or family favorites. The next page was filled with selections of various kinds, and with original matter interesting to farmers. Then came a page of advertisements, and then the editorial page, where my father had given his opinions of the political questions which interested him, and which he thought it the duty of the country press to discuss, with sometimes essays in the field of religion and morals. There was a letter of two columns from Washington, contributed every week by the congressman who represented our district; and there was a letter from New York, written by a young lady of the county who was studying art under a master of portraiture then flourishing in the metropolis; if that is not stating it too largely for the renown of Thomas Hicks, as we see it in a vanishing perspective. The rest of this page, as well as the greater part of the next, was filled with general news, clipped from the daily papers, and partly condensed from them. There was also such local intelligence as offered itself, and communications on the affairs of village and county; but the editor did not welcome tidings of new barns and abnormal vegetation, or flatter hens to lay eggs of unusual size or with unusual frequency by undue public notice. All that order of minute neighborhood gossip which now makes the country paper a sort of open letter, was then unknown. He published marriages and deaths, and such obituary notices as the sorrowing fondness of friends prompted them to send him; and he introduced the custom of publishing births, after the English fashion, which the people took to kindly.

We had an ambition, even so remotely as that day, in the direction of the illustration which has since so flourished in the newspapers. Till then we had never gone further in the art than to print a jubilant raccoon over the news of some Whig victory, or, what was to the same purpose, an inverted cockerel in mockery of the beaten Democrats; but now we rose to the notion of illustrated journalism. We published a story with a woodcut in it, and we watched to see how that cut came out all through the edition with a pride that was perhaps too exhaustive; at any rate, we never tried another.

Of course, much of the political writing in the paper was controversial, and was carried on with editors of other opinions elsewhere in the county, for we had no rival in our own village. In this, which has always been the vice of American journalism, the country press was then fully as provincial as the great metropolitan journals are now. These may be more pitilessly personal in the conduct of their political discussions, and a little more skilled in obloquy and insult; but the bickering went on in the country papers quite as idly and foolishly. I fancy nobody really cared for our quarrels, and that those who followed them were disgusted when they were more than merely wearied.

The space given to them might better have been given even to original poetry. This was sometimes accepted, but was not invited; though our sixth page commonly began with a copy of verse of some kind. Then came more prose selections, but never at any time accounts of murder or violent crimes, which the editor abominated in themselves and believed thoroughly corrupting. Advertisements of various kinds filled out the sheet, which was simple and quiet in typography, wholly without the hand-bill display which now renders nearly all newspapers repulsive to the eye. I am rather proud, in my quality of printer, that this was the style which I established; and we maintained it against all advertisers, who then as now wished to out-shriek one another in large type and ugly woodcuts.

It was by no means easy to hold a firm hand with the ''live business men'' of our village and county, who came out twice a year with the spring and fall announcements of their fresh stocks of goods, which they had personally visited New York to lay in; but one of the moral advantages of an enterprise so modest as ours was that the counting-room and the editorial-room were united under the same head, and this head was the editor's. After all, I think we lost nothing by the bold stand we made in behalf of good taste, and at any rate we risked it when we had not the courage to cut off our delinquent subscribers.

We had business advertising from all the villages in the county, for the paper had a large circle of readers in each, and a certain authority, in virtue of representing the county seat. But a great deal of our advertising was of patent medicines, as the advertising still is in the country papers. It was very profitable, and so was the legal advertising, when we could get the money for it. The money

292

had to come by order of court, and about half the time the order of court failed to include the costs of advertising. Then we did not get it, and we never got it, though we were always glad to get the legal advertising on the chance of getting the pay. It was not official, but was made up of the lawyers' notices to defendants of the suits brought against them. If it had all been paid for, I am not sure that we should now be in a position to complain of the ingratitude of the working-classes, or prepared to discuss, from a vantage of personal experience, the duty of vast wealth to the community; but still we should have been better off for that money, as well as the money we lost by a large and loyal list of delinquent subscribers. From time to time there were stirring appeals to these adherents in the editorial columns, which did not stir them, and again the most flattering offers to take any kind of produce in payment of subscription. Sometimes my brother boldly tracked the delinquents to their lairs. In most cases I fancy they escaped whatever arts he used to take them; many died peacefully in their beds afterward, and their debts follow them to this day. Still, he must now and then have got money from them, and I am sure he did get different kinds of "trade." Once, I remember, he brought back in the tail of his wagon a young pig, a pig so very young that my father pronounced it "merely an organization." Whether it had been wrought to frenzy or not by the strange experiences of its journey, I cannot say, but as soon as it was set down on the ground it began to run madly, and it kept on running till it fell down and perished miserably. It had been taken for a year's subscription, and it was quite as if we had lost a delinquent subscriber.

Upon the whole, our paper was an attempt at conscientious and self-respecting journalism; it addressed itself seriously to the minds of its readers; it sought to form their tastes and opinions. I do not know how much it influenced them, if it influenced them at all, and as to any effect beyond the circle of its subscribers, that cannot be imagined, even in a fond retrospect. But since no good effort is altogether lost, I am sure that this endeavor must have had some tacit effect; and I am very sure that no one got harm from a sincerity of conviction that devoted itself to the highest interest of the reader, that appealed to nothing base, and flattered nothing foolish in him. It went from our home to the homes of the people in a very literal sense, for my father usually brought his exchanges from the office at the end of his day there, and made his selections or wrote his editorials while the household work went on around him, and his children gathered about the same lamp, with their books or their jokes; there were apt to be a good many of both.

Our county was the most characteristic of that remarkable group of counties in northern Ohio, called the Western Reserve, and forty years ago the population was almost purely New England in origin, either by direct settlement from Connecticut, or indirectly after the sojourn of a generation in New York State. We were ourselves from southern Ohio, where the life was then strongly tinged by the adjoining life of Kentucky and Virginia, and we found these transplanted Yankees cold and blunt in their manners; but we did not undervalue their virtues. They formed in that day a leaven of right thinking and feeling which was to leaven the whole lump of the otherwise proslavery or indifferent State; and I suppose that outside of the antislavery circles of Boston, there was nowhere in the country a population so resolute and so intelligent in its political opinions. They were very radical in every way, and hospitable to novelty of all kinds. I imagine that they tested more new religions and new patents than have been even heard of in less inquiring communities. When we came among them they had lately been swept by the fires of spiritualism, which had left behind a great deal of smoke and ashes where the inherited New England orthodoxy had been. A belief in the saving efficacy of spirit phenomena still exists among them, but not, I fancy, at all in the former measure, when nearly every household had its medium, and the tables that tipped outnumbered the tables that did not tip. The old New York *Tribune,* which was circulated in the county almost as widely as our own paper, had deeply schooled the people in the economics of Horace Greeley, and they were ready for any sort of millennium, religious or industrial, that should arrive, while they looked very wisely after the main chance in the meantime. They were temperate, hardworking, hard-thinking folks, who dwelt on their scattered farms, and came up to the County Fair once a year, when they were apt to visit the printing-office and pay for their papers. In spite of the

English superstition to the contrary, the average American is not very curious, if one may judge from his reticence in the presence of things strange enough to excite question; and if our craft surprised these witnesses they rarely confessed it.

They thought it droll, as people of the simpler occupations are apt to think all the more complex arts, and one of them once went so far in expression of his humorous conception as to say, after a long stare at one of the compositors dodging and pecking at the type in his case, "Like an old hen pickin' up millet." This sort of silence, and this sort of comment, both exasperated the printers, who took their revenge as they could. They fed it full, once, when a country subscriber's horse, tied before the office, crossed his hindlegs and sat down in his harness like a tired man, and they proposed to go out and offer him a chair, to take him a glass of water, and ask him to come inside. But fate did not often give them such innings; they mostly had to create their chances of reprisal, but they did not mind that.

There was always a good deal of talk going on, but although we were very ardent politicians, the talk was not political. When it was not mere banter, it was mostly literary; we disputed about authors among ourselves, and with the village wits who dropped in. There were several of these who were readers, and they liked to stand with their backs to our stove and challenge opinion concerning Holmes and Poe, Irving and Macaulay, Pope and Byron, Dickens and Shakespeare.

It was Shakespeare who was oftenest on our tongues; indeed, the printing-office of former days had so much affinity with the theatre that compositors and comedians were easily convertible; and I have seen our printers engaged in hand-to-hand combats with column-rules, two up and two down, quite like the real bouts on the stage. Religion entered a good deal into our discussions, which my father, the most tolerant of men, would not suffer to become irreverent, even on the lips of law-students bathing themselves in the fiery spirit of Tom Paine. He was willing to meet anyone in debate of moral, religious, or political questions, and the wildest-haired Comeouter, the most ruthless sceptic, the most credulous spiritualist, found him ready to take them seriously, even when it was hard not to take them in joke.

295

It was part of his duty, as publisher of the paper, to bear patiently with another kind of frequenter: the type of farmer who thought he wished to discontinue his paper, and really wished to be talked into continuing it. I think he rather enjoyed letting the subscriber talk himself out, and carrying him from point to point in his argument, always consenting that he knew best what he wanted to do, but skilfully persuading him at last that a home-paper was more suited to his needs than any city substitute. Once I could have given the heads of his reasoning, but they are gone from me now. The editor was especially interested in the farming of the region, and I think it was partly owing to the attention he called to the question that its character was so largely changed. It is still a dairy country, but now it exports grain, and formerly the farmers had to buy their flour.

He did not neglect any real local interest in his purpose of keeping his readers alive to matters of more general importance, but he was fortunate in addressing himself to people who cared for the larger, if remoter, themes he loved. In fact, as long as slavery remained a question in our politics, they had a seriousness and dignity which the present generation can hardly imagine; and men of all callings felt themselves uplifted by the appeal this question made to their reason and conscience. My father constantly taught in his paper that if slavery could be kept out of the territories it would perish, and, as I have said, this was the belief of the vast majority of his readers. They were more or less fervid in it, according to their personal temperaments; some of them were fierce in their convictions, and some humorous, but they were all in earnest. The editor sympathized more with those who took the true faith gayly. All were agreed that the Fugitive Slave Law was to be violated at any risk; it would not have been possible to take an escaping slave out of that county without bloodshed, but the people would have enjoyed outwitting his captors more than destroying them. Even in the great John Brown times, when it was known that there was a deposit of his impracticable pikes somewhere in our woods, and he and his followers came and went among us on some mysterious business of insurrectionary aim, the affair had its droll aspects which none appreciated more keenly than the Quaker-born editor. With his cheerful scepticism, he could never have believed that any harm or danger would come of it all; and I think he would have been hardly surprised to wake up any morning and find that slavery had died suddenly during the night, of its own iniquity.

He was like all country editors then, and I dare say now, in being a printer as well as an editor, and he took a full share in the mechanical labors. These were formerly much more burdensome, for twice or three times the composition was then done in the country offices. At the present day the country printer buys of a city agency his paper already printed on one side, and he gets it for the cost of the blank paper, the agency finding its account in the advertisements it puts in. Besides this patent inside, as it is called, the printer buys stereotyped selections of other agencies, which offer him almost as wide a range of matter as the exchange newspapers he used to choose from. The few columns left for local gossip and general news, and for whatever editorial comment he cares to make on passing events, can be easily filled up by two compositors. But in my time we had three journeymen at work and two or three girl-compositors, and commonly a boy-apprentice besides. The paper was richer in a personal quality, and the printing-office was unquestionably more of a school. After we began to take girl-apprentices it became coeducative, as far as they cared to profit by it; but I think it did not serve to widen their thoughts or quicken their wits as it did those of the men. They looked to their craft as a living, not as a life, and they had no pride in it. They did not learn the whole trade, as the journeymen had done, and served only such a brief apprenticeship as fitted them to set type. They were then paid by the thousand ems, and their earnings were usually as great at the end of a month as at the end of a year. But the boy who came up from his father's farm, with the wish to be a printer because Franklin had been one, and with the intent of making the office his university, began by sweeping it out, by hewing wood and carrying water for it. He became a roller-boy, and served long behind the press before he was promoted to the case, where he learned slowly and painfully to set type. His wage was forty dollars a year and two suits of clothes, for three years, when his apprenticeship ended, and his wander-years (too often literally) began. He was glad of being inky and stained with the marks of his trade; he wore a four-cornered paper cap, in the earlier stages of his service, and even an apron. When he became a journeyman, he clothed himself in black doeskin and broadcloth, and put on a silk hat, and the thinnest-soled boots that could be found, and comported himself as much like a man of the world as he knew how to do. His work brought him acquainted with a vast variety of interests, and kept his mind as well as hands employed; he could not help thinking about them, and he did not fail to talk about them. His comments had generally a slightly acid flavor, and his constant survey of the world, in the "map of busy life," always under his eye, bred in him the contempt of familiarity. He was none the less agreeable for that, and the jokes that flew about from case to case in our office were something the editor would have been the last man to interfere with. He read or wrote through them all, and now and then turned from his papers to join in them.

The Man of Letters as a Man of Business *

I THINK that every man ought to work for his living, without exception, and that, when he has once avouched his willingness to work, society should provide him with work and warrant him a living. I do not think any man ought to live by an art. A man's art should be his privilege, when he has proven his fitness to exercise it, and has otherwise earned his daily bread; and its results should be free to all. There is an instinctive sense of this, even in the midst of the grotesque confusion of our economic being; people feel that there is something profane, something impious, in taking money for a picture, or a poem, or a statue. Most of all, the artist himself feels this. He puts on a bold front with the world, to be sure, and brazens it out as Business; but he knows very well that there is something false and vulgar in it; and that the work which cannot be truly priced in money cannot be truly paid

* *Scribner's*, October, 1893.

in money. He can, of course, say that the priest takes money for reading the marriage service, for christening the new-born babe, and for saying the last office for the dead; that the physician sells healing; that justice itself is paid for; and that he is merely a party to the thing that is and must be. He can say that, as the thing is, unless he sells his art he cannot live, that society will leave him to starve if he does not hit its fancy in a picture, or a poem, or a statue; and all this is bitterly true. He is, and he must be, only too glad if there is a market for his wares. Without a market for his wares he must perish, or turn to making something that will sell better than pictures, or poems, or statues. All the same, the sin and the shame remain, and the averted eye sees them still, with its inward vision. Many will make believe otherwise, but I would rather not make believe otherwise; and in trying to write of Literature as Business I am tempted to begin by saying that Business is the opprobrium of Literature.

Literature is at once the most intimate and the most articulate of the arts. It cannot impart its effect through the senses or the nerves as the other arts can; it is beautiful only through the intelligence; it is the mind speaking to the mind; until it has been put into absolute terms, of an invariable significance, it does not exist at all. It cannot awaken this emotion in one, and that in another; if it fails to express precisely the meaning of the author, if it does not say *him*, it says nothing, and is nothing. So that when a poet has put his heart, much or little, into a poem, and sold it to a magazine, the scandal is greater than when a painter has sold a picture to a patron, or a sculptor has modelled a statue to order. These are artists less articulate and less intimate than the poet; they are more exterior to their work; they are less personally in it; they part with less of themselves in the dicker. It does not change the nature of the case to say that Tennyson and Longfellow and Emerson sold the poems in which they couched the most mystical messages their genius was charged to bear mankind. They submitted to the conditions which none can escape; but that does not justify the conditions, which are none the less the conditions of hucksters because they are imposed upon poets. . . .

There are several men of letters among us who are such good men of business that they can command a hundred dollars a thousand words for all they write. It is easy to write a thousand words a day, and supposing one of these authors to work steadily, it can be seen that his net earnings during the year would come to some such sum as the President of the United States gets for doing far less work of a much more perishable sort. If the man of letters were wholly a business man, this is what would happen; he would make his forty or fifty thousand dollars a year, and be able to consort with bank presidents, and railroad officials, and rich tradesmen, and other flowers of our plutocracy on equal terms. But, unfortunately, from a business point of view, he is also an artist, and the very qualities that enable him to delight the public disable him from delighting it ininterruptedly. "No rose blooms right along," as the English boys at Oxford made an American collegian say in a theme which they imagined for him in his national parlance; and the man of letters, as an artist, is apt to have times and seasons when he cannot blossom. Very often it shall happen that his mind will lie fallow between novels or stories for weeks and months at a stretch; when the suggestions of the friendly editor shall fail to fruit in the essays or articles desired; when the muse shall altogether withhold herself, or shall respond only in a feeble dribble of verse which he might sell indeed, but which it would not be good business for him to put on the market. But supposing him to be a very diligent and continuous worker, and so happy as to have fallen on a theme that delights him and bears him along, he may please himself so ill with the result of his labors that he can do nothing less in artistic conscience than destroy a day's work, a week's work, a month's work. I know one man of letters who wrote to-day and tore up to-morrow for nearly a whole summer. But even if part of the mistaken work may be saved, because it is good work out of place, and not intrinsically bad, the task of reconstruction wants almost as much time as the production; and then, when all seems done, comes the anxious and endless process of revision. These drawbacks reduce the earning capacity of what I may call the high-cost man of letters in such measure that an author whose name is known everywhere, and whose reputation is commensurate with the boundaries of his country, if it does not transcend them, shall have the income, say, of a rising young physician, known to a few people in a subordinate city.

In view of this fact, so humiliating to an author in the presence of a nation of business men like ours, I do not know that I can establish the man of letters in the popular esteem as very much of a business man after all. He must still have a low rank among practical people; and he will be regarded by the great mass of Americans as perhaps a little off, a little funny, a little soft! Perhaps not; and yet I would rather not have a consensus of public opinion on the question; I think I am more comfortable without it.

There is this to be said in defence of men of letters on the business side, that literature is still an infant industry with us, and so far from having been protected by our laws, it was exposed for ninety years after the foundation of the republic to the vicious competition of stolen goods. It is true that we now have the international copyright law at last,[1] and we can at least begin to forget our shame; but literary property has only forty-two years of life under our unjust statutes, and if it is attacked by robbers the law does not seek out the aggressors and punish them, as it would seek out and punish the trespassers upon any other kind of property; but it leaves the aggrieved owner to bring suit against them, and recover damages, if he can. This may be right enough in itself; but I think, then, that all property should be defended by civil suit, and should become public after forty-two years of private tenure. The Constitution guarantees us all equality before the law, but the law-makers seem to have forgotten this in the case of our literary industry. So long as this remains the case, we cannot expect the best business talent to go into literature, and the man of letters must keep his present low grade among business men.

As I have hinted, it is but a little while that he has had any standing at all. I may say that it is only since the war that literature has become a business with us. Before that time we had authors, and very good ones; it is astonishing how good they were; but I do not remember any of them who lived by literature except Edgar A. Poe, perhaps; and we all know how he lived; it was largely upon loans. They were either men of fortune, or they were editors, or professors, with salaries or incomes apart from the small gains of their pens; or they were helped out with public offices; one need not go over their names, or classify them. Some of them must have made money by their books, but I question whether any one could have lived, even very simply, upon the money his books brought him. No one could do that now, unless he wrote a book that we could not recognize as a work of literature. But many authors live now, and live prettily enough, by the sale of the serial publication of their writings to the magazines. They do not live so nicely as successful tradespeople, of course, or as men in the other professions when they begin to make themselves names; the high state of brokers, bankers, railroad operators, and the like is, in the nature of the case, beyond their fondest dreams of pecuniary affluence and social splendor. Perhaps they do not want the chief seats in the synagogue; it is certain they do not get them. Still, they do fairly well, as things go; and several have incomes that would seem riches to the great mass of worthy Americans who work with their hands for a living—when they can get the work. Their incomes are mainly from serial publication in the different magazines; and the prosperity of the magazines has given a whole class existence which, as a class, was wholly unknown among us before the war. It is not only the famous or fully recognized authors who live in this way, but the much larger number of clever people who are as yet known chiefly to the editors, and who may never make themselves a public, but who do well a kind of acceptable work. These are the sort who do not get reprinted from the periodicals; but the better recognized authors do get reprinted, and then their serial work in its completed form appeals to the readers who say they do not read serials. The multitude of these is not great, and if an author rested his hopes upon their favor he would be a much more embittered man than he now generally is. But he understands perfectly well that his reward is in the serial and not in the book; the return from that he may count as so much money found in the road—a few hundreds, a very few thousands, at the most. . . .

It is not common, I think, in this country, to publish on the half-profits system, but it is very common in England, where, owing probably to the moisture in the air, which lends a fairy outline to every prospect, it seems to be peculiarly alluring. One of my own early books [2] was published there on these terms, which I accepted with the insensate joy of the young author in getting any terms from a publisher. The book sold, sold every copy of the small first edition, and in due time the publisher's statement came. I did not think my half of the profits was very great, but it seemed a fair division after every imaginable cost had been charged up against my poor book, and that frail venture had been made to pay the expenses of composition, corrections, paper, printing, binding, advertising, and editorial copies. The wonder ought to have been that there was anything at all coming to me, but I was young and greedy then, and I really thought there ought to have been more. I was disappointed, but I made the best of it, of course, and took the account to the junior partner of the house which employed me, and said that I should like to draw on him for the sum due me from the London publishers. He said, Certainly; but after a glance at the account he smiled and said he supposed I knew how much the sum was? I answered, Yes; it was eleven pounds nine shillings, was not it? But I owned at the same time that I never was good at figures, and that I found English money peculiarly baffling. He laughed now, and said, It was eleven shillings and ninepence. In fact, after all those charges for composition, corrections, paper, printing, binding, advertising, and editorial copies, there was a most ingenious and wholly surprising charge of ten per cent commission on sales, which reduced my half from pounds to shillings, and handsomely increased the publisher's half in proportion. I do not now dispute the justice of the charge. It was not the fault of the half-profits system; it was the fault of the glad young author who did not distinctly inform himself of its mysterious nature in agreeing to it, and had only to reproach himself if he was finally disappointed.

But there is always something disappointing in the accounts of publishers, which I fancy is because authors are strangely constituted, rather than because publishers are so. I will confess that I have such inordinate expectations of the sale of my books which I hope I think modestly of, that the sales reported to me never seem great enough. The copyright due me, no matter how handsome it is, appears deplorably mean, and I feel impoverished for

several days after I get it. But then, I ought to add that my balance
in the bank is always much less than I have supposed it to be, and
my own checks, when they come back to me, have the air of having
been in a conspiracy to betray me. . . .

The English writers seem largely to suspect their publishers;
. . . but I believe that American authors, when not flown with
flattering reviews, as largely trust theirs. Of course there are
rogues in every walk of life. I will not say that I ever personally
met them in the flowery paths of literature, but I have heard of
other people meeting them there, just as I have heard of people
seeing ghosts, and I have to believe in both the rogues and the
ghosts, without the witness of my own senses. I suppose, upon
such grounds mainly, that there are wicked publishers, but in the
case of our books that do not sell, I am afraid that it is the graceless
and inappreciative public which is far more to blame than the
wickedest of the publishers. It is true that publishers will drive
a hard bargain when they can, or when they must; but there is
nothing to hinder an author from driving a hard bargain, too,
when he can, or when he must; and it is to be said of the publisher
that he is always more willing to abide by the bargain when it is
made than the author is; perhaps because he has the best of it.
But he has not always the best of it; I have known publishers too
generous to take advantage of the innocence of authors; and I
fancy that if publishers had to do with any race less diffident than
authors, they would have won a repute for unselfishness that they
do not now enjoy. It is certain that in the long period when we
flew the black flag of piracy there were many among our corsairs
on the high seas of literature who paid a fair price for the stranger
craft they seized; still oftener they removed the cargo and released
their capture with several weeks' provision; and although there
was undoubtedly a good deal of actual throat-cutting and scut-
tling, still I feel sure that there was less of it than there would
have been in any other line of business released to the unrestricted
plunder of the neighbor. There was for a long time even a comity
among these amiable buccaneers, who agreed not to interfere with
each other, and so were enabled to pay over to their victims some
portion of the profit from their stolen goods. Of all business men
publishers are probably the most faithful and honorable, and

are only surpassed in virtue when men of letters turn business men. . . .

However, the most important question of all with the man of letters as a man of business is what kind of book will sell the best of itself, because at the end of the ends, a book sells itself or does not sell at all; kissing, after long ages of reasoning and a great deal of culture, still goes by favor, and though innumerable generations of horses have been led to the water, not one horse has yet been made to drink. With the best, or the worst, will in the world, no publisher can force a book into acceptance. Advertising will not avail, and reviewing is notoriously futile. If the book does not strike the popular fancy, or deal with some universal interest, which need by no means be a profound or important one, the drums and the cymbals shall be beaten in vain. The book may be one of the best and wisest books in the world, but if it has not this sort of appeal in it the readers of it, and worse yet, the purchasers, will remain few, though fit. The secret of this, like most other secrets of a rather ridiculous world, is in the awful keeping of fate, and we can only hope to surprise it by some lucky chance. To plan a surprise of it, to aim a book at the public favor, is the most hopeless of all endeavors, as it is one of the unworthiest; and I can, neither as a man of letters nor as a man of business, counsel the young author to do it. The best that you can do is to write the book that it gives you the most pleasure to write, to put as much heart and soul as you have about you into it, and then hope as hard as you can to reach the heart and soul of the great multitude of your fellow-men. That, and that alone, is good business for a man of letters. . . .

The man of letters must make up his mind that in the United States the fate of a book is in the hands of the women. It is the women with us who have the most leisure, and they read the most books. They are far better educated, for the most part, than our men, and their tastes, if not their minds, are more cultivated. Our men read the newspapers, but our women read the books; the more refined among them read the magazines. If they do not always know what is good, they do know what pleases them, and it is useless to quarrel with their decisions, for there is no appeal from them. To go from them to the men would be going from a higher

305

to a lower court, which would be honestly surprised and be-wildered, if the thing were possible. As I say, the author of light literature, and often the author of solid literature, must resign himself to obscurity unless the ladies choose to recognize him. Yet it would be impossible to forecast their favor for this kind or that. Who could prophesy it for another, who guess it for himself? We must strive blindly for it, and hope somehow that our best will also be our prettiest; but we must remember at the same time that it is not the ladies' man who is the favorite of the ladies. . . .

I hope that I have not been hinting that the author who ap-proaches literature through journalism is not as fine and high a literary man as the author who comes directly to it, or through some other avenue; I have not the least notion of condemning my-self by any such judgment. But I think it is pretty certain that fewer and fewer authors are turning from journalism to litera-ture, though the *entente cordiale* between the two professions seems as great as ever. I fancy, though I may be as mistaken in this as I am in a good many other things, that most journalists would have been literary men if they could, at the beginning, and that the kindness they almost always show to young authors is an effect of the self-pity they feel for their own thwarted wish to be authors. When an author is once warm in the saddle, and is riding his winged horse to glory, the case is different: they have then often no sentiment about him; he is no longer the image of their own young aspiration, and they would willingly see Pegasus buck under him, or have him otherwise brought to grief and shame. They are apt to gird at him for his unhallowed gains, and they would be quite right in this if they proposed any way for him to live without them; as I have allowed at the outset, the gains *are* unhallowed. Apparently it is unseemly for an author or two to be making half as much by their pens as popular ministers often receive in salary; the public is used to the pecuniary prosperity of some of the clergy, and at least sees nothing droll in it; but the paragrapher can always get a smile out of his readers at the gross disparity between the ten thousand dollars Jones gets for his novel and the five pounds Milton got for his epic. I have always thought Milton was paid too little, but I will own that he ought not to have been paid at all, if it comes to that. Again I say that no

THE WRITER AS WORKER

man ought to live by any art; it is a shame to the art if not to the artist; but as yet there is no means of the artist's living otherwise and continuing an artist. The literary man has certainly no complaint to make of the newspaper man, generally speaking. I have often thought with amazement of the kindness shown by the press to our whole unworthy craft, and of the help so lavishly and freely given to rising and even risen authors. To put it coarsely, brutally, I do not suppose that any other business receives so much gratuitous advertising, except the theatre. It is enormous, the space given in the newspapers to literary notes, literary announcements, reviews, interviews, personal paragraphs, biographies, and all the rest, not to mention the vigorous and incisive attacks made from time to time upon different authors for their opinions of romanticism, realism, capitalism, socialism, Catholicism, and Sandemanianism. I have sometimes doubted whether the public cared for so much of it all as the editors gave them, but I have always said this under my breath, and I have thankfully taken my share of the common bounty. A curious fact, however, is that this vast newspaper publicity seems to have very little to do with an author's popularity, though ever so much with his notoriety. . . .

After all, and in spite of my vaunting title, is the man of letters ever a business man? I suppose that, strictly speaking, he never is, except in those rare instances where, through need or choice, he is the publisher as well as the author of his books. Then he puts something on the market and tries to sell it there, and is a man of business. But otherwise he is an artist merely, and is allied to the great mass of wage-workers who are paid for the labor they have put into the thing done or the thing made; who live by doing or making a thing, and not by marketing a thing after some other man has done it or made it. The quality of the thing has nothing to do with the economic nature of the case; the author is, in the last analysis, merely a workingman, and is under the rule that governs the workingman's life. If he is sick or sad, and cannot work, if he is lazy or tipsy and will not, then he earns nothing. He cannot delegate his business to a clerk or a manager; it will not go on while he is sleeping. The wage he can command depends strictly upon his skill and diligence.

I myself am neither sorry nor ashamed for this; I am glad and proud to be of those who eat their bread in the sweat of their own brows, and not the sweat of other men's brows; I think my bread is the sweeter for it. In the mean time I have no blame for business men; they are no more of the condition of things than we working-men are; they did no more to cause it or create it; but I would rather be in my place than in theirs, and I wish that I could make all my fellow-artists realize that economically they are the same as mechanics, farmers, day-laborers. It ought to be our glory that we produce something, that we bring into the world something that was not choately there before; that at least we fashion or shape something anew; and we ought to feel the tie that binds us to all the toilers of the shop and field, not as a galling chain, but as a mystic bond also uniting us to Him who works hitherto and evermore.

I know very well that to the vast multitude of our fellow-work-ingmen we artists are the shadows of names, or not even the shadows. I like to look the facts in the face, for though their linea-ments are often terrible, yet there is light nowhere else; and I will not pretend, in this light, that the masses care any more for us than we care for the masses, or so much. Nevertheless, and most distinctly, we are not of the classes. Except in our work, they have no use for us; if now and then they fancy qualifying their ma-terial splendor or their spiritual dulness with some artistic pres-ence, the attempt is always a failure that bruises and abashes. In so far as the artist is a man of the world, he is the less an artist, and if he fashions himself upon fashion, he deforms his art. We all know that ghastly type; it is more absurd even than the figure which is really of the world, which was born and bred in it, and conceives of nothing outside of it, or above it. In the social world, as well as in the business world, the artist is anomalous, in the actual conditions, and he is perhaps a little ridiculous.

Yet he has to be somewhere, poor fellow, and I think that he will do well to regard himself as in a transition state. He is really of the masses, but they do not know it, and what is worse, they do not know him; as yet the common people do not hear him gladly or hear him at all. He is apparently of the classes; they know him, and they listen to him; he often amuses them very much; but he

THE WRITER AS WORKER

is not quite at ease among them; whether they know it or not, he knows that he is not of their kind. Perhaps he will never be at home anywhere in the world as long as there are masses whom he ought to consort with, and classes whom he cannot consort with. The prospect is not brilliant for any artist now living, but perhaps the artist of the future will see in the flesh the accomplishment of that human equality of which the instinct has been divinely planted in the human soul.

THE TEACHER, THE CRITIC,
AND "THE VITAL WORD"

❧❧

WHEN in 1882 Howells received an invitation from President
Daniel Coit Gilman to lecture at Johns Hopkins University, he
was tempted to accept it. Not only was Howells, a nonuniversity
man, flattered by the honor extended to him, but he had previously
experienced the rewards of being a university lecturer at Harvard
from 1869 to 1871. Howells' letter to President Gilman shows that
he was a "born teacher," capable of enjoying his contact with
younger people. Something of this teacher-pupil relationship
Howells had known in the office of the *Atlantic*, which he had
left only the year before. Should he now turn to teaching rather
than editing? Would he, as a teacher, have more time for novel
writing? Could he "give students ideas of literary art and criticise their work"? And would he be relieved of the necessity of
marketing his manuscripts? Gilman's invitation posed these questions at a time in Howells' career when the future was not clear
to him. Two weeks later Howells wrote to Lowell for advice and
said of the offer: "It looks like Fortune, but who knows Fortune's real face?"

Howells was in Switzerland when he received the letter from
President Gilman, which he discussed further with him in his reply of December 3, 1882. By the following July the decision still
hung fire: "The Johns Hopkinses are after me again tempting me
to try it for a year!", Howells wrote to Lowell. After his return
to Boston later in the same month, his letter to John Hay makes it
clear that the possibility of teaching still invited him. He wrote:

Something that happened to me may interest you. President Gilman of
Johns Hopkins renewed that offer to me with such kind insistence and

310

concession that I am presently much tempted to go to Baltimore three or four months of the winter. It will depend upon whether the President and I can come to an understanding about the time and length of time.

When, after several years in Boston no understanding was reached, Howells signed a contract with *Harper's* and entered upon the second chapter of his life as an editor. In 1886 he refused the Smith Professorship at Harvard, perhaps without as much hesitation as he felt when he received the offer from Johns Hopkins.

In 1889 the Howellses returned to Boston for two years, and there they met a handsome young man with whom Howells already had an acquaintance, Barrett Wendell, who was at that time teaching English composition at Harvard. Eighteen years younger than Howells, he moved in the same literary circles of Cambridge and Boston and knew and admired Fields, Norton, Holmes, and Lowell. We know from Wendell's letters that they met in the drawing rooms and studies of their many common acquaintances, and that, though both men were interested in literature from other lands, their tastes were poles apart. Did Howells perhaps have Wendell in mind when he remarked in *Criticism and Fiction* that the critics of the day were apt to be young people, "and young people are necessarily conservative in their tastes and theories," because they are only repeating what they have recently learned from their instructors?

The temperamental differences between these two American critics, one a novelist and the other a teacher, is most strikingly suggested by the fact that in 1891 Howells published *Criticism and Fiction,* in which he encouraged the new generation of writers to break with the outworn tradition of England, and that in the same year Wendell published *English Composition,* in which he urged upon several generations of American students the most polished rhetorical precepts for writing as exemplified by the English classics. To the young teacher of English 12 there simply were no American classics on which he might draw. "To put the question bluntly," said Wendell in an address at Vassar College on January 27, 1893, "what does American literature amount to?"—a question to which Howells had been giving a positive answer for more than twenty-five years through the columns of the *Atlantic* and *Harper's Monthly*.

The year 1900 is another date that marks a curious parallel—and divergence—between Howells and Wendell. The same year in which the older man, then occupying "The Editor's Easy Chair" of *Harper's*, published *Literary Friends and Acquaintance*, Wendell gathered up the lecture notes of the course in American literature that he had introduced at Harvard in 1898 and published them under the title *A Literary History of America*. Howells did not allow much time to elapse before he published in the *North American Review*, not a mere book notice of Wendell's history—which, incidentally, made no mention of Howells, not even in a chapter on the *Atlantic Monthly*—but a lengthy essay in which Howells allowed himself the critic's privilege of rolling up his sleeves and getting to work on "Professor Barrett Wendell's Notions of American Literature."

Howells' opening remarks in this essay, the only one he ever wrote on any of Wendell's books, indicate that he accepted the *Literary History of America* as a sort of challenge and that he expected the reader to "choose between my author and me" in this battle between two critic-teachers, the one looking backward to the lost values of an aristocratic culture, the other peering into the "democratic vistas" ahead. "Wherever Professor Wendell scents democracy or perceives the disposition to value human nature for itself and independently of the social accidents, he turns cold, and his intellectual tradition gets the better of his nature, which seems sunny and light and friendly. Something, then, like a patrician view of the subject results."

From this "patrician view" comes a "priggish and patronizing" attitude toward the New England writers, eliciting from Howells a fine defense of "the absolute and final and august simplicity" of such a man as Emerson, whom Wendell thought of as a village rustic. Not only did Howells defend the great names of New England, but he also pointed out that even in Emerson's time good writing had begun to come from the West and the South and the Middle States, which Wendell had failed to recognize.

Such men as De Forest, Harte, Eggleston, Clemens, and others, Howells had known and encouraged, and in his view to omit these names from an account of the literary history of the United States was to lend oneself "to the measurements of worldly-minded criticism," and "to leave the vital word unsaid." The critic, rather than the teacher, seemed to Howells equipped to guide the new generation of readers and writers. In his letter to Gilman, almost twenty years earlier, Howells had pondered the relationship of the teacher and the critic to the "vital word." Wendell's *Literary History of America* seemed to him to indicate that at least this teacher had become "ossified in tradition."

Letter to Daniel Coit Gilman *

Villeneuve, Dec. 3, 1882.

MY DEAR MR. GILMAN:

I do not know what to say in answer to your most kind and gratifying letter of the 14th ult., and I feel the disadvantage of trying to talk the matter over with you at this prodigious distance. I am afraid in the first place that you do not know how rich and various are my disqualifications for such a position as that you offer me; and I am most anxious, before the negotiation goes farther, to be perfectly frank about them. I have a literary use of Spanish, French, German and Italian, and I have some knowledge of the literature and the literary history of those languages; but I have not a *scholarly* acquaintance with them, and could not write any of them correctly, not even Italian. Greek literature I know only by translations, and not fully; under *peine forte et dure*, I might read Latin. As to English literature, why of course I know it in a sort of way, but rather in the order and degree of preference than thoroughly and systematically. And I do not even know our own language scientifically,—that is from the Anglo-Saxon up; and I might often be unable to give a philological reason for the faith that was in me.

* *Life in Letters*, I (1928), pp. 330–31.

Nevertheless, I do feel strongly and deeply, the art of literature, and I believe I could make others feel its beauty and importance. I have fancied myself confronting a class of young men,—and also young women,—and I have thought that I should begin by making each one tell me what he had read, in whatever language. Then I should inquire into his preferences and require the reasons for them. When I had acquainted myself fully with the literary attainments and opinions of the class and come perfectly into *rapport* with them, I should want to see their work, to criticize it with them and correct it—not in detail but "by sample." All the time I should be giving illustrative readings and lectures, which would be rather to the point of what we were doing than in any order of time, or critical or historical sequence. Often I should read a poem, or an essay or passage from a novel or history, and prove to them—for such things are perfectly susceptible of proof—why it was good or bad; but I should always give them the first chance to analyze: I should seek at every step to make them partners in the enterprise, and not treat them as bottles to be filled with so much literary information and opinion. Sometimes I should turn to one literature and sometimes to another; if a new book were making much talk, I would read it and talk about it with them. In every way I would try to emancipate them from the sense of drudgery, and yet teach them that work—delightful work—was perpetually necessary in literary art as in every other. My idea is that the sum of this art is to speak and to write simply and clearly, and I should labor in every way to make them feel that this was also to write beautifully and strongly. Is any such system or no-system practicable with you? I could not and would not *teach* by any sort of *text-book* in any branch.

Now, how much of my time must I give to such work? How many hours a week?

I am by trade and by affection a writer of novels, and I cannot give up my trade, because, for one reason, I earn nearly twice as much money by it as you offer me for salary. But I feel the honor and distinction of being connected with such an institution as yours, and I own that your offer tempts me.

Yours sincerely,

W. D. HOWELLS

P.S. If it were at all possible to leave this matter open till my return next August, it would be best. I don't see how we can arrive at each other's ideas clearly and fully by letter.

Professor Barrett Wendell's Notions of American Literature *

IF THE critic were to set down the psychology of his acquaintance with an important book, he would probably do a greater service to his reader than he does by merely recording his opinions of it. The best sort of criticism is that which gives the critic, as well as the author, to the reader's knowledge, so that he may judge not only the critic's opinions, but the motives behind his opinions, and value the opinions or not as he finds the motives worthy or not. I am going, therefore, to lay bare the facts of my personal history with regard to the present review, and to let the reader choose between my author and me, and enable or disable my judgment at the points where he thinks I have gone right from a just cause or wrong from an unjust cause. I do regard the book which Professor Wendell somewhat indescriptively calls "A Literary History of America" as an important book, and have found it impossible to ignore the sort of challenge it gives to one interested in the matter it treats of.

I had seen, I confess at second hand, a praise of the book so sweeping, so overwhelming, from a critical authority which I value, that I at once made up my mind against it; and when, later, I came upon certain expressions from it, again at second hand, I was not distressed to find them priggish and patronizing, but fortified myself in my dislike upon evidence which, if it had been my own book, I should have thought partial. When, still later, I came to the book itself, I was not able to dispatch it so promptly as I had expected, not because I was wrong concerning its intellectual

* *A Literary History of America*, by Barrett Wendell, 1900. Review in *The North American Review*, April, 1901.

quality, but because I was not sufficiently right. It *is* priggish and patronizing, but it is several other things so very much better that one must not, on one's honor, on one's honesty, fail to recognize them. It is, throughout, the endeavor of a narrow mind to be wide, and the affair in hand receives a species of illumination in the process which is novel and suggestive. It is not the kind of mind I like, but I like it better than I did before I was so well acquainted with it. It has an elasticity which I had not suspected, and the final result is a sort of instruction which the author seems to share with the reader. One is tempted to say that if Professor Wendell had not produced in his present book the best history of American literature, he had educated himself, in writing it, to produce some such history.

His general attitude toward his subject is the attitude of superiority, but not voluntary superiority; every considered volition of his is towards a greater equality with his theme. It is as if, having been born a gentleman, he wished conscientiously to simplify himself, and to learn the being and doing of his inferiors by a humane examination of their conditions, and a considerate forbearance toward their social defects. He has his class feeling against him, but he knows it, and he tries constantly to put it aside. All this is temperamental; but, besides, Professor Wendell has certain disadvantages of environment to struggle with, and in this he exemplifies the hardship of such Bostonians as have outlived the literary primacy of Boston. A little while ago and the air was full of an intellectual life there, which has now gone out of it, or has taken other than literary forms; and, in the recent ceasing of the activities that filled it, the survivor is naturally tempted to question their greatness. The New England poets and essayists and historians who gave Boston its primacy, are in that moment of their abeyance when the dead are no longer felt as contemporaries, and are not yet established in the influence of classics. It is the moment of misgiving, or of worse, concerning them; and it is altogether natural that this doubt should be most felt where their past greatness was most felt. Elsewhere, they are still measurably Emerson and Longfellow, Whittier and Holmes and Lowell; but on their native ground, where they lately walked with other men, and the other men are still walking and they not, the

TEACHER, CRITIC, AND "THE VITAL WORD"

other men can hardly fail to ask themselves whether they were not unduly oppressed by a sense of the vanished grandeur. These other men, looking abroad, and seeing little such question elsewhere, cannot help feeling it a proof of discernment in themselves, and governing themselves accordingly. They occupy the places of those illustrious men, and though they no longer find them so very illustrious as people once fancied, still they cannot resist the belief that they inherit them and have somehow the right to administer upon their estates.

The office has its difficulties, which will realize themselves to the imagination of any reader who has had the experience of looking over the papers of a person recently deceased, and has felt the insidious slight for the deceased which inevitably mingles with the conventional awe that all mankind pretend for the dead. The problem is how best to conceal the slight, not only from others but from one's self. If one keeps silence, one may partially succeed; but if one speaks, one inevitably takes on that air of superiority which affects the witness so disagreeably, no matter how involuntary it is. Another hard condition of such a work as Professor Wendell's is, that the author, in order to widen his survey of the subject, must get a bird's eye view of it, and if the resulting map or picture is not satisfactory to an observer on the terrestrial level, he accuses the bird of strabismus or astigmatism. But such an observer ought to guard himself from hasty censure, and ought to take into account the variety of obstacles overcome, as well as the defective character of the result. He ought to consider the exhaustive athletics by which Professor Wendell, for instance, places himself in a position to get a bird's eye view of Emerson, for instance. Then, I think, the observer on the terrestrial level will allow that he has done surprisingly well, and that the great wonder is that he should not have done worse.

Much that he suggests of Emerson is just, though I doubt if he does justice to the absolute and final and august simplicity from which the greatness of Emerson rises. He sees that, on the social side, Emerson was a villager; but he does not see that this sort of social outlook is compatible with universal and secular citizenship. He complains that, to the end, Emerson "never lost his . . . exuberantly boyish trick of dragging in allusions to all sorts of personages and matters which he knew only by name"; but he alleges no proof that Emerson was so audaciously ignorant. He bids us "take that sentence . . . 'Pythagoras was misunderstood and Socrates, and Jesus, and Luther, and Copernicus, and Galileo and Newton.' These great names he mentions with all the easy assurance of intimacy; he could hardly speak more familiarly of seven Concord farmers, idling in a row on some sunny bench." But here, in the absence of proof from the critic, there is no internal evidence of the intimacy and familiarity ascribed to "the juvenile pedantry of renascent New England at a moment when Yankees . . . did not yet distinguish between such knowledge and the unpretentious mastery of scholarship." He gives, upon the whole, a notion of Emerson which would be creditable to a scholarly gentleman straining a point for the sake of liberality, in the direction of things offensive to his class instincts. It is such a view as would be acceptable to one dining well with an unusually cultivated company of people, not too critical of saws or instances that seemed to glitter or illustrate, and only very amiably contrary-minded when the praise went too far.

The paper on Holmes is more adequate, because the subject is one that may be more adequately handled in the spirit of Professor Wendell's criticism; but slighter and lighter as Holmes's meaning was in literature, the criticism has not the value in the retrospect that it had in the prospect. There is always the promise of vital consideration, which somewhere, somehow, fails to fulfill itself. One perceives that little which is true in it is new; and that little which is new is true. At first, one is struck by the notion that Holmes is a sort of Bostonian Voltaire, and all the more profoundly impressed because of the critic's care in distinguishing between the authors in their conditions and temperaments. "Yes, yes," you say, to your neighbor at table, "that is true; I wonder I never thought of that." The next morning, the facts of their radical difference in feeling, thinking and saying, present themselves against the sole fact that they were both brilliant urban wits, and the notion is not at all convincing.

In the papers on Whittier and Longfellow, there is an exterior sense of their place in literature; but if the passages quoted from them as distinctive are to be taken as proof of the critic's penetration, there is little interior sense of their quality. Rather unexpectedly, the essay on Lowell satisfies one better. He was of greater intellectual range and weight than any of his contemporaries; he was more acquainted with books and with affairs; he had infinitely more humor, but on his social side he finally lent himself more to the measurements of worldly-minded criticism. Yet, through his humor he was apt at any time to pass impalpably into his poetry, where its divining rods were of no avail.

Professor Wendell's radical disqualification for his work seems the absence of sympathy with his subject. He is just, he is honest, he is interested, he is usually civil and too sincere to affect an emotion which he does not feel; he is versed in general literature, and he knows a great deal of his chosen ground. But he does not, apparently, know all of his ground; and his facts, when he ascertains them, are the cold facts, and not the living truth. Only those of like temperament can fail to be aware of this in him, and only those of like intellectual experience can fail to perceive the error of his ideals. The chief of these ideals is distinction, which he apparently thinks a man may seek with the same effect as if it had sought him. But distinction is something that comes by nature, like personal beauty, or lofty stature, or physical courage, or a gift for poetry or art. Short of it, one may be good, or clever, or wise; but one must be born distinguished. Most members of most aristocracies, most kings and emperors, are altogether undistinguished, and no breeding can make them so. For illustration in literature, one may say, without fear of contradiction, that the writer of the most distinction now writing English is Mr. Henry James. Every page, almost every sentence, of his testifies to his intellectual distinction. The very vulgarity which none of us escapes and which he occasionally fails to escape, has a sort of distinction. Contrast a passage of his criticism with a passage of Professor Wendell's, and you have the proof of what I am saying. Professor Wendell is so wanting in that distinction which is his ideal that his phrase is always in danger of wearing down to the warp of his undistinguished thought. This happens when, after some lumbering facetiation about ''those countless volumes of contemporary biography wherein successful men of business are frequently invited to insert their lives and portraits,'' he goes on to assure us that "Emerson's Representative Men were of a different *stripe* from these" men. His nerves do not instruct him that *stripe*, in this sense, has remained hopelessly rustic, plebeian, common, and so his ideal of distinction does not avail. It is somehow the same with his efforts for lightness; they affect one painfully as undignified, and of the sort that can be grateful only to the young gentlemen on the benches glad to relieve their overtaxed attention in a giggle.

When he is serious, Professor Wendell is always interesting and he is often very respectable. The best part of his book is formed by the essays on Bryant, Poe, Longfellow, Lowell, Whittier, Holmes, Whitman, and the essay on the change from Calvinism to Socinianism in New England, all papers of such good magazine quality that an editor would think twice before declining them, as a little wanting in form and a sort of final freshness. Their group is preceded by studies, varying in fulness, of our Colonial authors. Of these, one alone survives in literature; for, though Edwards is still a theologian whom the theologians cannot ignore, Franklin is the only literary man of that period whom lovers of literature can wish to know. The rest have the interest of quaintness, and of a significance among the origins of New England literature, which seems overrated in giving them a good fourth of "A Literary History of America." They were to be examined as the tough Calvinistic stock which flowered in the Unitarian poetry of the nineteenth century; but his notion of them, by no means original with Professor Wendell, is elaborated to the neglect of the truly American period which has followed the New England period of our literature. If he had called his book "A Study of New England Authorship in its Rise and Decline, with Some Glances at American Literature," one could not have taxed him with neglect, though one might still have found him wanting in proportion.

As a study of New England authorship, this book *has* value, as one may freely own, without disowning its valuelessness in specific instances. Its generalizations are at times excellent; though, from the passages of their literature which he gives, he would seem to have read about his authors rather than read them, the quotations are so far from representative. One of his most notable generalizations occurs when, after long fumbling over his material, he is able to say in summing up, "Then our ancestral America, which had so unwittingly lingered behind the mother country, awoke. In the flush of its awakening it strove to express the meaning of life; and the meaning of its life was the story of what two hundred years of inexperience had wrought for a race of Elizabethan Puritans"; and this is so well imagined, it is so challenging and suggestive, if not convincing, that, for the moment, you feel him fit to have written that history of our literature which he has not written. It is compensation and consolation for so much priggish banality that you almost forget the priggish banality, and you try to forgive him even for saying of Victoria's accession, "When her Majesty came to the throne," as if he were a subject of her Majesty, so devoted in his loyalty as to be insensible of the greatness of a theme essentially indignant of all ceremonial self-abasement. Still, this sort of lapse makes you doubt his fitness to treat his theme with the due breadth of feeling, as more than one page of his book makes you question his literary qualification. The man, you say, who could write such a sentence as, "The Southerners of the fifties were far more like their revolutionary ancestors than were the Northerners,"—a sentence so slovenly, so uncouth, so really inexpressive—is surely not qualified to judge even the mechanism of literature; but presently he gives you pause by declaring that "no one who lacks artistic conscience can write an effective short story, and . . . the artistic conscience may be called characteristic" of American authorship. He surprises you again when he declares that "in its beginning the American literature of the nineteenth century was marked rather by delicacy than by strength, by palpable consciousness of personal distinction rather than any such outburst of previously unphrased emotion as on general principles democracy might have been expected to excite." He surprises you still again, and still more, by his divination of the purity of soul in American literary art, as where he says: "In the literature of every other country you will find lubricity, in that of America hardly any. Foreigners are apt to think this trait hypocritical; whoever knows the finer minds of New England will be disposed to believe it a matter not of conscientious determination, but rather of instinctive preference." He perceives that while purity has been the instinct of our literature, excellence has been its ideal, and he enforces the fact with an aptness of expression which yet once more is surprising. To be sure, none of these notions is quite novel; and you may question Professor Wendell's originality, if you like. But if you like to do so, you will not be fair. He feels them originally and he imparts them cogently.

With as much reason you could say that his point of view in the study of Hawthorne was that chosen by Mr. Henry James, and perhaps sufficiently established twenty years ago; yet Professor Wendell does some thinking of his own on the subject, and he says some things which one cannot fail to heed without loss, as: "Comparing his work with the contemporary work of England, one is aware of its classically careful form, of its profoundly romantic sentiment, and of its admirable artistic conscience. One grows aware, at the same time, of its unmistakable rusticity, . . . monotony, provincialism, a certain thinness. . . . He was ideal, of course, in temper; he was introspective, with all the self searching instinct of his ancestry. . . . In a dozen aspects, then, he seems typically Puritan. His artistic conscience, however, as alert as that of any pagan, impelled him constantly to realize in his work those forms of beauty which should most beautifully embody the ideals of his incessantly creative imagination. . . . Beyond any one else, he expresses the deepest temper of that New England race which brought him forth, and which now, at least in the phases we have known, seems vanishing from the earth."

I do not think that, in my sense of the prevailing academic temper of Professor Wendell's work, I am attributing undue freshness to these remarks, though I confess that, in transferring them to my page, the freshness has seemed somehow to evaporate, and I hasten to restore my faith in their novelty by giving a passage from the paper on Irving: "One thing is pretty clear: the man had no message. From beginning to end he was animated by no profound sense of the mystery of existence. Neither the solemn eternities which stir philosophers and theologians, nor the actual lessons as distinguished from the superficial circumstances of human experience, ever much engaged his thought. Delicate, refined, romantic sentiment he set forth in delicate, refined, classic style. One may often question whether he had much to say; one can never question that he wrote beautifully."

TEACHER, CRITIC, AND "THE VITAL WORD"

I should object, of course, to the looseness and inaccuracy and tendency to tall talk in such phrasing as "the solemn eternities," and to a certain vagueness of statement, but I could not deny that a kind of truth about Irving, which is not the whole truth, was here strikingly expressed, while I should feel that the very perfection of his work was a sufficient "message."

I should be of the same divided mind, but more deeply divided, concerning Professor Wendell's saying of Poe: "From beginning to end his temper had the inextricable combination of meretriciousness and insincerity which marks the temperament of typical actors. Theirs is a strange trade wherein he does best who best shams." The first part of this saying appears to me true enough, and quite new; the last entirely false and wrong. The greatest actor is not he who best shams, but he who is the truest to reality. On the other hand, I should be inclined largely to agree with his saying, as far as it goes, about Longfellow: "Whether he ever understood his mission, it is hard to say; but what that mission was is clear; and so is the truth that he was a faithful missionary. Never relaxing his effort to express in beautiful language meanings which he truly believed beautiful, he revealed to the untutored new world the romantic beauty of the old." As far as it goes; for this saying does not get further in appreciation than the work of Longfellow's first period. As for his not knowing just what his mission was, I should hope not. Few men outside of the insane asylums are perfectly aware of what they are here for, and these are not usually at large. In such a saying as this, however, Professor Wendell does not mean any sort of unjust limitation, and if you come to his book of a *parti pris,* with the belief that he is altogether academic, and praises or blames by rule, you will find yourself mistaken. You may say that he is narrow-minded, but that he is not open-minded you cannot say. You must own again and again that he is very open-minded, and that he is not afraid to be generous when he conceives that generosity is justice. After long years of condemnation, when there was no question of Willis's abuse of hospitality in England by turning his hosts and his fellow-guests into newspaper copy,[3] his fame has a stout good word from an historian who does not think much of his poetry. "Superficial as you like, his letters are vivid, animated and carefully reticent of anything which might justly have displeased the persons concerned.'' But by far the most signal instance of Professor Wendell's open-mindedness is his recognition of Mark Twain's positive value as a talent almost unique, his relative importance in the literature of his country, and his representativity as a Westerner.

No man, and I least of all men, will wish to question such a characterization of a humorist whom I think the greatest that has lived; yet I strongly feel the inadequacy of Professor Wendell's general statement of the literary case as regards the region which gave Mark Twain to the world. He might defend it upon the ground that he has explicitly refused to deal with our literary history in men and women still living; but he is obliged to modify this refusal again and again. He names names and he imputes qualities in the case of writers still living quite inevitably, and it is by a volition disastrous to the completeness of his argument that he leaves unmentioned the writer in whom the brief glories of the literary movement on the Pacific slope culminated. I am not disposed to exaggerate the merits of Mr. Bret Harte, but it cannot be denied that he made one of the great impressions of his time, and that his once towering reputation was solidly based upon a real power. He still disputes European popularity with Mr. Clemens, and he long enjoyed the sort of perverse primacy on the Continent which confounds us in the case of Poe. Not to speak of such a principal writer in discussing the literature of his section is to cripple the criticism attempted, and not to speak of such another writer as Mr. James Whitcomb Riley, in dealing with Western effort in poetry, is to ignore what is most vital and indigenous in it. It is as if in treating of Scottish poetry, some Professor Wendell, contemporary with Robert Burns, should refrain from mentioning him because he was still living; and the like censure may be urged against his treatment of the chief Southern authors. The literary movement in the South since the war has been of the most interesting and promising character, and in the work of several men has been of most distinguished performance. Mr. Joel Chandler Harris's contributions to our imaginative literature are of absolute novelty, and Mr. G. W. Cable has written one of the few American fictions which may be called great. These men are not fully representative of the literary advance in the South, but not to name them, not to consider their work, is to leave the vital word unsaid. But the vital word concerning the rise of American fiction since the civil war is also left unsaid, and the South only suffers with the North.

As to that tendency in the North and East which, widening beyond the trend of the old New England endeavor for ideal excellence, resulted in the distinction of Mr. Henry James's work, how is any just notion of it to be given without some direct consideration of that work? Professor Wendell does not give any just notion of it, simply because he does not consider Mr. James's work either in itself or in relation to the general tendency. He has sworn to his hurt and changed not, though he swore to his hurt and changed in the case of Mark Twain with respect to the Western humor, and in the case of Miss Jewett and Miss Wilkins with respect to the New England short story. It is a pity that a critic so inconsistent should be so scrupulous, but it cannot now be helped, and Professor Wendell's history of our literature must remain so far imperfect.

If this were all, if it were imperfect only in this, it would not be so bad, but it is imperfect in so many other points as not to be a history of American literature, although it may be a literary history of America, if any one can say what that is. It is not only insufficient and apparently unintelligent at the points noted, but it conspicuously ignores some incidents which even a literary history of America ought to take account of. There is, for instance, nothing in it to betray consciousness of such a resurgent spirit as produced the first *Putnam's Magazine* at New York in the early fifties, though this was a literary event of as great importance as the founding of the *Atlantic Monthly* five years later at Boston. The earlier enterprise evolved and concentrated the literary elements which gave strength to the later undertaking, and it was, perhaps, more responsive and useful to the country at large. The great New England wits were contributors to *Putnam's*, while it revived and fostered the local and general literary aspiration. It completed the intellectual development of so important an American as George William Curtis, and gave American letters the humane and manly cast which it would be a pity they should ever lose. Almost more than any other agency in their annals, it dedicated them to liberty and democracy in the best and widest sense. They ceased with its coming to be servile at their worst, and to be merely elegant at their best.

But Professor Wendell ignores an incident of such prime significance, and whether he ignores it voluntarily or involuntarily it is to be regretted that he ignores it. He scarcely offers us compensation in the story of the founding of the *Atlantic Monthly*, and its mission to our literature. That periodical was imagined by Francis Underwood, the professional literary adviser of a successful publishing house, who had no conception of it as the avenue of Harvardized genius to the American public, or even as an outlet to the culture of New England, but who had an abiding faith in Lowell as the fittest man in the world to direct such a periodical. Lowell, as the first editor, divined that Holmes could do more than any living man to "float the *Atlantic*," and at his strong entreaty, the "Autocrat" papers were written, and the *Atlantic* was floated. Lowell, if any one, characterized the magazine. He gave it literary conscience and human responsibility, and the best that his successive successors could do was to keep it true to his conception of its mission. Fields, whose generous love of letters and wide intelligence Professor Wendell does not overrate, could do no more than this, and he did no more. He left the *Atlantic* what he found it, and what it has since remained with marvellous constancy to the original impulse from Lowell's great nature and liberal mind. It is ludicrously mistaken to suppose that after Fields left the magazine, it ceased to be in sympathy with Harvard. Fields had no special affinity with Harvard, and the young Harvard men—it is sufficient to name Mr. John Fiske alone —began writing for his successor in greater number than before, in proportion to their fitness or their willingness; if there was any change it was because Harvard was becoming less literary, and the country at large more literary. The good things began to come from the West and the South and the Middle States, and the editors took the good things wherever they came from.

No one can estimate the relative value of the New England episode of our literary growth more highly than I, but I cannot ignore the fact that our literary conscience, the wish for purity and the desire for excellence, which Professor Wendell recognizes as its distinguishing qualities, was not solely of Puritan origin. Before the New England renaissance, there was an American literature dignified by these qualities, and since the New England decadence (if he insists upon an appearance in which I do not find so much fact as he) here is a far larger body of American literature illustrated by their original and prominent characteristics. Clever and charming and even "distinguished" writing is now of an abundance in certain kinds which would have amazed the frugal sufficiency of the great New England days. In poetry only have we declined; but so has all the world.

Yet, even as a study of the New England episode of American literature, the work is not sympathetic. It is prevailingly antipathetic, with moments of kindness, and still rarer and more unexpected moments of cordial respect and admiration. Wherever Professor Wendell scents democracy or perceives the disposition to value human nature for itself and independently of the social accidents, he turns cold, and his intellectual tradition gets the better of his nature, which seems sunny and light and friendly. Something, then, like a patrician view of the subject results. Well, it is, perhaps, time that we should have the patrician view, for the patricians are usually not very articulate and it is interesting to know how they feel. The worst of it is, perhaps, that when the other patricians get this patrician view they will not care for it any more than they care for the subject. As a class, they have never, in any country, at any time, cared generally for literature, though they have been patrons of the objective arts, which could minister to their state in the decoration of their dwellings. Otherwise, they have been preoccupied with their dogs and horses, their yachts and villas; their recreations have been boyish or barbarous; their chance pleasure in a book has been almost a brevet of its badness. The American patriciate, so far as we have any, is like every other, and will not care, even unintelligently, for a patrician view of American literature. A large class of crude people, who do not know the ground, but have the belief that the things they do not know are not worth knowing, will, perhaps, in the harshness of their crudity, find Professor Wendell's history acceptable. It will not fundamentally disturb their ignorance, and it will please their vanity with the suggestion that not they alone are contemptible. The impression they will get from it is that American literature is not worthy the attention of people meaning to be really critical.

But I doubt if the American public needed any such recall as Professor Wendell has sounded from a mad pursuit of American authorship. I doubt if they have over valued it in the productions of our greatest poets, essayists, historians or novelists. I doubt if anything has been gained for a just estimation of Emerson by a patronizing allusion to his "guileless confusion of values," or for his interpretation by the elaborate explanation that in his saying, "hitch your wagon to a star," he had not in mind "a real rattling vehicle of the Yankee country, squalid in its dingy blue," or any such star "as ever twinkled through the clear New England nights," but that he used the "incomplete symbol" to bind together for an instant "the smallest things and the greatest." This had always been apparent to most people; and, throughout, Professor Wendell seems unaware of the fine, quaint humor lurking at the heart of Emerson's philosophy, and amusing itself with the fire it struck from such grotesque contrasts. There seems to have been a certain fantastic wilfulness in the Seer which would account for much that Professor Wendell treats as superficiality, and even ignorance. But Professor Wendell's strong point is not humor or the perception of it. His own intentions of lightness find an expression that does not add to the reader's gaiety, and he has so little humorous conscience that he can bring out that poor old moth-eaten anecdote of Emerson and Margaret Fuller watching Fanny Elssler's dancing and the one pronouncing it poetry, and the other religion. He should have been principled against this inhumanity, but he is not probably to blame for citing, in illustration of the old New Englander's sense of human equality, the story of Father Taylor's [4] saying of his interview with the Pope: "So the Pope blessed me and I blessed the Pope." Father Taylor was a saint who loved fun, and among the sailors to whom he preached there were often sinners who could take a joke. Perhaps, however, Professor Wendell knew that Father Taylor was joking, but in his need of an instance to support his position he pressed the old man's irony into the service.

One cannot often accuse him of uncandor; but no one can call his statement of the attack on Charles Sumner in the United States Senate a candid statement. "The first blow, to be sure, was struck from behind; it was struck, however, in the most public place in America," he says; and he gives the impression that Brooks's attack was made in full session of the Senate, in the midst of a crowd of spectators, when he ought to have known that the blow from behind was dealt a man sitting at his desk and busy over his papers, with only a few unfriendly people by.[5] This distortion of the fact is wholly needless, even to the unhandsome effect which the literary historian of America achieves. No man, except some such angelic minded man as Longfellow, ever met Charles Sumner without feeling the impact of his gross egotism almost like a blow in the face; and there can be no question that the speech which provoked Brooks's attack was insufferably outrageous in its insolence. One is amazed in reading it that any one should permit himself such brutal terms with an opponent; but the wish to minimize the far greater atrocity which it provoked cannot be justified, even in the interest of a patrician view of American literature. Mostly, however, Professor Wendell's uncandor goes no farther than that sort of noble aloofness with which self-conscious gentlemen begin their letters to editors in the formula, "Sir, my attention has been called to an article in your paper," and so forth. In the spirit of this fine detachment he acknowledges the persistent vitality of "Uncle Tom's Cabin," by owning that, "to this day, dramatized versions of it are said to be popular in the country," when he must have known, at first hand, that they were popular not only in the country, but in the suburbs of Boston itself, and wherever a summer pleasaunce large enough for the scene lent itself to the representation of a play requiring real bloodhounds in pursuit of fugitives escaping across a river of real water. At the moment I write, it is filling one of the largest New York theatres.[6]

Is it, then, the tone of Professor Wendell's book, rather than the matter of it, that I am finding fault with? I think it is largely the tone; for I believe that I have already done justice to the recurrent excellence of its matter. When he can keep himself from instances, he deals interestingly and often convincingly with his subject. It is when he illustrates his meaning by a quotation, and interprets the passage given by comment on it, that he is least fortunate. Then you see that he has judged the poet with a narrow mind, and has failed of his real significance through natural disability, or that he has wilfully obscured it. An unpleasing instance of this sort is his remark upon that poem of Longfellow's on the dead slave:

> Beside the ungathered rice he lay,
> His sickle in his hand; [7]

of which he says, "One may fairly doubt whether, in all anti-slavery literature, there is a more humorous example of the way in which philanthropic dreamers often constructed negroes by the simple process of daubing their own faces with burnt cork." Here the misconception of the artistic intention of the poet is so offensive, and put in terms of such jaunty vulgarity, that it is hard not to believe it a wilful misrepresentation. You ask yourself: "Could any one sincerely take that view of it?" and, for the credit of the human mind, you prefer to think not, bad as the insincerity would be.

Downright vulgarity Professor Wendell is not often guilty of; but something one must call commonness is rather common with him. His language is without distinction, as his thought is without precision, not always, but regrettably often. One finds it hard to forgive a writer who can suffer himself such a figure as, "Coal and oil, too, and copper and iron began to sprout like weeds." No writer of artistic sensitiveness could have written that sentence, and no critic of ultimate civility could say of Walt Whitman's "mad kind of rhythm" that it "sounds as if hexameters were trying to bubble through sewage." That is not graphic; it is simply disgusting. Yet the paper on Walt Whitman is almost the best of the whole collection, and is notable for some of the sanest and frankest and kindest criticism of a most difficult subject:

One begins to see why Whitman has been so much more eagerly welcomed abroad than at home. His conception of equality, utterly ignoring values, is not that of American democracy, but rather that of European. . . . The saving grace of American democracy has been a tacit recognition that excellence is admirable. . . . The glories and beauties of the universe are really perceptible everywhere, and into what seemed

utterly sordid Whitman breathed ennobling imaginative fervor. . . .
The spirit of his work is that of the old-world anarchy; its form has all
the perverse oddity of old world decadence; but the substance of which
his poems are made—their imagery, as distinguished from their form or
spirit—comes wholly from our native country. In this aspect, then,
though probably in no other, he may, after all, throw light on the
future of literature in America.

But what is literature in America? Almost any one can tell us
what it will be, but it wants a prophet to tell us what it is and has
been, and I doubt if Professor Wendell is that prophet. In the
first place, it does not appear to me that a prophet beginning to
prophesy would give you the feeling that the things he is about to
divine are not quite worthy of his powers, and I think that Professor Wendell gives you this feeling. In the next place, it does
appear to me that he mistakes the nature of our literature, or
seems to do so, in contrasting from time to time what we were
doing in America with what they were doing in England at the
same moment, and minifying our performance accordingly. Such
a method might be the means of useful spiritual exercise for
those vain Americans who suppose that our literature is the rival
or the sister of English literature. It is the daughter or the grand-
daughter of that literature, or, in terms less flowery, it is a condition of English literature; and it is not interesting in its equality or likeness to the other conditions, but in its inequality or
unlikeness. It has differenced itself from the mother or grand-
mother literature involuntarily, so far as it has differenced itself
valuably, and it is an error either in friend or foe to put it in the
attitude of rivalry. It would fail in that rivalry so far as it was
like English literature, just as English literature would show
itself in error where it was like American literature. Professor
Wendell, therefore, has not dealt wisely or kindly with it in the
contrasts he makes; and, largely speaking, I should say he was
not a kind or wise critic of it.

This is, of course, solely to his own disadvantage; the literature
will remain for every future student, while his criticism may,
perhaps, pass; and I should be sorry to pronounce him inimical
where the proof would be difficult. The best I could do toward
convincing the reader would be to recur again to his tone. "And
what," the reader might ask, "is his tone? Come," he might con-

tinue, "you have had your fling at his tone; you have tried to disable his supposed point of view; you have accused him of this, that and the other; but where is your proof?" I might retort that I preferred to leave the proof to Professor Wendell himself; but this seems rather sneaking, and I will not make that retort. I will allege the things I have quoted from him, and I may fairly, also, allege the impression of slight for his subject which he leaves with the reader. His subject is not, as I have represented, American literature, but that episode of our literary history which he calls the New England Renaissance. It cannot be questioned by any one who observes his attitude that he has the effect of looking down upon it. I will not suppose him capable of the charlatanry of wishing to surprise or shock his readers, or of the mistaken notion that they could be awakened to a just sense of New England literature by an occasionally rude or supercilious behavior to it. Clearly, he is sincere in not valuing it as it has been hitherto critically valued, and as it is still popularly valued. I cannot blame him for that; I myself have had my misgivings as to its perfection; and I have freely confessed them, but what I wish to make Professor Wendell observe is, that the New England literature uttered with singular adequacy the spirit of its time and place. I could also desire him to note that this spirit was generous and even sublime in its faith in humanity. He might answer me that it was weakened and intellectually dwarfed by this faith in humanity. In that case, I should say that I did not believe it, and I should like to ask what we should have faith in, if not in humanity. That would bring us to the *impasse* which people of different opinions must always come to.

THE GREAT AMERICAN NOVEL

❧

INTRODUCTION

JOHN W. DE FOREST'S essay "The Great American Novel,"
published in the *Nation* of January 9, 1868, proposed a discussion
that has reverberated down to our own day. Whether the country
was ready for a national novel, whether it ever would be—these
questions, and similar ones, were touched on frequently by Howells in his *Atlantic* and *Harper's* reviews, notably in his comments
on Mark Twain, Henry James, and Frank Norris. This section
contains several essays that reflect Howells' thinking on the subject of the American novel at the turn of the century.

As we have seen, Howells' editorial contact with another generation of writers, such as Garland, Bellamy, and later Crane and
Norris, kept him aware of changing aspects of American civilization on which the American novel must be based. So seriously
concerned was Howells during the 1890's with social problems that,
in spite of his dislike for the lecture platform, he addressed a meeting of the Twentieth Century Club on Bellamy's philosophy. The
Boston *Journal* of March 1, 1900, reported:

> William Dean Howells addressed the Twentieth Century Club last
> evening on Liberty and Equality, in the hall of the Boston University
> Law School, Ashburton Place. Every seat in the hall was occupied, and
> scores of people were standing. [He said] "We must not imagine our
> state perfect so long as there is one oppressed man in it. (Applause)
> We must not reason less than the greatest good to the whole."

By the time Howells lectured to this Boston audience he had
completed a series of articles in *Literature* in which he pondered
the impact of the "problems of existence" on "our faltering fiction." A "clever young writer" in Chicago, Lilian Bell, who had
suggested that the American novel did not dare deal with the

real problems of life, "tearing like wolves" at our hearts, moved Howells to define further his concept of realism in the novel. In his reply, "Problems of Existence in Fiction," Howells faced Miss Bell's criticism squarely and enumerated the sort of "economical" and "social" problems that he thought beset "ninety-nine hundredths of us."

The second essay from *Literature*, "An Opportunity for American Fiction," is a review of Thorstein Veblen's *Theory of the Leisure Class*, the first of two essays on a writer new to Howells and to most of his readers. Howells urged the novelist "with the seeing eye and the thinking mind, not to mention the feeling heart," to avail himself of the wealth of fresh material concerning the new "leisure class" and to illustrate the paradoxical fact that a moneyed patrician class has evolved in our democracy. "This is the supreme opportunity of the American novelist," said Howells. The absence of such a leisure class was, according to James, the reason why the American scene seemed to the novelist so empty; according to Veblen, the growth of such a class presented new social problems. Novelists have explored the American village and country life, Howells pointed out; Veblen offered a fresh field to the storyteller, "almost wholly unexplored," from which might emerge the great American novel. In urging upon writers this rich "opportunity" Howells suggested that they employ Veblen's spirit of scientific inquiry, that they assume the detachment and objectivity of the true realist. Just as Howells was quick to sense the unused materials suggested by Eggleston's frontier scenes, by De Forest's realistic treatment of the Civil War, by Hay's use of industrial strikes, by Crane's stark presentation of Bowery types, so here he perceived the opportunity opened up by this scientific study of the "leisure class"—a suggestion accepted by Norris and Dreiser. Howells' two essays on *The Theory of the Leisure Class*, in the words of Veblen's biographer, Joseph Dorfman, "not only helped to make the book a sensation, but helped to set the fashion of interpreting it as a withering criticism of aristocratic prejudice, as distinct from middle-class prejudice."

The difficulties of maintaining a modest respect for the factual truth of the actual American situation is pointedly stated by

THE GREAT AMERICAN NOVEL

Howells in the third selection below, "The Physiognomy of 'The Poor,'" written several years later for "The Editor's Easy Chair," in reply to a letter addressed to *Harper's Weekly*, October 25, 1902. "Why," asked the critic, Edith Baker Brown, "is Mr. Howells's democracy less convincing to the imagination than Tolstoy's? What makes the difference between Miss Wilkins's *Portion of Labor*, and, say, Hauptmann's *Weavers?*" Howells' reply, mock-modest in style, is a characteristic reproof to Miss Brown's romantic yearning for the great American novel.

In the last essay, "The Future of the American Novel," we see Howells again lifting his pen against the many-headed dragon of the romantic, this time in answer to a voice from England, that of Arnold Bennett, the so-called realist. Bennett's article "The Future of the American Novel," actually written for the *North American Review* in 1903, appeared for the first time in the January, 1912, issue of that magazine; Howells' reply was published in *Harper's Monthly* two months later.

Arnold Bennett looks first into the past of the American novel as viewed by an Englishman of 1903, and reports that until recently "the advertisements of English publishers contained scarcely any names save those of Mr. Henry James and Mr. William Dean Howells, and one or two more," so deep was the British disdain of American authors. Now, however, Norris' *Octopus* and Dreiser's *Sister Carrie* have awakened the reading world to the "phenomenon of American fiction." The great argument in favor of the American novel as opposed to the British "lies in the strenuousness, the variety, and the essential romance of American life." Howells might see "opportunities for American fiction" in the daily struggle of an ordinary family to earn a decent living; to Bennett the "intensity of competition, this interplay of warring activities, this havoc of operation in Wall Street, these monstrous concatenations of dollars, will lead to enterprises equally prodigious, fierce and astounding in the region of imaginative art." Were a Balzac on hand, writes Bennett, he would say: "'This country is simply steeped in romance; it lies about in heaps. Give me a pen, quick, for Heaven's sake!'" Howells did seize his pen as promptly as he could and with it attempted to pierce this latest version of the "romanticistic," asserting once

335

more that in fact the commonplace truth is superior to romantic bombast, no matter how real it pretends to be.

Problems of Existence in Fiction *

A CRY for "expansion" is no new thing in the voices from the West of these States. It is mainly in that section that the longing for our territorial enlargement beyond seas is felt; and from the cry which has lately made itself heard there, it seems that a sense of restriction is shared with the politician by the novelist. Apparently the present bounds of American fiction are not wide enough, or rather they are too strictly patrolled by the spirit of the young girl; and there are those who would give our fiction a Latin latitude, or free it from any sort of surveillance by the anxieties. The cry is a protest as well as a demand, and it is only a little more incoherent in the one quality than in the other.

The sum of it is the expression of a vehement belief, not to call it conviction, that "American novels are too expunged to be true to life. They are novels of clever details, of witty conversations, and delicate touches which give your brain little tingles of delight when you read them. But the great things of life, the problems of existence which are tearing like wolves at your hearts and mine, are never grasped and handled firmly. They are staggered around and hinted at, and the author stutters and coughs behind his hand until his readers are blushing for what he has purposely avoided." [8]

This expression may owe something of its headlong character to the impetuosity of the reporter, but in the absence of any other statement, it must be accepted as representative of the feeling, if not the thought, of the clever young writer said to have lately addressed it to a Chicago audience. In any case, however, the most interesting suggestion from it is the question whether it is true. It looks like the sort of hasty conclusion from the book last read

* *Literature,* March 10, 1899.

THE GREAT AMERICAN NOVEL

which disables so very much trenchant criticism, and makes the reader wish that the critic had acquainted himself a little better with his subject generally. If one considers the facts for one's self, they do not seem in this case to bear the construction put upon them. One may very well allow that American novels are full of clever details, witty conversations, and delicate touches, without at all allowing that the wolfish problems of existence are never grasped and handled firmly in them. One can at once recall a great number of the greatest of them which handle these problems without staggering around or stuttering. There are, for example, the two Chicago books of Mr. Henry B. Fuller, "The Cliff Dwellers" and "With the Procession"; and there is "The Money Captain," of Mr. William Payne,[9] in all its palpitant actuality. There is Mr. Herrick's "Gospel of Freedom." There are the books of Mr. Stephen Crane and the books of Mr. Harold Frederic, especially "The Damnation of Theron Ware." There is such a book as Miss Wilkins' "Jane Field." There is "The Grandissimes" of Mr. Cable. There are "What Maysie Knew" and "The Awkward Age," by Mr. James, and almost any of his fine strong studies of life. To go farther back, there is "Uncle Tom's Cabin"; there is "The Scarlet Letter," "The Blithedale Romance." In all these the literary expansionist would find the problems of existence grasped and handled firmly; and are not their writers the chief of those who make American novels and give them standing in the literary world?

There can be less question of this than of the real nature of the problems of existence, especially the sort that tear like wolves at our hearts. As to their nature, the critic of our faltering fiction shows something of its own disposition to stagger and stutter; and it is mainly by inference from some other possible impetuosities of the reporter that this critic may be understood to mean some of the more darkling affairs of the heart. But it would be so easy to work injustice by such an inference that a generous criticism of the critic would not press it; and I, for my part, should like to break altogether away from it and ask what the real problems of existence are.

They are, it seems to me, very largely economical. With those who have no money they are the question of a job, and the pay they shall get for it. This is of a far more vital significance and heart-rending consequence than the critic or the novelist, even, could often be persuaded to believe. With those who have money it is the question of losing it, and the anguish and squalor of coming down to narrower things; or it is the secret remorse for wasting it, the corroding shame for spending it selfishly while many hunger and freeze in sight of the riot. Then, for a real, wolfish, tearing problem, a mortgage is not a bad thing; and a note falling due at the bank and no money to pay it, is very well.

The problems are often social, as, whom shall one ask to dinner, or shall one be asked one's self to this or that house where one wishes to be seen. Whether a girl who has not a partner engaged for the german will have a good time at a ball, is a problem involving the keenest pathos. Such problems are really agonising, as people would own if they were honest.

The domestic problems are not alone those bound up in the behavior of the cook and the housemaid, but are also such crucial questions as to how one shall get on with a nagging wife or a brutal husband, and wear life out with the patience that brings peace at last. There are other domestic problems, such as a daughter's wish in her innocent heart to marry a fool or a drunkard, and how to prevent it; or a son's determination to bring a goose or a cat into the family circle, and how to keep him from doing it. Questions like these rob the nights of sleep, and turn the watcher's hair gray and age the soul itself. Or, there is a lingering, hopeless sickness, which must be borne by the sufferer, and by those who love the sufferer; how to bear this nobly is often a problem, which, if not wolfish, is inexpressibly lacerating.

There are civic and moral and religious problems, from which no life is exempt, though they may not spectacularly tear at the heart like wolves. You are sometimes tempted against your conscience to side with your country when your country is wrong, or to vote for your party when your party is false to your country. You are tempted to tell a lie which shall profit you; to profess openly a creed which secretly you deny.

Such are a few of the real problems of existence. They beset ninety-nine hundredths of us, and the other hundredth may be safely left to his question of conduct in matters which fiction, our

338

American fiction, our Anglo-Saxon fiction, staggers round and coughs at behind its hand. The books which deal with the problems noted and with kindred questions are as powerful and as important as any which treat the emotional, or hysterical, or even the equivocal questions; and they may be openly read by young people together and in all families.

This is not saying that the hundredth man's or woman's case may not be freely looked after also; it is perhaps important, too, though not so important as he or she thinks; and any one may treat it who chooses. But if one chooses to treat it, one cannot do it with open doors. If one does it, one shuts one's book to nine-tenths of those who read Anglo-Saxon novels unashamed; and if our novelists were generally to do it, their novels would be kept out of the hands of the young and inexperienced, as novels are in those Latin countries where novelists habitually grasp and handle problems of that sort.

There is not and there never has been anything to prevent the freest expansion in that direction, which our critic supposes forbidden. The young girl is not on guard there, but young girls may be very fitly guarded from looking for their knowledge of life to books that deal with the more darkling problems, because, for one thing, such books do not present a true picture of life, as a whole or in any large part.

An Opportunity for American Fiction *

ONE of the most interesting books which has fallen in my way since I read "The Workers" of Mr. Wyckoff [10] is Mr. Thorstein Veblen's "Theory of a Leisure Class." It does for the Idlers in terms of cold, scientific analysis the office which Mr. Wyckoff's book dramatically performs for the Workers; and I think that it is all the more important because it deals, like that book, with a class newly circumstanced rather than newly conditioned. The

* *Literature,* April 28, 1899.

workers and the idlers of America are essentially the same as the
workers and the idlers of occidental civilisation everywhere; but
there is a novelty in their environment peculiarly piquant to the
imagination. In the sociological region the spectacle has for the
witness some such fascination as geological stratification would
have for the inquirer if he could look on at its processes; and it
is apparently with as strong a zest as this would inspire that Mr.
Veblen considers the nature and the growth of the leisure class
among us.

His name is newer to me than it should be, or than it will hereafter be to any student of our status; but it must be already well
known to those whose interests or pleasures have led them into the
same field of inquiry. To others, like myself, the clear method, the
graphic and easy style, and the delightful accuracy of character-
isation will be part of the surprise which the book has to offer.
In the passionless calm with which the author pursues his in-
vestigation, there is apparently no animus for or against a leisure
class. It is his affair simply to find out how and why and what it is.
If the result is to leave the reader with a feeling which the author
never shows, that seems to be solely the effect of the facts. But I
have no purpose, as I doubt if I have the qualification, to criticise
the book, and it is only with one of its manifold suggestions that
this notice will concern itself.

The suggestion, which is rather a conclusion, is the curious fact,
noted less securely and less scientifically before, that the flower of
the American leisure class does not fruit in its native air, and perhaps can not yet perpetuate itself on our soil. In other words, the
words of Mr. Veblen, "the English leisure class being, for purposes
of reputable usage, the upper leisure class of this country," the
extraordinary impulse among us toward the aristocraticisation of
society can as yet fulfil itself only in monarchical conditions. A
conspicuous proof of this is the frequent intermarriage of our
moneyed bourgeoisie with the English aristocracy, and another
proof, less conspicuous, is the frequent absenteeism of our rich
people. The newspapers from time to time make a foolish and
futile clamor about both these things, as if they were abnormal,
or as if they were not the necessary logic of great wealth and
leisure in a democracy. Such things result as infallibly from wealth

and leisure as indigence and servility, and are in no wise to be deprecated. They are only representations on a wider stage of the perpetual and universal drama of our daily life. The man who makes money in a small town goes into the nearest large town to spend it—that is, to waste it; waste in some form or other being the corollary of wealth; and he seeks to marry his children there into rich and old families. He does this from the instinct of self-preservation, which is as strong in classes as in individuals; if he has made his money in a large town, he goes to some such inland metropolis as Chicago to waste his wealth and to marry his children above him. The Chicago, and San Francisco, and St. Louis, and Cleveland millionaires come to New York with the same ambitions and purposes.

But these are all intermediate stages in the evolution of the American magnate. At every step he discovers that he is less and less in his own country, that he is living in a provisional exile, and that his true home is in monarchical conditions, where his future establishes itself often without his willing it, and sometimes against his willing it. The American life is the life of labor, and he is now of the life of leisure, or if he is not, his wife is, his daughters and his sons are. The logic of their existence, which they cannot struggle against, and on which all the fatuous invective of pseudo public spirit launches itself effectlessly, is inter-marriage with the European aristocracies, and residence abroad. Short of this there is no rest, and can be none for the American leisure class. This may not be its ideal, but it is its destiny.

It is far the most dramatic social fact of our time, and if some man of creative imagination were to seize upon it, he would find in it the material of that great American novel which after so much travail has not yet seen the light.[11] It is, above all our other facts, synthetic; it sums up and includes in itself the whole American story: the relentless will, the tireless force, the vague ideal, the inexorable destiny, the often bewildered acquiescence. If the novelist were a man of very great imagination indeed, he might forecast a future in which the cycle would round itself, and our wealth would return from European sojourn, and dwell among us again, bringing its upper class with it, so that we should have a leisure class ultimated and established on our own ground. But for my part I should prefer the novel which kept itself entirely to the actualities, and studied in them the most profoundly interesting spectacle which life has ever offered to the art of fiction, with elements of equal tragedy and comedy, and a pathos through all which must be expressed, if the full significance of the spectacle were to be felt.

The Physiognomy of "The Poor" *

IN A polite periodical [12] we read the other day a suggestive communication from a correspondent urging us to have more and better criticism in all our periodicals. This is not so simple as the writer perhaps thinks, and it may be long from here to the abode of the prophets who shall expound such mysteries as "What are the conditions from which springs, we will say, Mr. Norris's theory of the novel? Why is Mr. Howells's democracy less convincing to the imagination than Tolstoy's? What makes the difference between Miss Wilkins's *Portion of Labor*, and, say, Hauptmann's *Weavers?*" The correspondent of the periodical in question seems to think that adequate literary journalism would tell us; but we do not know that we need wait for this altogether. Mr. Norris's theory of the novel is the Zolaesque theory, which he improved and adapted to conditions which it did not spring from; in his hands the theory of human documentation became more selective; he made the epic poetical again, and imbued it with the strong, fiery spirit of California soil and air which is as native as the California flavor of the grapes grown from the Spanish stocks. As for Mr. Howells, we hardly feel authorized to speak for him; but it may be tentatively said that his democracy does not convince the imagination so much as Tolstoy's because it is incomparably less powerfully imagined than Tolstoy's. But in coming to Miss Wilkins's work we fearlessly affirm that its difference from Haupt-

* *Harper's Monthly*, January, 1903.

mann's may possibly lie in the world-wide difference in the conditions from which it originates. Poverty is the same everywhere; like slavery it is still a bitter draught. But the physiognomy of the poor varies from land to land and from age to age. It expresses patience, and despair, or oblivion everywhere, but in our country there is conjecturable also a certain surprise, the bewilderment of people who have been taught to expect better things of life, and who have fallen to the ground through the breaking of a promise. Was this, their faces ask, really the meaning of the glad new world? If Miss Wilkins has caught this expression of our poor (we do not say she has) she has divined the difference between them and the poor of the old world, where misery is of such ancient date that all hope has died out of it, and the disappointment of defeated expectation has been long outgrown.

As the reader will bear witness we have been careful to defend our surmise as to the fact of Miss Wilkins's contribution to sociology by several very obvious ifs and ands. But when it comes to inferences from the possible or impossible fact, we have no hesitations, no provisions. Whatever the difference of fact between *The Portion of Labor* and *The Weavers,* the difference of effect needs no coming of a seer for its interpretation. Miss Wilkins's work is less impressive than Herr Hauptmann's because it is in a region less strange than his. Misery for misery, the average mind prefers that which is foreign to its observation or experience. The non-imaginative person is nowhere so much at home as in a voluntary exile; and this may be why it was sometimes said that travel is the fool's paradise. For such a person to realize anything, the terms are that he shall go abroad, either into an alien scene, or into a period of the past; then he can begin to have some pleasure. He must first of all get away from himself, and he is not to be blamed for that; any one else would wish to get away from him. His exaction is not a test of merit; it is merely the clew to a psychological situation which is neither so novel nor so important as to require of our hard-worked civilization the production of an order of more inspired criticism than it has worried along with hitherto.

It is not the key to the mystery of Frank Norris's great work now ended. He lived to give to us *McTeague* and *The Octopus,* two novels of such signal mastery, so robust, so compact, so vital, and yet so graced with the beauty of an art which came to its consciousness in full maturity, as to merit that comparison which they need not fear with the best of our time. He has died in the flower of his years, and has bereft us of a hope in fiction which no other now promises fully to restore. He did not invent his means; in a world already rather full of inventions we rather inherit our means; but he was in the divine secret of the supreme artists: he saw what was before him, with the things in their organic relations, and he made life live. Most people, however, do not like to see life living, especially life that they might know if they knew or could bear to know themselves, and so perhaps Frank Norris's mastery will remain a mystery to them.

It was the glad delusion of the Easy Chair in the days when it was the Study that the reader could be persuaded to ask nothing better of the writer than the truth about the facts. But this was a radiant error; the reader, in his immense majority, asks nothing worse of the writer. He desires only and ever that the pneumatic tires bearing him to eternity shall be constantly pumped full of the East wind; and that perhaps is one of the minor reasons why the democracy of one American author mentioned by the correspondent of that polite journal is "less convincing to the imagination than Tolstoy's." It is mainly but not merely because Tolstoy's imagination is incomparably more potent. It is also because the aspiration of the widely parted classes of Russia towards a human brotherhood is in a region of entrancing strangeness, where we can feel its pathos and its sublimity, and not be molested by any social likeness in it to our own experiences. It has the fascination of the thing *in posse,* which the thing *in esse* already lacks. It is conjecturable that democracy as we have realized it, and as that mistaken American author has studied and painted it, has a repulsiveness which the ideal does not wear. It looks ordinary, commonplace, uninteresting, as one's face and figure are apt to look in the glass when not made up for the ordeal. This, however, one may very well feel, is not the fault of one's self, but of the glass, and then one does well to smash it, or if not quite that, to impeach its veracity.

The Future of the American Novel *

WE HAVE just been reading Mr. Arnold Bennett's paper on "The Future of the American Novel," and fancying that which was written nine years ago, but only now printed, already obsolescent, almost obsolete, through the changing circumstances.[13] We do not say changing conditions, for these remain much the same in 1912 that they were in 1903. The novelist who is also an artist is still trying to write something good and great, or at least the best and greatest things he can; the publisher, who is a merchant, is seeking to bring out the thing that everybody is reading; the reader, who knows what he likes, is trying to find it in the book that the most people are liking. It is still the old lottery, with hazard apparently overruling law, but with the law, eternal and immutable, finding itself the animating force in hazard. "What is excellent, as God lives, is permanent," and in spite of all doubts whether God really lives, something supreme ordains the survival of the fittest in literature, in fiction, as in everything else. Since Mr. Bennett wrote his interesting paper a hundred big sellers have gone to the rag-bag, the ash-barrel. Having ceased to sell big, they have ceased to sell little, and some books that sold little are selling a little more. It is not much to brag of, but it is the most we have, and we make it our meek boast. We are still in the competitive age, the stone age, the mud age, as to our conditions, but our circumstances have improved. Occasionally a publisher who has grown rich in big-selling feels that he can print a good book because it is good, because he himself loves it. Occasionally an author produces a failure after the formula which has often warranted success; but more than ever, it seems to us, our authors are trying to do good work and taking their chances with it. Our criticism is more intelligent and better mannered; our public is more intelligent and better read than it was nine years ago. The friendly foreign

* *Harper's Monthly*, March, 1912.

observer has also advanced, and we take leave to think that Mr. Bennett would write in 1912 a better paper on the future of our novel than he wrote in 1903.

We do not believe, for instance, that he would now look at the phenomena of our enormous enterprise in all kinds, as the best material for fiction, as the material with which art would prosper most. That material is the stuff for the newspaper, but not for the novel, except as such wonders of the outer world can be related to the miracles of the inner world. Fiction can deal with the facts of finance and industry and invention only as the expressions of character; otherwise these things are wholly dead. Nobody really lives in them, though for the most part we live among them, in the toils of the day and the dreams of the night. We say this rather to the reader than to our hopeful critic, for nobody knows better than he how inanimate the material things are. The man who has written of the Five Towns and the heights and depths of the real life there ought not to indulge the illusion that there can be for the novelist elsewhere any lasting future except in writing of the real life which he knows. We do not think he would indulge this illusion now, because with him also the circumstances have changed in the last nine years. In that time he has found himself, and if the world had not found him, too, it would scarcely have mattered to him in his sense of the true work he has done. This sense is his triumph and his exceeding great reward, but when he wrote his paper on the future of our novel, he had not done the work which it crowns.

We must not, therefore, suppose that if he were writing now he would imply that our objective bigness was the stuff of our art. He must have learned from his own achievements that it could not be so, and that if we were ever to discover our greatness to others we must withdraw from our bigness to the recesses of that consciousness from which characters as well as camels are evolved. The American, no more than any other man, shall know himself from his environment, but he shall know his environment from himself. In the measure of his self-knowledge only shall he truthfully portray his neighbor,

and he shall instinctively keep to his neighborhood, to his experience of it for his chance of knowledge beyond it. This has
been instinctively so with the localists whom Mr. Bennett finds
to have written novels of the States, but not of the United
States. We for our part do not believe that the novel of the
United States ever will be, or ever can be, written, or that
it would be worth reading if it were written. In fiction, first
the provincial, then the national, then the universal; but the
parochial is better and more to be desired than either of the
others. Next to the Italians and the Spaniards the Americans
are the most decentralized people in the world, and just as
there can never be a national Italian fiction, or national Spanish
fiction, there can be no national American fiction, but only
provincial, only parochial fictions evermore. The English cannot imagine this because of their allegiance to a capital, such
as we feel to no supreme city of ours; and yet the English
have no national novel, no United Kingdom novel. Mr. Bennett,
who has written novels on a scale nobly vast, is strictly provincial in his scope; as provincial as Ibsen himself. When he
goes to Paris with his scene he takes the Five Towns folk with
him, and he realizes Paris to us through them, whom alone he
perfectly knows. We could not wish it otherwise, and if we
did we could not have it; or he, either.

Can any one, when he comes to it, really conceive of a United
States novel? No more than of a novelist who should make
our giant operations, our tremendous industries, our convulsive
finance, our seismic politics, our shameless graft, stuff of an
imaginative work. Mr. Bennett figures Balzac confronted with
our gross material marvels, and crying out: "This country
is simply steeped in romance; it lies about in heaps. Give me
a pen quick, for Heaven's sake!" The words are brave and
flattering to our vanity, but when we wake in the night and
wish we had not eaten so much for dinner, we must doubt
whether Balzac, bit of a quack as he was, would not have
paused and reflected before attempting to extract sunbeams
from our mammoth cucumbers. They are cucumbers, after all;
and the more precious fruits of our earth and air are those

that grow everywhere from the blossoms that mostly blush unseen. To seek them out and impart their color and perfume to his page is the true office of the artist. The simple structure of our society, the free play of our democracy in spite of our plutocracy, the ineradicable desire of the right in spite of the prevalence of the wrong, the generous instinct of self-sacrifice, the wish to wreak ourselves in limitless hospitality, the capacity for indefatigable toil, the will to make our achievement commensurate with our opportunity—these are the national things which the national novel might deal with, better than with Pittsburg chimneys and Chicago expresses. In the mean time we have the localists who have done and are doing far better work than any conceivable of a nationalist: Sarah Orne Jewett and Mrs. Wilkins Freeman for New England, Mr. Cable for New Orleans, Miss Murfree for the Tennessee mountains, Mr. Brand Whitlock for the older Middle West, Mr. Hamlin Garland for the younger and farther West, Mr. Henry B. Fuller and Miss Edith Wyatt for Chicago, Georg Schock for German Pennsylvania, Mr. Harben for Northern Georgia. We name a few out of many, and we would not leave unnamed Mr. William B. Trites, whose two very extraordinary books, *John Cave* and *Life,* are now making him known in England for the mastery of his treatment of local phases not before studied in Philadelphia journalism and the life of a small Pennsylvania town. *John Cave* is a tragedy of such proportions as is not easily predicable of an action commensurate with our geographical superficies, and in the brief compass of *Life,* the vast conception of a chain of Beauty Parlors stretching from ocean to ocean has its origin in the imagination of a village youth mean in everything but his generous passion for the village girl who studied with him in their small-town environment. If the story strays to capitals beside and beyond the sea it is with no purpose of the author to enlarge it to national dimensions. We do not forget what Frank Norris did and wished to do. His epic of the wheat was to have run from California to Chicago, and from Chicago to Paris; but he, too, was a localist, and *The Octopus* was better than *The Pit,* because he had lived more in California than in Chicago, and was more vitally intimate with his scene and action there. Closer, firmer, truer than even *The Octopus* is Norris's other great book, *McTeague*, which scarcely ever leaves the shabby San Francisco street where the irregular dentist hangs out his sign of a golden tooth.

Our novelists are each bound by the accident of birth to this locality or that; and we do not believe we shall ever have a truly United States novel till some genius is born all over the Union.

POETRY OR PROSE?

❧

AT THE request of the editor of *Harper's Bazar,* Howells in 1910 paused to consider what had been the turning point of his life—a question perennially fascinating to editors who wish to draw out famous authors. Howells' reply, in which he finally concludes that there was no one turning point, is of interest in a consideration of Howells as a critic. As he pondered the question, his mind went back to the moment in Venice when he knew that he was to be a writer of prose rather than of poetry, or at least that his prose would sell, whereas his poems plainly would not.

Howells, however, never ceased to write poetry and to review the poetry of others from Whitman to Frost. His devotion to both poetry and prose, as writer and reader, began as a child, when he listened to his father's reading of poetry or fiction in the evenings before the family hearth, and it continued all his life. The effect of this absorption in the sound of poetry on his own prose has never been fully studied; nor have Howells' critical judgments of poetry been considered in relation to the tension set up in him by this dual allegiance. Was his response to prose somewhat poetic; and on the other hand, was his reading of poetry frequently rather prosaic? These questions come to one's mind as one reads the lonely young consul's account of the faraway days in Venice when he received a letter from Lowell accepting a piece of his prose when other editors were rejecting his efforts in poetry.

James Russell Lowell, in 1864 when he wrote the welcome letter to Howells, was coeditor with Charles Eliot Norton of the *North American Review.* Howells had sent him a paper on "Recent Italian Comedy" on which he had "labored with great pains." Lowell had accepted the essay at the time when Howells was still smarting from the rejection by the *Atlantic* of his articles on Venice, which were at once serialized in the *Boston Daily Advertiser* and later appeared in book form as *Venetian Life*. Lowell had read and admired the sketches of Venice, and he said so in the letter, which soothed Howells' wounded spirits like balm, "consoling [him] in an instant for all the defeat [he] had undergone, and making it sweet and worthy to have lived through that misery."

So moved, in fact, was Howells by Lowell's letter that he poured out his heart to him in a reply from Venice, August 21, 1864, mingling his appreciation with reminiscences of "the cordial and flattering reception" Lowell had given "a certain raw youngster" four years ago in Boston, with his plans for sketches of Venetian customs and a personal account of his growing family. Perhaps because Lowell, as editor of the *Atlantic*, had printed five or six poems written by Howells when he was still a reporter in Columbus (and had warned him that he "must sweat the Heine out of him"), perhaps because Lowell had given him a letter of introduction to the great Hawthorne, perhaps because Howells had talked for long hours with Lowell in his study at Shady Hill—for these reasons and for many more—the young Howells felt the beginnings of a close relationship with Lowell even before he set out for Italy. It is the cordial letter from Lowell, which Howells received at a time of great discouragement and loneliness as "an almost expatriated" American in Venice in 1864, that Howells remembered over forty-six years later as "The Turning Point of My Life."

The "turns" in Howells' life were often made necessary by the need to support himself and his family, and this economic fact, never far from Howells' mind, is explored in the account he gives us of his pleasure in Lowell's letter. In his reply he tells his friend of his plans for his Venetian sketches and of his wish to establish himself: "I'm anxious to succeed with this book, for I've got to the point in life where I cannot afford to fail any more. Besides, I'm going to resign my office and go home . . . and as I have no prospect of place or employment in the State, I must try to make this book a pecuniary success.'' The remembrance of the need of those early Venetian days moved Howells, when he relived this period of his life, to disabuse ''the polite reader'' who thinks there is ''something sordid'' in referring to a writer's desire to earn a living.

Lowell's next letter to Howells clearly indicates into what a furor of planning Lowell's encouragement put him. After telling Howells that his article was in print and asking him to whom he should pay his ''honorarium,'' Lowell invited Howells to write another article for the *North American Review,* on Italian literature ''or on anything you like.'' In spite of the fact that Howells stressed his need to earn a living, something more than the hope of selling his manuscript moved him to turn from poetry to prose as he considered Lowell's second letter, which reads in part:

I don't forget my good opinion of you, and my interest in your genius. Therefore I may be frank. You have enough in you to do honor to our literature. Keep on cultivating yourself. . . . I have been charmed with your Venetian letters in the *Advertiser.* They are admirable, and fill a gap. They make the most carefully [sic] and picturesque *study* I have ever seen on any part of Italy. *They are the thing itself.*

In writing his father Howells quoted Lowell's letter in order to explain to him how loath he was to return home to take his brother Joe's place in the family printing enterprise, where of course the jobless young man would have been much more certain of earning a living than by embarking on the sea of literature. Instead of soberly entering the family business, then very much in need of his aid, Howells planned ''to make notes on all sorts of subjects for articles—I think of a dozen at least.''

Compelling as Lowell's letter was, we know that Howells never wholly gave up writing poetry. For, he admitted, looking back over the stretch of years, ''Brazen it out as we will in behalf of prose, there is a mystic power in verse which utters in a measured line the passion and the aspiration which a whole unmetered volume cannot express.'' At seventy-three the ''vista'' was still opening up for Howells, inviting him ''to stray apart'' into a region where the demarcation between poetry and prose is never quite fixed. Prose he preferred, for "when it is perfected . . . it will not have to hide the art of its construction; . . . it will be a thing born, not made, and will live from the pen as it lives from the lips . . . and yet—and yet—."

Howells was constantly under the exacting discipline of his artistic conscience in the effort to draw a line between his own poetry and his prose. H. H. Boyesen tells us in "Mr. Howells and His Work," written for the *Cosmopolitan*, February, 1892, that Howells "was his own severest critic": "I have known him to strike out the most beautiful passages (in spite of my entreaties) because they were 'meaninglessly poetic' and did not carry with absolute and unerring precision, the thought which they had been intended to embody. Sometimes they were sacrificed merely because they were too 'ornate and self-conscious.' "

Not to recognize in Howells' concept of realism the peculiar blend of poetry and prose that mark his writing is to join with those who "bray" at his "flowers picked from the fruitful fields of our common life, and turn aside among the thistles with keen appetites for the false and impossible," as Howells wrote to Brander Matthews in 1902. "I had hoped," he added, "I was helping my people know themselves in the delicate beauty of their every day lives, and to find cause for pride in the loveliness of an apparently homely average." Howells as a novelist and critic was subtly responsive to both poetry and prose, and to the blend that was realism.

The Turning Point of My Life *

WHEN I brought myself to book and fancied saying in definite words what had been the most fateful change in my life, I found a certain difficulty which I had not realized in first

* *Harper's Bazar*, March, 1910.

thinking of the matter. Then it was very simple, for I had supposed, in that dreamy remoteness from chapter and verse, that there was one great turning-point in my journey through life; now upon closer inspection I perceived that it was full of turning-points, that it bristled with finger-posts marking the intersections of ways, where it seemed to me I was always in danger of taking the wrong road. But if I went back a little from it, I had a moment of thinking that it was not that winding and crooked lane which it had seemed, but a fair highway, and that those admonitory finger-posts were the stately pillars which I had set up to mark the perspective of my undeviating progress toward the vanishing-point beyond which there is no shadow of turning.

It was in Venice when in the enjoyment of my consular stipend of fifteen hundred a year and ten per-cent. office-rent, I had still remained in my inveterate dream of living a poet by my poetry, that I came to the turning-point which I fancied the great one in my literary career, if I may call it by so strenuous a name. Much at that time had been done by adverse fate to rouse me from that dream. My verses had come back to me from the magazines of the whole English-speaking world with unfailing promptness, and yet I was not swerved from my purpose of making verses, and making a living by them. It seems very incredible, very preposterous, and yet it was not without its root, the fairy flower, in actuality, in the literary experience which was commoner then than now. *Hiawatha* had sold like a latter-day novel, and so had *Evangeline* before it; Tennyson was as popular as any of our newest romancers; Alexander's [Alexander Smith's] will-o'-the-wisp *Life Drama* [14] had swept the land like the wildfire it was; Tupper's [15] *Proverbial Philosophy* had breathed its rhythmical wisdom from the marble top of every centre table in the country; it might not yet have been the impassioned hour of Owen Meredith's *Lucille,* but his earlier poems were in every throbbing hand that was not in some other throbbing hand. My own later newspaper experience had given my self-knowledge the keen edge which may be noted in all young journalists, but in the lapse of my long, official leisure this sharpness had been lost, and I had reverted to the gentle ignorance of my primal literary intention. It wanted some kindlier touch from the hand of Destiny to break my illusion, and this came one morning in a letter from James Russell Lowell, accepting an article of mine for the *North American Review*. He was then the editor of that periodical, to which I am still contributing after nearly fifty years; and I suppose I had offered him my paper on "Recent Italian Comedy" in some interval between getting back a poem from one editor and sending it to another. I never failed to do this; but it took me a little time to catch my breath after each knock-down blow, and then I gaspingly set about doing something in prose. Usually I did so without relinquishing for a moment that prime purpose of out-Poping Pope with which I had started in literature but later relinquished for the intention of surpassing more modern masters; but now I must have distinctly faltered, or perhaps I ought to say wavered. I perceived that it was open to me to be a critic in a field where my solitude, if not my magnitude, would give me monumental distinction. No one else that I knew of was discussing contemporary Italian literature; I was always more or less filling myself up with its unstaying substance, and that kind, that overkind, letter of my *dolce duca* gave me an impulse which was not exhausted till it had eventuated in the studies and versions of the *Modern Italian Poets,* a volume largely reprinted from papers first written for the *North American*.

I will not burlesque, though it would be so easy to burlesque, the facts of my change from a supreme purpose of poetry to a supreme purpose of prose. All the time that I had been writing my verses in one dreamland, I had been making my sketches in another. But as yet I had only printed the sketches in a Boston newspaper,[16] after failing with them in the *Atlantic Monthly* and *Harper's Magazine;* and it was a distinct call to the larger criticism which I heard in Lowell's note. Book-notices enough I had written in Ohio newspapers and elsewhere, but I had not till now seen myself in the majestic proportions of quarterly reviewer which I had envied other men.

I wish I could impart the thrill of joy and hope and pride which that note gave me, a trumpet call to battle, which echoed and re-echoed in my soul and seemed to fill the universe with its reverberation. To be accepted by an editor has the advantage of being accepted by a woman, in that it may be almost indefinitely repeated, while, with all modern facilities of divorce, one cannot well be married more than half a dozen times; but in the tender glow of intimate satisfaction the two experiences are all but identical. For days and days, for weeks and weeks, I would not be parted from that letter which was all but frayed to tatters by my fondness. Life, which had been dimmed by fold on fold of editorial refusal, resumed its loveliness in the effulgence of this acceptance, and in the crepuscular promise of the new day my literary purposes shaped themselves anew. I renounced the intention of earning a livelihood by verse, and dedicated myself to prose with a constancy which has since been only occasionally corrupted. I have written many and many a *North American Review* paper, and every manner of study, sketch, tale, and novel, with essays and travels and plays; but I have turned aside so rarely to verse that one small volume would easily contain all I have done in that sort, against the forty or fifty that would hardly hold the things I have done in those other sorts.

I can still see myself coming out of the Gothic landgate of the Palazzo Giustiniani dei Vescovi, where I dwelt in less splendor than might be imagined from its name, receiving Lowell's letter from the postman with my own hand, and knowing it his at a glance by the beautiful superscription, and tremulously breaking the seal, and then going back up into the palace, and expanding to its utmost measure of height and breadth. I had meant to go somewhere, but I went nowhere that I can remember; in fact I do not know what became of me for days. Very likely I set to work on that historical study of Ducal Mantua, which I duly printed in succession to the "Recent Italian Comedy," as a contribution to the *North American*.

Verse became more and more "My shame in crowds, my solitary pride," as the immediate years passed, but when I came home to America I began thriftily to dispose of the old stock of poems which had been returned upon my hands by

356

those pitiless magazine editors. In the market which I found surprisingly open to me I sold one poem to the *Nation* [17] for enough to pay for my winter's coal, and I remember how the fact amused my father-in-law, who happened to be visiting us, and saw the coal putting into our cellar. I printed in book form a long story in hexameters; [18] and then on the publisher's complaint that he had lost money by it rather superroyally returned him my royalty. But another piece in hexameters brought me fifty dollars (to be sure in the pathetically depreciated paper of the day) from the *Galaxy* magazine, [19] long since "with God," as the pious old phrase is. So with other things of the deserted Muse, whose raiment was stripped from her till I could almost say in all literalness, "Povera e nuda vai, Filosofia." [20] In the end every scrap of metre was marketed; but even at the advanced rates I could hardly have lived upon the proceeds, and prose was a steady support. It was not that my heart turned from the Muse in her penury; she was all the dearer because she was poor, and would have kept me so, but because there were higher claims than hers, the higher and dearer claims of the common human lot which every man must first of all satisfy. Now and again, through those many intervening years since 1864, I have returned to her and invoked her divine forgiveness. In these recourses I have held that prose which sold so much better might also be poetry, if well imagined and carefully altered, while verse might play one false and be a masquerade of dull commonplace. So for the most part I have excused myself from constant and direct service to the Muse; but there has hardly been a year of those five-and-forty when I have not paid her my devoir; and as I have meant my life long to turn and be a professed Christian, to go to church and hear sermons, and say prayers, and the like, so I have never quite forsaken the hope of dwelling in that heavenly presence an avowed poet. Brazen it out as we will in behalf of prose, there is a mystic power in verse which utters in a measured line the passion and the aspiration which a whole unmetred volume cannot express.

Besides this turning-point, at which my two selves came face to face and had it out with each other, there were hours of terrible choice when I had to say and to do one of two alternative things on which my fate hung. Such an hour was that when once it was sharply borne in upon me that I must choose between literature and law, and cleave with my whole mind to one or the other. I cannot now remember just what had tempted me away from the current of my life, except, perhaps, that it had stagnated in the printing-office where I used to dream my dreams in a little village of northern Ohio.²¹ In that village a general love of literature existed, but such a thing as a literary career was hardly imagined outside of my brain-pan. You could be a business man of one sort or other, but if you wished to be somebody, you must study law. Then you could be a lawyer, and in the course of nature, a politician, and an office-holder, rising through lucrative county offices to memberships of the State Legislature, and of Congress, and culminating in the United States Senate, and—who knows? Heaven knows!— the White House itself, though Ohio men were not yet so habitually elected to the Presidency as they have been since. In the book recording *My Literary Passions* ²² I have already told how I was so daunted by learning from Blackstone that "the Law is a jealous mistress," that I fled from her exacting presence back to the tolerant affection of the Muse. I need not repeat the story here, nor twice tell the tale of yet another reversion, when I turned from an opening path of journalism to dedicate myself again to dreams of poetic glory. Those were the days when I imitated the Spanish *romancieros,* when I imitated Heine and Uhland, when I imitated Tennyson, when I imitated Longfellow, and Keats, and Kingsley, and whatever other poet lent himself to my unconscious homage.²³ It is a prime condition of this sort of self-teaching that you must always think yourself your own master, and debtor to none but nature for your inspirations and their expression.

All along with the successive renunciations of every service but that of poetry persisted the question of living by its favor. For the present it did not trouble me much; for I was really living by my handicraft of printer, which I loved and rejoiced in; but there was the future which did not fail to recall itself to me at times, and trouble the visions which swam round me in the long afternoons, when I was distributing my case. I do not know what golden hours the operator of a linotype machine may now know; I will not deny them; but I doubt if he is ever so rapt from the sense of work as a compositor might be fifty or sixty years ago when he was renewing the sources of his next day's work. It was a mechanical employment, yes, and it involved the shame which still waits on handiwork, but I was no more conscious of the flying types than the pianist is of the throbbing keys. If I could again be transported so far from myself, I would be glad of the same means; but, perhaps, one must be nineteen or twenty for the full effect of the magic; the force of that is not increased by the increase of the years to seventy-three.

I suspect in the polite reader a sense of something sordid in my talk of earning a livelihood, and I would like to disabuse him of it, if I may, while I still insist upon the necessity as a governing motive in my turning to prose at the moment when I most consciously gave myself to that form of literature, in its infinite variety. I should like to persuade him of the beauty which one perceives in earning one's keep, which is duly heightened by the greater handsomeness of the keep. Poverty is an ugly thing, so ugly that I wish there might more quickly be none of it in the world than I fear there is any just hope of, though I do believe that we can, and will, one day end it. There is but one thing which can justify a man in remaining poorer when he can become richer, and that is the sort of truth which we recognize by the name of honesty. Ugly is one's own poverty, uglier yet the poverty which one inflicts on those helplessly dependent upon him. He is to blame, to blame sorely, who does not use every fair and kind means to brighten and adorn his lot and theirs. Let him not cherish any beloved longings at the common cost; the beauty he will so make is not to be matched with the beauty he can live if he does his utmost for the common welfare.

The day will come, I believe, when there will be no money in the world, and when we shall all live in plenteous and graceful ease by mutual service, but well on toward that day we must each get as much money as he can without greed or theft, or any smallest hurt to his neighbor. Money justly earned is sweet, and its sweetness is quantitative as well as qualitative; though when the money earned passes immediate need we become insensible of it. That is right; it is a sign from Heaven that we have had enough. But short of that we shall taste the sweetness of it, the joy of having won through it a coign of peace and safety for those entrusted to our valor.

I could not honestly say that I was instantly sensible of a turning-point in my career with the coming of that letter from Lowell. Things do not happen so in real life, though they often happen so in fiction; and I like the reader to think that this confidence is a bit of real life. Perhaps, if I were to be more precise, to be quite accurate, I should say that there was not so much a fatal turning in the way as an opening, a widening of the perspective in a quarter where there had indeed been scope, which had not yet flattered my steps to penetrate it to the utmost verge. I have not yet reached that point; the vista has widened before me as I have advanced, and charmed me more and more. I have found it full of divine surprises, of invitations to stray apart, and break wild-flowery by-ways to the right and left. I know the witchery of verse, the mystery and the miracle of rhyme, which, when a word finds its mate, their marriage mothers an endless offspring of unexpected thoughts. I have known the still joy of patient working, of patient waiting, till somehow the broken pieces of color clung together in a kaleidoscopic pattern of loveliness in which seeming chance omnipotently befriended art. In translation of others' verse I have experienced this delight, as well as in my own, so that I have come almost to believe that if you will let a version have time, it will take the very form of the original, word for word, rhyme for rhyme, metre for metre, and to doubt whether the many, the most, renderings of poetry in paraphrastic diction and paraphrastic dimension are not the effect of indolence, or impatience.

To stay with one's endeavor for the English meaning, say,

of a German or Italian lyric, and watch the original passing through the alembic of one's mind, and distilling itself liquid, limpid, in an English poem perfectly responsive, after days, after weeks even, what greater bliss can there be for the soul of art? One is oneself translated to a region of pure bliss in the exercise of this patience, the fulfilment of this trust. Yet, sometimes I think there is a finer pleasure in divining the subtle offices, the exquisite potentialities of prose. It is like walking in a fair country over a path that wanders at will among waving fields, beside rambling brooks, through shadowy woods and sunny openings, all under a blue sky; and the birds flute and trill on every side, and when you will them, the shy words come trooping, come flying, and settle in their chosen places as of their own accord with no rhythmic compulsion and no metrical command. Prose, when it is perfected, will be as sweet as the talk of gracious-minded women, as simple and strong as the parlance of serious men; and it will not have to hide the art of its construction, for it will be a thing born, not made, and will live from the pen as it lives from the lips. It will then be the highest privilege of letters to serve it; and yet—and yet—if I must be honest at last, I have to own that there lurks in me the hope, the secret longing for work in the sort from which there seemed to be so vital a turning in me when that letter of Lowell's came. Looking at the fact a little more narrowly in the light of such self-knowledge as I have, as I have acquired in the present writing, I do not believe there has really been any such change in me as I began by pretending. From my earliest remembrance, from the time before I could read, when I made up stories to match the pictures in the first book I ever looked at, "one continuous purpose" of literature has run through my life. My work has always been so "lief and dear" to me that now in my seventy-third year a proof of the thing I have last written is as wondrously precious as that which I printed from the types put together with my childish hands, when I could have been about seven, in an essay on *Human Life*. The theme is one which in manifold phases has engaged me since, and I suppose will flatter my notice to the end, with the perpetual chance of turning out a song or turning out a sermon. But could I have my way with it, I might have it in form like my beloved Heine's *Reisebilder*, where the page of prose always tremulous with inner music, breaks now and again into open rhyme.

A BACKWARD AND
A FORWARD LOOK

✦

INTRODUCTION

WHEN Van Wyck Brooks, then a young reporter, asked the seventy-two-year-old Howells whether as a writer he took more delight in his fiction or in his criticism, he replied, with a good deal of warmth, "Oh, fiction, fiction. Writing novels is a kind of work in which you do not satisfy yourself entirely, but nothing could more nearly satisfy an honest man. I have never been really pleased with any of my criticism. Here and there would be a piece of luck—that is all."

Two years later, in an Easy Chair essay for *Harper's*, May, 1911, Howells expanded upon this brief comment. He is frankly personal, recalling the days on the Study when he was shocking the sensibilities of "that large class of dotards" who worshiped at the shrines of Scott, Dickens, and Thackeray, unwilling to hear the subtler appeal of Hardy, Valdés, Tolstoy, and others. Readers of the Study had been for the most part incensed by these monthly utterances, Howells tells us. Were the authors themselves "ever pleased with the form of a critic's censure?" Though "the critic is often quite right," concluded Howells, "he is right too late."

On March 2, 1912, Howells had an opportunity publicly to express his view of American literature based on fifty years of experience as both critic and writer. At that time George Brinton McClellan Harvey, then head of Harper and Brothers, arranged for a dinner at Sherry's to celebrate Howells' seventy-fifth birthday. "Of course," Howells wrote to his brother several weeks before the affair, "I would rather not have been 75 years old. I hear it is to be the largest dinner on record:

and I have begun to write out my few impromptu remarks.'' In his birthday speech Howells glanced backward at our literary tradition and forward to our literary future in a rapidly changing society. His address was first published in the March 9 issue of *Harper's Weekly* and then, together with a letter from Henry James, was reprinted in the April, 1912, issue of the *North American Review*, the version reproduced below.

The occasion itself, attended by President William Howard Taft, "was really something extraordinary," Howells wrote to James in thanking him for his congratulatory letter. "Four hundred notables swarmed about a hundred tables on the floor, and we elect sat at a long board on a dais." The letter from James, written to be read to the gathering, was laid aside, somewhat to the relief of Howells, who was throughout the evening, he told his old friend, "in a daze" from which he "wrenched" himself for twenty minutes to read his own remarks. James's letter was to Howells undoubtedly the most significant part of the "ghastly" occasion, which was "all, all wrong and unfit." The tribute from his friend and fellow craftsman sent him dreaming back to the old Cambridge days.

Your letter, meant for the public eye, brought before mine the vision of those days and nights in Sacramento street, "when my bosom was young," and swelled with pride in your friendship and joy in sharing your literary ambition, as if it were the "communion of saints." I do thank you for it, and I am eager for all men to read it in the *North American,* to which, as alone worthy of reporting it, it has been transferred from the *Weekly.*

James, in this letter—which is in fact a short essay—speaks for a host of young writers in referring to Howells' editorial kindness. In the *Atlantic* period of fifty years earlier Howells was "the making" of James's "confidence that required help and sympathy."

You showed me the way and opened me the door; you wrote to me and confessed yourself struck with me—I have never forgotten the beautiful thrill of *that.* You published me at once—and paid me, above all, with a dazzling promptitude; magnificently, I felt, and so that nothing since has ever quite come up to it. More than this even, you cheered me with a sympathy that was in itself an inspiration. I mean that you talked to me and listened to me—ever so patiently and genially and suggestively conversed and consorted with me. This won me to you irresistibly and made you the most interesting person I knew.

Howells' critical reviews and essays reprinted in this book give one only a suggestion of the many writers who were thus encouraged and published—and paid—by this editor who, at the same time, was eager to return to his own novel writing. Were it not for the fact that many a young contributor to the *Atlantic* and to *Harper's* walked into Howells' office and soon became involved in a literary discussion with the genial and patient editor, Howells might never have paused to formulate his critical theory. Against his better judgment he was persuaded by J. Henry Harper in 1885 to undertake a monthly contribution to "The Editor's Study," and here he expressed his unsystematized conclusions about the writing of novels, which he had reached after many years of talking with writers, reviewing their books, and experimenting with his own.

The battle for "truth" in novel writing is never won; nor did Howells delude himself with the belief that his voice had prevailed, in spite of the vigorous discussion stirred up by *Criticism and Fiction* on both sides of the Atlantic. In a "Bibliographical Note" written for the 1911 Library Edition of *My Literary Passions* and *Criticism and Fiction*, Howells referred to the essays collected in the 1891 edition of the latter book in these quiet words, which serve as a summing up of a controversy that was both of its period and of every period. The essays in this little book, writes Howells, deal with "the office of Criticism and the art of Fiction." They

may serve to recall to an elder generation than this the time when their author was breaking so many lances in the great, forgotten war between Realism and Romanticism that the floor of the "Editor's Study" in *Harper's Magazine* was strewn with the embattled splinters. The "Editor's Study" is now quite another place, but he who originally imagined it in 1886, and abode in it until 1892, made it at once the scene of such constant offense that he had no time, if he had the temper, for defense. The great Zola, or call him the immense Zola, was the prime mover in the attack upon the masters of the Romanticistic school; but he lived to own that he had fought a losing fight, and there are some proofs that he was right. The Realists, who were undoubtedly the masters of fiction in their passing generation, and who prevailed not only in France, but in Russia, in Scandinavia, in Spain, in Portugal, were overborne in all Anglo-Saxon countries by the innumerable hosts of Romanticism, who to this day possess the land; though still, whenever a young novelist does work instantly recognizable for its truth and beauty among us, he is seen and felt to have wrought in the spirit of Realism. Not even yet, however, does the average critic recognize this, and such lesson as the "Editor's Study" assumed to teach remains here [in *Criticism and Fiction*] in all its essentials for his improvement.

On the occasion of his seventy-fifty birthday Howells recalled for a younger generation the "forgotten war between Realism and Romanticism," which is the subject of *Criticism and Fiction*. He reminded his hearers that when he began his career, the United States had little literature of its own. Most of the reading of his youth came from the romantic novelists of England, and it was from the Continental masters that American fiction received the bent toward realism which it still keeps "wherever it is vital."

Mr. Howells's Speech *

SOME fifty-two years ago, come next summer, I sat with the great Hawthorne on the hill behind his house in Concord and heard him say several memorable things. The most memorable of these things was to the effect that there was nothing like recognition to make a man modest. At the time I supposed he was speaking of one of his neighbors, perhaps Thoreau, perhaps Alcott, who had not had recognition enough to make him modest. It has since occurred to me that he had the actual occasion in mind and was with a subtle prescience insinuating the kindly hope that I might profit by the insurpassable inducement to shrink into the background which has been given me here tonight. This, in fact, is what I propose to do when I have made you believe that I really mean it in putting away the

* *North American Review*, April, 1912.

crowns you have offered me on this little Lupercal of mine. I can do this the more easily when I remember that the occasion was no more the effect of my wishing than of my deserving, but was created solely by that genius for hospitality in our host which bends all wills to it when it frees itself in the motion of a seventy-fifth birthday dinner or the like. I can do it still more easily, if possible, when I recall myself to consciousness of the fact that whatever else has brought you here, you are glad and proud to be here supremely because the occasion is honored by the nation in the presence of the man who honors the high office of Washington and Lincoln.

If you ask me for some further conjecture of mine as to why our host or his chief guest should have united on this occasion so apparently, so evidently inadequate, I will urge in their defense that I do not come seventy-five years of age every day, and that if I should prove altogether unworthy of their kindness the occasion will not repeat itself though I should live to be a hundred. Except as a condition of being still alive, I would not have chosen to have a seventy-fifth birthday. It is something that both practice and precept would have forbidden me. I have never had a seventy-fifth birthday before in my life and I am keenly aware that in now venturing upon one I am transcending the psalmist's limit of threescore years and ten. Yet, with all this, I will not deny that there is some merit in having lived seventy-five years, in having outrun the psalmist with his hampering limit, though there is not so much merit as the man who has done it is apt to think. The very experience of life which has enlightened him on most points rather darkens him on this one and he has come to believe that somehow he has done the things he has witnessed, or, if he has not done them, that they have been done because of him. I should like you to keep this amiable peculiarity of our race in view when I say what great things of our literature I have personally known and what great things I hope of it.

To the backward glance the light of the past seems one great glow, but it is in fact a group of stellar fires; fixed stars not unaccompanied by wandering comets, not without the gaiety of aimless meteors. Perhaps, it is as some incandescent mass that the future will behold this present when it has become the past, and we who sit here tonight shall appear one great glow without distinction of age or sex or any qualitative difference in our several glory. But we who sit here tonight are keenly aware of distinctions and of differences. Such of us as are the fixed stars know very well which are the wandering comets and which are the aimless meteors kindly only in their passage through our atmosphere. It has been so in every period; and if I say that I knew at first hand the luminaries of a by-gone period it is not merely to attribute their greatness to my acquaintance with them, but it is also to affirm their consciousness of difference from one another. They differed as the stars differ in glory and always will, though the stars may not know it as these great men did. The list of them is very long, and I may say that if I missed the personal acquaintance of Cooper and Irving and Poe and Prescott I was personally acquainted with all the others in whom the story of American literature sums itself. I knew Hawthorne and Emerson and Walt Whitman; I knew Longfellow and Holmes and Whittier and Lowell; I knew Bryant and Bancroft and Motley; I knew Harriet Beecher Stowe and Julia Ward Howe; I knew Artemus Ward and Stockton and Mark Twain; I knew Parkman and Fiske. Names refulgent still, however the fire, never to be relumed, seems beginning to die out of some of them; names such as we have hardly the like of.

Hardly the like of? I say this, but I say it askingly and at the worst wistfully in fear of your response to a question which I should myself answer courageously rather than categorically. I should not want to be damped by your doubt or to have my ever-youthful faith dashed by your experience, and so before you can get in a word I make haste to declare; yes, we have many like them, but of no more identity with them than they felt with one another. As far as they were truly great they must have perceived that they were not so great as they had grown to seem and each must have perceived even more clearly that the others were not so great. But it is not this point that I care to insist upon, it is another; it is that difference in the present from the past which I think is inevitable from what seems the new conditioning of our lives. All of human life has turned more and more to the light of democracy, the light of equality, if you please. Literature, which was once of the cloister, the school, has become more and more of the forum and incidentally of the market-place. But it is actuated now by as high and noble motives as ever it was in the history of the world; and I think that in turning from the vain endeavor of creating beauty and devoting itself to the effort of ascertaining life it is actuated by a clearer motive than before. If we have no single name so sovereign as these names I have cited, we have many talents which do things impossible to the geniuses who wore these names on earth. Let us love them, let us honor them; we cannot worship them too much, but let us remember their limitations and consider the potentiality of the artists who now are and are to be. Let us recognize the fact that in the present vast output of literature the pure gold is not less in quantity because the mass of dirt and dross is so immeasurably greater than in the days of another sort of mining. I myself believe there is gold greater in quantity and that possibly in a critical analysis the report of the assayer will declare as high a percentage of the genuine metal. I am not dismayed by the numbers who have taken to literature in these days and found a living in it. At first it seems a little odd, a little droll to have a publisher announce a novel as "by a new writer"; but when there are so many new readers, why should not the new writers have their innings? The old ones have had theirs and even the old readers do not want them always. Ought not we old writers, who are confronting a new life elsewhere at such close range, try to be in love with the new literature here? I myself am going to cultivate an affection for it from this on.

The great men I have named could not do just the fine things, the brave things, the true things that are done now by the men I will not name lest I miss some in the long count. In my time I have seen a whole literature grow up and flourish into national proportions. Nearly all the writers I have been naming were New Englanders, but now our writers are of every sectional origin and constitute an American authorship. They are of the West and the South, as well as of the North and East, and more and more their work tastes of the soil that mothered them. Once we had a New England literature, now we have an American literature, and Indianapolis is, as Boston was, a city in which books are held dear and the art of them is prized above any other. The poets, the best of them, are of or from the West; our ablest living historian [24] is a Western man; our students of the human mind in the past and the human soul in the present—a very stellar group—are of the East; but our novelists and our novelettists are from every part of the country; and each is devoted wittingly, or unwittingly to the representation of the America that he knows best because he has lived it most.

A literature as authentic and distinctive as our journalism has grown up in the years since the Civil War; my years, which must seem almost antediluvian to some of you here, and with this literature as truly as with our commerce and our finance the American consciousness has increased. We makers of that literature may not always realize it and the readers of that literature very seldom knew it, but the fact remains; and its genius may be intelligibly traced, I think. We began our national career by having no literature of our own; our reading, except in the very noble political writing of the fathers, came from England; and then, as the rift between the two countries deepened and widened, it began to come from the European continent. When I commenced author it was yet coming very little from that continent. We still prayed at the old shrines; and our knees knocked together at the names of the awful gods of English criticism who scarcely even deigned an open contempt for our poor little offerings. Gradully the light which showed us the way dawned upon us and it dawned from the countenance of that most generous of the nations, from France, from the face of her who befriended us in our struggle to be an independent people; from France whose schools no less of literature than of art and science are freely open to any in the whole world who will learn. Some of you may not know this, but I know it, for I am of the generation that lived it and I would fain help to have it remembered that we studied from the French masters, the continental masters, to imitate nature, and gave American fiction the bent which it still keeps wherever it is vital. You may not know it, or, if you know it, you may not own it, but this is the fact, and though a flood of unreality followed us and swept us under, when that deluge went down there all over the land, the seed that we had planted, behold! it had sprouted and stood— "Fast-rooted in the fruitful soil." I would have you all, whatever esthetic thinking or feeling you are of, look about you and see whether every plant now bearing good and nourishing fruit is not of that growth.

There are many kinds of art, but there is only one best kind; and while every one ought to be freely suffered and cordially welcomed to do the thing he most likes to do, none of us should forget that there is only one best thing. Look about you, I say, not only in America, but in England, and you will see that what I say is true, for the English, too, have come to the right faith in their latest and greatest work. But we came to this faith first because we had opener minds than the English and because we brought a willingness to learn of those masters who could teach, because we also were somehow instinctively continental. Since then a world of continental art has offered itself to us. Masterpieces have come to us from everywhere—from Norway, from Russia, from Poland, from Spain, from Italy, from Portugal—and I know no higher joy than to recognize that our best work is a response in form and spirit to that best kind which these masterpieces exemplify. Our fiction so far as it really exists is of the European and not the English make and the newer English fiction, so far as it really exists, is not of the English, but of the European make, the American make.

If I come now to speak of poetry, I own there are no sources so sweet and pure as the English sources. But I do not willingly yield the primacy in poetry to the English poets contemporary with the American poets I knew. Longfellow and Bryant and Emerson and Whittier and Lowell and Holmes—"Touched the tender stops of various quills" to as beautiful effect of truth as the English poets of their time and, perhaps, in even wider range. But they belonged to an idealistic period when men dreamed of human perfectibility through one mighty reform. Their dream was that if the slaves were freed there could hardly be sorrow on the earth which our good-will could not easily assuage. Now long ago the slaves were freed, but through the rift of the poets' broken dream the faces of underwaged women and overworked children stare at us; and it does not seem as if it were a sufficient change that now those faces are white and not black. Has the real frightened the ideal from us? Is poetry so essentially of the ideal that it must go into exile with it? Or is it that our poetry is not equal to the claim which humanity has upon America beyond all other lands and shrinks from a duty which should be her solemn joy? They who dreamed that beautiful dream in other days were each at some moment realists in their lives as they were idealists in their art. Each according to his gift laid his offering on the altar of freedom; but has each of our later poets, according to his gift, laid his offering on the altar of justice? For equality, which is justice "writ large," is now the hope of humanity and its service is the condition which has effected itself even in the mystical sources where the inspirations of art have their rise. Yet I am ready, almost ready, to say that as much good poetry is written in this time as in the time that is past; but it is not the poetry of the few, it is the poetry of the many. We no longer have supremacies, we no longer have primacies; the gods, the half-gods, the heroes are gone, I hope not to return; and it is the high average which reigns in this as in all American things. Amidst the misgivings of our excellence in poetry we may console ourselves with the fact that the average in it is higher than ever before.

This I truly believe, though I could not allege the proofs as easily as I could allege these of our national advance in the art of the stage. Not less wonderful to me than the growth of the American novel in the fifty years which have now passed like a vision of the night is the growth of the American play. Scarcely less astonishing is that mood of ours, for it is only a mood, to which this fact is not apparent. I had greatly admired the modern English drama with hardly a question of its superiority to ours, but last summer, when I was expressing my high sense of it to an Englishman in London, he said: "Yes, but you know you are doing much better things at home," and though he gave me no instances he set me thinking, and I thought I perceived that in their very difference from the English things which I had so admired there was that which at least equaled our things with theirs. I thought I saw that while the English dramatists painted manners so wonderfully well, ours painted nature, our everyday American nature, which at the bottom of its heart is always human nature. If they did not paint manners so well it was perhaps because we had none to paint, or perhaps because our customs, which we make do for manners, change so rapidly from day to day, from Boston to Pittsburg, from to-morrow to the day after, and from Pittsburg to Oklahoma, that the kinematograph alone can catch them. Besides, our drama is still very new. Before the great Civil War which fertilized the fields of thought among us, as well as the fields of battle with the blood of its sacrifice, we had no drama which was essentially American except the wretched stage travesty of that most essentially American novel, *Uncle Tom's Cabin*. But now already we have a drama which has touched our life at many characteristic points, which has dealt with our moral and material problems and penetrated the psychological regions which it seemed impossible an art so objective should reach. Mainly it has been gay as our prevalent mood is; mainly it has been honest as our habit is in cases where we believe we can afford it; mainly it has been decent and clean and sweet as our average life is; and now that Ibsen no longer writes new plays, I would rather take my chance of pleasure and profit with a new American play than with any other sort of new play. We are still waiting our Shakespeare, but we can very well wait patiently for him; perhaps one Shakespeare is enough for all time; and in the mean while we may console ourselves in the drama as in poetry with that high or higher average which is the distinctive American thing.

It is this which most consoles me for our bereavement in a region where it seems irreparable. In that American humor which within the half-century of my observation developed itself in such proportion as almost to dwarf any other growth of our air, there was one humorist who when he died might well have given us the sense of Shakesperian loss, though we are not yet aware of a Shakesperian gain. But the soul of Mark Twain which divined and uttered the inmost and most immanent American mood has passed again so lastingly into the American consciousness that it will remain the inspiration of that high or higher average in humor which once again is the distinctively American thing. It will take many forms and offer many aspects to our glad recognition. But hereafter that high or higher average of our humor must always be generous and magnanimous; in its broadest clowning, its wildest grotesquery, it can never forget to be kind, to be kind to the whole world that the touch of nature makes kin, but especially kind to those that the world and the world's law seem to have kept strangers to the rest of the family.

If I had been witness to no other surpassing things of American growth in my fifty years of observation, I should think it glory enough to have lived in the same time and in the same land with the man whose name must always embody American humor to human remembrance. What has been my own influence on that time in that land I should like so much to say, so much to say! But the theme is too vast, if not for my powers, then for your patience. Regretfully, very sorrowfully, I turn from the alluring opportunity. I shall never be just seventy-five years old again, and the ripe occasion must go rot in these bins of oblivion where so much occasion has failed of even the sad immortality of cold storage. Yet, in the midst of my self-denial, in my poignant regret for having said so little about myself in my survey of things, "all which I was and part of which I saw," if I may so construe the Latin, I am very truly grateful for the lenient things that have been said of me here already and for those which I cannot help hoping some of you are still going to say of me. I must spend the rest of my days trying to puzzle out the reason of these things, unless I lay it at once to your compassion for a man who is seventy-five years old and still lives. But in venturing to live on I have the hope of returning those things in kind, for I understand that it is the purpose of our host to give you each a birthday dinner as fast as you become seventy-five years old, and that his most honored guest, still typifying the Nation at its best, will come to them all.

HOWELLS AND THE HOUSE
OF HARPER

≫⋘

INTRODUCTION

FEW OF the guests who gathered to honor Howells at Sherry's could have read "Mr. Howells's Paper," which had appeared barely two weeks before in J. Henry Harper's history, *The House of Harper*. So important did this statement seem to the literary world of that day, however, that the New York *Evening Post* reprinted the paper, May 11, 1912 (except for the last three paragraphs), so that it might reach a wider public than the four hundred guests who dined at Sherry's. We are including here the portion that appeared in the *Post*.

The paper is of interest because of the autobiographical light it casts on the author and, more particularly, because of the account Howells gives of the actual publication of the essays that comprised *Criticism and Fiction*. The stands Howells took for truth in literature in his advocacy of realism, and for truth toward humanity in his opposition to the execution of the Chicago Anarchists, are well known, but nowhere else than in the paper do we find Howells stating in so forthright a manner his realization of the defeat of his efforts in these years during which he wrote "The Editor's Study." Nor do we find anywhere else a clearer statement of the attitude of Harper's toward its outspoken contributor. In this paper one steps into the Franklin Square office of the House of Harper and listens to the conferences of "the man of letters" with "the man of business."

Howells had seriously injured his financial position by his courageous attitudes; he feared, for at least one sleepless night, that he would be in want. Through the good sense and kindliness of the Harpers, however, Howells kept as busy as ever for the decade of the nineties, and, finally, after the reorganization of the House of Harper in 1900, he secured a place on Harper's staff for the rest of his life.

In "Mr. Howells's Paper," which the *Evening Post* printed with the caption "Howells's Path Not Easy," Howells looked back to his early efforts to publish his poems in *Harper's* and then to the stirring days when, from "The Editor's Study," he was encouraging American writers to discover their own way of writing. But in his anniversary speech Howells also had commented on the new writers of the period. The *Post*, therefore, of March 27, featured an interview, entitled "With Mr. Howells," in which the novelist enlarged on his views of poets and storytellers appearing in the magazines of 1912. To recognize and encourage young writers, to remember that criticism is secondary to creativeness, to refuse to accept a false distinction between journalism and literature, to appreciate the native touch in writing—all these attitudes expressed more than twenty years earlier in *Criticism and Fiction*—Howells discussed with the *Post* interviewer with the old liveliness.

"And do you think that volume of production is a good thing, Mr. Howells?" asked the interviewer of the author of several shelves of books.

"Yes, to be sure, it is a good thing," Howells promptly replied. "Trying to restrict the volume of production on the plea that it is wise is the same as trying to restrict a man. No man can 'write himself out' unless there is nothing in him. Remember the old artists—it is the same with them—Valesquez, Tintoretto, and his wonderful pictures, Titian—they covered acres of canvas, and grew with their work. A man cannot write himself out."

Howells, at seventy-five, had not written himself out. He still felt the full, free creative vigor reflected in *Criticism and Fiction,* and this spirit he passed on to hosts of younger writers who helped to form our culture. Recognizing the position that Howells held in the world of letters, President William Howard Taft could tell the assembled dinner guests at Sherry's, "I have travelled from Washington to do honor to the greatest living American writer and novelist" (*New York Tribune,* March 3, 1912).

376

HOWELLS AND THE HOUSE OF HARPER

Mr. Howells's Paper *

AFTER I had printed five or six poems in the *Atlantic Monthly*, I made several unsuccessful attempts to contribute to *Harper's Magazine*, notably in the autumn of 1861, when, with the support of my friend, Richard Henry Stoddard, I moved personally upon the editor in Franklin Square with a poem which, after many vicissitudes, was at last printed in *The Nation*. He was proof against our joint forces, and I did not penetrate his stronghold until two years later, when I sent him a piece called "St. Christopher," with an illustration by my wife, who had sketched the figure over a garden gate in Venice, after I had made it the subject of my verse. I think the editor was then still Mr. Guernsey,[25] who had not hitherto liked my things, but who, when he later returned a prose paper (the reader will find "A Visit to Arqua" in *Italian Journeys* and in the early files of *The Nation*), graciously said that if he were making a magazine solely to please himself he would take it. It must have been nearly twenty years before I again offered anything to Harper's, when Mr. Alden accepted a long story in hexameters, again on a Venetian theme, which had languished many years in manuscript without finding editorial favor. It was called "Pordenone," and I still do not think it was very bad, though the reader who turns to it in my "Poems," so called, may not agree with me.

I had then ceased to be editor of the *Atlantic Monthly*, and was in the employ of the late James R. Osgood, who took everything I wrote and paid me a yearly salary for it. He sold the material wherever he could, mostly to *The Century*, where *A Modern Instance, The Rise of Silas Lapham,* and *The Minister's Charge* were serialized in the order given. In the mean time he had been asked for one of my novels by Mr. J. W. Harper,[26] who wanted "a Boston story" from him, and who, when he got the manuscript of *Indian Summer* and read the name Ponte Vecchio on the first page, was at no pains to hide his humorous disgust with

*Reprinted by permission from *The House of Harper*, published by Harper & Brothers, copyright 1912.

377

the Florentine scene. I remember his asking me, not very hopefully, I am afraid, whether I thought it as good as *The Minister's Charge,* which was a Boston story with a vengeance; and when I assured him that I did, he consoled himself as well as he could.

I now began to write frequently for the *Magazine,* or rather, regularly, sending a farce in time for every Christmas number. The farces really began in the *Atlantic Monthly,* and my first Harper farces were printed in the *Weekly.* I offered one of them to my late friend Laffan,[27] who was then the English manager for the House and whom I met in London; and when I went to Italy for the winter I gave him another, at increased rates—many other farces, as we joked it together, having been winter-killed. It is my impression that it was this increased expensiveness which led to their use in the *Monthly,* which could better afford to pay the prices. They made me a very amiable public there with the youth who played in drawing-rooms and church parlors; they never got upon the stage, though they were represented over the Union in private theatricals, and, as Mr. Alden gratifyingly told me, were asked for in the advance sheets months before their publication. One of them, indeed, enjoyed a most noble distinction in London, where *The Mouse Trap* was twice played with an all-star cast for a charity which naturally and rightly did not include the author; he thought it riches to have his play done by Miss Ellen Terry[28] and Mrs. Kendal[29] and the like planetary splendors.

By and by Osgood failed in business,[30] and through the good office of the late Charles Fairchild (so many of my friends are dead that I find it rather lonely to be alive myself) I was brought into the relation with the House of Harper & Brothers, which has existed, with a few years' interval at one time, for twenty-five years in practically the same form. Osgood had already come to the Harpers, and he was frankly vexed that I should not have come to them through his interest; but, as he said, the great matter was my being there, and Fairchild was his friend, too, and had long had dealings with them for paper; he was not yet a banker and broker. The *pour parlers* were by letter and telegram, and then I went on to New York for my final interview with the head of the House, then Mr. J. W. Harper. I lunched with him in the fine great room which still continues the supreme audience chamber at Franklin Square, under the roaring eaves of the elevated railroad, and we talked our affairs over in detail, with those digressions which he loved to make from any main topic. The detail was not very intricate; it consisted in my agreeing for a certain salary to write at least one short novel every year, with at least one farce, and as much more as I could or liked in the various kinds I was a supposed expert in. Then he made a set at me for something I had hitherto absolutely refused to do: which was to write a department in the *Magazine* every month, covering the whole ground of reviewing and book-noticing. Mr. Alden had proposed this to me by letter, and I had distinctly objected to it as forming a break in my fictioning; I should have to unset myself from that, and reset myself for it, and the effect would be very detrimental to me as a novelist. I still think I was right, and that turning aside to critical essaying at that period of my career, when all my mind tended to fictioning, had the effect I feared. A novelist should be nothing but a novelist, which, of course, included being a moralist if he is a man of any conscience; in art a man cannot serve two masters more than in religion. But in vain I urged my reasons against the insistence of the amiable chief, who went and came, after the manner of his talk, until I gave way. Then we had a little more talk, and it was understood that I was to make the department what I liked and to call it what I liked. My dear and honored predecessor [31] in the "Easy Chair" was then doing his beautiful work in that department, as well as writing his unrivaled leaders in the *Weekly,* and Mr. Harper skilfully led up to what a man might or might not say in the Harper periodicals. There appeared to be very few things: the only one I remember was that he might not deal, say, with the subject of capital punishment, which the House probably agreed about with Mr. Curtis, but at any approach to which it "rang a little bell." The phrase pleased me, and I readily censented to leave that matter untouched, not foreseeing that I should, within the next year, write a letter of ironical praise of the good old gallows-tree, then being supplanted by the electric chair, and that Mr. Curtis would print it in the *Weekly* [32] without a tinkle from the little bell.

This is as good a place as any to recognize the good business, to put it on the lowest ground, with which the House left me free to say what I pleased on whatever topic I chose to talk about. Their tolerance put me on my conscience, and I tried to catch the tinkle of the little bell when it was not actually sounded. There was, indeed, one moment when I would not have obeyed its behest, and that was when I protested against the condemnation of the Chicago anarchists as a grotesque perversion of law. My protest was not printed in any of the Harper periodicals, but I suppose it was as distasteful to the House as it was to the immeasurable majority of the American people. It raised a storm about my head, but no echo of the tempest ever reached me from Franklin Square any more than if the House there had quite agreed with me that it was wrong to hang five men for a murder never proved against one of them, because they were violently spoken enthusiasts. The case has already been revised by history, and I cannot feel hereafter in my position as I did then; but I cannot cease to remember the magnanimous forbearance of the House in the affair with regard to me.

I was already having trouble enough from my attitude in the "Editor's Study," as I had called my new department. From the first it was a polemic, a battle. I detested the sentimental and the romantic in fiction, and I began at once to free my mind concerning the romanticists, as well dead as alive. As I could not in conscience spare either age or sex the effect of my reasons, I soon had every lover of romanticism hating me and saying I had said worse things about it than I had ever said, whatever I had thought. In fact, I carefully kept myself from personalities; but that did not save me from them either on this shore of the sea or the other. I remember one English reviewer beginning a notice of my book of *Criticism and Fiction,* which grew out of "The Study" essays, by saying, "This man has placed himself beyond the pale of decency," and then, in proof, going on to behave indecently toward me. But that is all past; and since then one of the bitterest of my English enemies has generously written me that I was quite right in what I was always saying about romanticism, if not the romanticists. I am not sure that I was, now; but I was sure then, and I was so sure that I did not much mind the abuse showered upon me, though I would always have liked praise better. When after six years' warfare I gave up writing "The Study" I talked the matter over with J. Henry Harper, who had meanwhile assumed the position left vacant by the retirement of Joseph W. Harper, and I owned that it had been a rigorous experience which I was very willing to have end. I had felt that I had something to say in behalf of the truth, and I had conscientiously said it. I believe that we agreed the effect had been injurious to my books, which had not been so well liked or so much bought as they had before I began my long fight. The worst of it I did not then perceive, or know that my long fight had been a losing fight; I perceive now that the monstrous rag-baby of romanticism is as firmly in the saddle as it was before the joust began, and that it always will be, as long as the children of men are childish.

I was not young when our acquaintance began, but I was in the heyday of the early fifties, and I still had the spring of youth in me. When six years later our agreement came to an end and I gave up "The Study," it was not only because I had grown increasingly restive under the recurrent drain of that essaying, but because it had become more and more difficult for them to place even in their several periodicals the annual novel I gave them. I perceived myself that *toujours perdrix* was not essentially bettered because I was the partridge, and I had to own that they were right. Still they remained my most frequent customers for serial rights, and they remained the publishers of all my subsequent books. Under the contract which had been terminated I had not indeed given them a *Silas Lapham*, but I gave them more than one Boston story, and I gave them a Boston–New York story, which after its serialization in the *Weekly* became the most immediately successful of all my novels. This was *A Hazard of New Fortunes*, which, in spite of its clumsy name, had silently won itself a wide circle of friends. For breadth and depth I still think it my best book; although it has not the shapeliness of *Silas Lapham* or *Indian Summer*, or the intensity of

A Modern Instance. At the beginning I reeled about in it, for I had to write it while the heaviest sorrow I had known was a staggering load on heart and brain; but when I had struggled up, and found my footing, I believe I went forward with no uncertain tread.

It was preceded by *April Hopes*, and followed by *The Shadow of a Dream* and *An Imperative Duty*, and when our agreement lapsed they serialized for me *The World of Chance, The Landlord at Lion's Head, Ragged Lady*, and *Their Silver Wedding Journey* in the *Monthly*, the *Weekly*, and the *Bazar*, and perhaps other stories which I do not now recall. Now and then I serialized a story elsewhere, in *The Century*, in *Scribner's*, in *The Ladies' Home Journal;* but still the Harpers were the largest takers of my fiction. It was the day before the day of the wild efflorescence of the historic novel, written so largely by people who knew so little of history and read by people who knew it possibly less. There were certain English novelists who were pretty constantly represented in the Harper periodicals, and Mrs. Margaret Sangster,[33] who was then the editor of *Harper's Bazar*, and wanted a story of mine, said that she was tired of the succession of William Black and Thomas Hardy, and would like a little change to American flavors.

It seemed as if this order of things was to continue forever, when, one morning after the misery of a night in a sleeping-car on my way home from a Western lecturing tour, I read in the New York *Tribune*[34] that the House of Harper & Brothers had failed. It was as if I had read that the government of the United States had failed. It appeared not only incredible, but impossible; it was, as Mr. J. Pierpont Morgan said, a misfortune of the measure of a national disaster. Apart from the anxiety I felt for my own imaginable share in the ruin, there was a genuine grief for those whom it necessarily involved; they had been my friends so long that I could not help appropriating their misfortune and making it personal to myself. Before that, indeed, I had heard some intimation that things were not well with them, but I had not been uneasy, for the simple reason that what could not happen would not. Yet it had now, and I promptly reported myself at Franklin Square, and somehow amid the

chaos I contrived to arrange with the new strange powers for a
book to be serialized in the *Bazar,* which I learned was under
new management. I really do not know how the affair was contrived; I did not see the editor of the *Bazar;* a gentleman whom
I had never seen before went and came, and then said that they
would like *Heroines of Fiction* for the *Bazar.*

It was all very bewildering. In the vast space without, where
the kind Harper brotherhood and cousinhood had abounded at
low desks or high, I did not see one familiar face. It seemed to
me now that even the desks had been removed, and were not replaced till the House had fairly passed into the control where it
still remains. I had not the courage to climb the winding stairs
to the editorial rooms, but later I found my friend, Mr. J. Henry
Harper, who gave me comforting reassurances, which Mr. Alden
confirmed in due course. The great change which had come upon
Franklin Square was not the gravest which had threatened, and
it brought the energy and courage for the rehabilitation which
followed. Still, I went away for the summer with a very uncertain mind, and when I had renounced an editorial enterprise
which offered itself, I grew more and more anxious for the future, which stared at me rather vacantly. I had no work before
me except that on *Heroines of Fiction,* I who used to have con-
tracts for handsome thousands and the choice of more. I had
always had a salary until my agreement came to an end with
Harper & Brothers at the end of the year 1890,[35] when I spent a
sleepless night in view of a week without a check. It had proved
a needless fear, for during the next decade I had more work than
I could do, and mainly from the House that no longer paid me
a weekly wage. But now the House itself had come to an end, at
least in its former phase, and I had no invitations from editors;
some invitations from myself were met with their regrets for
previous engagements.

It seemed to me that I had better go up to New York and
look after my chances personally. I took with me the first chapters of the story which became *The Kentons,* and went with it to
Mr. Dodd,[36] of Dodd, Mead & Co., with the hope that the editor
of *The Bookman* might like it. The publisher did not forbid my
hope, and with some courage in my heart I went on down to

383

Franklin Square, and met there Col. George Harvey for the first time. He had become the president of the new House of Harper & Brothers, and he received me as if he had been the president of the old House; I could not say better. He asked me if I would come down to his home at Long Branch the next afternoon and pass the night. In the morning I went back to Mr. Dodd to confess the hope I permitted myself. The confession was the more difficult because he had told me that he thought they would like my story for *The Bookman;* but I managed, and he said, "I think Harvey will want you."

That night at Long Branch we talked generalities, and I began to fear Mr. Dodd was wrong, but the following day, after breakfast, Colonel Harvey called a session on his veranda, and then made me the offer which reunited my fortunes with those of Franklin Square. I was to give them so many thousand words for so much a year, and I was to be a literary adviser, however much or little that meant; only, as at a later time he expressed it, he wished me to belong to the shop. At that later time he also said that he did not want me to hold myself to any exact count of thousands in the words I was to furnish, and he intimated that he wished me to hold myself quite free in that matter. This seemed good business both for himself and me, and with the winter I came personally to Franklin Square. I had a room there for some months, like the other editors, and for a while I dealt with manuscripts as one of the readers for Harper & Brothers, as well as one of the writers. But that phase of the affair scarcely outlasted the winter. As an adviser I grew more and more reticent as I perceived that the general equipment of the house enabled it to deal more modernly with its literary enterprises than if I had counseled them. My functions in this sort were also curtailed by the successive absences, in England and in Italy, which resulted for me in the books of travel about those countries, and in which I have renewed the early practice of my life, for I was a traveler long before I was a noveler, and I had mounted somewhat timidly to the threshold of fiction from the high-roads and by-roads where I had studied manners and men. I am not yet sure which branch of the art I prefer.

NOTES TO PART I

CRITICISM AND FICTION

1. J. A. Symonds, *Renaissance in Italy: The Catholic Reaction*, Part II, pp. 230–31.
2. "Constant situation" or "unchanging relationship."
3. Howells' version is close to the translation of John S. Dwight, *Select Minor Poems of Goethe and Schiller* (1839), p. 179:
   > Wouldst know if blackberries taste well?
   > Ask boys and blackbirds—they can tell.

   On December 1, 1869, Lowell wrote in a letter to Howells, "Goethe tells us go ask boys and blackbirds which are the ripest cherries" (*Letters* [1894], I, 306). This is slightly nearer to Goethe's verses:
   > Wie Kirschen und Beeren behagen,
   > Musst du Kinder und Sperlinge fragen.

   Goethes Sämtliche Werke (1902), IV, 25.
4. See the account Agassiz gave of his own lecture on grasshoppers before a teachers' institute conducted by Horace Mann in 1847. On this occasion he distributed real grasshoppers to all the members of his class and thus taught the lesson of observation of nature at first hand Lane Cooper, *Louis Agassiz as a Teacher* (1945), p. 82; and Agassiz's *Methods of Study in Natural History* (1878), p. 237. For further comment by Howells on Agassiz's method see *Literary Friends and Acquaintance*, pp. 271–72.
5. Vicenzo Monti (1754–1828). This phrase, "the romantic was the cold grave of the Beautiful," which Howells had originally translated in the *North American Review*, CIII (1866), 327, as "the hard truth was the grave of the Beautiful," is a poor translation of *Sulla Mitologia. Sermone* (1825), ll. 92–93.
6. Cf. Henry Fielding's introductory essays in *Tom Jones*. See also the Prologue, mentioned by Howells, to *Sister Saint Sulpice* (*La Hermana San Sulpicio*), from the Spanish of Don Armando Palacio Valdés. Authorized translation by Nathan Haskell Dole, New York (1890), pp. 15–16, 31.
7. Frederic William Farrar (1831–1903), Anglican clergyman and critic. His article from which Howells quotes is "Literary Criticism," *Forum*, IX (1890), 284.

NOTES TO PART I: CRITICISM AND FICTION

8. *Ibid.*, p. 279; *Works of John Ruskin,* eds. E. T. Cook and Alexander Wedderburn (1908), XXXIV, 519.
9. Nickname of the public executioner of Paris.
10. *Journal,* March 14, 1826.
11. The quotation from *Sister Saint Sulpice* is from p. 19. Howells either paraphrased the translation of Valdés or made his own translation from the Spanish.
12. Octave Feuillet (1821–1890), Arsène Houssaye (1815–1896), Georges Ohnet (1848–1918), all French novelists.
13. This long passage in which Valdés defines "effectism" comes from the Prologue to *Sister Saint Sulpice*. The following, also from the Prologue, pp. 51–52, should be compared with it: "Here is another example [of effectism]. Not many months ago, the eminent novelist and critic of Harper's New Monthly Magazine, Mr. Dean Howells, wrote me about his impression of 'El Cuarto Poder' (The Fourth Estate). And, amid eulogies which I ought not to repeat here, he said: 'What does not please me, I must frankly confess, is the chapter in which Cecilia substitutes herself for her sister, to allay Gonzalo's jealousy. It strikes me as a false and romantic note, discordant with the truth existing in the rest of the work.' I will remark that this chapter is the one that had brought me the heartiest praise, and which had been celebrated more than anything else in the book. But, with all that, the illustrious American novelist's words were for me like a jar of cold water emptied over my head. I instantly perceived that he was wholly right, and I resolved to relapse no more into such effectism. It may be seen, therefore, how criticism, where it is rational and made in good faith, helps me." Howells remarks in "The Easy Chair," *Harper's,* May, 1911, that this is the only time an author ever openly acknowledged his indebtedness to Howells' criticism.
14. We cannot identify the source of this first quotation.
15. The later quotations in this paragraph come from several parts of Emerson's essays, including "The American Scholar" and "The Poet."
16. Valera y Alcala Galiano wrote *Pepita Ximenez* (1874); translated by Alcala Galiano into English, 1886. Howells' quotations are from p. 24.
17. Valdés writes in the Prologue to *Sister Saint Sulpice,* p. 23: "The idea of *Genius* in literature, as held by the public, is absolutely erroneous." He goes on to explain his point and concludes: "To call a literary man a genius one must be in a condition to know whether his work will or will not influence the generations to come, or, in other words, contemporaries can never know whether an artist is a genius or not." For his disbelief in "genius" Howells was taken to task by his friend Edmund C. Stedman, "Genius," *The New Princeton Review,* September, 1886, pp. 145–67. See also "Mr. Howells, Mr. Stedman and—Genius," *The Critic,* VI (1886), 121–22. This

debate began years before in the pages of the *Atlantic:* see William James, "Great Man, Great Thoughts, and Their Environment," *Atlantic Monthly,* XLVI (October, 1880), 441–59; and Grant Allen's reply, "The Genesis of Genius," *ibid.,* XLVII (March, 1881), 371–81.

18. *Critical and Miscellaneous Essays* (1900), III, 178.
19. "The Novel of Character," *The Speaker* (London), March 1, 1890, pp. 225–27. Allen talks of the "recrudescence" to which Howells refers and praises Howells as "by far the greatest and ablest exponent" of "the American school of character-painters in fiction."
20. "Popularity Not a Test of Merit," *Critic* (New York), August 9, 1884, p. 61.
21. Emerson, "Shakespeare; Or, The Poet," *Representative Men* (1850), p. 207.
22. Eilian Hughes, "Present-Day Novels: American Versus English," *Some Aspects of Humanity,* London, 1889. Howells' quotations begin on p. 15 and end on p. 77. James is never mentioned.
23. This expression (and the whole of *Criticism and Fiction*) offended the reviewer for the London *National Observer,* September 5, 1891, p. 408. See also the unfriendly review in the *Scots Observer,* July 12, 1891, pp. 194–95.
24. William E. Henley, *Views and Reviews* (1892, 2d ed.), p. 50.
25. The bell glass of an air pump from which the air has been exhausted.
26. George Du Maurier, *Pictures of English Society* (New York, 1884), pp. 22–23.
27. Preface to *The Marble Faun* (1860), p. viii.
28. In the summer of 1888 George Eastman patented the camera with a flexible film and called it a "Kodak." Howells' use of the term "snap-camera" in "The Editor's Study," November, 1888, may be the earliest example of this word.
29. Painted in 1863 by Christian Schussele (1826–1879); a large engraving made in 1864 by Thomas Oldham Barlow (1824–1887); engraved for *The Eclectic Magazine,* New Series, XV (1872), by George E. Perrine (1837–1885).
30. *New York Daily Tribune,* October 11, 1885, p. 3.
31. Translated from "Le Prime Storie," *Canti di Aleardo Aleardi* (Firenze, 1882, Sesta edizione), p. 56.
32. "Civilization in the United States," *Nineteenth Century,* XXIII (1888), 481–96.
33. *New York Herald,* March 24, 1889, p. 22, and editorial, p. 16; March 31, 1889, p. 12; *Critic,* XI (1889), 158, 251. The editor of the *Herald* had asked a number of American authors to express their views on "the tyranny of the Young Girl" in preventing writers from "depicting life" and from "frank treatment of the passions" in novels. In "The Editor's Study" of June, 1889 (*Criticism and Fic-*

NOTES TO PART I: CRITICISM AND FICTION

tion, Sections XXIV–XXV), Howells responded to the editor of the *Herald,* who had dicussed the Anglo-Saxon and the Gallic novels in his editorial. The *Herald* concluded by saying, "Let us have a rule of art that shall allow more Hawthornes and more George Eliots, but shall exclude the Zolas and all their tribe." In his defense of Zola and other Continental writers, Howells' views proved to be so liberal that one English reviewer of *Criticism and Fiction* said that he had put himself beyond the bounds of "decency." (Quoted by Howells in "Bibliographical," *My Literary Passions and Criticism and Fiction,* Library Edition (1911), p. xii.) In a second symposium in the *New York Herald,* March 29, 1891, p. 16, entitled "What Will Be the Future Novel?" Howells again speaks up for the European naturalists, as opposed to the English romantics, in giving his idea of "the novel of the future." He wrote: "In France, Émile Zola, Daudet and others are doing splendid work by their natural methods. Even in Spain and Italy the fiction writers are ahead of England in naturalness. They have caught the spirit of truth, and write it graphically." See also George Parsons Lathrop, "Literature in the United States," *New Review* (London), V (1891), 244–55; and Walter Besant, E. Lynn Linton, Thomas Hardy, "Candour in English Fiction," *ibid.,* II (1890), 6–21. That Howells' women continued to be a subject for discussion throughout the decade is apparent from the following: Howard W. Bell, "Mr. Howells's Women," *Chap-Book* (Chicago), December 1, 1897, and Hunt Cook, "The Wanton Cruelty of Mr. Howells," *ibid.,* January 1, 1898.

34. *Sappho,* Daudet's novel from which the editor of the *Herald* quoted the dedication, "To my sons when they shall have arrived at the age of twenty-one."

35. See Gordon N. Ray, *Letters and Private Papers of William Makepeace Thackeray* (1946), IV, 206–7; Geoffrey Tillotson, *Thackeray the Novelist* (1954), p. 124.

36. A year and a half before Howells wrote this section for *Harper's,* he had finished editing (with T. S. Perry) the *Library of Universal Adventure by Land and Sea* (1889), which seems still to have been running through his mind. If, as Howells goes on to suggest, Irving was the first to observe surviving Christmas rites and customs, Howells himself was a late follower in the tradition, for he wrote "Christmas Every Day" for *St. Nicholas,* January, 1886.

37. This paragraph, which first appeared in "The Editor's Study" of August, 1889, contains the essential thought of the Christian Socialists, with whom Howells was at this time associated. He sent a copy of their publication *The Dawn* to his father, April 27, 1890. *Life in Letters* (1928), II, 3. See "Howells and the Church of the Carpenter," by the present authors, *New England Quarterly,* March, 1959.

NOTES TO PART I: CRITICISM AND FICTION

38. William Morris, "Art and Socialism" (1884), *Collected Works* (1915), XXIII, 202.
39. Cf. *Les Miserables* (1862).
40. See the introduction to "Dickens and Thackeray" in this book, p. 93.
41. In reviewing *Their Wedding Journey* in the *North American Review*, CXIV (1872), 444–45, Henry Adams suggested that if a student a hundred years later wanted a true picture of the United States in 1871, he did not know where a better description could be found.

TEXTUAL NOTE

The variants made in the 1911 edition are listed below opposite the readings of the 1891 edition. Mere variations in spelling are not noticed. The page and line references are to the text on pp. 9–87.

Page	Line	1891 Edition	1911 Edition
15	31	romantic	romanticistic
22	4–6	If he . . . malice.	omitted
23	4–8	He ought . . . proceed	omitted
23	20–31	It is not . . . mistaken	omitted
23	31	to drop the others	omitted
24	5–6	which is often but a narrow field	omitted
25	14–24	I doubt if [to end of section]	omitted
28	24–26	Any author . . . escape	omitted
29	24–27	I venture . . . to him.	omitted
31	6–14	The temptation . . . taste.	omitted
31	15	In fine	omitted
38	13–14	the divine Jane	Jane Austen
39	22	caricaturist	omitted
39 40	37 to 6	Doubtless . . . as an art.	omitted
41	28–32	I fancy that . . . delicate irony	omitted
42 43	13 to 5	What is it that . . . to life and to art	omitted
43	6	as it does	omitted
49	5–7	More and more . . . demand	omitted
54	7	Henry James, Thomas Hardy	Mr. Henry James, Mr. Thomas Hardy

NOTES TO PART I: CRITICISM AND FICTION

Page	Line	1891 Edition	1911 Edition
57	17	The reversions . . . Mr. Hughes	omitted
61	31	notices.	Sec. XXI begins p. 61, l. 31
62	34–37	If we kept . . . intentions.	omitted
64	5 to	In other countries . . . used to be	
64	12	given.	omitted
			Sec. XXII omitted. Sec. XXIII becomes Sec. XXII.
64	30–33	M. Alphonse Daudet, in a conversation which Mr. H. H. Boyesen has set down in a recently recorded interview with him, said, in speaking of Tourgenief	Alphonse Daudet, in a conversation with H. H. Boyesen said, speaking of Tourgenief
65	30	Mr. Lowell	Lowell
		Sec. XXIII	Sec. XXII
		Sec. XXIV	Sec. XXIII
72	13–18	It attaches . . . of the popularity	omitted
		Sec. XXV	Sec. XXIV
75	20	After all [no paragraph]	Begins paragraph
76	12	Believe me	omitted
		Sec. XXVI	Sec. XXV
79	34 to	We need not [no paragraph]	Begins paragraph
80	3	Not all . . . with surprise	omitted
		Sec. XXVII	Sec. XXVI
81	1	If we cannot [no paragraph]	Begins paragraph
83	37	It was well [no paragraph]	Begins paragraph
84	22 to	It never did disappear . . . the	
85	11	American imagination.	omitted
		Sec. XXVIII	Sec. XXVII
85	32 to	This has long . . . do; and	omitted
86	1		
86	2–3	from him and from Morris	omitted
86	28–30	It is needless . . . them, that	omitted

NOTES TO PART II

EUROPEAN MASTERS

1. See verses by Edmund Gosse deriding Howells for his attack on Dickens in an article by the present authors, "An Enchanted Guest," *Journal of the Rutgers University Library*, XXII (June, 1959).
2. *Nation*, III (December 6, 1866), 453–54.
3. Pseudonym for Klara (Müller) Mundt, 1814–1873.
4. With this essay cf. "The Editor's Study," LXXVIII (December, 1888), 158–59.
5. Discussed in "The Postmaster-General and the Censorship of Morals," *Arena*, II (October, 1890), 540–52.
6. For the "comment" see the *New York Herald*, June 22, 1890, p. 22, and the editorial "Tolstoi on Marriage," p. 16; and July 5, 1891, p. 8, for careful statements by Tolstoy concerning his attitude and the contemporary reception of his view; see also L. N. Tolstoy, "Guy de Maupassant," *Arena*, II (1894), 15–26; *New York Herald*, April 26, 1891, p. 12.

NOTES TO PART III

AMERICAN WRITERS

1. Howells' memory is at fault. He became editor of the *Atlantic* in July, 1871 at the age of thirty-four, when Fields (born December 31, 1817) was still fifty-three.
2. The full names and dates of the less well-known writers whom Howells mentions are here given: Alice Cary (1820–1871), James Freeman Clarke (1810–1888), Abby Morton Diaz (1821–1904),

391

Henry Giles (1809–1882), Annie Douglas Greene Robinson, pseudonym "Marian Douglas" (1842–1913), George Stillman Hillard (1808–1879), Walter Mitchell (1826–1908), Fitz-James O'Brien (1828–1862), John Williamson Palmer (1825–1906), Norah Perry (1841–1896), W. J. Still (1828–1901), David A. Wasson (1823–1887), Adeline D. T. Whitney (1824–1906), Forceythe Willson (1837–1867).

3. Leonard Case (1820–1880).

4. Over and over one learns of Howells' helpfulness to young authors; see, for instance, the *New York Herald,* November 27, 1892, p. 31.

5. Howells perhaps refers to "A Light Man," which he had apparently advised James to submit to *Galaxy,* in which it appeared in July, 1869.

6. Sarah Butler Wister (1761–1804).

7. Jonas Lie (1833–1908), a well-known Norwegian writer.

8. Alexander Lange Kielland (1849–1906), Norwegian novelist.

9. Emerson's essay "The American Scholar."

10. Hiram Rich (1832–19—?).

11. William Henry Bishop (1847–1928).

12. Fiske dedicated *Myths and Myth-Makers* (1872) to Howells.

13. "L'Ecole du Flat-Creek," *Revue des Deux Mondes,* 102 (November, 1872), 125–76.

14. For a discussion of Howells and Bellamy's socialism see the *New York Herald,* September 23, 1894, section 6, p. 7. Cf. "Mr. Howells's Millenium," *American Fabian,* July, 1898, pp. 6–7.

15. Garland gives two dates for his first meeting with Howells. In "Meetings with Howells" (*Bookman,* March, 1917, p. 3), the date given is June, 1887. In "Meeting with Howells," *Roadside Meetings* (1930), pp. 55–56, the date is October, 1885. The date given in the *Bookman* is probably the more authentic because written nearer the event.

16. Garland took the word "veritism" from the French writer Eugène Véron (1825–1889), whose *Aesthetics* was translated into English by W. H. Armstrong (1879).

17. Garland reports a conversation held in 1890 between Howells and James A. Herne, *Bookman,* 45 (March, 1917), 6–7. Howells suggested to Herne that "he take a sail-loft, if necessary, and produce his new play Margaret Fleming." The result was the production of the play in Chickering Hall, Boston, in 1890. "Mr. and Mrs. Herne," *Arena,* IV (October, 1891), 543–60. According to the *New York Herald,* December 13, 1891, p. 12, "The reception of the play by the public in the modern Athens [Boston] hardly bore out Mr. W. D. Howells in his optimism."

18. One of these plays was *Under the Wheel, A Modern Play in Six Scenes* (1890).

19. *A Glance at New York,* by Benjamin Archibald Baker, produced in 1848.
20. In *The Minister's Charge,* p. 84, Howells defines this word, which is not found in his sense in dictionaries: "She was what they call whopper-jawed, and spoke a language almost purely consonantal, cutting and clipping her words with a rapid play of her whopper-●jaw till there was nothing but the bare bones left of them." "E. A." questioned Howells' usage and definition of the word. *Critic,* V (1886), 238.
21. "A name applied to a class of noisy young men of the lower ranks of society in the city of New York." *Dictionary of American English.*
22. This was Lilian Lida Bell (later Mrs. A. H. Bogue), 1865–1929, whose address to the Chicago Baptist Social Union was reported in *The New York Times,* February 19, 1899, p. 13, and the *Critic,* XXXI (1899), 310–11. Howells remarked on it in "Problems of Existence in Fiction," *Literature,* March 10, 1899 (see p. 336 in this book).

NOTES TO PART IV

FURTHER CRITICAL ISSUES

1. Passed in 1891.
2. *Venetian Life* (1866).
3. See the review by J. G. Lockhart, *Quarterly Review,* LIV (1835), 455–69, of *Pencillings by the Way,* by Nathaniel P. Willis.
4. Fanny Elssler (1810–1884). Edward T. Taylor (1793–1871).
5. Preston Smith Brooks (1819–1857), a member of the House of Representatives from South Carolina, entered the Senate Chamber and beat Senator Charles Sumner into unconsciousness after Sumner had made a bitter speech against Brooks's uncle, Senator A. P. Butler, on the slavery question.
6. *Uncle Tom's Cabin* was performed at the Academy of Music, 14th Street and Irving Place, New York, in April, 1901.
7. Longfellow, "The Slave's Dream."
8. *The New York Times,* February 19, 1899, p. 13; see note 22 above.
9. William Payne (1865–1954).
10. Walter Augustus Wyckoff (1865–1908). *The Workers* was published in 1897.

NOTES TO PART IV: FURTHER CRITICAL ISSUES

11. But the fact is that Howells had no faith in the great American novel: "For myself, I do not believe in what you term the 'American' novel. . . . We are too local. . . . We shall go on writing novels of New York, of Boston, of Georgia, of California. . . ." *New York Herald,* July 19, 1891, p. 9.

12. "A Plea for Literary Journalism," *Harper's Weekly,* October 25, 1902.

13. *North American Review,* January, 1912. The editors appended a note: "Written for the North American Review in 1903, and now published for the first time." No explanation was given for the nine-year delay in publication.

14. Alexander Smith (1830–1867) was the author of *A Life-Drama and Other Poems* (1859).

15. Martin Farquhar Tupper (1810–1889) wrote *Proverbial Philosophy,* 1838–1876.

16. *The Daily Advertiser,* between March 27, 1863, and May 3, 1865.

17. "Forlorn," issue of August 16, 1866.

18. *No Love Lost* (1869).

19. Issue of June 1, 1866.

20. Petrarch, Sonnet VII.

21. Jefferson, Ohio.

22. Chap. xix.

23. *Ibid.,* chap. xxiv.

24. One thinks of several candidates for this honor, but perhaps Wisconsin-born Frederick Jackson Turner (1861–1932) was in Howells' mind.

25. Alfred Hudson Guernsey (1825–1902) edited *Harper's* from 1856 to 1869.

26. Joseph Wesley Harper (1801–1870), one of the founders of the House of Harper.

27. William Mackay Laffan (1848–1909), journalist and publisher of the New York *Sun.* Representative of Harper's in London for two years.

28. Ellen Terry (1847–1928), English actress.

29. Madge Kendal (1849–1935), English actress.

30. Osgood failed in 1885.

31. This was George William Curtis (1824–1892).

32. "Execution by Electricity," *Harper's Weekly,* January 14, 1888.

33. Margaret Sangster (1838–1912), second editor of *Harper's Bazar* (1889–1899).

34. Howells probably read the *New York Tribune* of November 29, 1899, where the news first appeared. On November 30 a further news item and editorial were published.

35. This date seems confusing, but it is based on Howells' original con-

tracts with Harper's. See Robert W. Walts, "William Dean Howells and The House of Harper" (Doctoral dissertation, Rutgers University, 1953).
36. Frank Howard Dodd (1844–1916), publisher.

INDEX

꙰

A

397

INDEX

B

"Backward and a Foreward Look, A,"
  363–74
Bacon, Sir Francis, 255
Baker, Benjamin Archibald, 383
Baker, William M., 203
Balzac, Honoré, 12, 14, 15, 16, 18, 19,
  39, 54, 57, 82, 149, 155, 230,
  231, 232, 335, 347
Bancroft, George, xv, 368
Bankrupt, The (Björnson), 103
Barrett, Lawrence, 193
Beautiful, the, 33
"Beautiful war," 270
Beecher, Henry Ward, xv
Bell, Lilian Lida, 333
Bellamy Club. *See* Nationalist Club
Bellamy, Edward, 165, 246–55, 289,
  333
Bellamy, Francis, 246
Bennett, Arnold, 335, 345–49
Bennett, Emerson, 98
Bible, 26
Bishop, William Henry, 200
Bismarck, Otto Eduard Leopold, 45
Björnson, Björnstjerne, xiv, 20, 90,
  101–9, 111, 130, 139, 150, 196,
  222, 223, 224, 228
Blackstone, Sir William, 358
Bleak House (Dickens), 98
Blindman's World and Other Stories
  (Bellamy), 247
Bliss, William Dwight Porter, 249, 289
Blithdale Romance, The (Hawthorne),
  56, 337
Bogue, Mrs. A. H. *See* Bell, Lilian
  Lida
Boker, George Henry, 187
Bonheur, Rosa, 194
Bookman, 256, 257, 383–84
Book News, 96
Boston Daily Advertiser, 110, 351, 352
Boyesen, Hjalmar Hjorth, 64, 196, 353
Bread-Winners, The (Hay), 237–45
Briggs, Charles F., 98
Brontë, Charlotte, 38, 93
Brooks, Preston Smith, 329
Brooks, Van Wyck, 363
Brown, Edith Baker, 335
Brown, John, 296

Browning, Robert, 28, 198
Brunetière, Ferdinand, 156
Bryant, William Cullen, xv, 186, 320,
  368, 371
Bulwer. *See* Lytton
Bunyan, John, 26, 246
Burgess, Gelett, 276
Burke, Edmund, 11, 12
Burns, Robert, 324
Burroughs, John, 203
Byron, George Gordon, Lord, 80, 295

C

Cable, George Washington, 324, 337,
  348
Calvinism, 320
Captain Ben's Choice (Pratt), 195
Captain of the Gray-Horse Troop, The
  (Garland), 263, 265
Carlyle, Thomas, 50
Carol, The (Dickens), 82
Carter, Everett, 5
Cary, Alice, 187, 188
Case, Leonard, 188
"Case in Point, A," 279–82
Case of George Dedlock (S. W.
  Mitchell), 195
Castilian Days (Hay), 197
Catholicism, 307
Cavanagh (Garland), 263, 265
Cavour, Camillo Benso, Count di, 45
*Celebrated Frog of Calaveras County
  and Other Sketches, The* (Clem-
  ens), 213
Century, 94, 96, 181, 230, 238, 239,
  240, 247, 256, 268, 290
Cervantes, Saavedra Miguel, de, 36, 90,
  133, 271
Chance Acquaintance, A (Howells),
  102, 111, 112, 181
Channing, William Ellery, 233
Character
  according to Balzac, 16
  according to Thackeray, 99
  according to Valdés, 37
  outside fiction, xiii
  psychological study of, 132
Chesebro', Caroline, 187, 203
Chicago Anarchists, 4, 248, 380
Child, Lydia Maria, 187

INDEX

Childhood, Boyhood, and Youth (Tolstoy), 174
Chimes, The (Dickens), 82
Christianity, 162, 171
Christian Socialists. *See* Society of Christian Socialists
Christians, Tolstoy asks us to be, 162
Christmas story
defined, 76–79
humanitarian impulse of, 85
Chronicles, Book of. *See* Bible
Church of the Carpenter (Boston), 249
Circuit Rider, The (Eggleston), 223, 227, 228
Civilization, false concept of, 53
Clarín. *See* Alas, Leopoldo
Clarke, James Freeman, 187
Classes, authors not of, 308
Classic way, the, 34
Classicism, effete, 14
Classics
greatest sometimes not great, 14
three-fifths not alive, 69
Clemens, Mrs. Olivia Langdon, 214
Clemens, Samuel L., xv, 180, 197, 198, 213–20, 269, 312, 324, 325, 333, 368, 373
Cliff-Dwellers, The (Fuller), 337
Collins, Wilkie, 83
Columbus, Christopher, 45
Common sense
superior to power, 37
the unmoral and the immoral, 43
Complicity, defined in *The Minister's Charge*, 248
Comte, August, 248
"Contributors Club," 191
Conway, Moncure Daniel, 187
Cooke, Delmar G., 112
Cooke, Rose Terry, 64, 79, 187
Cooper, James Fenimore, 360
Cooperative Commonwealth (Gronlund), 165
Copernicus, Nikolaus, 318
Copyright law
international, 301, 303
passage of, 6
Cosmopolitan, The, 289
Cossacks, The (Tolstoy), 164, 174

"Country Printer, The" (Howells), 290–98
"Craddock, Charles Egbert." *See* Murfree, Mary N.
Craig, Mary A., 117
Cranch, Christopher, 187
Crane, Stephen, xv, 184, 267–75, 333, 337
Cricket on the Hearth, The (Dickens), 82
Crime and Punishment (Dostoevsky), 61
Critic
American, 21
often right too late, 363
should seek principles, 22–23
unwilling to learn from authors, 21–22
usefulness of, 24
Critic, The, 148, 149
Criticism
anonymous, 29
average of, 20
bad, 27
best sort of, 315
business of, 15
future of, 144
inferior to novels, 20
judging author without reference to his aims, 28
modern English, 36
most American bad, 27
put literary consciousness into books, 26
"vaster and powerfuler," 49
vested interests of, 11
Critics
ossified in tradition, 19
Symonds' view of, 9
use of, 24
Crumbling Idols (Garland), 258
Cuarto Poder, El (Valdés), 124
Cuestion Palpitante, La (Pardo-Bazán), 132, 135
Curtis, George William, 187, 325, 379–80

D

Damnation of Theron Ware, The (Frederic), 337

399

INDEX

INDEX

INDEX

Genius (*continued*)
   Howells' regard for, xv
   knows without learning, 144
   romantic spirit worships genius, 86
George, Henry, 261
George's Mother (Crane), 269, 273
Georgism, preached by Garland, 258, 261
Ghosts (Ibsen), 140, 141
Gibson, William M., x
Gilder, Jeannette L., 149
Gilder, Richard Watson, 94, 268
Giles, Henry, 187
Gilman, Daniel Coit, 310, 313–15
"Glance at New York, A" (Baker), 271
"Glut of the Fiction Market, The," 104
Goethe, Johann Wolfgang, 12, 17, 18, 43
Goetze, E., x
Gogol, Nicolas, 16, 122, 149, 155, 165, 172
Goldoni, Carlo, 91, 101
Goldsmith, Oliver, 16
Goncourt, Edmond Huot, de, and Jules, 95, 139, 154
Gospel of Freedom (Herrick), 337
Gosse, Edmund, 95
Grandissimes, The (Cable), 337
Grant, Ulysses S., 26, 45, 216
Grasshopper, the true and the false, 13
Graysons, The (Eggleston), 224
"Great American Novel," 230, 333–49, 394
Great Masters of Russian Literature, The (Dupuy), 165
Greeley, Horace, 227
Greene, Annie Douglas. *See* Robinson, Annie Douglas Greene
Griffith Gaunt (Reade), 198
Gronlund, Laurence, 165, 249
Guernsey, Alfred Hudson, 377
Gunnar (Boysen), 196

H

Haggard, Rider, 118
Haight, Gordon, 207
Hale, Edward Everett, 187, 203, 249, 289

Hale, Lucretia, 187
Hamilton, Gail, 187
Hamlet (Shakespeare), 116, 142, 143, 144
Handy Andy (Lover), 98
Happiness from labor, 168
Happy Boy, The (Björnson), 101, 106–7
Harben, William Nathaniel, 348
Hardy, Thomas, 39, 54, 57, 90, 93, 139, 148–53, 273, 363
Harper, J. Henry, 149, 287, 365, 375, 381, 383
Harper, J. W., 377, 379, 381
Harper & Brothers. *See* Howells and the House of Harper
Harper's Bazar, 131, 207, 350
Harper's Weekly, 90, 149, 165, 249, 269, 335, 364
Harrigan, Edward, 272
Harris, Joel Chandler, 324
Harte, Bret, xv, 184, 197, 214, 237, 312, 324
Harvard University, 101, 130, 311, 326
Harvey, George Brinton McClellan, 363, 384
Haunted Man, The (Dickens), 82
Hauptmann, Gerhart, 335, 342, 343
Hawthorne, Nathaniel, xv, 12, 20, 54, 57, 61, 73, 95, 179, 186, 199, 222, 230, 232–36, 247, 255, 322, 337, 351, 366, 368
Hay, John, 154, 197, 237–45, 310, 334
Hayes, Rutherford B., 238
Hayne, Paul H., 199
Hazard of New Fortunes, A (Howells), 5, 167, 240, 249, 381
Hearne. *See* Herne, James A.
Hearth and Home, 221, 222
Heine, Heinrich, 358, 362
Henley, William Ernest, 61
"Henry James, Jr." (Howells), 94, 230
Herald (New York), 213
Herne, James A., 262
Heroes and heroines
   Balzac's, 19
   "gaudy" hero and heroine, 46–47
Heroines of Fiction (Howells), 149, 150, 208, 383
Herrick, Robert, 337

402

INDEX

INDEX

James, Henry, Jr., xv, 6, 54, 57, 58, 59, 89, 94, 95, 96, 110, 154, 180, 187, 194, 195, 216, 229–36, 237, 262, 319, 322, 325, 333, 334, 335, 337, 364
James, Henry, Sr., 187
"James's Hawthorne," 229–36, 322
Jane Field (Wilkins), 337
Jefferson, Joseph, 32
Jefferson, Thomas, 200
Jesus Christ, 161, 166, 169, 170, 171, 318
Jewett, Sarah Orne, 64, 79, 184, 194, 325, 348
John Cave (Trites), 348
"John Hay in Literature" (Howells), 237
Johns Hopkins University, The, 130, 310
"John's Trial" (Deming), 197
Jones, Edith. *See* Wharton, Edith
Jones, Henry Arthur, 145
José (Valdés), 123
Journal (Boston), 333
Journal (New York), 269
Journalism
  from journalism to literature, 306
  opening path of, 358
  vice of American, 292
Jude the Obscure (Hardy), 149, 150, 273

K

Kate Beaumont (De Forest), 206
Keats, John, 10, 24, 28, 358
Kelley, Gilbert, xi
Kemble, Frances, 200
Kendal, Madge, 378
Kentons, The (Howells), 383
Kielland, Alexander Lange, 196
Kilmer, Joyce, 112, 166
King, Clarence, 203
Kingsley, Charles, 358
Kipling, Rudyard, 118
Kreutzer Sonata (Tolstoy), 166, 176

L

Lady of the Aroostook, The (Howells), 181, 257

Labor
  leaders, the new villains of American fiction, 239
  question, as dealt with by Hay, 240
Laffan, William Mackay, 378
Lang, Andrew, 93
Langdon, Olivia. *See* Clemens, Mrs. Olivia Langdon
Larcom, Lucy, 187, 199
L'Argent (Zola), 156
L'Assommoir (Zola), 154, 156
Lathrop, George Parsons, 110, 191, 200
Latin frankness
  "certain nudities which the Latin peoples seem to find edifying," 62
  in Valdés, 125
Law, a jealous mistress, 358
Lear of the Steppes (Turgenev), 228
Leisure class
  absence of, 334
  opportunity for American novelist, 334
  Veblen's idea of, 340
Leon Roch. See Familia de Leon Roch, La
Lerner, Anita Marburg, xi
"Letters of an Altrurian Traveler" (Howells), 289, 290
"Letter to Daniel Coit Gilman" (Howells), 313–15
Lever, Charles, 98
Library of the World's Best Literature (Howells and Perry), 164
"Lida Ann" (Deming), 197
Lie, Jonas, 196
Life (Tolstoy), 170
Life (Trites), 348
"Life and Letters" (Howells), 139, 269
Life Drama (Smith), 354
Life in Letters of W. D. Howells (M. Howells), 94, 268
"Life in the Brick Moon" (Hale), 203
"Light Man, A" (James), 392
Lincoln, Abraham, 45, 66, 237, 366
Literary
  art, "to speak and write simply and clearly," 314

404

INDEX

INDEX